LEARN HOW TO READ AND UNDERSTAND BODY MOVEMENTS!

Learn, for example:

- How to make advances without taking chances!

- How to read *shoulders*. (Is this person in a good mood? Angry? Frightened?)

- Body language between sex partners. How to communicate feeling and need without words.

- How to enter a room full of strangers, inventory body positions, and tell who the "important" people are.

- How to use Body Language to assume *leadership* of a group.

- How you can use this "new" language to *defeat* language.

BODY LANGUAGE
was originally published by
M. Evans and Company, Inc.

Body Language

by Julius Fast

PUBLISHED BY POCKET BOOKS NEW YORK

Acknowledgments

The author would like to express his appreciation to the following
for their help in preparing this book:
Dr. Arnold Buchheimer, *Psychologist and Professor of Education
at the City University of New York;* Dr. Albert E. Scheflen,
*Professor of Psychiatry at the Albert Einstein College of Medi-
cine;* Michael Wolff, *Doctoral candidate in Social Psychology,
City University of New York;* Jean Linden, *Research Associate,
Interscience Information, Inc.*

BODY LANGUAGE

M. Evans edition published May, 1970

POCKET BOOK edition published May, 1971
14th printing......December, 1972

This book is gratefully dedicated to all the passengers of the second car in the Independent Subway's F train, eastbound from Fifth Avenue at 5:22 P.M.

Contents

1
The Body
Is the Message

A Science Called Kinesics

Within the last few years a new and exciting science has been uncovered and explored. It is called body language. Both its written form and the scientific study of it have been labeled kinesics. Body language and kinesics are based on the behavioral patterns of nonverbal communication, but kinesics is still so new as a science that its authorities can be counted on the fingers of one hand.

Clinical studies have revealed the extent to which body language can actually contradict verbal communications. A classic example is the young woman who told her psychiatrist that she loved her boyfriend very much while nodding her head from side to side in subconscious denial.

Body language has also shed new light on the dynamics of interfamily relationships. A family sitting together, for example, can give a revealing picture of itself simply by the way its members move their arms and legs. If the mother crosses her legs first and the rest of the family then follows suit, she has set the lead for the family action, though she, as well as the rest of the family, may not be aware she is doing it. In fact her words may deny her leadership as she asks her husband or children for advice. But the unspoken, follow-the-leader clue in her action

1

gives the family setup away to someone knowledgeable in kinesics.

A New Signal from the Unconscious

Dr. Edward H. Hess told a recent convention of the American College of Medical Hypnotists of a newly discovered kinesic signal. This is the unconscious widening of the pupil when the eye sees something pleasant. On a useful plane, this can be of help in a poker game if the player is in the "know." When his opponent's pupils widen, he can be sure that his opponent is holding a good hand. The player may not even be conscious of his ability to read this sign, any more than the other person is conscious of telegraphing his own luck.

Dr. Hess has found that the pupil of a normal man's eye becomes twice as large when he sees a picture of a nude woman.

On a commercial level, Dr. Hess cites the use of this new kinesic principle to detect the effect of an advertising commercial on television. While the commercial is being shown to a select audience, the eyes of the audience are photographed. The film is then later carefully studied to detect just when there is any widening of the eye; in other words, when there is any unconscious, pleasant response to the commercial.

Body language can include any non-reflexive or reflexive movement of a part, or all of the body, used by a person to communicate an emotional message to the outside world.

To understand this unspoken body language, kinesics experts often have to take into consideration cultural differences and environmental differences. The average man,

2

unschooled in cultural nuances of body language, often misinterprets what he sees.

How to Tell the Girls Apart

Allen was a small-town boy who had come to visit Ted in the big city. One night, on his way to Ted's apartment and a big cocktail party, Allen saw a lovely young brunette walk across the street ahead of him and then start up the block. Allen followed her, marveling at the explicit quality of her walk. If ever Allen had seen a nonverbal message transmitted, this was it!

He followed her for a block, realizing that the girl was aware of him, and realizing too that her walk didn't change. Allen was sure this was a come-on.

Finally, at a red light, Allen summoned up his courage and catching up to the girl, gave her his pleasantest smile and said, "Hello."

To his amazement she turned a furious face to him and through clenched teeth said, "If you don't leave me alone I'll call a cop." Then as the light changed, she churned off.

Allen was stunned and scarlet with embarrassment. He hurried on to Ted's apartment where the party was in progress. While Ted poured him a drink he told him the story and Ted laughed. "Boy, you got the wrong number."

"But, hell, Ted—no girl at home would walk like that unless—unless she was asking for it."

"This is a Spanish-speaking neighborhood. Most of the girls—despite outward appearances—are very good girls," Ted explained.

What Allen didn't understand is that in a culture, such as that of many Spanish-speaking countries, in which

3

girls are chaperoned and there are strict codes of social behavior, a young girl can safely flaunt her sexuality without fear of inviting trouble. In fact, the walk that Allen took as a come-on would be considered only natural, and the erect, rigid posture of a proper American woman would probably be considered graceless and unnatural.

Allen circulated through the party and slowly forgot his humiliation.

As the party was breaking up, Ted cornered him and asked, "See anything you like?"

"That Janet," Allen sighed. "Man, I could really go for that—"

"Well, swell. Ask her to stay. Margie's staying too, and we'll have dinner."

"I don't know. She's just—like I couldn't get to first base with her."

"You're kidding."

"No. She's had the 'hands off' sign out all evening."

"But Janet likes you. She told me."

"But—" Bewildered, Allen said, "Then why is she so—so—I don't know, she just looks as if she didn't want me to lay a finger on her."

"That's Janet's way. You just didn't get the right message."

"I'll never understand this city," Allen said still bewildered, but happy.

As Allen found out, in Latin countries girls may telegraph a message of open sexual flirtation, and yet be so well chaperoned that any sort of physical "pass" is almost impossible. In countries where the chaperoning is looser, the girl will build her own defenses by a series of nonverbal messages that spell out "hands off." When the situation is such that a man cannot, within the rules of the

4

culture, approach a strange girl on the street, a girl can move loosely and freely. In a city such as New York where a girl can expect almost anything, especially at a cocktail party, she learns to send out a message saying "hands off." To do this she will stand rigidly, cross her legs demurely when sitting, cross her arms over her breasts, and use other such defensive gestures.

The point is that for every situation there must be two elements to body language, the delivery of the message and the reception of the message. Had Allen been able to receive the messages correctly in terms of the big city he would have been spared the embarrassment of one encounter and could have avoided much of the uncertainty of the other.

To Touch or Not to Touch

Body language, in addition to sending and receiving messages, if understood and used adroitly can also serve to break through defenses. A businessman who was trying a bit too hard to wind up a very profitable deal found that he had misread the signs.

"It was a deal," he told me, "that would have been profitable not only to me but to Tom as well. Tom was in Salt Lake City from Bountiful, which isn't far away geographically, but is miles away culturally. It's a damned small town, and Tom was sure that everyone in the big city was out to take him. I think that deep down he was convinced that the deal was right for both of us, but he just couldn't trust my approach. I was the big city businessman, way up there, wheeling and dealing, and he was the small-time boy about to get rooked.

"I tried to cut through his image of the big city busi-

5

nessman by putting my arm around his shoulder. And that darn touch blew everything."

What my businessman friend had done was violate Tom's barrier of defenses with a nonverbal gesture for which the groundwork had not been laid. In body language he was trying to say, "Trust me. Let's make contact." But he only succeeded in committing a nonverbal assault. In ignoring Tom's defenses, the overeager businessman ruined the deal.

Often the swiftest and most obvious type of body language is touch. The touch of a hand, or an arm around someone's shoulder, can spell a more vivid and direct message than dozens of words. But such a touch must come at the right moment and in the right context.

Sooner or later every boy learns that touching a girl at the wrong moment may turn her off abruptly.

There are people who are "touchers," compulsive touchers, who seem completely impervious to all messages they may get from friends or companions. They are people who will touch and fondle others when they are bombarded with body language requests not to.

A Touch of Loneliness

However, touching or fondling in itself can be a potent signal. Touching an inanimate object can serve as a very loud and urgent signal, or a plea for understanding. Take the case of Aunt Grace. This old woman had become the center of a family discussion. Some of the family felt she would be better off in a pleasant and well-run nursing home nearby where she'd not only have people to take care of her but would also have plenty of companionship.

The rest of the family felt that this was tantamount to putting Aunt Grace "away." She had a generous income

6

and a lovely apartment, and she could still do very well for herself. Why shouldn't she live where she was, enjoying her independence and her freedom?

Aunt Grace herself was no great help in the discussion. She sat in the middle of the family group, fondling her necklace and nodding, picking up a small alabaster paperweight and caressing it, running one hand along the velvet of the couch, then feeling the wooden carving.

"Whatever the family decides," she said gently. "I don't want to be a problem to anyone."

The family couldn't decide, and kept discussing the problem, while Aunt Grace kept fondling all the objects within reach.

Until finally the family got the message. It was a pretty obvious message too. It was just a wonder no one had gotten it sooner. Aunt Grace had been a fondler ever since she had begun living alone. She touched and caressed everything within reach. All the family knew it, but it wasn't until that moment that, one by one, they all became aware of what her fondling was saying. She was telling them in body language, "I am lonely. I am starved for companionship. Help me!"

Aunt Grace was taken to live with a niece and nephew, where she became a different woman.

Like Aunt Grace, we all, in one way or another, send our little messages out to the world. We say, "Help me, I'm lonely. Take me, I'm available. Leave me alone, I'm depressed." And rarely do we send our messages consciously. We act out our state of being with nonverbal body language. We lift one eyebrow for disbelief. We rub our noses for puzzlement. We clasp our arms to isolate ourselves or to protect ourselves. We shrug our shoulders for indifference, wink one eye for intimacy, tap our fingers for impatience, slap our forehead for forgetfulness.

7

The gestures are numerous, and while some are deliberate and others are almost deliberate, there are some, such as rubbing under our noses for puzzlement or clasping our arms to protect ourselves, that are mostly unconscious.

A study of body language is a study of the mixture of all body movements from the very deliberate to the completely unconscious, from those that apply only in one culture to those that cut across all cultural barriers.

2
Of Animals and Territory

The Symbolic Battle

The relationship between animal communication and human communication is only now beginning to be understood. Many of our insights into nonverbal communication have come from experiments with animals. Birds will communicate with each other by song, generation after generation singing the same set of notes, the same simple or complex melody. For many years scientists believed that these notes, these bird songs were hereditary accomplishments like the language of the porpoise, the language dances of certain wasps, and the "talking" of frogs.

Now, however, there is some doubt that this is completely so. Experiments seem to indicate that bird songs are learned. Scientists have raised certain birds away from any others of their own kind, and these fledglings have never been able to reproduce the species' typical songs.

Indeed the scientists who raised such birds were able to teach them a fragment of a popular song to replace the species song. Left alone, a bird like this would never be able to mate, for bird songs are involved with the entire mating process.

Another type of animal behavior that has long been termed instinctive is the symbolic fighting of dogs. When two male dogs meet they may react in a number of ways, but the most common is the snarling, snapping simulation of a fight to the death. The uninitiated onlooker will usually be alarmed by this behavior and may even try to separate the seemingly angry animals. The knowing dog owner simply watches, realizing how much of the fight is symbolic.

This is not to say that the fight isn't real. It is. The two animals are competing for mastery. One will win, because he is more aggressive, perhaps stronger and with harder drives than the other. The fight is over at the point when both dogs realize that one is the victor, though no skin has been broken. Then a curious thing happens. The vanquished dog lies down, rolls over and exposes his throat to the victor.

To this surrender, the victor reacts by simply standing over the vanquished, baring his fangs and growling for a definite period of time. Then both leap away and the battle is forgotten.

A nonverbal procedure has been acted out. The vanquished says, "I concede. You are the stronger and I bare my vulnerable throat to you."

The victor says, "Indeed, I am stronger and I will snarl and show that strength, but now let's get up and romp."

It is a curious aside to note that in almost no species of higher animal does one member of the species kill another for any reason, though they might fight with each other for many reasons. Among roe bucks at mating time such semi-symbolic fights can build up to the point of actual battle, and then, curiously, the animals will attack the nearby trees instead of each other.

Certain birds, after scolding and flapping in angry prelude to battle, will settle their differences by turning furiously to nest building. Antelope may lock horns and struggle for superiority, but the fight, however furious it may be, will end not always in death but in a ritual defeat. Animals have learned the art of acting out relationships in a kind of charade that is a first cousin to body language.

The controversial point about this symbolic battling behavior of dogs and other animals is whether this conduct, this type of communication, is inherited as instincts are inherited, imprinted in the genetic pattern of the species and handed down from generation to generation, or whether it is learned anew by each animal.

I mentioned that in some song birds the species' song must be learned; however, in others the songs are truly instinctive. Linnets learn their songs, while reed buntings inherit the ability to sing the characteristic species song whether or not they are in contact with other reed buntings during their growth. We must be careful in studying any behavior in the animal world not to generalize. What is true for one species of bird is not at all true for another. What is true for animals is not necessarily true for men. The symbolic battling of dogs is believed by many scientists to be an inherited thing, and yet I have had a dog trainer assure me that this behavior is learned.

"Watch a mother dog when her cubs are scrapping. If one is triumphant and tries to carry his victory to the point of damaging the other, the mother will immediately cuff him into neutrality, teaching him to respect the defeat of his brother. No, a dog must be taught symbolic behavior."

On the other hand there are dogs, such as the Eskimo dogs of Greenland, that seem to have a tremendous amount of difficulty learning symbolic behavior. Niko Tinbergen, the Dutch naturalist, says these dogs possess definite territories for each pack. Young male pups constantly violate the boundaries of these territories, and as a result they are constantly punished by the older males who have set the boundaries. The pups, however, never seem to learn just where the boundaries are. That is, until they reach sexual maturity.

From the time they experience their first copulation they suddenly become aware of the exact boundaries. Is this a learning process that has been reinforced over the years and now takes hold? Or is it some instinctive process that only develops with sexual maturity?

Can We Inherit Language?

The inheritance of instinct is not a simple matter, nor is the process of learning simple. It is difficult to pinpoint just how much of any system of communication is inherited and how much is learned. Not all behavior is learned, any more than it is all inherited, even in humans.

And this brings us back to nonverbal communication. Are there universal gestures and expressions which are culturally independent and true for every human in every culture? Are there things every human being does which somehow communicate a meaning to all other humans regardless of race, color, creed or culture?

In other words, is a smile always indicative of amusement? Is a frown always a sign of displeasure? When we shake our head from side to side, does it always mean no? When we move it up and down, does it always mean yes? Are all these movements universal for all people, and if so, is the ability to make these movements in response to a given emotion inherited?

If we could find a complete set of inherited gestures and signals, then our nonverbal communication might be like the language of the porpoises or like the nonverbal

12

language of the honeybee, who by certain definite motions can lead the entire hive population to a new-found supply of honey. These are inherited movements that the bee does not have to learn.

Have we an inherited form of communication?

Darwin believed that facial expressions of emotion are similar among humans, regardless of culture. He based his belief on man's evolutionary origin. Yet in the early 1950's, two researchers, Bruner and Taguiri, wrote, after thirty years of study, that the best available research indicated that there was no innate, invariable pattern accompanying specific emotions.

And then fourteen years later, three researchers, Ekman, Friesen (from California's Langley Porter Neuropsychiatric Institute) and Sorenson (from the National Institute of Neurological Diseases and Blindness) found that new research supported Darwin's own belief.

They had conducted studies in New Guinea, Borneo, the United States, Brazil and Japan, five widely different cultures on three different continents and discovered: "Observers in these cultures recognize some of the same emotions when they are shown a standard set of facial photographs."

According to the three men, this contradicts a theory that facial displays of emotion are socially learned. They also feel that there is agreement within a culture on recognizing different emotional states.

The reason they give for this universality of recognition is only indirectly related to inheritance. They cite a theory which postulates ". . . innate subcortical programs linking certain evokers to distinguishable universal facial displays for each of the primary affects—interest, joy, surprise, fear, anger, distress, disgust, contempt and shame."

In simpler words this means that the brains of all men

13

are programmed to turn up the corners of the mouth when they're happy, turn them down when they're discontent, wrinkle the forehead, lift the eyebrows, raise one side of the mouth, and so forth and so on, according to what feeling is fed into the brain.

In opposition to this, they list other "culturally variable expressions and rules learned early in life."

"These rules," they say, "prescribe what to do about the display of each affect in different social settings; they vary with the social role and demographic characteristics and should vary across cultures."

The study that the three conducted tried as much as possible to avoid the conditioning that culture inflicts. The spread of television, movies and written matter makes this very difficult, but the investigators avoided much of this by studying isolated regions and, where they could, preliterate societies.

What their work proved seems to be the fact that we can inherit in our genetic makeup certain basic physical reactions. We are born with the elements of a nonverbal communication. We can make hate, fear, amusement, sadness and other basic feelings known to other human beings without ever learning how to do it.

Of course this does not contradict the fact that we must also learn many gestures that mean one thing in one society and something else in another society. We in the Western world shake our head from side to side to indicate no, and up and down to indicate yes, but there are societies in India where just the opposite is true. Up and down means no, and side to side means yes.

We can understand then that our nonverbal language is partly instinctive, partly taught and partly imitative. Later on we will see how important this imitative element is in nonverbal and verbal communication.

"The Territorial Imperative"

One of the things that is inherited genetically is the sense of territory. Robert Ardrey has written a fascinating book, *The Territorial Imperative,* in which he traces this territorial sense through the animal kingdom and into the human. In this book he discusses the staking out and guarding of territories by animals, birds, deer, fish and primates. For some species the territories are temporary, shifting with each season. For other animal species they are permanent. Ardrey makes an interesting case for the fact that, in his belief, "the territorial nature of man is genetic and ineradicable."

From his extensive animal studies he describes an innate code of behavior in the animal world that ties sexual reproduction to territorial defense. The key to the code, he believes, is territory, and the territorial imperative is the drive in animals and in men to take, hold and defend a given area.

There may be a drive in all men to have and defend a territory, and it may well be that a good part of that drive is inborn. However, we cannot always interpolate from humans to animals and from animals to humans.

The territorial imperative may exist in all animals and in some men. It may be strengthened by culture in some of these men and weakened in still others.

But there is little doubt that there is some territorial need in humans. How imperative it is remains to be seen. One of the most frightening plays of modern times is *Home,* by Megan Terry. It postulates a world of the future where the population explosion has caused all notion of territory to be discarded. All men live in cells in a gigantic metal hive enclosing the entire planet. They live

15

out their lives, whole families confined to one room, without ever seeing sky or earth or another cell.

In this prophetic horror story, territory has been completely abolished. Perhaps this gives the play its great impact. In our modern cities we seem to be moving toward the abolition of territory. We find families crammed and boxed into rooms that are stacked one on another to dizzying heights. We ride elevators pressed together, and subway trains, packed in too tightly to move our arms or legs. We have yet to fully understand what happens to man when he is deprived of all territorial rights.

We know man has a sense of territory, a need for a shell of territory around him. This varies from the tight close shell of the city dweller through the larger bubble of yard and home in the suburbanite to the wide open spaces the country man enjoys.

How Much Space Does a Man Need?

We don't know how much space is necessary to any individual man, but what is important in our study of body language is what happens to any individual man when this shell of space or territory is threatened or breached. How does he respond and how does he defend it, or how does he yield?

I had lunch not too long ago with a psychiatrist friend. We sat in a pleasant restaurant at a stylishly small table. At one point he took out a pack of cigarettes, lit one and put the pack down three-quarters of the way across the table in front of my plate.

He kept talking and I kept listening, but I was troubled in some way that I couldn't quite define, and more troubled as he moved his tableware about, lining it up with his cigarettes, closer and closer to my side of the table. Then

16

leaning across the table himself he attempted to make a point. It was a point I could hardly appreciate because of my growing uneasiness.

Finally he took pity on me and said, "I just favored you with a demonstration of a very basic step in body language, in nonverbal communication."

Puzzled, I asked, "What was that?"

"I aggressively threatened you and challenged you. I put you in a position of having to assert yourself, and that bothered you."

Still uncomprehending, I asked, "But how? What did you do?"

"I moved my cigarettes to start with," he explained. "By unspoken rule we have divided the table in half, half for you and half for me."

"I wasn't conscious of any such division."

"Of course not. The rule remains though. We both staked out a territory in our minds. Ordinarily we would have shared the table by some unspoken and civilized command. However, I deliberately moved my cigarettes into your area in a breach of taste. Unaware of what I had done, you still felt yourself threatened, felt uneasy, and when I aggressively followed up my first breach of your territory with another, moving my plate and silverware and then intruding myself, you became more and more uneasy and still were not aware of why."

It was my first demonstration of the fact that we each possess zones of territory. We carry these zones with us and we react in different ways to the breaking of these zones. Since then I have tried out the same technique of cutting into someone else's zone when he was unaware of what I was doing.

At supper the other evening, my wife and I shared a table in an Italian restaurant with another couple. Experimentally I moved the wine bottle into my friend's "zone." Then slowly, still talking, followed up my intrusion by rearranging wine glass and napkin in his zone. Uneasily he shifted in his chair, moved aside, rearranged his plate, his napkin and finally in a sudden, almost compulsive lunge, moved the wine bottle back.

He had reacted by defending his zone and retaliating.

From this parlor game a number of basic facts emerge. No matter how crowded the area in which we humans live, each of us maintains a zone or territory around us—an inviolate area we try to keep for our own. How we defend this area and how we react to invasion of it, as well as how we encroach into other territories, can all be observed and charted and in many cases used constructively. These are all elements of nonverbal communication. This guarding of zones is one of the first basic principles.

How we guard our zones and how we aggress to other zones is an integral part of how we relate to other people.

How We Handle Space

A Space to Call Your Own

Among Quakers, the story is told of an urban Friend who visited a Meeting House in a small country town. Though fallen into disuse, it was architecturally a lovely building, and the city Quaker decided to visit it for Sunday meeting although he was told that only one or two Quakers still attended meetings there.

That Sunday he entered the building to find the meeting hall completely empty, the morning sun shafting through the old, twelve-paned windows, the rows of benches silent and unoccupied.

He slipped into a seat and sat there, letting the peaceful silence fill him. Suddenly he heard a slight cough and, looking up, saw a bearded Quaker standing near his bench, an old man who might well have stepped out of the pages of history.

He smiled, but the old Quaker frowned and coughed again, then said, "Forgive me if I offend, but thee art sitting in my place."

The old man's quaint insistence on his own space, in spite of the empty meeting house, is amusing, but very true to life. Invariably, after you attend any church for any period of time, you stake out your own spot.

In his home Dad has his own particular chair, and while he may tolerate a visitor sitting there, it is often with poor grace. Mom has her own kitchen, and she doesn't like it one bit when her mother comes to visit and takes over "her" kitchen.

Men have their favorite seats in the train, their favorite benches in the park, their favorite chairs at conferences, and so on. It is all a need for territory, for a place to call one's own. Perhaps it is an inborn and universal need, though it is shaped by society and culture into a variety of forms. An office may be adequate for a working man or it may be too small, not according to the actual size of the room but according to placement of desk and chair. If the worker can lean back without touching a wall or a bookcase, it will usually seem big enough. But in a larger room, if his desk is placed so that he touches a wall when he leans back, the office may seem to be cramped from his viewpoint.

A Science Called Proxemics

Dr. Edward T. Hall, professor of anthropology at Northwestern University, has long been fascinated by man's reaction to the space about him, by how he utilizes that space and how his spatial use communicates certain facts and signals to other men. As Dr. Hall studied man's personal space, he coined the word *proxemics* to describe his theories and observations about zones of territory and how we use them.

Man's use of space, Dr. Hall believes, has a bearing on his ability to relate to other people, to sense them as being close or far away. Every man, he says, has his own territorial needs. Dr. Hall has broken these needs down in an attempt to standardize the science of proxemics and he has come up with four distinct zones in which most men operate. He lists these zones as 1) intimate distance, 2) personal distance, 3) social distance and 4) public distance.

As we might guess, the zones simply represent different areas we move in, areas that increase as intimacy decreases. Intimate distance can either be *close,* that is, actual contact, or *far,* from six to eighteen inches. The close phase of intimate distance is used for making love, for very close friendships and for children clinging to a parent or to each other.

When you are at *close intimate* distance you are overwhelmingly aware of your partner. For this reason, if such contact takes place between two men, it can lead to awkwardness or uneasiness. It is most natural between a man and a woman on intimate terms. When a man and a woman are not on intimate terms the close intimate situation can be embarrassing.

Between two women in our culture, a close intimate state is acceptable, while in an Arab culture such a state is acceptable between two men. Men will frequently walk hand in hand in Arab and in many Mediterranean lands.

The far phase of intimate distance is still close enough to clasp hands, but it is not considered an acceptable distance for two adult male Americans. When a subway or an elevator brings them into such crowded circumstances, they will automatically observe certain rigid rules of behavior, and by doing so communicate with their neighbors.

They will hold themselves as stiff as possible trying not to touch any part of their neighbors. If they do touch them, they either draw away or tense their muscles in the touching area. This action says, "I beg your pardon for intruding on your space, but the situation forces it and I will, of course, respect your privacy and let nothing intimate come of this."

If, on the other hand, they were to relax in such a situation and let their bodies move easily against their neighbors' bodies and actually enjoy the contact and the body heat, they would be committing the worst possible social blunder.

I have often seen a woman in a crowded subway car turn on an apparently innocent man and snarl, "Don't do that!" simply because the man had forgotten the rules and had relaxed against her. The snarls are worse when a man relaxes against another man.

Nor must we, in the crowded car or elevator, stare. There is a stated time interval during which we can look, and then we must quickly look away. The unwary male who goes beyond the stated time interval risks all sorts of unpleasant consequences.

I rode an elevator down in a large office building recently with another man. A pretty young girl got on at the fourteenth floor, and my friend looked at her absently but thoroughly. She grew redder and redder, and when the elevator stopped at the lobby, turned and snapped, "Haven't you ever seen a girl before, you—you dirty old man!"

My friend, still in his thirties, turned to me bewilderedly as she stormed out of the car and asked, "What did I do? Tell me, what the hell did I do?"

What he had done was to break a cardinal rule of nonverbal communication. "Look, and let your eyes slide away when you are in far intimate contact with a stranger."

The second zone of territory charted by Dr. Hall is called the *personal* distance zone. Here, too, he differentiates two areas, a *close personal* distance and a *far personal* distance. The close area is one and a half to two and a half feet. You can still hold or grasp your partner's hand at this distance.

22

As to its significance, he notes that a wife can stay within the close personal distance zone of her husband, but if another woman moves into this zone she presumably has designs on him. And yet this is obviously the comfortable distance at cocktail parties. It allows a certain intimacy and perhaps describes an intimate zone more than a personal zone. But since these are simply attempts by Dr. Hall to standardize a baby science, there may be a dozen clarifications before proxemics gets off the ground.

The far phase of personal distance, Dr. Hall puts at two and one half to four feet and calls this the limit of physical domination. You cannot comfortably touch your partner at this distance, and so it lends a certain privacy to any encounter. Yet the distance is close enough so that some degree of personal discussion can be held. When two people meet in the street, they usually stop at this distance from each other to chat. At a party they may tend to close in to the close phase of personal distance.

A variety of messages are transmitted by this distance and they range from, "I am keeping you at arm's length," to "I have singled you out to be a little closer than the other guests." To move too far in when you are on a *far personal* relationship with an acquaintance is considered pushy, or, depending on the sexual arrangement, a sign of personal favor. You make a statement with your distance, but the statement, to mean anything, must be followed up.

Social and Public Space

Social distance too has a close phase and a far phase. The *close* phase is four to seven feet and is generally the distance at which we transact impersonal business. It is the distance we assume when, in business, we meet the client from out of town, the new art director or the office manager. It is the distance the housewife keeps from the repairman, the shop clerk or the delivery boy. You assume this distance at a casual social gathering, but it can also be a manipulative distance.

A boss utilizes just this distance to dominate a seated employee—a secretary or a receptionist. To the employee, he tends to loom above and gain height and strength. He is, in fact, reinforcing the "you work for me" situation without ever having to say it.

The *far* phase of social distance, seven to twelve feet, is for more formal social or business relationships. The "big boss" will have a desk large enough to put him this distance from his employees. He can also remain seated at this distance and look up at an employee without a loss of status. The entire man is presented for his view.

To get back to the eyes, at this distance it is not proper to look briefly and look away. The only contact you have is visual, and so tradition dictates that you hold the person's eyes during conversation. Failing to hold his eyes is the same as excluding him from the conversation, according to Dr. Hall.

On the positive side, this distance allows a certain protection. You can keep working at this distance and not be rude, or you can stop working and talk. In offices it is necessary to preserve this far social distance between the receptionist and the visitor so that she may continue working without having to chat with him. A closer distance would make such an action rude.

The husband and wife at home in the evening assume this far social distance to relax. They can talk to each other if they wish or simply read instead of talking. The impersonal air of this type of social distance makes it an

24

almost mandatory thing when a large family lives together, but often the family is arranged for this polite separation and must be pulled more closely together for a more intimate evening.

Finally, Dr. Hall cites *public* distance as the farthest extension of our territorial bondage. Again there is a close phase and a far phase, a distinction which may make us wonder why there aren't eight distances instead of four. But actually, the distances are arrived at according to human interaction, not to measurement.

The *close* phase of public distance is twelve to twenty-five feet, and this is suited for more informal gatherings, such as a teacher's address in a roomful of students, or a boss at a conference of workers. The *far* phase of public distance, twenty-five feet or more, is generally reserved for politicians where the distance is also a safety or a security factor, as it is with animals. Certain animal species will let you come only within this distance before moving away.

While on the subject of animal species and distance, there is always the danger of misinterpreting the true meaning of distance and territorial zones. A typical example is the lion and the lion tamer. A lion will retreat from a human when the human comes too close and enters his "danger" zone. But when he can retreat no longer and the human still advances, the lion will turn and approach the human.

A lion tamer takes advantage of this and moves toward the lion in his cage. The animal retreats, as is its nature, to the back of the cage as the lion tamer advances. When the lion can go no farther, he turns and, again in accordance with his nature, advances on the trainer with a snarl. He invariably advances in a perfectly straight line. The trainer, taking advantage of this, puts the lion's platform between himself and the lion. The lion, approaching in a straight line, climbs on the platform to get at the trainer. At this point the trainer quickly moves back out of the lion's danger zone, and the lion stops advancing.

The audience watching this interprets the gun that the trainer holds, the whip and the chair in terms of its own inner needs and fantasies. It feels that he is holding a dangerous beast at bay. This is the nonverbal communication of the entire situation. This, in body language, is what the trainer is trying to tell us. But here body language lies.

In actuality, the dialogue between lion and tamer goes like this—Lion: "Get out of my sphere or I'll attack you." Trainer: "I am out of your sphere." Lion: "All right. I'll stop right here."

It doesn't matter where *here* is. The trainer has manipulated things so that *here* is the top of the lion's platform.

In the same way the far public sphere of the politician or the actor on a stage contains a number of body language statements which are used to impress the audience, not necessarily to tell the truth.

It is at this far public distance that it is difficult to speak the truth or, to turn it around, at this far public distance it is most easy to lie with the motions of the body. Actors are well aware of this, and for centuries they have utilized the distance of the stage from the audience to create a number of illusions.

At this distance the actor's gestures must be stylized, affected and far more symbolic than they are at closer public, social or intimate distances.

On the television screen, as in the motion picture, the combination of long shots and close-ups calls for still another type of body language. A movement of the eyelid or the eyebrow or a quiver of the lip in a close-up can convey as much of a message as the gross movement of arm or an entire body in a long shot.

In the close-up the gross movements are usually lost. This may be one of the reasons televison and motion picture actors have so much trouble adapting to the stage.

The stage often calls for a rigid, mannered approach to acting because of the distance between actors and audience. Today, in revolt against this entire technique, there are elements of the theatre that try to do away with the public distance between actor and stage.

They either move down into the audience, or invite the audience up to share the stage with them. Drama, under these conditions, must be a lot less structured. You can have no assurance that the audience will respond in the way you wish. The play therefore becomes more formless, usually without a plot and with only a central idea.

Body language, under these circumstances, becomes a difficult vehicle for the actor. He must on the one hand drop many of the symbolic gestures he has used, because they just won't work over these short distances. He cannot rely on natural body language for the emotions he wishes to project no matter how much he "lives" his part. So he must develop a new set of symbols and stylized body motions that will also lie to the audience.

Whether this "close-up" lying will be any more effective than the far-off lying of the proscenium stage remains to be seen. The gestures of the proscenium or traditional stage have been refined by years of practice. There is also a cultural attachment involved with the gestures of the stage. The Japanese kabuki theater, for example, contains its own refined symbolic gestures that are so culture-oriented that more than half of them may be lost on a Western audience.

27

How Different Cultures Handle Space

There are, however, body languages that can transcend cultural lines. Charlie Chaplin's little tramp, in his silent movies, was universal enough in his movements to bring almost every culture to laughter, including the technologically unsophisticated cultures of Africa. However, culture is still a guiding factor in all body language, and this is particularly true of body zones. Dr. Hall goes into the cross-cultural implication of his proxemics. In Japan, for example, crowding together is a sign of warm and pleasant intimacy. In certain situations, Hall believes the Japanese prefer crowding.

Donald Keene, who wrote *Living Japan,* notes the fact that in the Japanese language there is no word for privacy. Still this does not mean that there is no concept of privacy. To the Japanese, privacy exists in terms of his house. He regards this area as his own and resents intrusion into it. The fact that he crowds together with other people does not negate his need for living space.

Dr. Hall sees this as a reflection of the Japanese concept of space. Westerners, he believes, see space as the distance between objects. To us, space is empty. The Japanese see the shape and arrangement of space as having a tangible meaning. This is apparent not only in their flower arrangements and art, but in their gardens as well, where units of space blend harmoniously to form an integrated whole.

Like the Japanese, the Arabs too tend to cling close to one another. But while in public they are invariably crowded together, in private, in their own houses, the Arabs have almost too much space. Arab houses are, if possible, large and empty, with the people clustered together in one small area. Partitions between rooms are usually avoided, because in spite of the desire for space, the Arabs, paradoxically, do not like to be alone and even in their spacious houses will huddle together.

The difference between the Arab huddling and the Japanese proximity is a deep thing. The Arab likes to touch his companion, to feel and to smell him. To deny a friend his breath is to be ashamed.

The Japanese, in their closeness, preserve a formality and an aloofness. They manage to touch and still keep rigid boundaries. The Arab pushes these boundaries aside.

Along with this closeness, there is a pushing and a sharing in the Arab world that Americans find distasteful. To an American there are boundaries in a public place. When he is waiting in line he believes that his place there is inviolate. The Arab has no concept of privacy in a public place, and if he can push his way into a line, he feels perfectly within his rights to do so.

As the Japanese lack of a word for privacy indicates a certain attitude toward other people, so the Arab lack of a word for rape indicates a certain attitude toward the body. To an American the body is sacred. To the Arab, who thinks nothing of shoving and pushing and even pinching women in public, violation of the body is a minor thing. However, violation of the ego by insult is a major problem.

Hall points out that the Arab at times needs to be alone, no matter how close he wishes to be to his fellow man. To be alone, he simply cuts off the lines of communication. He withdraws, and this withdrawal is respected by his fellows. His withdrawal is interpreted in body language as "I need privacy. Even though I'm among you, touching you and living with you, I must withdraw into my shell."

29

Were the American to experience this withdrawal, he would tend to think it insulting. The withdrawal would be interpreted in his body language as "silent treatment." And it would be further interpreted as an insult.

When two Arabs talk to each other, they look each other in the eyes with great intensity. The same intensity of glance in our American culture is rarely exhibited between men. In fact, such intensity can be interpreted as a challenge to a man's masculinity. "I didn't like the way he looked at me, as if he wanted something personal, to sort of be too intimate," is a typical response by an American to an Arab look.

The Western World's Way with Space

So far we have considered body language in terms of spatial differences in widely disparate cultures, the East and Near East as opposed to the West. However, even among the Western nations, there are broad differences. There is a distinct difference between the way a German, for instance, handles his living space, and the way an American does. The American carries his two-foot bubble of privacy around with him, and if a friend talks to him about intimate matters they will come close enough for their special bubbles to merge. To a German, an entire room in his own house can be a bubble of privacy. If someone else engages in an intimate conversation in that room without including him he may be insulted.

Perhaps, Hall speculates, this is because in contrast to the Arab, the German's ego is "extraordinarily exposed." He will therefore go to any length to preserve his private sphere. In World War II, German prisoners of war were housed four to a hut in one army camp. Hall notes that as soon as they could they set about partitioning their huts to gain private space. In open stockades, German prisoners tried to build their own private dwelling units.

The German's "exposed ego" may also be responsible for a stiffness of posture and a general lack of spontaneous body movement. Such stiffness can be a defense or mask against revealing too many truths by unguarded movements.

In Germany, homes are constructed for a maximum of privacy. Yards are well-fenced and balconies are screened. Doors are invariably kept closed. When an Arab wants privacy he retreats into himself but when a German wants privacy he retreats behind a closed door. This German desire for privacy, for a definite private zone that does not intrude on anyone else's, is typified by his behavior in line-ups or queues.

At a movie house in a German-American neighborhood I waited in line recently for a ticket and listened to the German conversation about me as we moved forward in neat and orderly fashion.

Suddenly, when I was just a few places from the ticket-seller's window, two young men who, I later learned, were Polish walked up to the head of the line and tried to buy their tickets immediately.

An argument broke out around us. "Hey! We've been waiting on line. Why don't you?"

"That's right. Get back in line."

"To hell with that! It's a free country. Nobody asked you to wait in line," one of the Poles called out, forcing his way to the ticket window.

"You're queued up like sheep," the other one said angrily. "That's what's wrong with you Krauts."

The near riot that ensued was brought under control by two patrolmen, but inside the lobby I approached the line crashers.

"What were you trying to do out there? Start a riot?"

One of them grinned. "Just shaking them up. Why form a line? It's easier when you mill around." Discovering that they were Polish helped me understand their attitude. Unlike the Germans, who want to know exactly where they stand and feel that only orderly obedience to certain rules of conduct guarantees civilized behavior, the Poles see civilized behavior as a flouting of authority and regulations.

While the Englishman is unlike the German in his treatment of space—he has little feeling for the privacy of his own room—he is also unlike the American. When the American wishes to withdraw he goes off by himself. Possibly because of the lack of private space and the "nursery" raising of children in England, the Englishman who wants to be alone tends to withdraw into himself like the Arab.

The English body language that says, "I am looking for some momentary privacy," is often interpreted by the American as, "I am angry at you, and I am giving you the silent treatment."

The English social system achieves its privacy by carefully structured relationships. In America you speak to your next door neighbor because of proximity. In England, being a neighbor to someone does not at all guarantee that you know them or speak to them.

There is the story of an American college graduate who met an English Lady on an ocean liner to Europe. The boy was seduced by the Englishwoman and they had a wild affair.

A month later he attended a large and very formal dinner in London and among the guests, to his delight, he saw Lady X. Approaching her he said, "Hello! How have you been?"

Looking down her patrician nose, Lady X drawled, "I don't think we've been introduced."

"But . . . ," the bewildered young man stammered, "surely you remember me?" Then emboldened, he added, "Why, only last month we slept together on the trip across."

"And what," Lady X asked icily, "makes you think that constitutes an introduction?"

In England relationships are made not according to physical closeness but according to social standing. You are not necessarily a friend of your neighbor unless your social backgrounds are equal. This is a cultural fact based on the heritage of the English people, but it is also a result of the crowded condition in England. The French, like the English, are also crowded together, but their different cultural heritage has produced a different cultural result. While crowding has caused the English to develop an inordinate respect for privacy, it has caused the French to be very much involved with each other.

A Frenchman meets your eyes when he is talking to you, and he looks at you directly. In Paris women are closely examined visually on the streets. In fact many American women returning from Paris feel suddenly unappreciated. The Frenchman, by his look, conveys a nonverbal message. "I like you. I may never know you or speak to you, but I appreciate you."

No American male looks at women like this. Instead of appreciation this would be interpreted as rudeness in an American.

In France the crowding is partly responsible for the Frenchmen's involvement with each other. It is also held responsible for their concern with space. French parks treat space differently than American parks do. They

33

have a reverence for their open areas, a reverence even in the city, for the beauty of architecture.

We react to space in a different fashion. In New York we are an intensely crowded city and because of this we have developed an individual need for privacy. The New Yorker is traditionally known for his "unfriendly attitude" and yet the unfriendly attitude is developed out of a respect for our neighbor's privacy. We will not intrude on that privacy, so we ignore each other in elevators, in subways, on crowded streets.

We march along in our own little worlds, and when those worlds are forced together we go into a catatonic state to avoid a misinterpretation of our motives.

In body language we scream, "I am being forced to rub up against you, but my rigidity tells you that I do not mean to intrude." Intrusion is the worst sin. Speak to a stranger in New York City and you get a startled, alarmed reaction.

Only in times of great crisis do the barriers fall down, and then we realize that New Yorkers are not unfriendly at all, but rather shy and frightened. During the Great Northeast Power Failure everybody reached out to everybody else, to help, to comfort, to encourage and for a few warm, long hours the city was a vital place.

Then the lights went on and we fell back into our rigid zones of privacy.

Out of New York, in small American towns, there is a more open friendly attitude. People will say, "Hello," to strangers, smile and often make conversation. However, in *very* small towns, where everyone knows everyone else and there is very little privacy, the stranger may be treated to the same stand-offish attitude that he receives in the very big city.

When Space
Is Invaded

Defending Body Zones

At first glance it might be hard to see the exact relationship between personal spaces, zones or territories and kinesics, body language. But unless we understand the basic principles of individual territories we cannot appreciate what happens when these territories are invaded. How we react to personal invasion of our territory is very much related to body language. We should know our own aggressive behavior and our reactions to others' aggressions if we are to become aware of what signals we are sending and receiving.

Perhaps the most touching account of the inviolability of body zones was a novel written almost half a century ago by H. DeVere Stacpool, called *The Blue Lagoon*. It is the story of a young child shipwrecked on a tropical island with an old sailor. The sailor raises the boy to self-sufficiency and then dies, and the child grows to manhood alone, meets a young Polynesian girl and falls in love with her. The novel deals with the boy's love affair with the Polynesian girl who has been declared taboo from infancy. She has grown up forbidden to allow herself to be touched by any man. The struggle between the two to break down her conditioning and allow him to touch her makes a fascinating and moving story.

35

It was the early recognition of just how defensive a human can become about his body zones and personal privacy that led Stacpool to explore this theme, but it has only been in the last decade that scientists have begun to understand the complex significance of personal space.

In an earlier chapter I told of a psychiatrist who, with the aid of a pack of cigarettes, taught me a lesson about the invasion of personal space. He in turn had learned much of what he knew from the reaction of patients in hospitals for the mentally ill. A mental hospital is a closed microcosm, and as such often reflects and exaggerates attitudes of the larger world outside. But a mental hospital is also a very special type of place. The inmates are more susceptible to suggestion and aggression than are normal men and women and often their actions distort the actions of normal people.

How aggressive a mental patient is to someone depends on the rank of the other person. It is a test of dominance. In any mental hospital one or two patients will attain superior rank by aggressive behavior, but they can always be cowed by one of the attendants. In turn, the attendant is beneath the nurse and she is subordinate to the doctor.

There is a very real hierarchy developed in these institutions and it is reflected in the outer world in organizations like the army, or in business where there is a definite order of dominance. In the army, dominance is achieved by a system of symbols, stripes for the noncommissioned officers and bars, leaves, birds and stars for the commissioned officers. But even without the symbols, the pecking order remains. I have seen privates in a shower room deferential to sergeants without knowing who they were or what their rank was. The sergeants, through their manner and bearing, were able to convey an obvious body language message of rank.

Advice for Status Seekers

In the business world, where neither stripes nor other obvious symbols are worn, the same ability to project a sense of superiority is the common attainment of the executive. How does he do it? What tricks does he use to subdue subordinates, and what tricks does he bring out for in-fighting in his own rank?

An attempt to study this was made by two researchers in a series of silent films. They had two actors play the parts of an executive and a visitor, and switch roles for different takes. The scene had one man at his desk while the other, playing the part of a visitor, knocks at the door, opens it and approaches the desk to discuss some business matter.

The audience watching the films was asked to rate the executive and the visitor in terms of status. A certain set of rules began to emerge from the ratings. The visitor showed the least amount of status when he stopped just inside the door to talk across the room to the seated man. He was considered to have more status when he walked halfway up to the desk, and he had most status when he walked directly up to the desk and stood right in front of the seated executive.

Another factor that governed status in the eyes of the observers was the time between knocking and entering, and for the seated executive, the time between hearing the knock and answering. The quicker the visitor entered the room, the more status he had. The longer the executive took to answer, the more status *he* had.

It should be obvious that what is involved here is a matter of territory. The visitor is allowed to enter the executive's territory, and by that arrangement the executive automatically achieves superior status.

How far into the territory the visitor penetrates, and how quickly he does it, in other words how he challenges the personal space of the executive, announces his own status.

The "big boss" will walk into his subordinate's office unannounced. The subordinate will wait outside the boss's office until he is permitted in. If the boss is on the phone, the subordinate may tiptoe off and come back later. If the subordinate is on the phone, the boss will usually assert his status by standing above the subordinate until he murmurs, "Let me call you back," and then gives the boss his full attention.

There is a continuous shifting or fighting for status within the business world, and therefore status symbols become a very necessary part of the shift or dance. The executive with the attaché case is the most obvious one, and we all know the joke of the man who carries only his lunch in his attaché case but insists on carrying the case simply because it is so important to the image he must project. I know of a black minister and educator in America who travels around the country a great deal. He told me that he would never go into any Southern city, into the downtown area or a hotel, without a business suit and an attaché case. These two symbols gave him a certain amount of authority that differentiated him from the "nigger" in the same city.

Big business sets up a host of built-in status symbols. A large drug firm in Philadelphia earned enough money through the sale of tranquilizers to put up a new building that would house their rapidly expanding staff. The building could have been designed with any number of offices and workrooms, but quite deliberately the company set up a built-in status symbol in the offices. The corner offices on the very highest floor were reserved for the very highest personnel. The corner offices on the floor below were reserved for the next rank of top personnel. Lesser, but still important executives had offices without corner windows. The rank below this had offices without windows at all. Below them were the men with partitioned cubicles for offices. These had frosted glass walls and no doors and the next rank down had clear glass cubicles. The last rank had desks out in an open room.

Rank was arrived at by an equation whose elements consisted of time on the job, importance of the job, salary and degree. The degree of M.D., for example, gave any man, no matter what his salary or time on the job, the right to have a closed office. Ph.D.'s might or might not have such an office, depending on other factors.

Within this system there was room for many other elements to demonstrate degree of status. Drapes, rugs, wooden desks as opposed to metal desks, furniture, couches, easy chairs, and of course, secretaries, all set up subhierarchies.

An important element in this set-up was the contrast between the frosted glass cubicles and the clear glass cubicles. By allowing the world to see in, the man in the clear glass cubicle was automatically reduced in importance or rank. His territory was that much more open to visual invasion. He was that much more vulnerable.

How to Be a Leader

Opening of territory and invasion of territory are important functions of rank in business. What about leadership? By what tricks or by what body language does a leader assert himself?

Back in the years just before World War II, Charlie Chaplin did a motion picture called *The Great Dictator*.

39

As with all of Chaplin's movies, it was filled with bits of body language, but the most delightful sequence was one that took place in a barber shop.

Chaplin as Hitler and Jack Oakie as Mussolini are shown getting shaves in adjacent chairs. The scene centers around the attempts of each to put himself in a dominant position to the other in order to assert his superior leadership. Trapped within their chairs, lathered and draped, there is only one way to achieve dominance, and that is by controlling the height of the chairs. They can reach down and jack them up. The higher man wins, and the scene revolves around the attempt of each to jack his own chair to a higher position.

Dominance through height is a truism that works from the animal kingdom to man. Among wolves, recent studies have shown that the pack leader asserts his dominance by wrestling a yearling or subordinate wolf to the ground and standing over him. The subordinate expresses his subservience by crawling beneath the pack leader and exposing his throat and belly. It becomes a matter of who is higher.

The same positioning occurs with humans. We are all aware of the tradition of abasement before a king, before idols, before altars. Bowing and scraping in general are all variations of superiority or inferiority by height. They are all actions to point out the body language message, "You are higher than I am, therefore you are dominant."

A young man I know, well over six feet tall, was extremely successful in business because of his ability to show empathy for his associates. Observing him in action in some successful business transactions I became aware that whenever possible he stooped, sloped his body, or sat, in order to allow his associate to achieve dominance and feel superior.

In family seatings the dominant member, usually the father, will hold sway at the head of a rectangle table or an oval table. Often the choice of a round table will tell something of the family set-up. In the same way in discussion groups around a table, the leader will automatically assume the head of the table position.

That this is no new concept is obvious in the story of King Arthur and his round table. The table was round so that there could be no question of dominance and every knight could share equally in the honor of being seated at the table. However, this whole idea was weakened by the fact that Arthur himself, wherever he sat, became the dominant figure and status decreased as the distance from the King increased.

The boss of a large drug company I have worked in has an office that contains, in addition to his desk and desk chair, a couch, an easy chair and a coffee table with one or two chairs around it. This man announces the formality or informality of a situation by where he sits during that situation. If a visitor comes whom he wants to treat in an informal manner, he will come around from his desk and guide the visitor to the couch, to the easy chair or to the coffee table. In this way, by his positioning, he indicates just what type of interview he will have. If it's to be an extremely formal one he will remain seated behind his desk.

The Space We Hold Inviolate

The need for personal space and the resistance to the invasion of personal space is so strong a thing that even in a crowd each member will demand a given amount of space. This very fact led a journalist named Herbert Jacobs to attempt to apply it to crowd size. Since estimation

41

of crowd size tends to vary according to whether the observer is for the crowd or against it, the size of political rallies, peace rallies and demonstrations are inflated by the marchers and deflated by the authorities.

Jacobs, by studying aerial photographs of crowds where he could actually count heads, concluded that people in dense crowds need six to eight square feet each, while people in loose crowds require an average of ten square feet. Crowd size, Jacobs finally concluded, could be gauged by the formula, *length* times *width* divided by a *correction factor* that took density of the crowd into account. This gave the actual number of people in any gathering.

On the subject of crowds, it is important to realize that the personal territory of the people in a crowd is destroyed by the very act of crowding. The reaction to this destruction can, in some cases, change the temper of the crowd. Men react very strongly when their personal space or territory is invaded. As a crowd gets larger and tighter and more compact, it may also get uglier. A loose crowd may be easier to handle.

The need for personal space was known to Freud, who always arranged his sessions so that the patient would lie on the couch while he sat in a chair out of the patient's sight. In this way there was no intrusion upon the patient's personal space.

The police are also well aware of this fact, and they take advantage of it in their interrogation of prisoners. A textbook on criminal interrogation and confessions suggests that the questioner sit close to the suspect and that there be no table or other obstacle between them. Any kind of obstacle, the book warns, gives the man being questioned a certain degree of relief and confidence.

The book also suggests that the questioner, though he

may start with his chair two or three feet away, should move in closer as the questioning proceeds, so that "ultimately one of the subject's knees is just about in between the interrogator's two knees."

This physical invasion of the man's territory by the police officer, the crowding in as he is questioned, has been found in practice to be extremely useful in breaking down a prisoner's resistance. When a man's territorial defenses are weakened or intruded upon, his self-assurance tends to grow weaker.

In a working situation the boss who is aware of this can strengthen his own position of leadership by intruding spatially on the man under him. The higher-up who leans over the subordinate's desk throws the subordinate off balance. The department head who crowds next to the worker while inspecting his work makes the worker uneasy and insecure. In fact, the parent who scolds the child by leaning over him is compounding the relationship between them, proving and reinforcing his own dominance.

Can we use this intrusion of personal space to arouse defensive measures in others, or can we, by avoiding it, also avoid the sometimes dangerous consequences of an intrusion? We know that tailgating a car is dangerous from a purely physical point of view. If the car ahead stops short we can smack into it, but no one talks about what the act of tailgating can do to the nerves of the driver ahead.

A man driving a car often loses an essential part of his own humanity and is, by virtue of the machine around him, once removed from a human being. The body language communication that works so well for him outside the car often will not work at all when he is driving. We have all been annoyed by drivers who cut in front of us, and we all know the completely irrational rage that can sometimes fill the driver who has thus had his space invaded. The police will cite statistics to show that dozens of accidents are caused by this cutting in, by the dangerous reaction of the man who has been cut off. In a social situation few men would dream of acting or reacting in this fashion. Stripped of the machine we adopt a civilized attitude and allow people to cut in front of us, indeed we step aside quite often to permit people to board a bus or elevator ahead of us.

A car, however, seems to act much like a dangerous weapon in the hands of many drivers. It can become a weapon that destroys many of our controls and inhibitions. The reason for this is obscure, but some psychologists have theorized that at least a part of it is due to the extension of our personal territories when we are in a car. Our own zones of privacy expand and the zone of privacy of the car becomes much greater and our reaction to any intrusion on that zone is greater still.

Of Space and Personality

There have been many studies attempted to find out just how the reaction to invasion of personal space is related to personality. One, a master's thesis by John L. Williams, determined that introverts tended to keep people at a greater conversational distance than extroverts. The man who is withdrawn needs greater defenses to insure the sanctity of his withdrawn state. Another study, for a doctoral thesis, by William E. Leipold arrived at the same conclusion by a clever experiment. Students were first given personality tests to see if they were introverted or extroverted, and then were sent to an office to be interviewed about their grades.

Three types of instructions to the students were given

by the experimenter. These were called *stress, praise* or *neutral* instructions. The stress instructions were geared to upset the man. "We feel that your course grade is quite poor and that you haven't tried your best. Please take a seat in the next room till the interviewer can speak to you."

The student then entered the room with a desk and two chairs, one in front of it and one behind it.

The praise interview started with the student being told that his grades were good and that he was doing well. In the neutral interview the instructions were simply, "We are interested in your feelings about the course."

Results of the study showed that the students who were praised sat closest to the interviewer's chair. The students under stress sat farthest away, and the ones receiving neutral instructions sat midway. Introverted and anxious students sat farther away than extroverted students under the same conditions.

With this much charted, the next step was to determine the reactions of men and women when their territory was invaded. Dr. Robert Sommer, professor of psychology and chairman of the Psychology Department at the University of California, describes a set of experiments conducted in a hospital environment where, dressed in a doctor's white coat to gain authority, he systematically invaded the patients' privacy, sitting next to them on benches and entering their wards and day rooms. These intrusions, he reported, invariably bothered the patients and drove them from their special chairs or areas. The patients reacted to Dr. Sommer's physical intrusion by becoming uneasy and restless and finally by removing themselves bodily from the area.

From his own observations and the observations of others Dr. Sommer has discovered a whole area of body language that the individual uses when his private territory is invaded. Aside from the actual physical retreat of picking up and going somewhere else, there will be a series of preliminary signals, rocking, leg swinging or tapping. These are the first signs of tension, and they say, "You are too near. Your presence makes me uneasy."

The next series of body language signals are closed eyes, withdrawal of the chin into the chest and hunching of the shoulders. These all say, "Go away. I do not want you here. You are intruding."

Dr. Sommer tells of another researcher into the field of spatial invasion, Nancy Russo, who used a library as her theater of operations. A library is a perfect place to observe reactions. It is a subdued atmosphere geared to privacy. In most cases a newcomer to a library will isolate himself from the other researchers by taking a seat some distance from anyone else.

Miss Russo would take an adjacent chair and then move closer to her victim, or sit across from him. While she found no single universal reaction to people sitting close, she found that most spoke with body language to transmit their feelings. She described "defensive gestures, shifts in posture, attempts to move away unobtrusively." Eventually, she concluded, if all of a man's body language signals are ignored, he will take off and move to another location.

Only one out of eighty students whose area was intruded on by Miss Russo asked her verbally to move away. The rest used body language to communicate their disapproval of the closeness.

Dr. Augustus F. Kinzel, who now works at the New York Psychiatric Institute, evolved a theory while working at the U.S. Medical Center for Federal Prisoners which may point the way toward detecting, predicting and even treating violent behavior in men.

In his early animal studies Dr. Kinzel noted that animals will often react with violence to any intrusion of their personal territory. While working at the prison in a population selected for violent action against society, he noticed that certain men preferred isolation cells despite the deprivations of such living. He found that these same men were sometimes troubled by senseless outbursts of violence. Could it be that these men required more space to maintain their self-control?

Dr. Kinzel found that many men who were guilty of assault with violence complained that their victims had "messed around with them," though a careful check disclosed that they had assaulted men who had done nothing but come close to them. The fits of violence were similarly provoked in and out of prison, so the prison atmosphere could not explain it. What could?

To find out, Dr. Kinzel conducted an experiment in the prison with fifteen volunteer prisoners. Eight had violent histories and seven didn't. The men were asked to stand in the center of an empty room while the "experimenter" approached them slowly. Each was to say, "Stop!" when the experimenter came too close.

When the experiment was repeated again and again, each man was found to have a definite body zone, territory or bubble, a personal space Dr. Kinzel labeled a "body buffer zone."

"The violent group," Dr. Kinzel said, "kept the experimenter at twice the distance the non-violent ones did." Their body buffer zones were four times larger in volume than the zones of the non-violent group. When someone got too close to one of these men, he resisted as though the intruder were "looming up" or "rushing in."

47

In this experiment the same feeling had been induced in the violent men as when they had assaulted other prisoners for "messing around." These men, Dr. Kinzel decided, went into an unreal panic when someone intruded upon their larger-than-normal body zones. This panic and its resulting violence occurred at a distance that other people would consider normal.

Much of what Dr. Kinzel calls "the quickly spiraling character of violence between 'overcrowded' ghetto groups and the police" may be due to a poor understanding by the police of the sanctity of body zones. Dr. Kinzel's study seems to indicate that we are only beginning to understand the origins of violent outbreaks in human beings, and how to detect and manage them, outbreaks which seldom occur in the animal kingdom where a tacit understanding of territorial needs exists until man interferes.

Sex and Non-Persons

There is, in the whole business of invasion, a strong sexual link. A girl moving into a man's territory encounters a different set of signals than if she were moving into a woman's territory. There is more acceptance and the possibility of a flirtation makes the man less likely to resent the intrusion. The same situation reversed, however, generally puts a woman on her guard.

The signal that invariably is sent by intruders is, "You are a non-person, and therefore I can move in on you. You do not matter."

This signal, in the context of a business situation between boss and employee, can be demoralizing to the employee and useful to the boss. It can in fact reaffirm the boss's leadership.

In a crowded subway there is a slightly different interpretation of the signals. There it is important that the two people regard each other as non-persons. Otherwise the fact that they are forced into such intimate terms may be awkward. The person who intrudes on another verbally in a crowded subway is guilty of a gaucherie. It may in fact be a little left of gauche. Here a rigid withdrawal is necessary in order to endure an uncomfortable situation. We have never seen any movies in which a boy and a girl meet on a crowded subway. It just isn't done, even in Hollywood.

The crowding in subway trains is only bearable, Sommer believes, because the riders tend to think of each other as non-persons. If they are forced to acknowledge each other's presence because of an abrupt stop, for instance, they may resent the situation in which they find themselves.

The reverse is also true. In an uncrowded situation a person will resent being treated as a non-person. Our library researcher noticed one man who lifted his head and stared at her coldly, signaling with body language, "I am an individual, by what right do you intrude?"

He was using body language to resist her intrusion and she all at once became the person aggressed against, instead of the aggressor. So strongly did she feel this man's disapproval that she was unable to follow through her experiment for the rest of that day.

Her inability to continue was because the man whose privacy she was invading suddenly cut through her own defenses and for the first time in the experiment she perceived him as a human instead of an object. This ability to realize humanity in another individual is an extremely important key to how we act and react in body language as well as in all relationships. Dr. Sommer points out that an object, a non-person, cannot invade someone else's personal space, any more than a tree or a chair can. Nor is there any problem with invading the personal space of a non-person.

As an example Sommer cites the hospital nurses who discuss the patient's condition at his bedside, or the black maid in the white household who serves dinner while the guests debate the race question. Even the janitor who empties the waste basket in an office may not bother to knock when he enters, nor does the occupant of the office mind this intrusion. The janitor is not a real person to him. He's a non-person just as the man in the office is a non-person to the janitor.

Ceremonies and Seating

How we recognize and react to invasions includes a number of what Sommer calls "recognition ceremonies." In normal circumstances when you invade another's territory in either a library or a cafeteria, you send out a set of deferential signals. Verbally you apologize and ask, "Is this seat taken?" In body language you lower your eyes when you sit down.

When you take a seat on a crowded bus the proper ceremony is to keep your eyes straight ahead and avoid looking at the person sitting next to you. For other situations there are other ceremonies.

Defending personal space, according to Dr. Sommer, involves using the proper body language signals or gestures and postures as well as a choice of a location. How do you sit at an empty table when you wish to discourage other people from joining you? What body language do you use? A study by Sommer among university students showed that sitting down at an empty table when you wanted privacy usually involved use of two procedures. Either you look for privacy by positioning yourself as far as possible from other distracting people, or you attempt to get privacy by keeping the entire table to yourself alone.

If you look for privacy by retreating from others, you approach the problem from an avoidance standpoint. You take a retreat position, usually at the corner of the table. In body language you say, "Share my table if you wish, but leave me alone. I am putting myself here at a corner so that the next person can sit as far from me as possible."

The other approach would be to try to keep the entire table to yourself. This is an offensive attitude and the aggressive person who chooses it would seat himself in the center of either side. He is saying, "Leave me alone. You cannot sit down without annoying me, so find another table!"

Among other findings of Dr. Sommer's study were the following: students who are in retreat, who wish to be as far away from others as they can get, will face away from the door. Students who wish to hog the entire table, who are in defense, will face the door. Most students, retreaters and defenders, preferred the back of the room, and most preferred small tables or tables against the wall.

In body language, students who sat squarely in the center of the table were asserting their dominance, their ability to handle the situation and also their desire to have the table to themselves.

The student who sat at the corner of the table signaled his wish to be left alone. "I don't mind if you share the table, but if you do, I have placed myself far away. You should do likewise. In that way we can both have our privacy."

51

The same is true of park benches. If you want privacy and you take a seat on an empty park bench you will most likely sit on the far end of either side indicating, "If you must sit here too, there is room enough to leave me alone."

If you don't want to share the bench you will position yourself in the center and communicate, "I want this bench as my own. Sit and you are intruding."

If you are willing to share your bench and your privacy then you will sit to one side, but not at the far end.

These approaches to the struggle for privacy reflect our inner personality. They indicate that the extroverted man will tend to go after his privacy by holding off the world. The introverted one will look for his by sharing his place with others, but keeping them at a distance. In both cases the body language involved includes a different set of signals, not a signal of body movement, but rather a signal of placement. "I put myself here and by doing so I say, 'Keep off' or 'Sit here but do not intrude.'"

This is similar to the signal transmitted by arranging the body in various postures relating to the environment: behind the desk in an office, to signal, "Keep off, I am to be respected"; at the top of a judge's bench, the highest point in a courtroom, to signal, "I am far above you and therefore my judgment is best"; or close to someone else, violating their zone, to say, "You have no rights of your own. I move in on you at will and therefore I am superior."

The Masks
Men Wear

The Smile that Hides the Soul

There are many methods with which we defend our personal zones of space, and one of these is masking. The face we present to the outer world is rarely our real face. It is considered exceptional, almost peculiar behavior to show what we really feel in our facial expressions or in our actions. Instead we practice a careful discipline when it comes to the expression of our faces and bodies. Dr. Erving Goffman, in his book, *Behavior in Public Places,* states that one of the most obvious evidences of this discipline is the way we manage our personal appearance, the clothes we select and the hairdos we affect.

These carry a body language message to our friends and associates. Dr. Goffman believes that in public places the standard man of our society is expected to be neatly dressed and clean-shaven, with his hair combed and his hands and face clean. His study, written six years ago, didn't take into account the long hair, unshaven and careless or freer look of today's young people, a look that is slowly gaining acceptance. But this look too is one that is expected or formalized. It conforms to a general ideal.

Dr. Goffman makes the point that there are times, such as during the subway rush hour, when the careful masks we wear slip a bit, and "in a kind of temporary, uncaring,

53

righteous exhaustion," we show ourselves as we really are. We let the defenses down and out of weariness or exasperation we forget to discipline our faces. Play the game of looking about a crowded bus, subway, or train during the rush hour after a day's work. See how much of the bare human being is allowed to show in all the faces.

Day after day we cover up this bare human being. We hold ourselves in careful control lest our bodies cry out messages our minds are too careless to hide. We smile constantly, for a smile is a sign not only of humor or pleasure but it is also an apology, a sign of defense or even an excuse.

I sit down next to you in a crowded restaurant. A weak smile says, "I don't mean to intrude, but this is the only vacant place."

I brush against you in a packed elevator and my smile says, "I am not really being aggressive, but forgive me anyway."

I am thrown against someone in a bus by a sudden stop, and my smile says, "I did not intend to hurt you. I beg your pardon."

And so we smile our way through the day, though in fact we may feel angry and annoyed beneath the smile. In business we smile at customers, at our bosses, at our employees; we smile at our children, at our neighbors, at our husbands and wives and relatives, and very few of our smiles have any real significance. They are simply the masks we wear.

The masking process goes beyond the facial muscles. We mask with our entire body. Women learn to sit in a certain way to conceal their sexuality, especially when their skirts are short. Men wear underwear that often binds their sexual organs. Women wear brassieres to keep their breasts in place and mask too much sexuality. We hold ourselves upright and button our shirts, zip up our flies, hold in our stomachs with muscle and girdle, and practice a variety of facial maskings. We have our party faces, our campus faces, our funeral faces and even in prison we have particular faces to wear.

In a book called *Prison Etiquette,* Dr. B. Phillips notes that new prisoners learn to "dogface," to wear an expression that is apathetic and characterless. When the prisoners are alone, however, in a reaction to the protective dogfacing of the day, they overreact and exaggerate their smiles, their laughter and the hate they feel toward their guards.

With advancing age the masks we use often become more difficult to wear. Certain women, who have relied on facial beauty all their lives, find it hard in the mornings of their old age to "get their faces together." The old man tends to forget himself and drools or lets his face go lax. With advancing years come tics, sagging jowls, frowns that won't relax and deep wrinkles that won't go away.

Take Off the Mask

Again, there are certain situations in which the mask drops. In a car, when our body zones are extended, we often feel free to drop the masks, and if someone cuts in front of us or tailgates us, we may loose tides of profanity that are shocking in their out-of-proportion emotions. Why do we feel so strongly in such minor situations? What great difference does it make if a car cuts us off or comes too close?

But here is a situation where we are generally invisible and the need to mask is gone. Our reactions can be all the greater because of this.

The dropping of the mask tells us a great deal about

the need to wear a mask. In mental institutions the mask is often dropped. The mental patient, like the aging person, may neglect the most commonly accepted masks. Dr. Goffman tells of a woman in a ward for regressed females whose underwear was on wrong. She started, in full view of everybody, to adjust it by lifting her skirt, but when this didn't work she simply dropped her dress to the floor and fixed it, then pulled her dress up again quite calmly.

This attitude of ignoring the common devices of masking, such as clothes, of neglecting appearance and personal care, is often one of the most glaring signs of approaching psychotic behavior. Conversely, getting better in mental institutions is often equated with taking an interest in one's appearance.

Just as approaching psychotic behavior causes the patient to lose touch with reality and become confused in his verbal communication, causes him to say things that are divorced from reality, it also causes confusion in his body language. Here too he loses touch with the real world. He broadcasts statements that normal people keep hidden. He lets the inhibitions imposed by society slip, and he acts as if he were no longer conscious of an audience watching.

And yet this very loosening of body language may hold the key to a greater understanding of the mentally disturbed patient. While a person can stop talking, the same person cannot stop communicating through his body language. He must say the right thing or the wrong thing, but he cannot say nothing. He can cut down on how much he communicates by body language if he acts in the proper fashion, or acts normally, the way people are supposed to act. In other words, if he behaves sanely, then he will send out the least amount of body language information.

But if he acts sanely, then of course he is sane. What

other criteria do we have for sanity? So by definition, the insane man must act out his insanity and by so doing send a message to the world. This message, in the case of the mentally disturbed, is usually a cry for help. This puts an entirely new face on the strange actions of mentally disturbed people, and it opens up new avenues for therapy.

Masking cannot cover involuntary reactions. A tense situation may cause us to perspire, and there is no possible way to mask this. In another uncomfortable situation our hands may shake or our legs tremble. We can cover these lapses by putting our hands in our pockets, by sitting down to take the weight off our trembling legs, or by moving so quickly that the tremor isn't visible or noticed. Fear can be concealed by throwing yourself vigorously into the action you fear.

The Mask that Won't Come Off

The need to mask is often so deep that the process becomes self-perpetuating, and the mask cannot be taken off or let down. There are certain situations, such as sexual intercourse, where the masking should be stopped in order to enjoy love-making to its fullest, and yet many of us are only able to unmask in complete darkness. We are so afraid of what we may tell our partners by body language, or of what we may reveal with our faces, that we attempt to cut off the visual end of sex completely and we raise moral bulwarks to help us do this. "It's not decent to look." "The sexual organs are ugly." "A nice girl doesn't do that by daylight." And so on.

For many other people darkness is not enough to allow unmasking. Even in the dark they cannot drop the shields they have put up to protect themselves during sexual intercourse.

57

This, Dr. Goffman speculates, may be partly responsible for the large amounts of frigidity found in middle-class women. But in terms of sexual practice, Kinsey has shown that there are just as many shields, if not more, among the working classes. If anything, the middle class tends to be more experimental and less apt to shield its emotions.

The key to most masking in our society is often contained in books of etiquette. These will dictate what is proper and what isn't in terms of body language. One book suggests that it is wrong to rub our faces, touch our teeth or clean our fingernails in public. What to do with your body and your face when you meet friends or strangers is carefully spelled out by Emily Post. Her book of etiquette even describes how to ignore women. She discusses the "cut direct" and how to deliver it, "only with the gravest cause if you are a lady, and never to a lady if you are a man."

Part of our knowledge of masking is thus learned or absorbed from our culture, and part is taught specifically. But the technique of masking, though it is universal among mankind, varies from culture to culture. Certain aborigines, to be polite, must talk to each other without looking at each other's eyes, while in America it is polite to hold a partner's eyes while talking to him.

When Is a Person Not a Person?

In any culture there are permissible moments when the mask may slip. Blacks in the South are well aware of the "hate stare" that a Southern white can give to them for no obvious reason except skin color. The same stare or naked show of hostility without masking can be given to another white by a white only under the greatest provocation and it is never permitted in America's Southern cultures to be given by a black to a white.

One of the reasons why the mask may be dropped, in this case, by the Southern white is because the Southern white sees the black as a non-person, an object not worth concerning himself about. In the South, however, the blacks have their own private signs. One black, by a certain signal of the eye, may tell another that he too is a brother, a black, even though his skin is so light that he could pass as a white. By another type of eye signal he may warn off a black and tell him, "I am passing as a white man."

Children, in our society, are treated as non-persons quite often and so are servants. We feel, perhaps consciously, perhaps unconsciously, that before these non-persons no mask is necessary. We cannot worry about hurting the feelings of a non-person. How can he have feelings to hurt?

This attitude is usually seen as a class-oriented thing. A class in society will apply it to the class beneath; higher-status people will apply it to lower-status people. The boss may not bother to mask in front of his employee, nor the lady in front of her maid any more than a father will mask in front of his child.

I sat in a restaurant recently with my wife, and a table away two dowager-type women were having cocktails. Everthing about them from their furs to their hairdos cried out "wealth" and their bearing confirmed the fact. In the crowded restaurant they talked in voices so loud that they carried to every corner, yet their talk was private and intimate. The embarrassing result to the rest of the diners was that in order to maintain an illusion of privacy we all had either to pretend not to hear or to conduct ourselves and our own conversations so intently that we could block out the two dowagers.

In body language these two women were saying, "You are all of no real importance to us. You are all, in fact, not really people at all. You are non-persons. What we wish to do is all that matters, and so we cannot really embarrass anyone else."

Incidentally, instead of using their bodies to signal this message, these dowagers used voice volume, and it was not the intelligence of what they said but the amount of sound they used to say it that conveyed the message. Here we have the unusual technique of having two messages transmitted by one medium, the meaning of the words transmits one message, and the loudness of the voice transmits another.

These are cases where the mask is dropped but the dropping is almost contemptuous. Unmasking in front of a non-person is often no unmasking at all. In most cases we keep our masks on and the reason we keep them on is important. It is often dangerous in one way or another to unmask. When we are approached by a beggar in the street, if we do not wish to give him anything, it is important that we pretend he is not there and we have not seen him. We firm up the mask, look away and hurry past. If we were to allow ourselves to unmask in order to see the beggar as an individual not only would we have to face our own consciences, but we would also leave ourselves open to his importuning, pleading and possible attempt to embarrass us.

The same is true of many chance encounters. We cannot afford the time involved to exchange words and pleasantries, at least in urban areas. There are just too many people around us. In the suburbs or in the country it is different, and there is correspondingly less masking.

Also, by showing our real selves, we open ourselves to unpleasant interpretation. Dr. Goffman makes this clear in the setting of a mental institution. He describes a middle-aged man, a mental patient, who walked about with a folded newspaper and a rolled umbrella, wearing an expression of being late for an appointment. Keeping up the front that he was a normal businessman was overwhelmingly important to this patient, though in point of fact he was deceiving no one but himself.

In Eastern countries the masking procedure may be a physical one. The custom of women wearing veils is primarily to allow them to conceal their true emotions and so protect them from any male aggression. In these countries body language is so well recognized that it becomes an accepted fact that a man, with the slightest encouragement, will try to force sexual intercourse upon a woman. The veil allows the woman to hide her lower face and any unintentionally encouraging gesture. In the seventeenth century women used fans and masks on sticks for the same purpose.

The Masochist and the Sadist

In many cases masking can be used as an instrument of psychological torture. Take the case of Annie, married to Ralph, an older man, older and better educated and very conscious of the fact that Annie, intellectually and socially, was not his equal. Yet in a strange and somewhat perverted way Ralph loved Annie and realized she was the best wife for him. This did not prevent him from playing his own type of game with Annie, a game that involved masking to an intricate and exact degree.

When Ralph came home from work each day there was a well-standardized ritual. Annie must have his supper ready and waiting at exactly six-thirty, neither later nor earlier. He would arrive home at six, wash and read the afternoon paper until six-thirty. Then Annie would call him to the table and take her seat, watching his face furtively. Ralph knew she was watching him. She realized that he knew. But neither admitted to this.

Ralph would in no way indicate that the meal was either good or bad and as they ate Annie would construct a soap opera in her head. She would feel a sick despair in the pit of her stomach. Does Ralph like the food or doesn't he? If he doesn't, she knows what to expect: a cold upbraiding and a silent, miserable evening.

Annie would eat uneasily, watching Ralph's impassive face. Did she prepare the dish correctly? Did she season it properly? She followed the recipe, but she added some spices of her own. Was that a mistake? Yes, it must have been! She would feel her heart sink, her whole body tighten with misery. No, Ralph doesn't like it. Isn't his lip twisting in the beginning of a sneer?

Ralph, living the same soap opera, would look and for a long moment keep his face inscrutable while Annie would die a thousand deaths, and then he would smile his approval. And suddenly, miraculously, Annie's entire being would sing with happiness. Life is wonderful, and Ralph is her love and she is terribly, terribly happy. She would go back to her meal, enjoying the food now, ravenously hungry and delightfully pleased.

By careful manipulation of his mask, by timing his body language, Ralph has contrived a delicate torture and reward. He uses the same technique at night when he and Annie are in bed. He gives her no hint or indication of what he feels, of whether he will make love to her or not, and Annie goes through the same elaborate game of "Will he touch me? Does he still love me? How will I stand it if he rejects me!"

When finally Ralph does reach over and touch her Annie explodes in passionate ecstasy. Now the question of whether Annie is a victim or an accomplice is not for us to decide. The use of a mask to achieve the torture is the point to consider. The sado-masochist relationship of Annie and Ralph benefits both of them in a strange way, but for most mask wearers the benefits of wearing the mask are more realistic.

How to Drop the Mask

The benefits of masking, real or imagined, make us reluctant to drop the mask. We might, among other things, be forcing a relationship other people do not want. Or we might risk being rejected. Yet the very wearing of the mask can cheat us of relationships we want. Do we gain as much as we lose?

Take the case of Claudia. In her early thirties, Claudia is attractive in a thin, intense way. Because of her job in a large investment firm Claudia comes in contact with many men during the course of her day, and she dates a great deal. But she is still single and, though she hates to admit it, still a virgin.

It's not for want of desire, Claudia insists. She is a passionate girl and looks ahead with horror to the prospect of a sterile old maid's life. Why then can't she become involved with a man emotionally and sexually? Claudia doesn't understand why, but the men she dates can.

"She turns you off," one of them explained. "Hell, I like Claudia. At work she's a great gal and I've taken her out, but the moment something begins to develop she freezes up and the message is very clear. Don't touch. I'm not having any. Who needs that?"

Who indeed? Who can see past Claudia's forbidding façade to the warm and passionate woman underneath? Claudia, in terror of rejection, does the rejecting first before anything can develop. In that way she's never hurt. She's never refused because she does the refusing first.

Stupid? Perhaps, but effective if being rejected is the worst thing in the world that can happen to you. For Claudia it is. So rather than take a chance she'll live out her days in loneliness.

Claudia's masking is unnecessary and wasteful, but there are necessary maskings decreed by the society. The person who masks according to this rule may desperately want to use body language to communicate, but isn't allowed to by custom.

An example of this masking is a nubile young friend, a girl of seventeen, who came to my wife with her problem.

"There's this boy I ride home with on the bus every day, and he gets off at my stop and I don't know him, but he's cute and I'd like to know him, and I think he likes me, but how can I get to be friendly?"

My wife, out of the wisdom of experience, suggested a couple of awkward, heavy packages for the next bus ride plus a carefully rehearsed stumble to send all the packages flying as she left the bus.

To my amazement it worked. The accident called forth the only possible response, since they were the only two passengers who left the bus at that stop. He helped her with the packages, and she was obliged to drop the mask. He, too, could now unmask, and by the time they reached her house she was able to ask him in for a Coke, and so it went.

At the proper time, then, the mask should often be

dropped, must indeed be dropped if the individual is to grow and develop, if any meaningful relationship is to come about. The big problem with all of us is that after wearing a mask for a lifetime it is not so easy to drop it.

Sometimes the mask can only be dropped when further masking takes place. The man who dresses up in a clown suit for some amateur theatrical project often sheds his inhibitions as he dons his costume, and he is able to cavort and joke and "clown around" with perfect looseness and freedom.

The masking of darkness allows some of us the freedom to make love without masks, and for others the mask of anonymity serves the same purpose.

I have had male homosexuals tell me that they have had encounters with men, complete from pickup to sexual satisfaction, without even divulging their own names or learning their partners' names. When I asked how they could be so intimate without ever knowing their partners' names, the answer was invariably, "But that adds something to it. I can be relaxed and do what I want to. After all, we didn't know each other, and who cares what we did or said?"

To an extent, the same is true when a man visits a prostitute. The same anonymity may hold and bring with it a greater freedom.

But these are simply cases of double masking, of putting up another defense so that one may drop the mask. Along with the constant need to guard our body language, to keep a tight reign on the signals we send out, there is also a paradoxical need to transmit wildly and freely, to tell the world who we are and what we want, to cry out in the wilderness and be answered, to drop the mask and see if the hidden person is a being in his own right, in short, to free ourselves and to communicate.

6

The Wonderful World of Touch

Come Hold My Hand

Some time ago I volunteered to teach a young people's creative writing class at our local church. Harold, one of the young men who attended the class, was fourteen and a born troublemaker. Handsome, big for his age and very vocal, Harold made enemies without even trying, though usually he tried.

By the fifth session everyone hated him and he was well on his way to breaking up the group. For my part I was desperate. I tried everything from kindness and friendliness to anger and discipline, but nothing worked and Harold remained a sullen, disruptive force.

Then one evening he went a little too far in teasing one of the girls, and I grabbed him with both hands. The moment I did it, I realized my mistake. What could I do now? Let him go? Then he would be the victor. Hit him? Hardly, with the difference in age and size.

In a flash of inspiration I wrestled him to the ground and started to tickle him. He squealed with anger at first and then with laughter. Only when he gaspingly promised to behave did I let him up and found, to my own mixed reactions, that I had created a Frankenstein-type of monster. By tickling him I had invaded his body zone and prevented him from using it for defense.

Harold behaved himself from that time on, but Harold also became my devoted companion and buddy, hanging on my arm or my neck, pushing me or pummeling me and getting as close to me, physically, as he could.

I returned the closeness, and somehow we both made it through the session. What fascinated me was that by invading his personal sphere, by violating the sanctity of his territory, I had communicated with him for the first time.

What I learned from this encounter was that there are times when the masks must come down and communication must be by physical touch. We cannot achieve emotional freedom in many cases unless we can reach through our personal space, through the masks we set up as protection, to touch and fondle and interact physically with other people. Freedom perhaps is not an individual thing but a group function.

An awareness of this fact has led a group of psychologists to the formation of a new school of therapy, a school based very much on body language, but also concerned with breaking through the masking process by body contact.

The Crippling Masks

Children, before they are taught the inhibitions of our society, explore their world by touch. They touch their parents and cuddle into their arms, touch themselves, find joy in their genitals, security in the texture of their blankets, excitement in feeling cold things, hot things, smooth things and scratchy things.

But as the child grows up, his sense of awareness through touch is curtailed. The tactile world is narrowed. He learns to erect body shields, becomes aware of his territorial needs in terms of his culture, and discovers that masking may keep him from being hurt even though it also keeps him from experiencing direct emotions. He comes to believe that what he loses in expression, he gains in protection.

Unfortunately, as the child grows into adulthood, the masks all too often harden and tighten and change from protective devices to crippling devices. The adult may find that while the mask helps him to keep his privacy and prevents any unwanted relationship, it also becomes a limiting thing and prevents the relationships he wants as well as those he doesn't want.

Then the adult becomes mentally immobilized. But because mental qualities are easily translated into physical qualities, he becomes physically immobilized as well. The new therapy based on the experiments at the Esalen Institute at Big Sur in California, on research done among isolated groups of men living in Antarctica, and on group seminars all over the world called encounter groups, seeks to break through these physical immobilizations and work backward to the mental immobilization.

Dr. William C. Schutz has written a great deal about the new technique of encounter groups, a technique for preserving man's identity in the pressure of today's society. To show how much of feeling and behaving are expressed in body language, Dr. Schutz cites a number of interesting expressions that describe behavior and emotional states in body terms. Among these are: shoulder a burden; face up; chin up; grit your teeth; a stiff upper lip; bare your teeth; catch your eye; shrug it off; and so on.

The interesting thing about these is that they are all also body language phrases. Each of them expresses an emotion, but also expresses a physical body act that signals the same emotion.

When we consider these phrases we can understand Dr.

Schutz's suggestion that "psychological attitudes affect body posture and functioning." He cites Dr. Ida Rolf's speculation that emotions harden the body in set patterns. The man who is constantly unhappy develops a frown as a set part of his physical being. The aggressive man who thrusts his head forward all the time develops a posture with head thrust forward and he cannot change it. His emotions, according to Dr. Rolf, cause his posture or expression to freeze into a given position. In turn, this position pulls the emotions into line. If you have a face frozen in an habitual smile, Dr. Rolf believes it will affect your personality and cause you to smile mentally. The same is true for a frown and for deeper, less obvious body postures.

Dr. Alexander Lowen, in his book *Physical Dynamics of Character Structure,* adds to this fascinating concept by stating that all neurotic problems are shown by the structure and function of the body. "No words are so clear as the language of body expression once one has learned to read it," he says.

He goes on to relate body function to emotion. A person with a sway back, he believes, can't have the strong ego of a man with a straight back. The straight back, on the other hand, is less flexible.

You Are What You Feel

Perhaps it is the knowledge of this linking of posture to emotion that makes an army direct its soldiers to stand straight and stiff. The hope is that eventually they will become immovable and determined. Certainly the cliché of the old soldier with the "ramrod up his back" and a rigid personality to go with it has some truth.

Lowen feels that retracted shoulders represent sup-

70

pressed anger, raised shoulders are related to fear, square shoulders indicate shouldering responsibility, bowed shoulders carrying a burden, the weight of a heavy load.

It is difficult to separate fact from literary fancy in many of these suggestions of Lowen's, especially when he states that the bearing of the head is a function of ego strength and quality. He speaks of a long, proud neck or a short, bull neck.

Nevertheless there seems a great deal of sense in Lowen's relation of emotional states to their physical manifestations. If the way in which a person walks, sits, stands, moves, if his body language, indicates his mood and personality and ability to reach others, then there must be ways of causing a person to change by changing his body language.

Schutz, in his book *Joy*, notes that groups of people often sit with arms and legs crossed to indicate tightness and withdrawal, resistance against anyone else reaching them. Asking such a person to unlock himself, uncross his legs or arms, Schutz believes, will also open this person to communication with the rest of the group. The important thing is to know what the person is saying with his crossed arms and legs, what message he is sending. It is also important for the person himself to know what message he intends. He must be aware of the reasons for his own tension before he can break it.

How to Break Out of a Shell

How do you break out of your shell? How do you reach out to others? The first step in breaking free must be understanding that shell, understanding the defenses you have set up. Recently, at a counselor training center at New York University, I was shown a number of video-

71

tapes of interviews between counselors who were learning the counseling technique and troubled children who were being counseled.

In one tape, a pleasant-featured, well-dressed white woman who reeked of gentility was interviewing a disturbed and extremely introverted black girl of fourteen. The girl sat at a table with her head down, her face hidden from the woman, her left hand further covering her eyes and her right hand stretched across the table top.

As the interview progressed, the girl's left hand still shielded her eyes. She would not look up though she was quite articulate, but her right hand stole out across the table top toward the counselor, the fingers walking the hand along, retreating then advancing, cajoling and inviting, crying with an almost audible shriek of body language, "Touch me! For heaven's sake—touch me! Take my hand and force me to look at you!"

The white counselor, inexperienced in counseling techniques and thoroughly frightened by the entire experience, one of her first interviews, sat upright with her legs crossed and her arms folded across her chest. She smoked and moved only when she needed to tap the ash of her cigarette, but then her hand came back defensively across her chest. As plain as sight her physical attitude mirrored her mental attitude. "I am frightened and I cannot touch you. I don't know how to handle the situation, but I must protect myself."

How do you unlock such a situation?

Dr. Arnold Buchheimer, professor of education at the university, explained that the first step in unlocking came through showing the videotape (taken without the knowledge of either the counselor or the counselee) to the counselor. Along with this went an in-depth discussion of how she had reacted and why. She would then be encouraged to examine her own fears and hesitations, her own rigidity and tightness, and to attempt at the next session to achieve physical contact with the girl first and then verbal contact.

Before the series of counselor sessions was over, the counselor by training and analyzing her own behavior was able not only to reach the core of the girl's trouble on a verbal level, but also on a physical level; she was able to put her arm around her, hug her and give her some of the mothering she needed.

Her physical reaction was the first step toward opening a verbal reaction, and in due course toward helping the girl to help herself. In this situation the girl had asked in obvious body language for some physical contact. Her head down and her hand covering her eyes had said, "I am ashamed. I cannot face you. I am afraid." Her other hand, reaching across the table, said, "Touch me. Reassure me. Make contact with me."

The counselor by clasping her arms across her breast and sitting rigidly had said, "I am afraid, I cannot touch you nor permit you to invade my privacy."

Only when a mutual invasion became possible and there was direct physical contact could these two meet, then give and receive help.

The contact or invasion of privacy necessary to break down the barriers and strip away the masking need not always be physical. It can also be verbal. At a recent trip to Chicago I met a remarkable young man who was staying at my hotel. He had the unusual ability of verbally demolishing people's masks and barriers. Walking along the street with him one evening, we passed a restaurant in the style of the mid-nineteenth century. The doorman was dressed in a costume suitable to the period and physically was an imposing man.

My new friend stopped and to my intense embarrassment began the most intimate conversation with the doorman, intimate in terms of his family, his hopes in life and his achievements. To me it seemed the worst breach of good taste. One just does not intrude on a man's privacy in this way.

I was sure the reaction of the doorman would be to take offense, to be embarrassed and to withdraw. To my amazement, it was none of these. The doorman responded after only a moment's hesitancy, and before ten minutes were up, he had confided his hopes, ambitions and problems to my friend. We left him delighted and enthusiastic. Stunned, I asked my new friend, "Do you always come on that strong?"

"Why not?" he asked. "I care about that man. I was willing to ask about his problems and give him advice. He appreciated that. I feel better for doing it, and he feels better for my having done it."

The Silent Cocktail Party

It was true, but the ability to cut across the lines of taste and privacy is a rare thing. Not all of us have it, and not all of those who have it can avoid giving offense. I wonder too if my friend would have been as successful with someone who was his superior. Doormen are seen by many of us as non-persons and may react with gratitude to any notice.

But even if we cannot reach out verbally, we can devise methods of reaching each other in nonverbal ways, ways that may or may not include physical contact. One very successful way was a cocktail party given recently by a psychologist friend. He invited his guests with little invitations that informed them this was to be a nonverbal gathering.

"Touch, smell, stare and taste," his invitation read, "but don't speak. We're spending an evening in nonverbal communication."

My wife and I groaned at the precious quality of the invitation, but we couldn't gracefully get out of it. We went and to our surprise found it fascinating.

The room had been rearranged so that there were no available seats. We all stood and milled around, danced, gestured, mimed and went through elaborate charades, all without talking.

We knew only one other couple, and all our introductions were self-made and handicapped, or helped, by the imposed silence. We had to really work at getting to know each other, and amazingly enough we ended the evening with a clear and deep knowledge of our new friends.

What happened of course was that the verbal element of masking was taken away. All the rest of our masks were only half supported. They slipped easily and we found that we had to do without them to make our best contacts, and the contacts were physical for the most part.

In the silence, all accents and speech inflections and their link to status were eliminated. I shook hands with one man and noticed the callouses on his palm. This led to an acted-out version of his job with a construction crew and, without the barrier of words, to a closer understanding than is usually possible between two men in different class situations.

This is very much a parlor game, but a parlor game with a difference. There are no losers, and the total result is a more meaningful understanding of the people with whom you play. There are other games designed to enhance communication, to make body language understandable and to break down the barriers we erect to protect ourselves.

Playing Games for Health's Sake

Dr. Schutz has put together a number of these "parlor games," some garnered from the California Institute of Technology, some from the UCLA School of Business and some from the National Training Laboratories at Bethel, Maine. They are all designed to break down barriers, to unmask yourself and others and to make you aware of body language and its message.

One of them Schutz calls "Feeling Space." He instructs a group of people to sit together on the floor or in chairs and, with eyes closed, stretch out their hands and "feel" the space around them. Inevitably they will contact each other, touch and explore each other and react to that contact and their neighbor's intrusion upon their own bodies.

Some people, he notes, like to touch others and some do not. Some like being touched and some do not. The possible interactions, combinations, and permutations will often bring hidden emotions to the surface. If these are discussed afterward, the touchers and touchees can find a new awareness of themselves and their neighbors.

Another game Schutz calls "Blind Milling." Here, again with eyes closed, the group moves around a room encountering, touching and exploring each other with their hands. The end result is similar to that in Feeling Space.

Beyond these tentative explorations, Schutz suggests techniques that put emotional feeling into body language. As an example, he tells of a young man who withdrew from any direct relationship that might hurt him. It was easier for him to run away than to risk being hurt. To make him aware of what he was actually doing, his therapy group tried to get him to tell the person he disliked most in the group his true feelings about him. When he protested that he just could not do this, he was told to leave the group and sit in a corner. The physical acting out of his usual withdrawal made him realize he would rather withdraw than face a person directly and truthfully. He would rather remove himself from a group than risk doing something that might end up in an unpleasant situation, that might make someone else dislike him.

Much of the technique of the encounter groups is based on the physical acting out of an emotional problem.

On another level it is putting into body language what has already existed in emotional terms. Saying it with your body, however, allows you to understand it more completely.

In Schutz's technique, the man who has a suppressed hatred mixed with a very real love for his father, can best realize and deal with these conflicting emotions by pretending some other malleable object, say a pillow, is his father. He is encouraged to hit the pillow while expressing his anger and rage.

Often the furious beating of the pillow (if it does not come apart and fill the air with feathers) will carry the beater into an emotional state where his hostility to his father can empty out of him. Having expressed himself this way, in blatant physical terms, he may no longer feel in deep conflict, may indeed be able to express his love for his father, a love that has always been smothered by resentment and hostility.

What has happened to him is a freeing of emotion and the ability to hate as well as love. Often, instead of an inanimate object such as a pillow, the emotions can be freed in interaction between actual people.

Another technique for exposing a man to himself is for a group of people to form a circle with closed arms and let the person who is struggling to understand himself fight his way into the circle. The way in which he handles himself in this situation can help him to understand his real self and his real needs.

Some people will force and butt their way in to become part of a circle. Some will talk their way in, and others will use sly and devious techniques, such as tickling one member of the circle till he moves aside and lets the tickler join.

When a new encounter group is being formed, one interesting technique, Schutz suggests, is to have the members, one by one, brought up before the group to be examined physically, to be prodded, pushed, watched, touched and smelled. This he feels makes the reality of the person much greater to his fellow group members.

I would suggest that another technique could be based on body language. One member of a group could be watched by the others and then described in terms of body language. What is he saying by his walk, by his stance, by his gestures? Is what we think he is saying the same as what he is actually saying?

A discussion of the signals sent and the signals received might enable a person to gain new insights. What messages do you send? Does your walk express the way you really feel, the way you think you feel, or the way others see you? We send out certain signals of body language and it is possible to learn more about ourselves by listening to others interpret the signals that we send.

Psychologists have been aware of this for a long time, and the technique of filming a man in a relationship with others, then showing the film to him and discussing his own signals, his own body language, has proved effective in opening his eyes to reality.

Without the sophisticated techniques of film and videotape, how can we begin to understand our own signals? There are a number of ways, and perhaps the most obvious and the easiest is through a parlor game like charades—but different.

One man or woman at a gathering or group goes out of the room and then enters and without words tries to get across an idea or an emotion such as happiness, ecstasy, mourning or chagrin. Without resorting to the symbolic gestures and abbreviations of charades, this becomes a problem of personality projection. The one trying to project the idea suddenly becomes aware of himself, of his own gestures and signals, of how he holds himself and how he moves.

Afterward, when the group discusses the success or failure of his attempt to speak with body language, he becomes aware of their reaction to his signals. Has he tried to signal shyness and succeeded instead in getting haughtiness across? Has he sent out amusement for pain, assurance for uncertainty? In the larger mirror of life itself does he also confuse his signals? Or are his signals correctly interpreted?

This is a matter we should all take some time to consider. Do we present our real selves to the world? Are the messages our friends receive the same as the ones we think we send? If they aren't, this may be part of our failure to integrate into the world. This may be a clue toward understanding our failures in life.

Another parlor game that can help toward self-understanding is to ask a group to give one of its members a new name, a name that is suited to his body movements.

Then the person is asked to act in accordance with the new name the group has given him. Often the sudden freedom to act in a new fashion, to accept a new personality, will serve as a liberating force and will clear away inhibitions, allowing the newly named person to understand himself on a different level. This is acting out a new personality, but also a personality he would prefer to the one he has.

There are other variations of "acting out" that can cut to the heart of a situation. A friend of mine told me recently that in his own family he was having some very serious problems between his seventeen-year-old daughter and his fourteen-year-old son. "They've gotten to the stage where they can't be in the same room without exploding. Everything he does is wrong in her eyes, and she's always at him."

At my suggestion he tried a nonverbal game with the two of them and told them to do whatever they wanted, but not to use words.

"For a few moments," he told me later, "they were at a loss. Without words she couldn't scold him, and it seemed as if she didn't know what else to do, what other way to relate to him. Then he came over to where she was sitting and grinned at her, and all at once she caught him, pulled him down on her lap and actually cuddled him to the amazement of the rest of the family."

What came out of this in a discussion later was that the entire family agreed that by her actions she had seemed to be mothering him. She did indeed feel like a mother to him, and her constant scolding was less in the nature of criticism and more in the nature of possessive mother-love. Her body language action of cuddling made her aware of this and opened his eyes as well. Afterward, my friend reported, while they continued their bickering, it was hardly as serious as before and underlying it on both parts was a new warmth and understanding.

What often happens in any relationship is that language itself becomes a mask and a means of clouding and confusing the relationship. If the spoken language is stripped away and the only communication left is body language, the truth will find some way of poking through. Spoken language itself is a great obscurer.

In love and in sexual encounters, the spoken word can act as a deterrent to the truth. One of the most useful therapeutic exercises for a couple in love is to attempt, in complete darkness, to transmit a definite message to each other with only the tactile elements of body language. Try to tell your lover: "I need you. I will make you happy." Or "I resent you. You do not do this or that properly." "You are too demanding." "You are not demanding enough."

Stripped of words, these exercises in sexuality and love can become intensely meaningful and can help a relationship develop and grow. The same communication without words, but with the visual instead of the tactile sense, can be a second step in the maturing of a love affair. Somehow it is a great deal easier for many people to look at each other's bodies after having touched them.

7

The Silent Language of Love

Stance, Glance and Advance

Mike is a ladies' man, someone who is never at a loss for a girl. Mike can enter a party full of strangers and within ten minutes end up on intimate terms with one of the girls. Within half an hour he has cut her out of the pack and is on his way home with her—to his or her place, depending on which is closer.

How does Mike do it? Other men who have spent half the evening drumming up enough courage to approach a girl, will see Mike come in and take over quickly and effectively. But they don't know why.

Ask the girls and they'll shrug. "I don't know. He just has his antennae out, I guess. I get signals, and I answer them, and the first thing I know. . . ."

Mike is not particularly good looking. He's smart enough, but that's not his attraction. It seems that Mike almost has a sixth sense about him. If there's an available girl Mike will find her, or she will find him.

What does Mike have?

Well, if he hasn't looks or brilliance, he has something far more important for this type of encounter. Mike has an unconscious command of body language and he uses it expertly. When Mike saunters into a room he signals his message automatically. "I'm available, I'm masculine. I'm aggressive and knowledgeable." And then when he zeroes in on his chosen subject, the signals go, "I'm interested in you. You attract me. There's something exciting about you and I want to find out what it is."

Watch Mike in action. Watch him make contact and signal his availability. We all know at least one Mike, and we all envy him his ability. What is the body language he uses?

Well, Mike's appeal, Mike's nonverbal clarity, is compounded of many things. His appearance is part of it. Not the appearance he was born with, that's rather ordinary, but the way Mike has rearranged that appearance to transmit his message. There is, when you look at Mike carefully, a definite sexuality about him.

"Of course," a knowing woman will say, "Mike is a very sexy man." But sexy how? Not in his features.

Pressed further, the woman will explain, "It's something about him, something he has, a sort of aura."

Actually it's nothing of the sort, nothing so vague as an aura. In part it's the way Mike dresses, the type of pants he chooses, his shirts and jackets and ties, the way he combs his hair, the length of his sideburns—these all contribute to the immediate picture, but even more important than this is the way Mike stands and walks.

One woman described it as an "easy grace." A man who knew Mike was not so kind. "He's greasy." What came through as pleasing to the woman was transmitted as disturbing or challenging and therefore distasteful to the man, and he reacted by characterizing the quality contemptuously.

Yet Mike does move with grace, an arrogant sort of grace that could well arouse a man's envy and a woman's excitement. A few actors have that same movement, Paul Newman, Marlon Brando, Rip Torn, and with it they can transmit an obvious sexual message. The message can be broken down into the way they hold themselves, their stance or posture, and the easy confidence of their motion. The man who has that walk needs little else to turn a woman's head.

But Mike has more. He has dozens of little gestures, perhaps unconscious ones, that send out elaborations of his sexual message. When Mike leans up against a mantel in a room to look around at the women, his hips are thrust forward slightly, as if they were cantilevered, and his legs are usually apart. There is something in this stance that spells sex.

Watch Mike when he stands like this. He will lock his thumbs in his belt right above the pockets, and his fingers will point down toward his genitals. You have surely seen the same stance a hundred times in Western movies, usually not taken by the hero, but by the sexy bad guy as he lounges against a corral fence, the picture of threatening sexuality, the villain the men hate and the women— well, what they feel is a lot more complex than hate or desire or fear, and yet it's a mixture of all these things. With his blatant body language, his leather chaps, his cantilevered groin and pointing fingers he is sending out a crude, obvious but effective signal. "I am a sexual threat. I am a dangerous man for a woman to be alone with. I am all man and I want you!"

On a minor scale, less blatant, Mike sends out the same message.

But his body language doesn't stop there. This much serves to signal his intentions, to create an atmosphere, an aura if you will. This fascinates the available women and interests or even irritates the non-available ones.

Mike himself explained how he proceeded after this. "I size up the women, the ones who want it. How? It's easy.

By the way they stand or sit. And then I make my choice and I catch her eye. If she's interested she'll respond. If not, I forget her."

"How do you catch her eye?"

"I hold the glance a little longer than I should, since I don't really know her. I won't let her eyes slide away, and I narrow mine—sort of."

But there is even more to Mike's approach than the insistent eye, as I observed one evening at a party. Mike has an uncanny instinct for sizing up a woman's defensive body language and insistently breaking it down. Are her arms clasped defensively? He opens his. Is her posture rigid? He relaxes as they talk. Is her face pinched and drawn? He smiles and loosens his face.

In short, he answers her body signals with opposite and complementary signals of his own, and by doing this intrudes himself into her awareness. He brushes aside her body language pretenses, and because unconsciously she really wants to open herself up, she opens up to Mike.

Mike moves in on a woman. When he has made signal contact, when his body language gets the message of his availability across, his next step is physical invasion, but physical invasion without touch.

He cuts into the woman's territory or body zone. He comes close enough for her to be uneasy, and yet not close enough for her to logically object. Mike doesn't touch his victim needlessly. His closeness, his intrusion into her territory, is enough to change the situation between them.

Then Mike carries his invasion even further by visual intrusion as they talk. What they say really doesn't matter much. Mike's eyes do far more talking than his voice. They linger on the woman's throat, on her breasts, her body. They linger sensuously and with promise. Mike touches his tongue to his lips, narrows his eyes, and invariably, the woman becomes uneasy and excited. Remember, she's not just any woman, but that particular susceptible woman who has responded to Mike's opening gambit. She has returned his flattering attentions, and now she is in too deep to protest.

And anyway, what could she protest against? Just what has Mike done? He hasn't touched her. He hasn't made any suggestive remark. He is, by all the standards of society, a perfect gentleman. If his eyes are a bit too hot, a bit too bold, this is still a matter of interpretation. If the girl doesn't like it she has only to be rude and move off.

But why shouldn't the girl like it? Mike is flattering her with his attention. In effect he is saying, "You interest me. I want to know you better, more intimately. You're not like other women. You're the only woman here I care about."

For, in addition to his flattering attention to this woman, Mike never makes the mistake of spreading his interest. He narrows his focus and speaks to only one woman, and he makes the impact of his body language all the stronger for it. Half the time, when Mike leaves with the girl of his choice, she hardly needs any persuasion. By that time a simple, "Let's go!" is enough.

Is She Available?

How does Mike single out his victim? What body language does an available girl at a party use to say, "I'm available. I'm interested. I can be had"? There must be a definite set of signals because Mike rarely makes a mistake.

A girl in our society has an additional problem in this game of sexual encounters. No matter how available she may be, it's considered pretty square to let anyone know it. This would instantly put her value down and cheapen her. And yet, unconsciously, she must let her intent be known. How does she do it?

A big part of the way she transmits her message is also in stance, posture or movement. An available woman moves in a studied way. A man may label it posing, another woman, affection, but the movement of her body, hips and shoulders telegraphs her availability. She may sit with her legs apart, symbolically open and inviting, or she may affect a gesture in which one hand touches her breast in a near caress. She may stroke her thighs as she talks or walk with a languorous roll to her hips. Some of her movements are studied and conscious, some completely unconscious.

A few generations ago female availability was broadly burlesqued by Mae West's "come up and see me sometime" routine. A later generation turned to the baby-face and hushed and breathless voice quality of a Marilyn Monroe—a tarnished innocence. Today, in a more cynical age, it is again blatant sexuality. Someone like Raquel Welch spells out the message. But these are the obvious, motion picture messages. On a subtler, living-room level, the level on which Mike operates, the message is more discreet, often so discreet that the man who is ignorant of body language misses it completely. Even the man who knows a little about the subject may be misled. For example, the woman who crosses her arms across her chest may be transmitting the classic signal, "I am closed to any advance. I will not listen to you, or hear you."

This is a common interpretation of closed arms, and it is one with which most psychologists are familiar. As an example of this, there was a recent story in the papers about Dr. Spock addressing a class at the Police Academy. The audience of police were extremely hostile to the good doctor, in spite of the fact that he was responsible for the way most of them and their children had been brought up. They demonstrated their hostility verbally in their discussion, but also much more obviously in body language. In the news photo, every policeman sat with his arms crossed tightly over his chest, his face hard and closed.

Very clearly they were saying, "I am sitting here with a closed mind. No matter what you say I'm unwilling to listen. We just can't meet." This is the classical interpretation of crossed arms.

But there is another equally valid interpretation. Crossed arms may say, "I am frustrated. I am not getting what I need. I am closed in, locked in. Let me out. I can be approached and am readily available."

While the man who knows only a little about body language may misinterpret this gesture, the man well educated in body language will get the correct message from the accompanying signals the girl sends out. Is her face pinched and tight with frustration? Is she sitting stiffly instead of in a relaxed position? Does she avert her eye when you try to catch it?

All the body signals must be added up to a correct total if a man is to use body language effectively.

The aggressively available woman acts in a predictable fashion too. She has a number of effective tricks of body language to telegraph her availability. As Mike does, she uses territorial intrusion to make her point. She will sit uncomfortably close to the man she is after, taking advantage of the uneasiness such closeness arouses. As the man shifts and fidgets, unaware of why he is disturbed, she will move in with other signals, using his uneasiness as a means of throwing him off balance.

While a man on the make cannot touch the woman if he is to play the game fairly, it is perfectly permissible for a woman on the make, at this stage of the game, to touch the man. This touch can exaggerate the uneasiness of the man into whose territory she has cut.

A touch on the arm can be a disarming blow. "Do you have a match?" Steadying the hand that holds it to her cigarette can allow a moment of flesh-to-flesh contact that may be effectively troubling.

The contact of a woman's thigh, or her hand carelessly brushed against a man's thigh can be devastating if it is applied at just the right moment.

The aggressive approach by a woman can utilize not only body language—the adjustment of a skirt as she sits close, the uncrossing of her legs, the thrusting forward of her breasts, a pouting mouth—it can also utilize smell. The right perfume in the right amount, to give an elusive but exciting scent, is an important part of the aggressive approach.

Is the Face Worth Saving?

But sight, touch and smell are still less than the complete arsenal of the woman on the warpath. Sound is a very definite part of the approach. It is not always what she says, but the tone of her voice, the invitation behind the words, the pitch and the intimate, caressing quality of the sound.

The French actresses understand this well, but French is a language that lends itself to sexuality, no matter what is being said. One of the most amusing off-Broadway revue sketches I have ever seen consisted of an actor and actress doing a "scene" from a French movie. Each recited a list of vegetables in French, but the tone of voice, cadence and vocal innuendo dripped sexuality.

This, as we described earlier in the book, is the use of one communication band to carry two messages. In the area of love and sex it is a very common use. For the aggressively available woman it can serve to throw a man off guard. This is a trick used by both men and women in the aggressive sexual pursuit. If you throw your quarry off balance, make him or her uneasy, moving in for the kill becomes relatively easy.

The trick of using the voice to carry one innocuous spoken message and another more meaningful, and much stronger, unspoken message is particularly effective because the quarry, male or female, cannot protest by the rules of the game. The aggressor, if protest is made, can always draw back and say, with some truth, "But what did I do? What did I say?"

There is a face-saving device in this, for no matter how hot the pursuit of love or sex, it cannot be done with the risk of losing face. For many people, particularly if they are insecure, losing face is a devastating and humiliating occurrence. The sexual aggressor, if he or she is truly successful at the trade, is concerned with face-saving in his victim only as a means of manipulating his quarry. To be sexually aggressive, a man or woman must have enough self-assurance, enough security, to function without the need of face-saving devices.

On the opposite side of the coin, the sexually insecure person, the quarry in the inevitable hunt, desperately needs to avoid humiliation, to save face. This puts her at a tremendous disadvantage in the game. The aggressor can manipulate the quarry, holding loss of face as a threat.

When, for example, the aggressor moves in on the quarry's territory and, using a sexually seductive voice, speaks in obvious banalities, what is the quarry to do? Move back and risk the raised eyebrow. "What did you think I wanted?"

To assume that the aggressor is after *her* sexually is to import more worth to *herself* than *she* truly believes *she* has. To be let down after this would be too humiliating to bear. Suppose *she* were truly misinterpreting *his* motives? So, in most cases, the aggressor gets away with *his* ploy.

The same type of interaction is used by the deviate sexual aggressor outside of a social situation. The male subway-sexual deviate who attempts to fondle or touch a female rider in a crowd depends on her fright and insecurity to keep her quiet. The same dynamics are in action, and the fear of losing face may prevent her from protesting. She endures the minor annoyance of a groping pervert or an exposing pervert in order not to attract attention to herself.

This is so much an expected reaction that many sexual perverts who achieve satisfaction from exposing themselves count on the embarrassment and shame of their victims. Should the victim react by laughing or by any show of amusement, or even by aggressively approaching him, it would be a devastating experience for the deviate.

Pickups, AC and DC

On the theme of deviates, among both male homosexuals and lesbians there are definite body language signals that can establish intimate communication. Homosexuals "cruising" on a street can identify a sympathetic soul without exchanging a word.

92

"Making contact is relatively simple," a young homosexual recently explained in a survey. "The first thing to do is to identify your man, and it's hard to tell you how it's done, because there are so many little signals. Some of it is the way he walks, though many of us walk like perfectly normal men. Mostly, I guess, it's the eye contact. You look and you know. He holds your eye just a little too long, and then his eye may travel down your body. The quick glance to the crotch and away is a sure giveaway."

Discussing his own signals, he explains, "I walk past and then look back. If there's any interest he'll look back too. Then I slow down, stop to look at a store window. Then we'll drift back towards each other . . . and contact!"

The signals are rigid and formalized, and sometimes they are unspoken but on the verbal band, though not related to the words. Dr. Goffman tells of a homosexual who stopped into a "gay" bar for a drink but had no interest in picking anyone up. He took out a cigarette, but found he had no matches. He suddenly realized that to ask anyone at the bar for a match was the understood signal, "I am interested. Are you?"

In the end he bought a pack of matches from the bartender.

The homosexual's signals for initiating contact are not far divorced from the normal man's signals for picking up a girl. A long time ago, when I was a soldier on leave in Boston, a soldier friend cajoled me into coming out with him to "pick up some dames."

I had had no experience at this, but I had to play the "bigshot" since I couldn't admit my ignorance. I went along and watched my friend carefully. Within half an hour he had "picked up" five girls and selected two for us. His technique was built on body language.

Walking along the street, or more properly, sauntering along, he would catch a prospect's eye, hold it a bit longer than was necessary and lift one eyebrow. If the girl faltered in her stride, stopped to look at her compact, to fix her stockings or window-shop down the street, it was one of a number of return signals that meant, "I am aware of you and possibly interested. Let's pursue this further."

My friend would then break stride, turn and follow behind the girl for a block. The following without making contact was a necessary part of the ritual and allowed him to begin vocal contact, to comment to me, a third party, on her dress, her walk, her looks—all in semi-humorous terms, a face-saving device to avoid offense.

At first she would pretend his advances were unwelcome. If this stage lasted too long it would be mutually agreed that his advances really were unwelcome. If, however, she giggled or answered him, or commented on him to her girl friend, if she had one, then it indicated a growing interest.

Eventually the pickup ended with my friend side-by-side with the girl, talking her into an apparently reluctant familiarity. I have seen the very same technique used today among teen-agers and it is one in which every step is rigidly outlined and the game must be played out from start to finish. At any point negotiations can be easily broken off by either partner without loss of face to the other. This is a stringent requirement of a successful and smooth pickup.

There is something ritualistically similar to this in the opening ceremony of certain encounters among animal species. Watch two pigeons in the park as the male circles, pouts and goes through a formal pickup while the female pretends indifference. A very definite body language is in use and in the same way humans approach each other in courtship with definite body language.

Dr. Gerhard Nielsen of the Psychological Laboratory at the University of Copenhagen describes in his book, *Studies in Self-Confrontation,* the extremely important use of body language in what he calls the "courtship dance" of the American adolescent.

Breaking the procedure of courtship down to a cold, clinical level, Dr. Nielsen found twenty-four steps between the "initial contact between the young male and female and the coitional act." These steps by the man, he decided, and the counter steps taken by the girl had a "coercive order." He explains this by saying that when a boy takes the step of holding a girl's hand, he must wait until she presses his hand, signaling a go-ahead, before he can take the next step of allowing his fingers to intertwine with hers.

Step must follow step until he can casually put his arm around her shoulder. He may move his hand down her back then and approach her breast from the side. She, in turn, can block this approach with her upper arm against her side.

After the initial kiss, and only then, he may try to move toward her breast again, but he does not really expect to reach it until a good deal of kissing has taken place. Protocol forbids him to approach the breast from the front, even as it forbids the first kiss before the initial hand-holding.

Dr. Nielsen suggests that the boy or girl is labeled "fast" or "slow" in terms of the order of each step, not the time taken for each step. "Skipping steps or reversing

95

their order is fast," in the same way that ignoring the signal to move on to the next step, or not permitting the next step, is slow.

Choose Your Posture

Dr. Albert E. Scheflen, professor of psychiatry at the Albert Einstein College of Medicine in New York City, has studied and charted patterns of courtship and what he calls "quasi-courtship" in human beings. This quasi-courtship is the use of courting or flirting or sex to achieve non-sexual goals.

All human behavior is patterned and systematic, according to Dr. Scheflen, and it is also made up of regular, small segments arranged into larger units. This is equally true for sexual behavior, and in a study of the elements that make up our sexual relations to each other, Dr. Scheflen found that in business meetings, at parties, in school and in many other gatherings, people used these sexual elements, even though they had no sexual goal in mind.

He came to the conclusion that either Americans behave sexually when they get together on a non-sexual basis, or else—and more likely—the sexual behavior has certain qualifying body language signals when it is not used with the ultimate goal of sexual intercourse.

Just what are these sexual patterns of behavior? Well, according to Dr. Scheflen's investigations, when a man and a woman prepare for a sexual encounter, although they are unaware of what they are doing, they go through a number of body changes that bring them into a state of readiness.

The muscles of their bodies become slightly tensed and "ready for action." Body sagging disappears, and they stand up straighter, more erect and alert. There is less "jowling" in their faces and "bagging" around their eyes. Their posture becomes more youthful, and their stomachs are pulled in, their leg muscles tightened. Even their eyes seem brighter while their skins may blush or grow pale. There may even be changes in their body odors, harking back to a more primitive time when smell was a tremendously important sense in sexual encounters.

As these changes take place, the man or woman may begin to use certain gestures which Dr. Scheflen calls "preening behavior." A woman will stroke her hair or check her makeup, rearrange her clothes or push her hair away from her face, while a man may comb his hair, button his coat, readjust his clothes, pull up his socks, arrange his tie or straighten the crease in his trousers.

These are all body language signals that say, "I am interested. I like you. Notice me. I am an attractive man—an attractive woman. . . ."

The second step in these sexual encounters consists of positioning. Watch a man and a woman at a party, a couple who are getting to know one another and feel a mounting sexual interest in each other. How do they sit? They will arrange their bodies and heads to face one another. They will lean toward each other and try to block off any third person. They may do this by using their arms to close a circle, or by crossing their feet toward each other to block out anyone else.

Sometimes, if such a couple are sharing a sofa and a third person is on a facing chair, they will be torn between two compulsions. One is the desire to close in their own spaces, to include only themselves, and the other is the social responsibility of having to include the third person. They may solve their dilemma by having the best of both worlds. They may cross their legs to signal to each other that they are a closed circle. The one on the right will cross his right leg over his left. The one on the left will cross her left leg over her right. In effect this closes the two of them off from the third—from the waist down. However, social responsibility to the third person may make them arrange the top parts of their bodies directly facing him, thus opening themselves to him.

When one woman at a gathering wants to get a man into an intimate situation where the two of them can form a closed unit, she acts as the sexually aggressive woman does, but to a lesser degree. She utilizes body language that includes flirting glances, holding his eyes, putting her head to one side, rolling her hips, crossing her legs to reveal part of her thigh, putting a hand on her hip or exposing her wrist or palm. All of these are accepted signals that get a message across without words. "Come and sit near me. I find you attractive. I would like to know you better."

Now let us take a situation without sexual overtones. In a conference room at a big industrial firm, a male and a female executive discuss production costs with other officials. They may go through what appear to be these same sexual encounter signals. They are using body language that in other circumstances would invite sexual advances, and yet quite obviously these two have their minds entirely on the business matter at hand. Are they masking their true feelings and do they really have a sexual desire for each other? Or are we misinterpreting their body language?

In a college seminar it appears, to an uninitiated eye, that one of the girl students is using body language to send signals to the professor, signals that invite a sexual encounter. He in turn reacts as if he were agreeable. Are they in fact flirting, or are these really non-sexual signals?

98

Or is there something wrong with our interpretation of body language?

A group psychotherapy seminar has a group therapist who uses body language to make "advances" to one of the women. Is he stepping out of line and violating his code of ethics? Or is this part of his therapy? Or again, are the signals confused?

After careful study of these and similar situations, Dr. Scheflen found that often sexual signals were sent out when the people involved had no intention of getting into any sexual encounter. However, he found that the body language signals sent out when a sexual encounter was expected as the end result of a meeting were not quite the same as those sent out for non-sexual endings. There were subtle differences that announced, "I am interested in you and I want to do business with you, but this is not a sexual matter."

Semi-Sexual Encounters

How do we make it clear to each other that the encounter is to be non-sexual? We do it by sending another sign along with the signal, a bit of body language over and above the obvious body language, another case of two signals on one communications band.

One method for letting a partner know that the sexual signals are not to be taken seriously is to refer, in some way, to the fact that this is a business meeting, or a classroom, or a psychotherapy group. It could be something as simple as a gesture or a movement of the eyes or head toward someone in authority, or toward the other members of the gathering.

Another trick to separate sex from business is to make the sexual body language signal incomplete, to omit an

99

important part of it. Two people sitting close together at a business meeting may adopt a sexual relationship by facing each other, but may turn part of their bodies away, or put their arms out to include others in their private circle. They may break partner contact with their eyes, or raise their voices to include everyone else in the room.

In each case a vital element must be missing from the sexual encounter. The missing element may be eye linkage, a low and private voice, arms arranged to include only the partner or any of a number of other intimacies.

Another way of putting the situation on a non-sexual level is to use disclaimers, to refer in talk to a wife, a boyfriend, a fiancée. This brings the situation into proper focus and tells the partner, "We are friends, not lovers."

This goes back to Dr. Scheflen's belief that behavior occurs in specified units that make up whole patterns. If some of the units are omitted, the finished pattern is different. In this case it is changed from sexual to non-sexual, but still with a strong man-woman interaction. A certain business routine takes place, but it is spiced by a strong flavor of half-teasing sexuality. The participants, without any expectation of sexual gratification, are still exploiting the fact that there is a sexual difference between them. The businessman uses sexual body language signals to get a certain relationship across. The intellectual uses it as a teaching aid, and the therapist uses it to help a psychological situation, but they are all aware that they are simply manipulating their genders, not aiming at sexual gratification.

There is, however, no guarantee that in any of these situations sexuality will not develop. There have been enough teachers responding sexually to pupils, businessmen to businesswomen and therapists to patients to give all of these encounters a certain piquancy and even promise.

These semi-sexual encounters occur so frequently that they are an innate part of our culture. Not only do they take place out of the home, but they also occur between parents and children, hosts and guests, even between two women or two men. The one thing that must always be made clear in this sexual-non-sexual relationship is that it is not for real. From the beginning the qualifications or disclaimers must be in effect. There should, if it is done properly, be no possibility of one partner suddenly waking up to say, "But I thought you meant . . ."; and of the other having to protest, "Oh no, it wasn't that way at all."

Dr. Scheflen notes that there are some psychotherapists who use this flirtation behavior very consciously to involve their patients. A disinterested female patient may be made to talk openly by a sexual approach on the part of her therapist, sexual of course in terms of body language. He may arrange his tie, his sock or his hair in a preening manner to transmit sexual interest, but he must, of course, make his true non-sexual position known.

Dr. Scheflen describes a situation of a family visiting a therapist, a mother, daughter, grandmother and father. Whenever the therapist would talk to the daughter or grandmother, the mother, who sat between them, would begin to transmit sexual signals in body language. This would serve to draw the therapist's attention back to her, a sort of flirting procedure that is very common among women when they are not the center of attention. She would pout, cross her legs and extend them, place her hand on her hips and lean her body forward.

When the therapist unconsciously responded to her "advances" by arranging his tie or hair or leaning forward, both the girl and the grandmother on either side of

101

the mother would cross their legs, placing the crossed leg in front of the mother from either side and, in effect, "boxing her in." She, in turn, would stop her sexual signals and lean back.

Perhaps the most interesting thing about this entire charade was that the "boxing in" by daughter and grandmother was always done at a signal from the father. The signal—waving his crossed foot up and down! And all of this was done by therapist, women and father without any of them being aware of their own signaling.

From a carefully study of sexual-non-sexual behavior, Scheflen concludes that it usually occurs between two people when one becomes preoccupied or turns away from the other for some reason. In a large group, a family, a business gathering or a classroom, it also happens when one member is ignored or excluded by the others. The excluded member may "preen" in a sexual way to get back into the group. When one member of a group withdraws it may also be used by the rest of the group to call him back.

The important part in all of this is to know the signals, to know the limiting or qualifying signals that separate real sexual advances from non-sexual. The two, Scheflen believes, are easily confused. Indeed there are people who regularly confuse both the sending and receiving of these sexual signals and their qualifiers. There are people who, for psychological reasons, cannot follow through a sexual encounter, but still act in a sexually seductive manner, particularly when they should not.

These people not only provoke sexual advances, but see such advances in others when no such advances are intended. This is the typical "tease" all of us know or the girl who is sure everyone has designs on her.

On the other hand, Scheflen lists those people who are

not aware of the qualifying signals telling them that the advance is not really sexual. These people freeze up in ordinary non-sexual situations and withdraw.

How the body language for these situations is learned and how we know the correct interpretations, the correct disclaimers and qualifiers to make sexual advances nonsexual, how we learn all of this is hard to explain. Some is taught and some is absorbed from the culture. When, for one reason or another, an individual has been divorced from his society and hasn't been taught the proper interpretations of these signals, he may face a good deal of trouble. For him body language may be unknown on a conscious level and unused on an unconscious level.

Positions, Points and Postures

A Cry for Help

The patient was hardly more than a boy, seventeen years old, but he looked younger. He was pale and thin and he had a curious, uncertain quality to his face, as if someone had thought better about creating him and tried to erase his features but had only succeeded in smudging them. He was dressed carelessly and sloppily, and he sat in a listless way, his arms crossed, his eyes vague. When he moved, his motions were tight and restricted. When he came to rest he was slumped over and passive.

The therapist glanced at his watch surreptitiously, grateful that the hour was at an end, and he forced a smile. "That's all then, till tomorrow."

The boy stood up and shrugged. "What tomorrow? Don't you worry about tomorrow. I'm sure not going to after tonight. There won't be any tomorrow for me."

At the door the therapist said, "Now come on, Don. You've threatened suicide every week for the past six months."

The boy looked at him dully and then left, and the therapist stood watching the door uncertainly. Don was his last patient for the day, and he should have felt relieved. Instead he was filled with an uneasiness that steadily grew worse. He tried to work at his records for awhile, but he couldn't. Something bothered him, something about the boy. Was it the way he talked, his threat of suicide? But he had threatened to kill himself before, many times. Why was this threat any different?

Why was he disturbed now? He remembered his uneasy feeling during the session, how passive the boy had been. He recalled his gestures, the limited range of motion when he moved, his inability to hold his eye.

Uneasily the therapist cast back over the hour. Somehow, in some way, he had become convinced that this time was different, that this time the boy meant suicide. Yet what had he said that was different? What had he said that he hadn't said in every other session?

The therapist went to the console with the concealed tape recorder, his way of preserving each session, and he played back the tape of the past hour. Nowhere in any of the boy's words was there a hint of anything different or unusual, but the tone of voice was flat, lifeless, passive.

His uneasiness grew. Somehow a message had come across during the session. He had to trust that message even without knowing what it was. Finally, half annoyed at himself and yet half relieved, he called his wife and said he'd be home late and then set out for the boy's home.

The rest of the story is simple and direct. The therapist was right. The boy had attempted suicide. He had gone straight home, taken a bottle of pills from the family's medicine cabinet and locked himself in his room. Fortunately the therapist was in time. The parents were readily convinced, and the family physician was able to clean out the boy's stomach with an emetic. The bright lining to the cloud was that this event became the turning point in the boy's therapy. Progress was all uphill after that.

"But why?" the therapist's wife asked later. "Why did you go to the child's house?"

"I don't know, except—damn it all, it wasn't anything he said, but something screamed at me that this time he meant to kill himself. He signaled me but I don't know now—maybe it was in his face or his eyes or his hands. Maybe even the way he held himself and the fact that he didn't laugh at a joke I made, a good joke. He didn't have to use words. Everything about him told me that this time he meant it."

This incident happened not today nor within the last ten years, but twenty years ago. Today almost any good therapist would not only receive the message, but also know just how the message was sent, just what clue the boy had given him.

The empty face, the listless posture, the crossed hands, would all have spelled out a meaning as clearly as any speech. In body language the boy was telling the therapist what he meant to do. Words were no longer of any use. He had used them to cry out to no avail too often and had to fall back on a more primitive, more basic way of conveying his message.

What Does Your Posture Say?

In the twenty years since this incident took place, psychologists have become increasingly aware of how useful and important body language is in therapy. Interestingly enough, while many of them use body language in their practice, few are aware of doing so and many have no idea of all the work that has been done in the field of kinesics by men like Dr. Scheflen and Dr. Ray L. Birdwhistell.

Dr. Birdwhistell, professor of research in anthropolgy

at Temple University, who has initiated most of the basic work in developing a notational system for the new science of kinesics, warns that "no body position or movement, in and of itself, has a precise meaning." In other words, we cannot always say that crossed arms mean, "I will not let you in," or that rubbing the nose with a finger means disapproval or rejection, that patting the hair means approval and steepling the fingers superiority. These are naïve interpretations of kinesics, and tend to make a parlor game out of a science. Sometimes they are true and sometimes they are not, but they are only true in the context of the entire behavior pattern of a person.

Body language and spoken language, Dr. Birdwhistell believes, are dependent on each other. Spoken language alone will not give us the full meaning of what a person is saying, nor for that matter will body language alone give us the full meaning. If we listen only to the words when someone is talking, we may get as much of a distortion as we would if we listened only to the body language.

Psychiatrists particularly, according to Dr. Birdwhistell, must listen to both the body language and the spoken language. In an attempt to teach them how to do this, he published a paper called "Communication Analysis in the Residency Setting," in which he explains some of the methods he has used to make residents, young learning doctors, aware of the communication potential of body language.

It is an interesting aside that Dr. Birdwhistell has helped develop the concept of a "moral looking time." He believes that one person can observe another's eyes, face, abdomen, legs and other parts of the body for only so long before tension is created in both observer and observed.

In his advice to residents he points out that almost every moving part of the body can contain some message for the doctor, but when all else fails he falls back on two classic examples of body language that can communicate.

One, he explains, is the young adolescent girl who has to learn what to do with her newly developed breasts. How should she hold them? Thrust proudly forward with her shoulders back? Or should she pull her shoulders forward and hide her breasts by flattening them out? What should she do with her arms and shoulders, and what should she do about her mother who tells her half the time, "Hold yourself straight. Be proud of your body," and the rest of the time says, "Don't go around sticking out like that! You mustn't wear such tight sweaters."

I have a young teen-age friend who is particularly uninhibited and self-assured. Catching sight of herself in a mirror while trying on a bikini, she told her mother, "Aren't they great? Never mind cremation if I die. I'm going to have them bronzed for posterity!"

Most girls in their teens haven't this kind of body pride, and the carrying of their newly developed breasts becomes a real problem. The resident doctor can be made aware that changes in a girl's posture may signal depression, excitement, courtship, anger, or even an appeal for help. Eventually, in his own practice, he will be able to recognize and interpret some of the different problems of his teen-age patients by their stance.

Another example Dr. Birdwhistell uses for residents is what he calls the "remarkable distensibility and contractibility of the male abdomen and belly."

In courtship we have seen that the male will tighten his abdominal muscles and pull in his belly. In depression he may over-relax these muscles and let his stomach hang out. The degree of tension of these muscles can tell a great deal about the emotional and mental condition of a man. We must realize that the entire body is to body language as the speech organs are to the spoken language.

Dr. Paul L. Wachtel of the Downstate Medical Center, State University of New York, has studied nonverbal communication in psychiatric patients and has published an article titled, "An Approach to the Study of Body Language in Psychotherapy."

Each movement or position of the body, according to Dr. Wachtel, has adaptive, expressive and defensive functions, some conscious and some unconscious. "We seek," he said, "a thorough clinical evaluation of the significance of the patient's use of his body."

To obtain his data Dr. Wachtel filmed psychiatric interviews and then played and replayed the films, matching body language to verbal communication. One thing he learned from watching the films was when to look for significant gestures. Theoretically you could tell by listening to a patient, but actually the movements are too fast and are often missed in an interview. Film can be slowed down and replayed, serving as a time machine to recall any part of an interview at will.

An example of how body language helps, Dr. Wachtel said, came about in an interview with an extremely troubled person who did not know how she felt about a friend with whom she was involved.

In the film he noticed that whenever she was angry she made certain gestures. When she repeated these same gestures at the mention of the friend's name he was able to show her graphically how she felt toward that friend. Understanding your emotions is, of course, the first step in handling them.

Dr. Wachtel regards body language as a conscious or unconscious attempt by the patient to communicate with the therapist. One patient he studied would lean back and clasp her hands as the therapist reached certain troublesome areas. "Perhaps," Dr. Wachtel said, "this is a relatively common expression of resistance."

Different Places, Different Postures

Accepting the idea that man uses more than one form of communication has some very definite advantages to both the psychiatrist and the ordinary citizen. The psychiatrist can learn what to expect from his patient and the ordinary citizen can learn a great deal about what to expect from his fellow men if he understands that they react on a body language level as well as on a spoken level.

This awareness of body language is often a key to personal relationships and it may be the secret so many men use in handling others. Some men seem able to interpret body language and manipulate people with their bodies as well as with their voices.

Beyond this, the awareness of someone else's body language and the ability to interpret it create an awareness of one's own body language. As we begin to receive and interpret the signals others are sending, we begin to monitor our own signals and achieve a greater control over ourselves and in turn function more effectively.

However, it is very difficult to gain control of all the different methods of communication. There are literally thousands of bits of information exchanged between human beings within moments. Our society programs us to handle these many bits of data, but on an unconscious level. If we bring them up to our consciousness we run the risk of mishandling them. If we have to think of what we are doing, it often becomes much more difficult to do

111

it. An aware mind is not necessarily as effective as an un-aware one.

In spite of this psychiatrists continue to study all aspects of body communication. Dr. Scheflen has been particularly interested in the significance of posture in communication systems. In an article in the journal *Psychiatry* he notes that the way people hold their bodies tells us a great deal about what is going on when two or more people get together.

"There are no more than about 30 traditional American gestures," Dr. Scheflen writes and adds that there are even fewer body postures which carry any significance in communication, and that each of these occurs in a limited number of situations. To make his point, he notes that a posture such as sitting back in a chair is one rarely taken by a salesman who is trying to sell something to a more influential client.

While everyone in America is familiar with all of the different postures Americans may take, this doesn't mean that everyone uses all of them. A nineteen-year-old college student from New York will use different postures than a Midwestern housewife, and a construction worker in the state of Washington will use different postures than a salesman in Chicago. Dr. Scheflen believes that a real expert in body language could tell us just what part of the country a man came from by the way he moved his brow when he talked. Such an expert, however, has not yet been developed.

We are all aware of this regional difference in body language when we watch a talented mime. By specific gestures the mime can tell us not only what part of the world his character comes from, but also what he does for a living. When I was a college student in the days when football players were college heroes, many of the non-athletic boys at school would imitate the football-player walk realistically enough to arouse the girls' interest.

The Movement and the Message

Dr. Birdwhistell, in his work in kinesics, has tried to pinpoint just what gesture indicates what message. One of the things he has uncovered is that every American speaker moves his head a number of times during a conversation. If you film a typical conversation between two Americans and then slow down the film to study the elements of posture in slow motion you will notice a head movement when an answer is expected. The head movement at the end of each statement is a signal to the other speaker to start his answer.

This is one of the ways in which we guide our spoken conversations. It enables a back-and-forth exchange without the necessity of saying, "Are you finished? Now I'll talk."

Of course the signals for other regions of the world will be different. In theory it would follow that watching two people talk would give a good clue to their nationality.

In our language, a change in pitch at the end of a sentence can mean a number of things. If there is a rise in pitch, the speaker is asking a question. Ask, "What time is it?" and notice how your voice goes up on "it." "How are you?" Up on "you." "Do you like your new job?" Up on "job."

This is a linguistic marker. Dr. Birdwhistell has discovered a number of kinesic markers that supplement the linguistic markers. Watch a man's head when he asks a question. "What time is it?" His head comes up on "it." "Where are you going?" His head comes up on the "ing"

113

in going. Like the voice, the head moves up at the end of a question.

This upward movement at the end of a question is not limited to the voice and head. The hand, too, tends to move up with the rise in pitch. The seemingly meaningless hand gestures in which we all indulge as we talk are tied in to pitch and meaning. The eyelid, too, will open wider with the last note of a question.

Just as the voice lifts up at the end of a question, it also drops in pitch at the end of a statement. "I like this book." With "book" the voice goes down. "I'd like some milk with my pie." Down on "pie."

The head also accompanies the voice down at the end of a statement, and according to Dr. Birdwhistell, so do the hand and the eyelid.

When a speaker intends to continue a statement, his voice will hold the same pitch, his head will remain straight, his eyes and hands unchanged.

These are just a few of the changes in position of the eyes, head and hands as Americans speak. Rarely, if ever, do we hold our heads in one position for longer than a sentence or two. Writers are aware of this and also aware that head movement is tied not only to what we are saying but to emotional content as well. To characterize a "cool" person, one who shows and feels no emotion, a writer will have him appear stolid, physically unmoving. James Bond, in the movies made from Ian Fleming's 007 stories, was played by Sean Connery in a motionless style. His face rarely moved, even in the face of extinction. It was an excellent characterization, since he played a man who felt no emotion.

In Jewish folklore a golem is a being who shows no expression and, of course, feels no emotion. The high-fashion model holds herself in a rigid, unnatural pose to communicate no emotional overtones. When the normal man or woman talks, however, he looks to the right, to the left, now up, now down. He blinks his eyes, lifts his eyebrows, bites his lips, touches his nose—and each movement is linked to what he is saying.

Because of the tremendous variation in individual movements it is often difficult to link a specific movement to a specific message, but it is still true enough, to paraphrase Marshall McLuhan, the movement is the message. Dr. Scheflen, in studying psychiatric therapy sessions, has found that when a therapist explains something to a patient he may use one head position, but when he interprets some remark or behavior he uses another position. When he interrupts the patient he uses still a third and he has a fourth head position for listening.

The patient, too, when listening to the therapist, takes certain definite positions. In one situation studied by Dr. Scheflen, the patient put his head to the right when he acted in a childish fashion, and he kept his head erect when he spoke aggressively and maturely.

The difficulty in studying and interpreting these movements is that they are personal kinesic motions, related to events in the background of this or that particular patient. Not all patients put their heads to one side when they act childishly, and not all therapists make the same head motion when they listen. Yet it is pretty certain that the same man will repeat the same motion over and over. Dr. Scheflen was surprised that these head movements which were repeated again and again during a thirty-minute interview were so stereotyped and rigid, yet he emphasizes that in this, as well as in many other sessions he has studied, the patient and doctor rarely used a great range of movement.

It should not then be too difficult to find specific positions for a person and then relate them to statements or types of statements, questions, answers, explanations, etc.

Postures and Presentations

Movements of the head, the eyelids and the hands are not really postural movements, and Dr. Scheflen calls them "points." A sequence of several points he labels a "position" which is much closer to a posture. A position, he says, consists of "a gross postural shift involving at least half the body." A position can last for about five minutes.

Most people in a social situation will run through two to four positions, although Dr. Scheflen has observed psychotherapists in a treatment situation hold one position for as long as twenty minutes.

To illustrate the use of positions, imagine a situation in which one man is holding forth on a particular subject. The listener leans back in his chair, arms and legs crossed, as he listens to the speaker's ideas. When the listener reaches a point where he disagrees with the speaker, he shifts his position in preparation for delivering his protest. He may lean forward and uncross his arms and legs. Perhaps he will raise one hand with the forefinger pointed as he begins to launch a rebuttal. When he is finished he will again lean back into his first position, arms and legs crossed—or perhaps into a third, more receptive position where his arms and legs are uncrossed as he leans back, signaling that he is open to suggestion.

If you take all the positions a man or a woman goes through during the course of a conversation, you have what Dr. Scheflen labels a "presentation." A presentation can last up to a few hours, and is terminated by a complete change in location. Leaving the room, going to make a phone call, to get cigarettes, to the washroom—any move to cut the conversation short ends a presentation. If the person returns, then a new presentation starts.

The function of posture in communication, Dr. Scheflen believes, is to mark these units, points, positions, and presentations. The units themselves serve as punctuation for a conversation. Different positions are related to different emotional states, and often emotional states can be recaptured when a person resumes the original position in which they occurred. The careful and observant psychotherapist will realize, after a while, what postures are associated with what emotional states. This reflects the same thing Dr. Wachtel found. The woman he studied made a definite gesture when she was angry.

The ordinary citizen who understands body language very well, and uses it, has a grasp of these postures, though he may be unaware of it, and he can relate them to the emotional states of the people he knows. In this way he can actually keep a step ahead of other people in his dealings with them. This art can be taught to people for it is a function of careful observation but it can only be learned if one is aware that it exists.

Before posture was analyzed this carefully, psychiatrists were aware of it. The therapist in the anecdote at the beginning of this chapter was aware of a postural change in his patient. He didn't consciously know that severe suicidal depression is linked to a definite posture, a lack of animation and humor, a passivity and general drooping, but unconsciously he was aware of it, aware enough to be bothered and finally to take the steps necessary to save his patient.

Just as the lowering of the head indicates the end of a statement, or the raising of the head the end of a question, so larger postural changes indicate end points in interactions, the end of a thought, the end of a statement. For example, a shift in posture so that you are no longer facing the person to whom you are talking, often means you have finished. You want to turn your attention somewhere else for a while.

We are all familiar with this in the exaggerated form it takes when a child has had enough of a parental lecture. His, "Yeah, yeah, I know!" is accompanied by an actual, physical turning away that signals, "Enough already! Let me go!"

However, Scheflen, like Birdwhistell and the other researchers, warns that we must not try to tie up specific posture changes to specific vocal statements. We should beware of deciding that one postural shift always means this, another always that. "The meaning or function of an event," he explains, "is not contained in itself, but in its relation to its context." A shift in posture means that something is happening. It does not always tell us what is happening. We must study the shift in relation to the entire incident to find that out.

These shifts also vary from culture to culture. In Latin countries the arms may play a greater part in communication. Every statement is accompanied with sweeping hand motions. In the tighter northern countries we move our hands very little when we talk.

The other night I watched the evangelist Billy Graham on television, and I realized that he has a number of rigid, body language postural shifts. One of his favorites is the sweeping finger. His right index finger accompanies his words, pointing upward when he promises heavenly rewards and swooping down in a giant circle when he "nails" a point. Another favorite is both hands parallel and open, in front of his chest, moving up and down with chopping motions. The size of his audience and the number of conversions for which he is responsible leave no doubt about the effectiveness of his postures, though an objective look makes it clear that these are all well-rehearsed posturings rather than unconscious postures. The point is that they do convey an emotional context to accompany his words, they do create an "aura."

The famous movie *King Kong* had some scenes in which the giant ape moved in a surprisingly lifelike fashion. Much of this was because of the understanding of body language by the moviemakers. When Kong held Fay Wray in his palm and looked at her, he cocked his head to one side in what was a touching copy of a completely human "point."

A recognition of how important body language is in projecting a human or friendly image has led men in politically high places to adopt various body language generalities in an attempt to achieve that indefinable something we call charisma.

John Kennedy had it, and no matter what he said, a few gestures, a correct posture, captivated his audience. Robert Kennedy, not at all a tall man, came on very tall through his manipulation of posture. Johnson took lessons in body language and tried unsuccessfully to change his image and Richard Nixon, too, is very conscious of the importance of body language and tries to use it consciously to manipulate his audience. This use of body language is a blessing to the actor who mimics these politicians. David Frye, the mimic, relies heavily on these postures and posturings to make his characterizations perfect.

Jockeying for Position

Posture is not only a means of punctuating a conversation, it is also a way in which people can relate to each other when they are together. Dr. Scheflen has divided all postures that people take when they are with others into three groups: 1) inclusive-non-inclusive, 2) vis-à-vis or parallel body orientation and 3) congruence-incongruence.

Inclusiveness or *non-inclusiveness* describes the way members of a group include or do not include people. They do this by placing their bodies, arms or legs in certain positions. At a cocktail party, a group of people may form a little circle that excludes all others. If three members of a group are sitting on a couch, the two at each end can "bookend," turn inward to enclose the one in the center, and exclude others. In this way they achieve inclusiveness. They may also cross their legs to lock in their central member or members.

In the previous chapter we saw how the grandmother and daughter in a therapeutic group "bookended" the mother in order to keep her away from the advances of the therapist. This is a device often used to keep non-members out of a group, or to keep members in.

The arms and legs of group members are often unconsciously used to protect the group from intrusion. If you observe groups at any function, at weddings, parties, meetings or evenings at home, you will notice the number of curious ways group members protect their group. A man at a social gathering may place his foot up on a coffee table to act as a barrier against outsiders. Sometimes sex will determine the way in which group members exclude others. Dr. Scheflen tells of a seminar at a hospital where male staff members arranged themselves between

120

female staff members and a male visitor. It was as if they were protecting their prized possessions from outsiders, and yet there may be no sexuality involved in this device. The female staff members are just part of a group that is automatically protected by the males.

A key to group status may be found when a group is arranged in a line on a couch, along a wall, or at a conference. The most important members will tend to be at either end.

In our discussion of personal territories we explained the significance of body zones in different cultures. When American men are in a situation where their zones or territories are violated by crowding, they often react in curious ways. Two men pushed together on a crowded couch at a party may turn their bodies away from each other, and cross their legs away. Each may put the arm that is next to his neighbor up to his face to act as a further barrier.

If a man and a woman are forced to sit very close and face to face and they are not on intimate terms, they may cross their arms and legs protectively and lean away from each other. A good way to observe these and other defenses is to experimentally move in on other people's territories at parties and see the way they react, what defenses they put up.

The second category of posture involvement, Dr. Scheflen calls *vis-à-vis* or *parallel body orientation*. Quite simply, this suggests that two people can relate to each other, posturally, by either facing each other or by sitting side by side, parallel, perhaps oriented toward a third person. If three people are involved, two will always be parallel and one facing. In groups of four, two parallel couples will face each other.

If circumstances prevent people from arranging their

121

entire bodies in these positions, they will settle for head, and arm and leg arrangements.

The face-to-face arrangement usually occurs in a teacher-student, doctor-patient, or lover-lover relationship, where feeling or information is exchanged. Parallel arrangements usually indicate activities which require only one person. Reading, listening to a story, watching television or a show can all be done by one person alone and are also done in parallel when more than one person is involved.

Face-to-face arrangements indicate a reaction between the two people involved. Side-by-side arrangements, when they are freely taken, tell us the two people are more apt to be neutral to each other, at least in this particular situation. The way in which a couple at a party or a social gathering postion themselves tells us a great deal about their relationship. In a side-by-side situation intimacy can still be achieved by facing one another with the upper half of the body.

The last category, *congruence-incongruence,* covers the ability of members of a group to imitate each other. When a group is in congruence, their body positions will be copies of each other, in some cases, mirror images.

It is interesting to note that when one member of a congruent group shifts, the others will shift with him. In general, congruence of position in a group indicates that all members are in agreement. If the group has two points of view, the advocates of each viewpoint will take different positions. Each subgroup will be congruent in itself, but non-congruent to the other subgroup.

Old friends when arguing or discussing something will adopt congruent positions to show that, in spite of the discussion, they are still friends. A husband and wife who are very close will adopt congruent postures when one is under attack. In body language, the other is saying, "I support you. I'm on your side."

People who wish to show that they are a cut above the rest of a group may deliberately take a non-congruent position. In doctor-patient, parent-child, teacher-student relationships, the postures will be non-congruent, again to show status or importance. The man at a business meeting who deliberately adopts an unusual position does this in an attempt to indicate his higher status.

I know of a top editor in a publishing house who adopts a most curious position during conferences. He leans back and clasps his hands high above his head, then keeps them behind his head, his elbows extended like wings. This at once sets him apart and indicates his status. It makes him higher than the other men at the conference.

It was pointed out to me, however, that a close subordinate of this man's will often, after a stated interval, copy the editor's exact position, saying in body language, "I am on your side. I am faithful to you, my leader." He may also be saying, "I am trying to bask in your reflected importance." There is also the possibility that he is saying, "I am trying to take over from you."

The leader at any gathering, family or social, often sets the position for the group and one by one the others fall in. In a family, if the wife sets the position, then the chances are that she has the strongest hand in decision-making and, in effect, wears the pants in the family.

Three Clues to Family Behavior

Study the table arrangement of a family carefully. Who takes a seat first and where? A psychologist friend of mine who has made a study of table seating analyzed the positioning of a family of five in terms of the family relationships.

"In this family," he explained, "the father sits at the head of the table, and he is also the dominant member of the family. His wife is not in competition with him for dominance, and she sits to his immediate right. The rationale is that they are close enough to share some intimacy at the table, and yet they are also close to the children.

"Now the positioning of the children is interesting. The eldest girl who is in competition with the mother for the father's affection, on an unconscious level, sits to the father's left, in congruence with the mother's position.

"The youngest, a boy, is interested in his mother, a normal situation for a boy, and he sits to her right, a space away from his father. The middle child, a girl, sits to her sister's left. Her position at the table, like her position in the family, is ambivalent."

What is interesting about this arrangement is the unconscious placement of all the members in accordance with interfamily relationships. This selecting position can start as early as the selecting of a table. There is more jockeying for dominance possible around an oblong table than around a round one.

The positioning of the husband and wife is important in understanding the family set-up. A husband and wife at either end of a long table are usually in conflict over the dominant position in the family, even if the conflict exists on an unconscious level.

When the husband and wife choose to sit cater-cornered, they are usually secure in their marital roles and have settled their conflict one way or the other. Which one sits at the head?

Of course if the table is small and they face each other

124

across it, this may be the most comfortable position for intimacy.

Positions at a table can give a clue to dominance within a family. Another clue to interfamily relationships lies in the tightness or looseness of a family.

A photographer friend of mine was recently assigned to shoot some informal pictures of a mayoral candidate in a large Midwestern city. He spent a day with the family and came away muttering unhappily.

"Maybe I got one decent shot," he told me. "I asked him to call his dog and it was the only time he relaxed."

Asked to explain, my friend said, "The house was one of those up-tight places, the tightest one I've ever been in. Plastic covers on the lamp shades, everything in place, everything perfect—his damned wife followed me around picking up flashbulbs and catching the ashes from my cigarettes in a tray. How could I get a relaxed shot?"

I knew what he meant for I have seen many homes like that, homes that represent a "closed" family. Everything about the family is closed in, tight. Even the postures they take are rigid and unbending. Everything is in place in these neat, formal homes.

We can usually be sure that the family in such a home is less spontaneous, more tense, less likely to have liberal opinions, to entertain unusual ideas and far more likely to conform to the standards of the community.

By contrast the "open" family will have a lived-in look to their house, an untidy, perhaps disorganized appearance. They will be less rigid, less demanding, freer and more open in thought and action.

In the closed family each member is likely to have his own chair, his own territory. In the open family it seldom matters who sits where. Whoever gets there first belongs.

On a body language level the closed family signals its

125

tightness by its tight movements, its formal manner and careful posture. The open family signals its openness by looser movements, careless postures and informal manners. Its body language cries out, "Relax. Nothing is very important. Be at ease."

The two attitudes are reflected in a tactile sense by the mother's behavior with her children. Is she a tense, holding mother or a relaxed, careless one? Her attitude influences her children and is reflected in their behavior.

These, of course, are the two extreme ends. Most families fall somewhere in between, have some amount of openness and some closedness. Some are equally balanced and some incline toward one or the other end of the scale. The outsider studying any family can use openness or closedness as a clue to understanding it. A third and equally significant clue is family imitation.

Who imitates whom in the family? We mentioned before that if the wife sets the pace by initiating certain movements which the rest of the family follow, then she is probably the dominant partner.

Among brothers and sisters dominance can be easily spotted by watching the child who makes the first move and noticing those who follow.

Respect in a family can be understood by watching how body language is copied. Does the son copy the father's gestures? The daughter the mother's? If so we can be reasonably sure the family set-up is in good shape. Watch out when the son begins to copy the mother's movements, the daughter her father's. These are early body language warnings. "I am off on the wrong track. I need to be set straight."

The thoughtful psychologist, treating a patient, will try to discover something of the entire family set-up and, most important, of the place of his patient in the family.

To treat a patient as an individual aside from his family is to have little understanding of the most important area of his life, his relationship to his family.

Some psychologists are beginning to insist on therapy that includes the entire family, and it is not unlikely that someday therapists will only treat patients within the framework of the family so that they can see and understand all the familial relationships and understand how they have influenced the patient.

Our first relationship is to our family, our second to the world. We cannot understand the second without thoroughly exploring the first.

Winking, Blinking and Nods

The Stare that Dehumanizes

The cowpuncher sat his horse loosely and his fingers hovered above his gun while his eyes, ice cold, sent chills down the rustler's back.

A familiar situation? It happens in every Western novel, just as in every love story the heroine's eyes *melt* while the hero's eyes *burn* into hers. In literature, even the best literature, eyes are *steely, knowing, mocking, piercing, glowing* and so on.

Are they really? Are they ever? Is there such a thing as a burning glance, or a cold glance or a hurt glance? In truth there isn't. Far from being windows of the soul, the eyes are physiological dead ends, simply organs of sight and no more, differently colored in different people to be sure, but never really capable of expressing emotion in themselves.

And yet again and again we read and hear and even tell of the eyes being wise, knowing, good, bad, indifferent. Why is there such confusion? Can so many people be wrong? If the eyes do not show emotion, then why the vast literature, the stories and legends about them?

Of all parts of the human body that are used to transmit information, the eyes are the most important and can transmit the most subtle nuances. Does this contradict the

129

fact that the eyes do not show emotion? Not really. While the eyeball itself shows nothing, the emotional impact of the eyes occurs because of their use and the use of the face around them. The reason they have so confounded observers is because by length of glance, by opening of eyelids, by squinting and by a dozen little manipulations of the skin and eyes, almost any meaning can be sent out.

But the most important technique of eye management is the look, or the stare. With it we can often make or break another person. How? By giving him human or nonhuman status.

Simply, eye management in our society boils down to two facts. One, we do not stare at another human being. Two, staring is reserved for a non-person. We stare at art, at sculpture, at scenery. We go to the zoo and stare at the animals, the lions, the monkeys, the gorillas. We stare at them for as long as we please, as intimately as we please, but we do not stare at humans if we want to accord them human treatment.

We may use the same stare for the side-show freak, but we do not really consider him a human being. He is an object at which we have paid money to stare, and in the same way we may stare at an actor on a stage. The real man is masked too deeply behind his role for our stare to bother either him or us. However, the new theater that brings the actor down into the audience often gives us an uncomfortable feeling. By virtue of involving us, the audience, the actor suddenly loses his non-person status and staring at him becomes embarrassing to us.

As I said before, a Southern white may stare at a black in the same way, making him, by the stare, into an object rather than a person. If we wish pointedly to ignore someone, to treat him with an element of contempt, we can give him the same stare, the slightly unfocused look that does not really see him, the cutting stare of the socially elite.

Servants are often treated this way as are waiters, waitresses and children. However, this may be a mutually protective device. It allows the servants to function efficiently in their overlapping universe without too much interference from us, and it allows us to function comfortably without acknowledging the servant as a fellow human. The same is true of children and waiters. It would be an uncomfortable world if each time we were served by a waiter we had to introduce ourselves and indulge in social amenities.

A Time for Looking

With unfamiliar human beings, when we acknowledge their humanness, we must avoid staring at them, and yet we must also avoid ignoring them. To make them into people rather than objects, we use a deliberate and polite inattention. We look at them long enough to make it quite clear that we see them, and then we immediately look away. We are saying, in body language, "I know you are there," and a moment later we add, "But I would not dream of intruding on your privacy."

The important thing in such an exchange is that we do not catch the eye of the one whom we are recognizing as a person. We look at him without locking glances, and then we immediately look away. Recognition is not permitted.

There are different formulas for the exchange of glances depending on where the meeting takes place. If you pass someone in the street you may eye the oncoming person till you are about eight feet apart, then you must look away as you pass. Before the eight-foot distance is reached, each will signal in which direction he will pass. This is done with a brief look in that direction. Each will veer slightly and the passing is done smoothly.

For this passing encounter Dr. Erving Goffman in *Behavior in Public Places* says that the quick look and the lowering of the eyes is body language for, "I trust you. I am not afraid of you."

To strengthen this signal, you look directly at the other's face before looking away.

Sometimes the rules are hard to follow, particularly if one of the two people wears dark glasses. It becomes impossible to discover just what they are doing. Are they looking at you too long, too intently? Are they looking at you at all? The person wearing the glasses feels protected and assumes that he can stare without being noticed in his staring. However, this is a self-deception. To the other person, dark glasses seem to indicate that the wearer is always staring at him.

We often use this look-and-away technique when we meet famous people. We want to assure them that we are respecting their privacy, that we would not dream of staring at them. The same is true of the crippled or physically handicapped. We look briefly and then look away before the stare can be said to be a stare. It is the technique we use for any unusual situation where too long a stare would be embarrassing. When we see an interracial couple we use this technique. We might use it when we see a man with an unusual beard, with extra long hair, with outlandish clothes, or a girl with a minimal mini-skirt may attract this look-and-away.

Of course the opposite is also true. If we wish to put a person down we may do so by staring longer than is acceptably polite. Instead of dropping our gazes when we lock glances, we continue to stare. The person who dis-

approves of interracial marriage or dating will stare rude-
ly at the interracial couple. If he dislikes long hair, short
dresses or beards he may show it with a longer-than-ac-
ceptable stare.

The Awkward Eyes

The look-and-away stare is reminiscent of the problem
we face in adolescence in terms of our hands. What do we
do with them? Where do we hold them? Amateur actors
are also made conscious of this. They are suddenly aware
of their hands as awkward appendages that must somehow be used gracefully and naturally.

In the same way, in certain circumstances, we become
aware of our glances as awkward appendages. Where
shall we look? What shall we do with our eyes?

Two strangers seated across from each other in a rail-
way dining car have the option of introducing themselves
and facing a meal of inconsequential and perhaps boring
talk, or ignoring each other and desperately trying to
avoid each other's glance. Cornelia Otis Skinner, describing such a situation in an essay, wrote, "They re-read the
menu, they fool with the cutlery, they inspect their own
fingernails as if seeing them for the first time. Comes the
inevitable moment when glances meet, but they meet only
to shoot instantly away and out the window for an intent
view of the passing scene."

This same awkward eye dictates our looking behavior
in elevators and crowded buses and subway trains. When
we get on an elevator or train with a crowd we look
briefly and then look away at once without locking
glances. We say, with our look, "I see you. I do not know
you, but you are a human and I will not stare at you."

In the subway or bus where long rides in very close

circumstances are a necessity, we may be hard put to find some way of not staring. We sneak glances, but look away before our eyes can lock. Or we look with an unfocused glance that misses the eyes and settles on the head, the mouth, the body—for any place but the eyes is an acceptable looking spot for the unfocused glance.

If our eyes do meet we can sometimes mitigate the message with a brief smile. The smile must not be too long or too obvious. It must say, "I am sorry we have looked, but we both know it was an accident."

Bedroom Eyes

The awkward eye is a common enough occurrence for all of us to have experienced it at one time or another. Almost all actions and interactions between humans depend on mutual glances. The late Spanish philosopher José Ortega y Gasset, in his book *Man and People,* spoke of "the look" as something that comes directly from within a man "with the straight-line accuracy of a bullet." He felt that the eye, with its lids and sockets, its iris and pupil, was equivalent to a "whole theatre with its stage and actors."

The eye muscles, Ortega said, are marvelously subtle and because of this every glance is minutely differentiated from every other glance. There are so many different looks that it is nearly impossible to name them, but he cited, "the look that lasts but an instant and the insistent look; the look that slips over the surface of the thing looked at and the look that grips it like a hook; the direct look and the oblique look whose extreme form has its own name, 'looking out of the corner of one's eye.' "

He also listed the "sideways glance" which differs from

any other oblique look although its axis is still on the bias.

Every look, Ortega said, tells us what goes on inside the person who gives it, and the intent to communicate with a look is more genuinely revealing when the sender of the look is unaware of just how he sends it.

Like other researchers into body language Ortega warned that a look in itself does not give the entire story, even though it has a meaning. A word in a sentence has a meaning too, but only in the context of the sentence can we learn the complete meaning of the word. So too with a look. Only in the context of an entire situation is a look entirely meaningful.

There are also looks that want to see but not be seen. These the Spanish philosopher called sideways glances. In any situation we may study someone and look as long as we wish, providing the other person is not aware that we are looking, providing our look is hidden. The moment his eyes move to lock with ours, our glance must slide away. The more skilled the person, the better he is at stealing these sideways glances.

In a charming description Ortega labels one look "the most effective, the most suggestive, the most delicious and enchanting." He called it the most complicated because it is not only furtive, but it is also the very opposite of furtive, because it makes it obvious that it is looking. This is the look given with lidded eyes, the sleepy look or calculating look or appraising look, the look a painter gives his canvas as he steps back from it, what the French call *les yeux en coulisse.*

Describing this look, Ortega said the lids are almost three-quarters closed and it appears to be hiding itself, but in fact the lids compress the look and "shoot it out like an arrow."

"It is the look of eyes that are, as it were, asleep but which behind the cloud of sweet drowsiness are utterly awake. Anyone who has such a look possesses a treasure."

Ortega said that Paris throws itself at the feet of anyone with this look. Louis XV's DuBarry was supposed to have had it, and so was Lucien Guitry. In our own Hollywood, Robert Mitchum certainly had it and it set him up for years as a masculine sex symbol. Mae West copied it and the French actress Simone Signoret has it so perfectly controlled that even in middle age she comes across as a very sexy and attractive woman.

Other Cultures, Other Looks

The recognition of the eye as a means of communication, or of a look as having special significance is nothing new. Looking is something that has always had strong emotions attached to it and has been forbidden, under certain circumstances, in prehistory and legend. Lot's wife was turned to a pillar of salt for looking back, and Orpheus lost Eurydice by looking at her. Adam, when he tasted the fruit of knowledge, was afraid to look at God.

The significance of looking is universal, but usually we are not sure of just how we look or how we are looked at. Honesty demands, in our culture, that we look someone straight in the eye. Other cultures have other rules, as a principal in a New York City high school recently discovered.

A young girl at the high school, a fifteen-year-old Puerto Rican, had been caught in the washroom with a group of girls suspected of smoking. Most of the group were known troublemakers, and while this young girl, Livia, had no record, the principal after a brief interview was convinced of her guilt and decided to suspend her with the others.

"It wasn't what she said," he reported later. "It was simply her attitude. There was something sly and suspicious about her. She just wouldn't meet my eye. She wouldn't look at me."

It was true. Livia at her interview with the principal stared down at the floor in what was a clear-cut guilty attitude and refused to meet his eyes.

"But she's a good girl," Livia's mother insisted. Not to the school, for she was too much of a "troublemaker" the principal felt, to come to the authorities with her protest. Instead, she turned to her neighbors and friends. As a result there was a demonstration of Puerto Rican parents at the school the next morning and the ugly stirrings of a threatened riot.

Fortunately, John Flores taught Spanish literature at the school, and John lived only a few doors from Livia and her family. Summoning his own courage, John asked for an interview with the principal.

"I know Livia and her parents," he told the principal. "And she's a good girl. I am sure there has been some mistake in this whole matter."

"If there was a mistake," the principal said uneasily, "I'll be glad to rectify it. There are thirty mothers outside yelling for my blood. But I questioned the child myself, and if ever I saw guilt written on a face—she wouldn't even meet my eyes!"

John drew a sigh of relief, and then very carefully, for he was too new in the school to want to tread on toes, he explained some basic facts of Puerto Rican culture to the principal.

"In Puerto Rico a nice girl, a good girl," he explained, "does not meet the eyes of an adult. Refusing to do so is

137

a sign of respect and obedience. It would be as difficult for Livia to look you in the eyes as it would be for her to misbehave, or for her mother to come to you with a complaint. In our culture, this is just not accepted behavior for a respectable family."

Fortunately the principal was a man who knew how to admit that he was wrong. He called Livia and her parents and the most vocal neighbors in and once again discussed the problem. In the light of John Flores' explanation it became obvious to him that Livia was not avoiding his eyes out of defiance, but out of a basic demureness. Her slyness, he now saw, was shyness. In fact, as the conference progressed and the parents relaxed, he realized that Livia was indeed a gentle and sweet girl.

The outcome of the entire incident was a deeper, more meaningful relationship between the school and the community—but that of course is another story. What is of particular interest in this story is the strange confusion of the principal. How did he so obviously misinterpret all the signals of Livia's behavior?

Livia was using body language to say, "I am a good girl. I respect you and the school. I respect you too much to answer your questions, too much to meet your eyes with shameless boldness, too much to defend myself. But surely my very attitude tells you all this."

How could such a clear-cut message be interpreted as, "I defy you. I will not answer your questions. I will not look you in the eyes because I am a deceitful child. I will evade your questions slyly—"

The answer of course is a cultural one. Different cultures have different customs and, of course, different body language. They also have different looks and different meanings to the same looks.

In America, for instance, a man is not supposed to

look at a woman for any length of time unless she gives
him her permission with a body language signal, a smile,
a backward glance, a direct meeting of his eye. In other
countries different rules apply.

In America, if a woman looks at a man for too long a
period of time, she commits herself to a verbal approach.
Her signal says, "I am interested. You can approach me."
In Latin countries, though freer body movements are
permissible, such a look might be a direct invitation to a
physical "pass." It becomes obvious then why a girl like
Livia would not look the principal in the eye.

Again, in our country, two men are not allowed to
stare at each other for more than a brief period of time
unless they intend to fight or to become intimate. Any
man who looks at another man for too long embarrasses
and annoys him and the other man begins to wonder just
what he wants.

This is another example of the rigidity of the rules of
looking. If someone stares at us and we meet his eye and
catch him staring, it is his duty to look away first. If he
does not look away as we engage his eye, then we become
uncomfortable and aware that something is wrong. Again
we become embarrassed and annoyed.

A Long Look at Oneself

In an attempt to discover just how some of these rules
for visual communication work, Dr. Gerhard Nielson of
Copenhagen analyzed the "looks" of the subjects in his
self-confrontation studies. To discover just how long, and
when, the people being interviewed looked at the interviewer, he filmed interviews and replayed them a number
of times in slow motion.

While he started with no clear-cut idea of how long

one man would look at another during an interview, he was surprised to find how little looking there actually was. The man who looked at his interviewer the most, still looked away 27 per cent of the time. The man who looked at his interviewer the least looked away 92 per cent of the time. Half of the people interviewed looked away for half of the time they were being interviewed.

Dr. Nielson found that when people spoke a lot they looked at their partners very little; when they listened a lot they also looked a lot. He reports that he expected people to look at each other more when they listened more, but he was surprised to find them looking less when they spoke more.

He found that when people start to speak, they look away from their partners at first. There is a subtle timing, he explains, in speaking, listening, looking and looking away. Most people look away either immediately before or after the beginning of one out of every four speeches they make. A few look away at the beginning of half their speeches. As they finish speaking, half the people look at their partners.

As to why so many people refuse to meet the eyes of their partners during a conversation, Dr. Nielson believes this is a way of avoiding distraction.

How Long Is a Glance?

Another study, carried out by Dr. Ralph V. Exline at the University of Delaware, involved 40 men and 40 women, all freshmen and sophomores. In the study a man interviewed 20 men and 20 women and a woman interviewed the other 20 of each sex. Half the students were questioned by both interviewers about intimate subjects, their plans, desires, needs and fears. The other half were asked about recreational interests, reading, movies, sports.

Dr. Exline found that when the students were interviewed about personal subjects, they didn't look at the interviewer as often as they did when they were interviewed about recreational subjects. Women, however, in both types of interview, looked at the interviewers more frequently than men did.

What seems to come across from both these studies, and others of a similar nature, is that when someone looks away while he's speaking, it generally means he's still explaining himself and doesn't want to be interrupted.

A locking of his gaze with his partner's at this point would be a signal to interrupt when he paused. If he pauses and is not looking at his conversational partner, it means he hasn't yet finished. He is signaling, "This is what I want to say. What is your answer?"

If you look away from the person who is speaking to you while you are listening, it is a signal, "I am not completely satisfied with what you are saying. I have some qualifications."

If you look away while you are speaking it may mean, "I am not certain of what I am saying."

If while you are listening, you look at the speaker, you signal, "I agree with you," or "I am interested in what you are saying."

If while you are speaking, you look at the listener, you may be signaling, "I am certain of what I am saying."

There are also elements of concealment in looking away from your partner. If you look away while he is speaking, you signal, "I don't want you to know what I feel." This is particularly true if the partner is critical or insulting. It is something like an ostrich burying his head in the sand. "If I cannot see you, you cannot hurt me."

141

This is the reason children will often refuse to look at you when you are scolding them.

However, there are more complexities here than meet the eye . . . or the glance. Looking away during a conversation may be a means of concealing something. Therefore when someone else looks away, we may think he is concealing something. To practice deceit we may sometimes deliberately look at our partner instead of refusing to meet his glance.

In addition to length and direction of glances, there is a good deal of signaling involved in the act of closing the lid. In addition to the half-lidded look Ortega described, Birdwhistell states that five young nurses, in a series of tests, reported twenty-three different positions of lid closure that they could distinguish.

But they all agreed that only four out of the twenty-three "meant anything." Retesting allowed Dr. Birdwhistell to label these four positions, "open-eyed, droopy-lidded, squinting, eyes-closed-tight."

Working from the opposite end, trying to get the girls to reproduce the lid positions, was not so successful. All could reproduce five of the twenty-three positions, but only one could reproduce more than five.

Using a group of men in the same type of experiment, he found that all could reproduce at least ten positions. Unexpectedly men were more facile at winking. Some of the men could reproduce fifteen different positions, and one—fantastically eloquent in body language—came up with thirty-five different eyelid positions.

Branching out into cultural comparisons Dr. Birdwhistell found that among the Japanese both sexes were similar in the number of eyelid positions they could reproduce. But even the Japanese could recognize, in others, more positions than they could assume themselves.

When movement of the eyebrows is added to movement of the lids, many more recognizable signals are produced. Some scientists have found as many as forty different positions of the brows alone, though most agree that less than half of them are significant. It is only when the significant eyebrow movements are combined with the significant lid movements and we add forehead creases that the permutations and combinations are endless.

If each combination has a different implication, then there is no end to the number of signals we can transmit with our eyes and the skin around them.

An Alphabet
for Movement

Is There a Language of Legs?

As kinesics and body language became more generally known and understood, what started as a curiosity soon became a science, what started as an observable fact soon became a measurable fact, and also, unfortunately, what became a science also became an exploitable situation.

The fact that in times of stress a baby will suck his thumb, a man will bite his nails or knuckle, a woman will spread her hand across her chest are all curious gestures but an understanding of body language makes us realize that the child is sucking his thumb for security in a symbolic return to the comfort of the mother's breast. The man has substituted the socially acceptable nail-biting or knuckle-biting for the unacceptable thumb-sucking, and the woman spreads her hand across her chest in a defensive manner, covering and protecting her vulnerable breasts. An understanding of the forces behind these gestures is the point at which a curiosity becomes a science.

Knowing that people lift their eyebrows or lower their lids part way to express an emotion is an observable fact. Knowing the exact degree of lift or the angle of lowering makes the fact a measurable one. Dr. Birdwhistell has written, " 'droopy lidded' combined with 'bilaterally raised median portion depressed brows' has an evident

145

differential meaning from 'droopy lidded' combined with a 'low unilateral brow lift.' " This is a measured explanation of the observed fact that when the eyes are half closed and both the eyebrows are raised at the ends and lowered in the centers the face looks different than it does when the eyes are half closed and one eyebrow is slightly raised.

Unfortunately, something like kinesics, related facts on the way to becoming a science, also runs the risk of being exploited. For example, just how much can we really tell from crossed legs? Earlier in the book we spoke of the use of crossed legs to unconsciously include or exclude members of a group. We have seen how they can also be used in congruent sittings where one person in a room will set a postural pattern and the others will imitate it. If the leader crosses his legs, the others will cross theirs.

Can crossed legs also express character? Do we, in the way we hold our legs when we sit, give a clue to our inner nature?

As with all body language signals, there is no simple yes-or-no answer. Crossed legs or parallel legs can be a clue to what the person is feeling, to the emotional state *at the moment,* but they may also mean nothing at all. I have a friend who is a writer and writes in longhand. He only crosses his legs from left to right, the left leg on top, never the other way. At a recent social evening my friend was sitting to the left of his wife, his left leg over his right pointing to her. Her right leg, crossed over her left knee, pointed to him.

An amateur psychologist in the group nodded at the couple and said, "See, they form a closed circle, their crossed legs pointing to each other and excluding the rest of the group—a perfect illustration of body language."

I took my writer friend aside later and said, "I know

146

you get along well with your wife, but I wonder about this leg crossing."

Grinning, he explained. "I can only cross my left leg over my right. It's because I write my first drafts in longhand, not on a typewriter."

Puzzled, I asked, "But what does that have to do with it?"

"I can only cross from left to right because all my life I've crossed my legs that way, and my leg muscles and bones have become adapted to it. If I cross the other way I am uncomfortable. Automatically now, I cross my left leg over my right knee."

"But how does writing in longhand . . . ?"

"Simple. I don't write at a desk. I compose in an easy chair. I write on a clipboard which I balance on my knee. To bring the clipboard high enough to write, I must cross my knees. Since I am right-handed, I write toward the left side. I therefore cross my legs so my left leg will be higher, left over right. I always have, and now it's the only position I'm comfortable in. So much for your body language. By chance I sat to the left of my wife tonight. On other nights I've happened to sit on her right."

The moral here is that before making any scientific judgment, all the facts should be known. If we are to attach any significance to leg crossing, we must also be aware of the physiological condition of the body. The same is true of arm crossing. There is a terrible temptation to fix a host of meanings to the direction in which we cross our arms. It seems to have been established that crossing the arms is sometimes a defensive gesture, a signal that you don't want to accept another's point of view, or a sign that you are insecure and want to defend yourself. Now these and a few others are valid interpretations,

147

but when we come to the direction of the cross, left over right or right over left, we are on tricky ground.

Cross your arms without thinking. Some of you will put your left arm outside, some your right arm outside and, most important of all, you will always cross your arms the same way. Crossing them the other way just "feels wrong." This is because the way in which we cross our arms, left over right or right over left, is a genetic trait, an inborn trait, in the same way that using your left or right hand to write with is genetic. Folding the hands and intertwining the fingers is also genetic. Is your right thumb or left thumb on top?

Taking these points into consideration, we may be on safe ground when we use the gesture itself as a signal, but we are on uncertain ground when we speak of direction.

Most serious studies of body language have concerned themselves with the emotions transmitted by movement, not with the innate nature of the person transmitting the message. At best, the signal sent out, the body language, has been used to make a person understand himself. When it is used to try to determine personality or character rather than behavior, it seems fraught with contradictions.

The ABC of Body Language

In an attempt to outline certain aspects of body language and unify the science, or perhaps make body language into a science, Dr. Ray Birdwhistell has written a preliminary research manual on the subject, a manual he calls *An Introduction to Kinesics*. Basically, he has attempted to put together an annotational system for kinesics or body language, to break all relevant movements

148

down to their basics and give a symbol—much the way a choreographer breaks the dance down into basic steps and gives each a symbol.

The result is a little like Egyptian pictographs, but hopefully not as hard to read. Starting with the eyes, since they are the most common source of communication in body language, he has decided that ⬯ is the best symbol for the open eye, —— for the closed eye. A wink of the right eye then becomes (—— ⬯), of the left eye (⬯ ——). Open eyes are (⬯ ⬯) and so on. Dr. Birdwhistell calls each of these movements a kine, or the smallest recordable movement.

The first premise in developing this type of notational system for body language, Dr. Birdwhistell says, is to assume that all movements of the body have meaning. None are accidental. Once this is accepted, we can proceed to a study of every movement, its significance and a means of labeling it.

I find that this basic assumption is the most difficult one to accept. Perhaps scratching the nose is an indication of disagreement, but it may also be an indication of an itchy nose. This is where the real trouble in kinesics lies, in separating the significant from the insignificant gestures, the meaningful from the purely random, or from the carefully learned.

When a woman sits with her legs slanted, parallel and slightly crossed at the ankles it may indicate an orderly mind, but it is far more likely to be an affected positioning or even charm school training. Certain charm schools believe that this is a graceful and womanly pose and suggest that women condition themselves to fall into it when they sit. It is also a pose that allows a woman with a mini skirt to sit in a comfortable but unrevealing position. It was also a pose our grandmothers considered "very lady-like."

These are some of the reasons we must approach kinesics with caution and study a motion or a gesture only in terms of the total pattern of movement, and we must understand the pattern of movement in terms of the spoken language. The two, while sometimes contradictory, are also inseparable.

To standardize body movements before making them into kinesic pictographs, we must have a zero point or a resting point. An arm movement, for example, is only significant if we know how much distance it covers. We can only know this if we set up a standard zero point.

In Dr. Birdwhistell's work, he set a zero point for "middle-class Americans." This is the semi-relaxed state of the body, head balanced and facing forward, arms at the side and legs together. Any perceptible position is a motion away from this zero point.

It is significant that Dr. Birdwhistell limits his own work to middle-class Americans. He recognizes that even in our culture there is a surprising lack of uniformity in body movement. Working-class people will give certain interpretations to movements, and these interpretations will not apply in middle-class circles.

However, in America there is, I think, a greater ethnic difference in gesture than there is a class difference. Although he does not say so specifically, I would assume that Dr. Birdwhistell is primarily concerned with body language among middle-class white Anglo-Saxon Protestant Americans. If this is so it presents serious students of the subject with an overwhelming amount of data to learn. They must absorb not only a system of interpretation for white Anglo-Saxon Protestant Americans, but also one for Italian-Americans, Jewish Americans, American Indians, black Americans and so on. Then there would be class lines in each of these categories, and the total number of systems would become overwhelming. What must be found is one common system that will work for all cultures and all ethnic groups, and I suspect that, with some variation, Dr. Birdwhistell's system will.

Dr. Birdwhistell also points out that a body movement may mean nothing at all in one context, and yet be extremely significant in another context. For example, the frown we make by creasing the skin between our eyebrows may simply mark a point in a sentence or, in another context, it may be a sign of annoyance or, in still another context, of deep concentration. Examining the face alone won't tell us the exact meaning of the frown. We must know what the frowner is doing.

Another point Dr. Birdwhistell makes is that all of our movements, if they are significant, are learned. We pick them up as a part of our society. As an illustration of the learning power of humans he considers the most common kinesic motion, that of the eyelid. We tend to think that eyelid movements are reflex movements. We squint to guard against too much light, or we blink to keep out dust and to cleanse our eyeballs.

Contradicting this, Dr. Birdwhistell cites the numerous cases of learned eyelid movement. Fakirs in Indian religious cults can learn to look at the sun without blinking or face a dust storm without closing their lids. Girls in our society learn to "bat their eyelashes" in flirting, even when there is no need to clean the eyeball. He suggests that examples like these prove that not all lid movement is instinctive and, he adds, that lid behavior varies from culture to culture, the same as language.

151

An interesting fact here is that when a bilingual person changes his language, he also changes his body language, his gestures and lid movements.

Labeling the Kines

Even if, as we showed in an earlier chapter, some gestures are genetic and not learned—smiles, for example—Dr. Birdwhistell stresses that among men communication *is* a learned art, and since kinesics is concerned with those body movements that communicate, we can assume that most of kinesics is learned too.

In spite of the fact that most of Dr. Birdwhistell's analyses of body motion have come from the study of films played over and over till all casual traits are recognized and labeled, he warns against putting too much reliance on this method. If we must film motion and slow it down and replay it again and again to analyze it before we can notice certain movements—how much value is there to the motion we discover? A motion can only be meaningful if it is easily signaled and easily received. He believes that the small gestures picked up by film and missed by the human eye cannot be of much significance in communication.

There is, however, a possible subliminal value to these gestures. We have found that often images sent too rapidly to be perceived by the conscious eye are still recognized and absorbed by the unconscious eye. This is the whole point behind the field of subliminal communication.

Dr. Birdwhistell not only makes a distinction between those gestures we notice and those we don't, but also between those we are aware of making and those we make unconsciously. There are so many possible motions we can and do make from minute to minute, that almost no one is aware of either making them or observing them. Still we send out these continual signals and we receive them and, in relation to our reception, we send out more.

The most important thing to realize about body language, according to Dr. Birdwhistell, is that no single motion ever stands alone. It is always part of a pattern. A novelist may write, "She winked at him." But the statement only has meaning because the reader is aware of all the other gestures that go with a wink, and knows, in the context of the written situation, that that particular wink means an invitation to a flirtation.

The wink alone is called by Dr. Birdwhistell a kine, the smallest measurement of body language. This particular kine can be described as "a lowering of one lid while holding the other relatively immobile." This type of description, incidentally, tends to drain the kine of all attached emotion. It becomes a simple closing of one eye instead of a signal to flirtation.

In developing a system of "writing" body language, it is necessary to drain all emotion from the movement noted. It is also necessary to work out an experimental system for recording and duplicating kines. For this Dr. Birdwhistell uses an actor or a student skilled in body language to try to project different motions and their significance to a group of students. The group is asked to differentiate between the motions, but not to guess what each motion means.

"Does this mean something different from this?" is the usual question. In this way the recorder discovers when a small range of motion projects a different impression. To that extra motion he can then assign a meaning.

From a large series of such experiments Dr. Birdwhistell has managed to separate different kines, to tell at what point an additional kine makes the whole movement different.

For example, an actor was told to face the group of students and give the following expression.

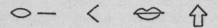

Translated into descriptive terms, this expression would be a wink with the left eye closed and a squint at the corner of the left eye. The mouth is normal, but the tip of the nose is depressed. A second, similar expression is then tried on the group of observers. Diagrammed, it would go like this:

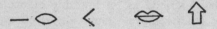

Described: it is a wink with the right eye, a squint at the corner of the left eye, the mouth held normal and the nose depressed.

The observers were asked the difference, and their comment was, "They look different, but they don't mean anything different."

A pertinent piece of information is then added to the growing body of data about kinesics. *It doesn't matter which eye is winked. The meaning is the same. Nor does it matter if one side of the eye is squinted.*

A third instruction is then tried out on the observers.

Essentially, this is the first wink without the squint and with the tip of the nose depressed. The group of observers decided that this was the same as the first expression. The science of kinesics now understands that a squint doesn't usually mean anything in body language. Finally, a fourth variation is tried.

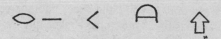

In this expression the wink is the same and the squint is kept at the closed eye. The tip of the nose is depressed, but the mouth is changed. It is drawn down into a pout. When this expression is shown to the group, their comment is, "Well, that changes things."

The datum that then goes into the kinesic file is, *a change in mouth position causes a change in meaning.*

Here a careful scientific study confirms the fact that communication is less likely to come from any change in the eye itself, than it is from a change in the face. We would think that squinting and alternate winking would convey different meanings, but Dr. Birdwhistell shows that they don't. A real change in expression is only reached when the mouth changes.

Of course he did not evaluate eyebrow change in this sequence. If he had, a slight change in either eyebrow might have signaled a very different meaning. A lift to one eyebrow is a classic signal of doubt, a lift to both eyebrows, of surprise and a lowering of both, uneasiness or suspicion.

The doctor found that winking, or closing one eye was significant in conveying an emotion. Squinting was not significant when the mouth was held in a normal position. A squint with a pout, however, was significant. A depressed nose tip was not significant in the context of winked eyes, but in other contexts it was meaningful.

Culture and Kinesics

The face, we can see, has a tremendous possible variety of expressions, and when we draw back a bit to consider the head, over and beyond the face, another set of motions become possible. One nods, shakes, pivots, bounces; and all are meaningful. But all hold different meanings when combined with different facial expressions and in different cultural situations.

A friend of mine teaches in a large graduate school which has many students from India. These students, he tells me, move their heads up and down to signify no, and from side to side to signify yes. "I'm sometimes driven to distraction," he complained, "when I explain a particularly complicated point and they sit there signaling what I understand to be 'no' as they accept it, and what I understand to be 'yes' when they don't accept it. Yet I know it's only a cultural problem. They are really signaling the opposite of what I receive, but that doesn't make it any easier for me. I'm so culturally indoctrinated myself that I just cannot accept the contradiction."

Cultural indoctrination in terms of body language is very difficult to overcome. I know a professor of mathematics at a nearby university who was originally a Talmudic student in Germany and left in the early 30's. To this day, when he lectures he falls back into the culture-oriented "davening" posture of the Talmudic student. He leans forward, bending his body from the waist, then rises on his toes and straightens up, arching his body backwards.

Even when this was pointed out to him in a joking manner, the professor was unable to control his body movement. We cannot underestimate the strength of cultural ties in body language. In Germany, during the Nazi years, Jews who were trying to pass as non-Jews often gave themselves away by their body language. Their hand movements were freer and more open than the Germans' hand movements, and of all the elements of their disguise, these hand movements were the hardest to control.

Because of this cultural difference, an observer of one nationality may see things in body language that are completely missed by someone of a different nationality.

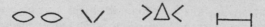

The above description, open eyes with a medial brow contraction, pinched nostrils and a mouth in repose, would be the same to an American as the one below.

However, to someone from Italy, there would be a subtle difference in omitting the medial brow contraction. The first expression might suggest uneasiness or apprehension. The final clue in each case would have to come from the context in which the expression occurred.

It is always, Dr. Birdwhistell emphasizes, a case of one complementing the other, body language in the context of the spoken language giving the clue to action and understanding. And yet, no matter what the spoken language, body language can often give a clue to the dynamics of the true situation.

Follow the Leader

Dr. Birdwhistell cites the case of a gang of adolescent boys. Three boys in the gang were what the doctor called "heavy vocalizers," what we might call "loud mouths."

Filming the action of this group, he found that within the gang the three "loud mouths" were responsible for from 72 to 93 per cent of all the words spoken.

There were two leaders in the gang. One of them belonged to the "loud mouths." Let's call him Tom. The other leader was a quiet fellow, Bob. In fact he was one of the quietest boys in the group. Careful analysis showed that Bob was responsible for only about 16 per cent of the words spoken. What then made him a leader?

In answering this question, we might also help to answer the more general question, what makes leadership? Is it the ability to give orders and talk others down? If that is so, as we might suspect from Tom's leadership, what about Bob who spoke so little and yet was a leader too?

The answer, Dr. Birdwhistell suspected, might lie in body language. Bob's leadership, he decided, seemed to be a kinesic one.

Studying the filmed records of the gang in action it was found that Bob, compared to the other boys, "engaged in few unrelated acts." Unrelated acts, Dr. Birdwhistell explains, are acts that try to start something new, that is, unrelated to what's being done. "Let's go fishing," when the gang is headed for a baseball game; or "Let's go downtown to the drugstore and hang around," when the gang is headed for a nearby beach.

Bob rarely took the chance of asking the gang to do something it wasn't ready to do or inclined to do. He would steer the gang in a direction it wanted to go, instead of trying to force it in a completely new direction. "Come on, let's go for a swim," if they were all sitting around on the beach, or "Let's go down to the drugstore," when they were headed for town.

There's a good lesson here in leadership. The most

successful leader, in gangs or in politics, is always the one who anticipates the desired action and leads people toward it, who makes people do what they want to do. Bob was an old hand at this.

But more interesting from a body language point of view, Bob was "kinesically mature." He had less wasteful body motions than the other boys. He didn't shuffle his feet needlessly. He didn't put his hand to his mouth, scratch his head or tap his fingers. The difference between maturity and immaturity is often telegraphed by body language. Too much body movement without real meaning is immature. A mature person moves when he has to, and moves purposefully.

The type of boy who is a born leader, who leads a gang in the direction it wants to go, is also mature enough to channel his body movements into useful areas. Listening is one of these areas. Kinesically, Bob was a good listener. He would copy the posture of the boy who was talking. He would steer the conversation along with the proper facial and head movements, and he wouldn't jiggle his leg or his foot or indulge in all the youthful body language signals which mean "I am restless, bored, disinterested."

Because of his listening ability in a body language sense, the rest of the gang were apt to go to Bob with their problems and to trust him when he made a suggestion. Oddly enough, or perhaps obviously enough, Bob, though he spoke less than the others, was a good conversationalist. It is possible that the traits of body language that made him a leader were reflected in his speech. When he did talk what he said was effective.

With this in mind. Dr. Birdwhistell has divided the body into eight sections to make these "little movements" easier to investigate. In addition to the *head,* and to the *face* with its pictographic symbols, he has the *trunk and*

159

shoulders, the *arm and wrist* area, the *hands and fingers,* the *hip, leg and ankle* area, the *foot* and the *neck.*

The special signs for movement in each of these parts are combined with a number of directional signals. These include ↑ to a higher position, ↓ to a lower position, ——→ forward, ←—— backward and ——⊣ which signals continuity of any motion or position.

But when all is said and done, the question inevitably arises: just how much does a system of notation contribute to the study of body language? How important is it to record an incident in kinesic terms? Even when the notation is combined with a record of the spoken words, there is surely only a limited use for the combination and that use is probably limited to only a few scholars.

However, such a notational system need not be confined to recording situations for study. It could, like the notational system for the dance, be used to "score" speeches and generate maximum effectiveness in fields such as politics or teaching. It could be used by therapists to "score" therapy sessions and refer back to what the patient said with his body as well as with his mouth. It could be used by actors and entertainers and even by businessmen.

In fact, when you begin to think about it, there are very few situations where such a notational system would not come in handy. Whether Dr. Birdwhistell's system will catch on or not remains to be seen, but eventually some such system will be needed.

11

Body Language:
Use and Abuse

Let's Talk to the Animals

A sign of the antiquity of body language and its supremacy over the spoken word has come from the studies of a husband and wife team of researchers, R. Allen and Beatrice T. Gardner of the University of Nevada. Pondering the many failures of psychologists to teach the anthropoid apes to speak, the Gardners decided to try gestures instead. Body language is a natural part of all animal behavior, they reasoned, and apes are familiar enough with body language to learn to use gestures for communication. This is particularly true of anthropoid apes, because they are initiative and manually dexterous.

The Gardners decided to teach a young female chimpanzee named Washoe the sign language used by the deaf in North America. The chimp was given the freedom of the Gardner house along with toys and large doses of tender loving care, and she was surrounded by humans who used only sign language to communicate.

Washoe, in true chimp fashion, very quickly imitated her human friends' sign language gestures, but it took months of patient work before she could reproduce them on command. She was urged to "speak up" by touching her hand, and any "faulty diction" was improved by repeating the sign in an exaggerated way. When Washoe learned a sign correctly she was rewarded with tickling. If she was forced to work too hard, she would rebel by running away or throwing a tantrum or by biting her teacher's hand.

After two years of patient work, Washoe learned about thirty signs. She was judged to have learned a sign if she used it of her own accord in a proper fashion at least once each day for fifteen days. Washoe learned to bring her fingertips over her head to signal "more," to shake her open hand at the wrist for "hurry" and to draw her palm across her chest for "please."

She also learned the signs for hat, shoes, pants and other articles of clothing and the signs for baby, dog and cat. Surprisingly enough, she used these latter signs for new babies, dogs or cats when she met them. Once she even used the sign for dog when she heard a bark. She has also invented some simple sentences: "Go sweet" when she wants to be carried to a raspberry bush, and "Open food drink" when she wants something from the refrigerator.

The experiment is still continuing, and Washoe is learning new gestures and putting them into new sentences. The old Dr. Dolittle idea of talking to the animals may yet be possible with body language.

However, some blasé naturalists point out that body language among animals is no new thing. Birds signal sexual willingness by elaborate courtship dances, bees signal the direction of a honey supply by involved flight patterns and dogs will indulge in a host of signals from rolling over and playing dead to sitting up and begging for food.

What is new in the case of Washoe is the teaching of a language to an animal, and the animal's initiation of signs in that language. It is logical that the deaf sign language should have succeeded where a spoken language failed. Loss of hearing and the cutting off of the world of sound apparently make an individual much more sensitive to the world of gestures and motions. If this is so, then someone who is deaf should have a more sensitive understanding of body language.

Symbols in a World Without Sound

With this in mind, Dr. Norman Kagan of Michigan State University conducted a study among deaf people. They were shown films of men and women in various situations and asked to guess at the emotional state of these people and describe what body language clues they used to convey this state. Because of technical difficulties they were unable to use lip reading.

"It became apparent to us," Dr. Kagan said, "that many parts of the body, perhaps every part to some extent, reflect a person's feeling-state."

As an example, talking while moving the hands or playing with a finger ring and moving restlessly were all interpreted by the deaf as nervousness, embarrassment and anxiety. When the eyes and face suddenly "came down," when the person seemed to "swallow back" his expression, or when his features "collapsed" it was interpreted as guilt.

Excessively jerky movements were labeled frustration, and a shrinking body movement, as if "hiding oneself," spelled out depression. Forcefulness was seen as the snapping forward of the head and whole body including the arms and shoulders, and boredom was inferred when the head was tilted or rested at an angle and the fingers doodled. Reflectiveness was linked to intensity of gaze, a

163

wrinkled forehead and a downcast look. Not wanting to see or to be seen was signaled by taking off eyeglasses or looking away.

These interpretations were given by deaf people, and sound played no part in transmitting clues, yet the interpretations were accurate. The gestures were interpreted within the total context of a scene, but the scene was played without any words. Body language alone, it seems, can serve as a means of communication if we have the ability to understand it, if we are extremely sensitive to all the different movements and signals. But this requires the supersensitivity of a deaf person. His sense of vision has become so heightened, his search for supernumerary clues so intense, that the total context of a scene can be transmitted to a deaf person through body language alone.

The real value of body language, however, still remains in a blending of all levels of communication of the spoken language, and whatever else is transmitted on the local wavelength, with the visual language including body language and self-imagery, with communication along any other bands. One of these other bands is the tactile, which sometimes overlaps the visual but is really a more primitive and basic form of communication.

According to the late Dr. Lawrence K. Frank of Harvard, a child's knowledge of his world starts with the touch of his mother, with caressing and kissing, the oral touch of her nipple, the warmth and security of her arms. His education proceeds with a "don't touch" indoctrination to fit him into the "property rights" aspect of his culture, to teach him a sense of possession and belonging. As a child and as an adolescent his touching of his own body, his adventures with masturbation—the ultimate self-touch—his exploration in young manhood of the touching of love, the mutual body exploration with his love partner, are all aspects of tactile communication.

But these are obvious aspects. We also communicate with ourselves tactually by scratching, patting or pressing against objects. We say, "I am aware of myself. I am giving myself pleasure and satisfaction." We communicate with others by hand-holding, handshaking and all kinds of touching, saying, "Be reassured. Be comforted. You are not alone. I love you."

Just where body language leaves off and tactile communication takes over is difficult to pinpoint. The barriers are too hazy and uncertain.

Mental Healing Through Body Language

Perhaps the greatest value of an understanding of body language lies in the field of psychiatry. Dr. Scheflen's work has shown us how important it is for therapists to use body language consciously, and Dr. Buchheimer and others have carried an understanding of body language into the areas of self-confrontation.

Dr. Buchheimer tells of a group of adult patients who were given finger paint to use as a therapeutic device. "The feel of the paint as they smeared it over the paper would free them, we hoped, from some of the inhibitions that slowed up the therapeutic process. To help them understand what was happening, we filmed them at work and then showed them the films."

One woman patient, he said, had had a bad first marriage, destroyed in part by her inability to enjoy sex. Now in her second marriage she felt that her sexual life was much better, but her marriage was still "coming apart at the seams."

165

Producing a violent scarlet and purple smear with her finger paints, she suddenly cried out, "How sexy that looks!" and at the same moment she crossed her legs.

When the film was played back to her and she was confronted with her own reaction to the tactile concept of sexuality, she couldn't believe that she had reacted that way. But in a discussion of the significance of leg crossing in terms of body language she agreed that this was one way of shutting out and refusing sex symbolically. This was particularly true in the context of her other actions, her comment on the "sexy" picture. She admitted that she herself still had sexual conflicts. She began to understand, from that time on, that her second marriage was suffering from the same problems as her first, and understanding this she was able to take the proper steps toward solving her problem.

Here is a classic example of how the understanding of her own use of a body language symbolic gesture opened a woman's eyes to the extent of her problems. Dr. Fritz Perls, the psychologist who originated Gestalt therapy (the psychiatric therapy that uses body language as one of its basic tools), says of his technique, "We try to get hold of the obvious, of the surface of the situations in which we find ourselves."

The basic technique of Gestalt therapy, according to Dr. Perls, is not to explain things to the patient, but to provide him with the opportunity to understand and discover himself. To do this, Dr. Perls says, "I disregard most of the content of what the patient says and concentrate mostly on the nonverbal level, as this is the only one which is less subject to self-deception." The nonverbal level, of course, is the level of body language.

As an example of what Dr. Perls means, let's eavesdrop on one of his sessions with a thirty-year-old woman. These conversations were taken from a psychiatric training film.

PATIENT: Right now I'm scared.

DOCTOR: You say you're scared, but you're smiling. I don't understand how one can be scared and smiling at the same time.

Confused, the patient's smile becomes tremulous and fades.

PATIENT: I'm also suspicious of you. I think you understand very well. I think you know that when I get scared I laugh or I kid to cover up.

DOCTOR: Well, do you have stage fright?

PATIENT: I don't know. I'm mostly aware of you. I'm afraid that—that you're going to make such a direct attack that I'm afraid you're going to get me in a corner and I'm afraid of that. I want you to be on my side.

As she says this the patient unconsciously hits her chest.

DOCTOR: You said I'd get you in a corner and you hit yourself on the chest.

Dr. Perls repeats her gesture of hitting and she stares at her hand as if seeing it for the first time, then repeats the gesture thoughtfully.

PATIENT: Uhuh.

DOCTOR: What would you like to do? Can you describe this corner you'd like to go to?

Turning to stare at the room's corners the patient is suddenly aware of it as a place she might be in.

PATIENT: Yeah. It's back in the corner, where you're completely protected.

DOCTOR: Then you would be safer there from me?

167

PATIENT: Well, I know that I wouldn't really. A little safer, maybe.

Still staring at the corner she nods.

DOCTOR: If you could make believe that you were in this corner, what would you do there?

For a moment she considers. A chance phrase, in a corner, has now become a physical situation.

PATIENT: I'd just sit.

DOCTOR: You'd just sit?

PATIENT: Yeah.

DOCTOR: How long would you sit?

Almost as if she were in an actual corner, the patient's position becomes that of a little girl on a stool.

PATIENT: I don't know, but it's funny that you're saying this. This reminds me of when I was a little girl. Every time I was afraid I'd feel better sitting in a corner.

DOCTOR: Okay, are you a little girl?

Again confused that her remark has been made graphic.

PATIENT: Well, no, but it's the same feeling.

DOCTOR: Are you a little girl?

PATIENT: This feeling reminds me of it.

Forcing her to face the feeling of being a little girl, the doctor continues.

DOCTOR: *Are* you a little girl?

PATIENT: No, no, no!

DOCTOR: No. How old are you?

PATIENT: Thirty.

DOCTOR: Then you're not a little girl.

PATIENT: No!

In a later scene, the doctor says:

DOCTOR: If you play dumb and stupid you force me to become more explicit.

PATIENT: That's been said to me before, but I don't buy it.

DOCTOR: What are you doing with your feet now?

PATIENT: Wiggling.

She laughs because the wiggling motion of her feet makes her realize she is pretending. The doctor laughs too.

DOCTOR: You joke now.

Later on the patient says:

PATIENT: You're treating me like I'm stronger than I am. I want you to protect me more, to be nicer to me.

Her voice is angry, but even as she says it she smiles. The doctor imitates her smile.

DOCTOR: Are you aware of your smile? You don't believe a word you're saying.

He smiles too, disarmingly, but she shakes her head.

PATIENT: Yes, I do.

She tries to keep from smiling, but the doctor has made her recognize the fact of her smile.

PATIENT: I know you don't think I'm——

DOCTOR: Sure. You're bluffing. You're a phony.

PATIENT: Do you believe—do you mean that seriously?

Now her smile is uncertain, fading.

DOCTOR: Yeah. You laugh and giggle and squirm. It's phony.

He mimics her motions, making her see them reflected in him.

DOCTOR: You put on a performance for me.

PATIENT: Oh, I resent that very much.

The smiles and giggles are gone and she is angry in voice and body.

DOCTOR: Can you express it?

PATIENT: Yes. I most certainly am not being phony. I'll admit it's hard for me to show my embarrassment. I hate being embarrassed, but I resent you calling me a phony.

169

Just because I smile when I'm embarrassed or put in a corner doesn't mean I'm being phony.

DOCTOR: You've been yourself for the last minute.

PATIENT: Well, I'm mad at you.

She smiles again.

DOCTOR: Now that! That!

He imitates her smile.

DOCTOR: Did you do that to cover up your anger with yourself? At that minute, at that moment, you had what emotion?

PATIENT: Well, at that minute I was mad, though I wasn't embarrassed.

The important thing about this particular session is the way in which Dr. Perls picks up body language on the part of the patient, her smile, her wiggling, even her desire to sit in a corner, and holds them up to her, forcing her to face the symbolism of her own body language. He shows her that her smile and laughter are only a defense to soften her real feelings, the anger she doesn't permit herself to feel because it might be too destructive. Only at the end does she get sufficiently mad to drop her defensive smile and really express herself. This is a self-confrontation in action.

What body language combined with self-confrontation can do, as these incidents show, is to make a person aware of what he is doing with his body that contradicts what he is saying with his mouth. If you are aware of what you are doing with your body, your understanding of yourself becomes much deeper and more significant. On the other hand, if you can control your body language you can cut through many of the defensive barriers with which you surround yourself.

170

Faking Body Language

Recently I watched a very beautiful teen-age girl at a dance and saw her stand near the wall with a girl friend, haughty, aloof and unapproachable, for all the world like the snow maiden in the fairy tale.

I knew the girl, and I knew that she was anything but cold and aloof. I asked her later why she had been so distant.

"I was distant?" she said in genuine amazement. "What about the boys? Not one of them came up and talked to me. I was dying to dance but no one asked me." A bit tragically she added, "I'm the only teen-age old maid in school. Look at Ruth. She's my age and she danced every dance, and you know her. She's a mess."

Ruth is a mess. Fat and unattractive, but ah, the secret! Ruth smiles at every boy. Ruth cuts through all shields and all defenses. Ruth makes a boy feel comfortable and assured. He knows if he asks her to dance she'll say yes. Her body language guarantees it. My beautiful young friend, so icy calm on the surface, hides the wistful shyness she feels. She signals, "Stay away. I am unapproachable. Ask me to dance at your own risk." What teen-age boy will take a chance at such a rejection? They obey the signals and turn to Ruth.

With practice my young friend may learn to smile and soften her beauty and make it attainable. She'll learn the body language to signal boys, "I can be asked, and I'll say yes." But first she must understand the signals. She must see herself as she appears to others, she must confront herself and only then can she change.

All of us can learn that if we express the *we* that we want to be, the *we* that we are hiding, then we can make ourselves more available and free ourselves.

There are many ways of doing this, ways of "faking" body language to achieve an end. All the books on self-improvement, on how to make friends, on how to make people like you, are aware of the importance of body language and the importance of faking it properly to signal, "I am a great guy. I am cool. I want to be your friend. Trust me." Learn and apply the proper signals for these messages and you guarantee social success.

The charm schools are aware of this and use the same technique to teach girls how to sit and walk and stand gracefully. If you doubt it watch a Miss America contest and see how the girls have been trained to use body language to seem charming and attractive. Sometimes it comes across as garish, but you must give them an A for trying. Their gestures are tested and accurate. They know how much can be signaled by body language.

Politicians have learned just how important body language is, and they use it to emphasize and dramatize their speeches and also to achieve a more pleasant and more acceptable personality or image. Franklin D. Roosevelt and Fiorello LaGuardia both had instinctive command of it. In spite of the fact that Roosevelt was handicapped and never allowed his body to appear in a handicapped position (well aware of the body language impact of such an appearance), he was able to use body language to transmit a controlled and self-assured image. LaGuardia transmitted another image, homey and down-to-earth, a son of the people, and all through gestures and body movement, through a startling knowledge of the vocabulary of body language, not only in English but also in Italian and Yiddish.

Some men cannot master the grammar of body language no matter how they try. Lyndon Johnson never quite got the hang of it. His arm motions were always too studied, too mannered, too much as if he were running through a memorized program.

The exaggerated use of a limited amount of body language makes Richard Nixon fair game to mimics, such as David Frye, who only need to pick up one or two of his gestures and heighten them to convey a startling imitation.

Dr. Birdwhistell, in his contribution to the book *Explorations in Communication,* states that a well-trained "linguistic-kinesiologist" should be able to tell what movements a man is making simply by listening to his voice.

If this is true then there is a rigid link between words and movements. When an orator points in a certain way he should make a corresponding statement. When, for example, Billy Graham thunders, "You will risk heaven . . . ," he points upward with one finger; and when he adds, "You will go straight to hell!" the finger descends just as we know we shall.

This is a very obvious and crude signal-to-word linkage, but nevertheless it is a proper one and the audience accepts it and is moved by it.

Just because there are proper linkages it stands to reason that some men will distort these linkages and use them inconsistently. Some men do this with words. They stutter or stammer or pitch their sound too high or too low and take all the strength out of what they say. It is just as easy to stutter or stammer kinesically and use the wrong gesture for the wrong word.

The audience may hear your words and understand them, but a good percentage of the message will be missing or distorted and you will be facing a "cold" audience. There will be no emotion in your speech, no empathy or none of that vague word, "charisma."

173

Just how confusing the wrong body language can be was made very clear a few years ago by the comedian Pat Paulson. Pretending to be a candidate for political office he did some delightful spoofing of the then-current candidates by flattening his voice to strip it of all emotion, deadpanning his face to further eliminate emotion and then, very cleverly, feeding the wrong body movements into his performance. The total result was a pseudopolitical disaster.

Unfortunately the same disaster can take over in earnest when a politician is either too inhibited and awkward to use the correct gestures, or just does not know them. William J. Fulbright and Arthur Goldberg have both made searching and important political contributions, but their deliveries are so lacking in the basics of proper body language that they come across as flat and uninspired. The same is true of George McGovern and to a lesser degree of Eugene McCarthy.

McCarthy's popularity is greatest among the young people who are able to cut through the way he says things to what he says. But for the bulk of the American people it is the unfortunate truth that often the way things are said, the body language used, is more important than what is being said.

The other McCarthy, Joseph McCarthy, a few decades back, had a frighteningly effective delivery, and the same grasp of the fundamentals of body language that many fundamentalist evangelists have.

George Wallace, though his politics were hard for many people to swallow, used body language during the Presidential campaign to project an "honest" image. A careful analysis of him in action, especially with the sound turned off, makes it clear that his body language shouted down the contents of his speeches.

174

New York's William Buckley is a man whose political philosophy is far to the right of center, but he has always had a large audience for his television appearances, an audience that is only partly right of center. His appeal is in his delivery rather than in what he delivers. In addition to the more obvious body language of hands and posture that serves politicians who must be viewed from a distance, Buckley has an excellent command of the subtler nuances of kinesics. He uses his face with remarkable facility, lifts his eyebrows, shields his eyes, twists his lips and cheeks and presents a constant variety of expressions.

The total effect is one of liveliness and animation, and adds sincerity to his statements.

John Lindsay projects the same sincerity, but his kinesic movements are turned off a bit, toned down, less exaggerated than Buckley's and with the sincerity we get a sense of calm and reassurance and something more—an engaging ingenuousness that comes from the very toning down of kinesic motion.

Ted Kennedy has the same kinesic facility, helped out as in Lindsay's and Buckley's cases with good looks. It enables him to project a boyish sincerity that may be completely at odds with what he's doing, but still melts our defenses.

Pierre Trudeau of Canada has the same sincerity, but a greater degree of animation—probably a reflection of his French ancestry—allowing him to add another dimension to his political image. This is the sophisticate, the man-about-town, even the playboy, but all in a good sense. His body language tells us, "Look I'm enjoying all the things you would like to enjoy. Share them vicariously."

Once you begin to look for the styles in the man, the gestures and motions and facial twists, you begin to understand just how heavily all political figures rely on body

175

language to make their words and images acceptable. The really good ones, good in the sense that they can project any emotion with their bodies, never had to bother about what they said. It was always the way they said it that mattered.

They were all good actors, and good actors must all be experts in the use of body language. A process of elimination guarantees that only those with an excellent command of the grammar and vocabulary get to be successful.

Of course there have been notorious exceptions. Nelson Eddy was one. He became an actor in the 30's because of his singing ability, and as is the case with many singers, he never learned the basics of body language. Some of his performances (still visible on the late late late shows) show the wooden quality of his gestures, the robotlike sawing of his arms. Contrast him with Gary Cooper. Cooper also had a wooden quality, but he used it to project solidity and masculine dependability through an unconscious grasp of the proper body language movements.

Putting It All Together

As the facts about body language are studied and analyzed and it is gradually elevated to a science, it becomes available as a tool in the study of other sciences. There was a recent report, from the Fifty-fifth Annual Convention of the Speech Association of America, by Professor Stanley E. Jones in which he applied body language principles to challenge Dr. Hall's statement that a basic difference between cultures lies in the way they handle space. Latin Americans, he said, stand closer when they talk than Chinese or Negroes, and Arabs stand even closer than Latins do.

Professor Jones, after working for two years in Harlem, Chinatown, Little Italy and Spanish Harlem, all ethnic areas of Manhattan in New York City, produced evidence that this pattern changes. He believes that conditions of poverty have forced these people to change some of their cultural behavior. According to him, there is a culture of poverty that is stronger than any ethnic subcultural background.

Professor Jones, discussing his paper in a press interview, said, "When I began studying the behavior patterns for subcultures living in New York's so-called melting pot, I expected to find that they would maintain their differences. Instead I was tremendously surprised to discover that poverty conditioned them to behave with remarkable similarity."

In overcrowded areas with poor housing, Professor Jones found that virtually everybody, regardless of their ethnic background, stood about one foot apart.

Here is a sociological use of the growing science of body language in an attempt to discover how poverty affects culture. What Professor Jones's findings seem to indicate is that the culture of the American poor overrides ethnic and national distinctions. America has become a melting pot, but it is the quality of poverty that melts down the barriers to produce a common body language.

It would be interesting to take this work further and see what other areas besides space are influenced by poverty, or to carry it in the other direction and see if wealth also breaks down the ethnic rules of body language. Are the forces of economics stronger than those of culture?

There are any number of possible studies open to the

future student of body language, and the beauty of it all is that a minimum amount of equipment is necessary. While I know of a number of sophisticated studies that have been done with videotape and sixteen millimeter film and dozens of student volunteers, I also know of a perfectly charming project done by a fourteen-year-old boy whose bedroom overlooked a street telephone booth in New York City.

He used an eight millimeter motion picture camera to film as much footage of people using the booth as his allowance would permit, and he then used the family projector to slow up motion while he noted and identified each movement.

I know another, older student who is working toward his doctorate by studying the way people avoid each other on a crowded street and on a not-so-crowded street.

"When there is enough space," he explained, "they wait till they're about ten feet apart and then each gives the other a signal so they can move around each other in opposite directions." He hasn't yet discovered the exact signal or how it is used to convey which direction each will take.

Sometimes of course the signals are confused and the two people come face to face and both move to the right and then to the left in unison and keep up this silly dance till they stop, smile apologetically and then move on. Freud called it a sexual encounter. My friend calls it kinesic stuttering.

Body language as a science is in its infancy, but this book has explored some of the ground rules. Now that you know them, take a close look at yourself and your friends and family. Why do you move the way you do? What does it signify? Are you dominant or subservient in your kinesic relationship to others? How do you manage space? Are you its master or do you let it control you?

How do you manage space in a business situation? Do you knock on your boss's door and then walk in? Do you come up to his desk and dominate him, or do you stop at a respectful distance and let him dominate you? Do you allow him to dominate you as a means of placating him or as a means of handling him?

How do you leave an elevator when you are with business associates? Do you insist on being the last one off because of the innate superiority such a gracious gesture gives you? Or do you walk off first, allowing the others to please you, taking their courtesy as if it were your due? Or do you jockey for position? "You first." "No, you."

Which of all of these is the most balanced behavior? Which does the perfectly secure man indulge in? Think about each one. Your guess is as good as a trained psychologist's. This is still a beginning science.

Where do you position yourself in a lecture hall? At the back where there is a certain amount of anonymity, even though you may miss some fine points of the lecture, or up front where you can hear and see comfortably but where you are also conspicuous?

How do you function at an informal gathering? Do you tie up your nervous hands with a drink? Do you lean against a mantel for security? It can serve as an immobilizing force for half your body and you needn't be concerned about what to say in body language—or only half concerned. Except that the very way you lean is betraying you!

Where do you sit? In a chair in the corner? In a group of your friends, or near a stranger? Which is safe and which is more interesting? Which spells security and which spells maturity?

Start observing at the next party you go to: Who are the people who dominate the gathering? Why? How much is due to body language and what gestures do they use to do it?

Notice how people sit in subway cars: How do they space themselves when the car is uncrowded? How do they cross their legs, feet and arms?

Hold the glance of a stranger a fraction longer than is necessary and see what happens. You may be in for a rude experience, and on the other hand, you may have a few good experiences. You may find yourself speaking to perfect strangers and liking it.

You know the groundwork and some of the rules. You've been playing the game of body language unconsciously all of your lifetime. Now start playing it consciously. Break a few rules and see what happens. It will be surprising and sometimes a bit frightening, adventurous, revealing and funny, but I promise you it won't be dull.

Selected References

ARDREY, R., *The Territorial Imperative*. New York: Atheneum, 1966.

BIRDWHISTELL, R. L., Background to Kinesics, *ETC: A Review of General Semantics,* Vol. 13, No. 1, Autumn 1955.

—Introduction to Kinesics. University of Louisville Press, 1952.

—The Kinesic Level in the Investigation of the Emotions. *Expression of the Emotions in Man.* New York: International Universities Press, 1963.

BRUNER, J. S.; TAGUIRI, R., The Perception of People. *Handbook of Social Psychology.* Cambridge, Mass.: Addison Wesley, 1954.

CARPENTER, C. R., Territoriality: A Review of Concepts and Problems. *Behavior and Evolution.* New Haven: University Press, 1958.

CARPENTER, E.; McLUHAN, M., *Explorations in Communication.* Boston: Beacon Press, 1968.

CHERRY, C., *On Human Communication.* New York: Science Editions, Inc., 1961.

DARWIN, C., *The Expression of the Emotions in Man and Animals.* London, Murray, 1872.

181

DEUTSCH, F., Analytic Posturology, *Psychoanalytical Quarterly,* Vol. 21, 1952.

DITTMAN, A.; PARLOFF, M.; BOOMER, D., Facial and Bodily Expression: A Study of Receptivity of Emotional Cues, *Psychiatry,* Vol. 28, 1965.

EKMAN, P.; SORENSON, E. R.; FRIESEN, W. V., Pan-Cultural Elements in Facial Displays of Emotion. *Science,* Vol. 164, No. 3875, April 4, 1969.

FRANK, L. K., Tactile Communications. *ETC, A Review of General Semantics,* Vol. 16, 1958.

GOFFMAN, E., *Behavior in Public Places.* The Free Press, 1969.

—*Encounters.* Indianapolis: Bobbs-Merrill, 1961.

—*Interaction Ritual.* Garden City, N.Y.: Anchor Books, 1967.

—*Presentation of Self in Everyday Life.* Garden City, N.Y.: Anchor Books, 1959.

HALL, E. T., *The Hidden Dimension.* Garden City, N.Y.: Doubleday, 1966.

—Proxemics—a Study of Man's Spatial Relationship. *Man's Image in Medicine and Anthropology.* International Universities Press, 1963.

—*The Silent Language.* Garden City, N.Y.: Doubleday and Co., 1959.

KINZEL, A. F., Towards an Understanding of Violence. *Attitude,* Vol. 1, No. 1, 1969.

KOFFKA, K., *Principles of Gestalt Psychology,* New York: Harcourt, 1935.

LORENZ, K., *On Aggression.* New York: Harcourt Brace, 1966.

MAHL, G. F., Gestures and Body Movements in Interviews. *Research in Psychotherapy,* Vol. 3. A.P.A., 1966.

MEHRABIAN, A.; WIENER, M., Non-Immediacy Between Communication and Object of Communication in a

SELECTED REFERENCES

Verbal Message. *Journal of Consulting Psychology,* Vol. 30, No. 5, 1966.

NIELSEN, G., *Studies in Self-Confrontation.* Munksgaard, Copenhagen, Howard Allen, Cleveland.

ORTEGA Y GASSET, J., *Man and People.* New York: W. W. Norton and Co., 1957.

SCHEFLEN, A. E., Human Communication. *Behavioral Science,* Vol. 13, 1968.

—Non-Language Behavior in Communication, *Address to New York Chapter of American Academy of Pediatrics.* Sept. 2, 1969.

—Significance of Posture in Communications Systems, *Psychiatry,* Vol. 27, No. 4, Nov. 1964.

—Quasi-Courtship Behavior in Psychotherapy, *Psychiatry,* Vol. 28, 1965.

SOMMER, R., *Personal Space.* Prentice Hall, 1969.

TINBERGEN, N., *Curious Naturalists.* New York: Basic Books, 1958.

WACHTEL, P. L., An Approach to the Study of Body Language in Psychotherapy. *Psychotherapy,* Vol. 4, No. 3, August 1967.

"Would you please help me get this costume off?" Gypsy requested, with a tiny clutch in her throat.

Chase sat on the arm of the couch, unable to control his silent laughter. "Sorry," he said, wiping his eyes with one hand. "But, Gypsy, Cyrano de Bergerac couldn't romance you with a straight face!"

"Oh, really," Gypsy responded haughtily.

"Really," he said, pulling her onto his lap. Both of them watched, totally deadpan, as the costume's hoop skirt shot into the air and poised there like a quivering curtain.

"You may have a point," Gypsy muttered.

"Yes."

"This never happens to heroines in the movies."

"Uh-huh." Chase looked as though his expressionless face was the result of all the control he could muster.

"They *never* get stuck in their dresses," Gypsy persisted solemnly.

"Nope."

"Or lose control of their hoops."

He choked.

"Or have to put their corsets on backwards."

Chase struggled even harder to keep a straight face.

"Or ask a man, with absolutely no delicacy, to take their clothes off."

There was a moment of silence, broken only by a peculiar sound.

Gypsy looked down at her tightly corseted stomach, disgusted. "Or have stomachs that growl like volcanos . . ."

WHAT ARE *LOVESWEPT* ROMANCES?

They are stories of true romance and touching emotion. We believe those two very important ingredients are constants in our highly sensual and very believable stories in the *LOVESWEPT* line. Our goal is to give you, the reader, stories of consistently high quality that may sometimes make you laugh, sometimes make you cry, but are always fresh and creative and contain many delightful surprises within their pages.

Most romance fans read an enormous number of books. Those they truly love, they keep. Others may be traded with friends and soon forgotten. We hope that each *LOVESWEPT* romance will be a treasure—a "keeper." We will always try to publish

*LOVE STORIES YOU'LL NEVER FORGET
BY AUTHORS YOU'LL ALWAYS REMEMBER*

The Editors

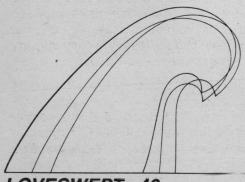

LOVESWEPT • 46

Kay Hooper
Something Different

BANTAM BOOKS • TORONTO • NEW YORK • LONDON • SYDNEY

SOMETHING DIFFERENT

A Bantam Book / May 1984

LOVESWEPT *and the wave device are trademarks of*
Bantam Books, Inc.

ISBN 0-553-21650-3

Published simultaneously in the United States and Canada

Bantam Books are published by Bantam Books, Inc. Its
trademark, consisting of the words "Bantam Books" and the
portrayal of a rooster, is Registered in U.S. Patent and Trade-
mark Office and in other countries. Marca Registrada. Bantam
Books, Inc., 666 Fifth Avenue, New York, New York 10103.

PRINTED IN THE UNITED STATES OF AMERICA

O   0 9 8 7 6 5 4 3 2 1

A writer is only as good as those rare and unrewarded friends who bolster, cheer (or jeer), criticize, question, applaud—or just listen in sympathetic silence. Ideas bounce off these friends, plots are tried for effect, character motivation explored. Discussions go on over the phone; across coffee tables or dinner tables; and in the presence of baffled, bemused spouses.

And you thought I wrote alone.

Pam and Bob, this one's for you.

One

Gypsy hit her brakes instinctively and swerved as the small brown rabbit darted across the road in front of her car. Satisfaction and relief at not hitting the creature were short-lived, however, as a sudden and savage jolt informed her that her already battered VW had been rear-ended.

Her head snapped back and then forward, banging into the steering wheel with enough force to give her a brief view of stars in broad daylight. She found herself fighting various laws of motion in an effort to bring the car and herself safely to the side of the road. Her heart lodged in her throat for one flashing instant, because the side of the road was a narrow strip of dirt bordering on a sheer drop. And, Gypsy thought, neither she nor the car had wings.

Sputtering, the VW's engine voiced an unmistakable death rattle and expired as the little blue car with its bright yellow daisy decals lurched onto the strip of dirt. Gypsy heard a more powerful engine rumble into silence behind her. Automatically and needlessly she pulled up the emergency brake and turned off the ignition switch.

Although her forehead throbbed painfully, and the sickening fear at her near-maiden flight over the cliff hadn't quite faded, Gypsy's thoughts were crystal-clear and crazily detached.

Not again. This could *not* be happening to her again. It was the third time in six months, and poor Daisy was certainly *dead.* Judging by the sound of the impact, not even the best body-and-fender man would be able to pound the dents out. And Daisy's engine had quite definitely been mortally wounded.

Gypsy abruptly became furious at whomever had murdered poor Daisy.

The sound of the other car's door slamming was followed swiftly by a startlingly deep and coldly controlled masculine voice. "Are you all right?" it demanded, and then added icily, "Don't you know that it's illegal as well as unsafe to drive a car without brake lights?"

Gypsy fumbled for Daisy's door handle and struggled out, letting her anger at Daisy's assassin have full rein. "*You* hit *me*, dammit, and Daisy *did* have a brake light—the left one! Now you've killed her—" She broke off abruptly as she got her first clear look at Daisy's assassin. He didn't look like a killer.

He was slightly under six feet tall, wide-shouldered but slender, and finely muscled. His burnished copper hair was thick and slightly shaggy, a bit longer than collar length. Eyes of an astoundingly intense shade of jade-green shot icicles at her. But his obvious anger couldn't hide the shrewdness behind his eyes, and the rigidly held expression only emphasized his marvelous bone structure.

Not a bit like a killer, Gypsy mused. . . .

Recovering from her initial surprise, Gypsy was just about to light into the handsome stranger when he aimed the first thrust.

"My God! I thought the last of the flower children grew up years ago!"

She automatically looked down at herself; there was nothing unusual. Faded, colorfully patched jeans, a tie-dyed T-shirt, ragged sneakers, and a silver peace sign dangling around her neck on a leather thong. She supposed that his description fit, but the thrust didn't go home. In the first place one did not normally dress neatly to perform the errand Gypsy had just completed, and in the second place she didn't much care how she looked—and this man's distaste did nothing to change that.

She rather pointedly eyed his neat, three-piece business suit, spending a long moment gazing at extremely shiny shoes. Then she let her gaze wander briefly to the gleaming silver-gray Mercedes before returning it to his face. Satisfied with his reaction—a slight reddening beneath the tan of his cheeks—she let the matter drop, refusing to correct his first impression.

Dropping the easily assumed dignity, she spoke heatedly. "You hit Daisy from behind, and that makes it your fault!"

He sent a faintly bewildered glance toward Daisy's crumpled rear end, but said shortly, "You had no brake lights."

"Big deal!" she snapped. "If you'd been watching where you were going, you would have seen me swerve to miss that rabbit, and— Oh! Corsair!" Hastily she turned back to her car.

"Corsair?" the man muttered blankly, standing where she'd left him between their two cars and watching her open her car door and extract a bundle of cream-colored fur from inside. As she turned back toward him, he saw that the bundle was a large—a very large—Himalayan cat. Its face, paws, and tail were a dark chocolate color, and its broad face wore what seemed to be a permanently sulky expression.

"Just look at him!" she said angrily. "It's not enough that you killed poor Daisy; you nearly gave Corsair a heart attack!"

To the man's clear, jade eyes, Corsair didn't look as though he'd ever be—or had ever been— startled by anything short of a massive earthquake. He started to make that observation out loud, then realized that by participating in this ridiculous conversation, he'd only prolong it.

"Look—" he began, but she cut him off fiercely. "This is all your fault!"

Jade eyes narrowed in sudden suspicion. "You're certainly hell-bent to prove this was my fault, aren't you? I'll bet you don't even— How old are you?" he demanded abruptly.

Gypsy drew herself up to her full height of five nothing and deepened her glare. "You should never ask a woman her age! Where did you learn your manners?"

"Where you learned yours!" he retorted irritably.

Into that tense confrontation came a slow, grinding *thunk*, and Daisy's entire engine hit the ground in a little puff of dust.

Gypsy stared rather blankly for a moment and then began to giggle. "Poor Daisy," she murmured.

The man was leaning back against the low hood of his car chuckling quietly, his icy temper apparently gone. "Why don't we start over?" he suggested wryly. "Hello, I'm Chase Mitchell."

"Gypsy Taylor," she returned solemnly.

"Gypsy? Now, why doesn't that surprise me?"

"No reason at all, I'm sure." Gypsy sighed, her amusement brief. "How am I going to get home? Daisy isn't going anywhere without the aid of a tow truck."

"I'll take you. We have to exchange insurance information anyway." He was looking down disgustedly at the slightly crumpled hood that he'd just stopped leaning against, then looked up quickly as a thought apparently occurred to him. "You *are* insured?" he asked carefully.

Knowing full well that Daisy's lack of brake lights made her at least partially to blame for the accident, Gypsy had stopped protesting. "Certainly I'm insured," she responded with dignity. After a beat she added, "At least . . . well, I think I am."

"How can you not be sure?"

"Well, I move around a lot." Unconsciously Gypsy had gravitated closer to the dented Mercedes. "Sometimes the notices from the insurance company get lost in the mail or—" She broke off hastily as she noted a disconcertingly icy storm gathering in his jade eyes. Gypsy loved a good storm, but she wasn't an idiot. "I'm insured. I know I'm insured."

"Right." As pointedly as she had done before, Chase looked from the top of her short black curls to the toes of her sneaker-clad feet. In between he noted a petite but nicely curved figure that in no way belonged to a teenager, and a face that was lovely—with fine bone structure and wide, dreamy gray eyes. "I thought you were about fifteen," he murmured almost to himself, "but I think I was wrong."

Gypsy blinked. "You certainly were." She was neither flattered nor insulted. "By about thirteen years. I'm twenty-eight." She blinked again, and added in a scolding voice, "And that was a sneaky way to find out!"

He grinned suddenly, and Gypsy was astonished at the change it wrought in his stern face. The jade eyes gleamed with amused satisfaction, laugh lines appearing at their corners, and white teeth flashed in a purely charming and surprisingly boyish smile.

"Well, I had to find out," he said. Before she could ask why, he was going on briskly. "Hop in and I'll take you home."

Having always relied on her instincts about people, Gypsy didn't worry about getting into a car with a stranger. Not this stranger. For some reason she instinctively trusted him. With a sigh and a last lingering glance toward the fallen Daisy, she started around to the passenger side of the Mercedes. Then she hesitated and went back to her car long enough to pull the keys from the ignition.

"Shouldn't you lock it up?"

"Why?" Gypsy asked wryly, heading back to the Mercedes. "Daisy isn't going anywhere."

Conceding the point, he got in the driver's side of his car, shut the door, and started it up. "Where to?"

Gypsy pointed along the winding, steadily uphill road. "Thataway. Follow the yellow brick road."

As the Mercedes pulled onto the road and began to climb smoothly, Chase distinctly felt baleful eyes on him. He risked a glance sideways, and found that it was the cat's gaze he was feeling.

Because of a childhood allergy—and no inclination since then—he'd had little experience with cats. But he recognized the expression on this one's face. Only cats and camels could stare through supposedly superior human beings with such utter and complete disdain. It gave him a disconcertingly invisible feeling.

Caused by a cat, it was a hell of a reaction, Chase thought.

"Your cat doesn't like me," he observed, eyes firmly back on the tricky business of negotiating the road's hairpin curves.

Gypsy looked at him in surprise, and then glanced down at the cat resting calmly in her lap. Corsair was fixedly regarding one chocolate paw. "You're imagining things," she scoffed lightly. "Corsair's never met anybody he didn't like."

Chase risked another glance, and then wished he hadn't. "Uh-huh. So why is he glaring at me?"

Gypsy glanced down again. "He isn't. He's looking at his paw." Her voice was mildly impatient.

Chase decided not to look again. He also decided that Corsair was a sneaky cat. "Never mind. Tell me, Miss Taylor—"

"Gypsy," she interrupted.

"As long as you'll return the favor."

"Fine. I hate formality."

"Gypsy, then. Where exactly do you live? I know this road, and it dead-ends a mile or so further up. There are two houses—"

"One of them's mine," she interrupted again.

"Yours?" He sounded a bit startled.

"I'm house-sitting," she explained absently, looking out the window and thinking as she always did, that it was nice to have the Pacific for a backyard. "The owners were temporarily trans-ferred to Europe—six months. I'll be sitting for them another four months."

"I see."

He sounded rather faint, and Gypsy looked over at him in amusement. "I'm not quite as dis-reputable as I look," she said gently. "I'm dressed like this because I had to take Corsair to the vet."

"And the peace sign?"

His mind obviously wasn't on the conversation, and Gypsy wondered why. "It was a gift from some friends. Sort of a private joke," she explained automatically, gazing at him searchingly. She thought that he had the look of a man who had bitten down on something and wasn't quite sure what it was. Odd. Before she could attempt to probe the cause of his strange expression—Gypsy wasn't at all shy—he was speaking again.

"Do you live around here? When you're not house-sitting, I mean."

"I live wherever I happen to be house-sitting. Before this, I was in Florida for three months, and before that was New England. I like to move around."

"Obviously."

"Not *your* favorite life-style, I see," she said wryly.

"No." Abruptly, he asked, "Do you live alone?"

Gypsy thought briefly of all the bits of infor-mation a single woman generally didn't reveal to strange men—like whether she lived alone. However, if she was any judge of character, this man hardly had rape or robbery on his mind. "Usually I don't. A housekeeper usually lives with me; she's a good friend and practically raised me.

But she's visiting relatives right now, so I'm on my own. Why do you ask?"

"Just wondering." He sent a sidelong glance her way. "You aren't wearing a ring, but these days asking a woman if she's single doesn't automatically preclude a live-in 'friend.' "

Gypsy looked at him thoughtfully and tried to ignore the sudden bump her heart had given. She'd been on the receiving end of enough male questions to know what that one was pointing to, and it was not a direction she wanted to explore. As handsome as Chase Mitchell undoubtedly was, Gypsy nonetheless told herself firmly that she wasn't interested. At this point in her life, a man was a complication she hardly needed.

And Chase Mitchell would prove to be more of a complication than most, she decided shrewdly. They obviously had nothing in common, and he wouldn't be the sort of man who could fit in with her offbeat life-style.

Frowning, Gypsy wondered at the trend of her own thoughts. Why on earth was she hesitating? Usually she disclaimed interest immediately in order to avoid complications before they arose.

Before she could further explore her inexplicable hesitation, Chase was going on in a smooth voice.

"Of course, you could have a 'friend' who doesn't live with you." It was definitely a question, she thought.

Gypsy answered wryly, "The way I move around?"

"Some men would consider plane tickets a small price to pay," he murmured.

She wondered if that was a compliment, but decided not to ask. With that kind of fishing she was half afraid of what she might catch. Instead, she chose a nice, safe, innocuous topic. "Do you live around here?" she asked casually.

He nodded, his eyes again on the road. The road was still both winding and tricky, but it no longer bordered on the cliffs. Trees hid the ocean now as they progressed further inland. "I've always lived on the West Coast," he said. "Apart from school years, that is."

Gypsy nodded and sought about for more safe topics. "Nice car," she finally managed inanely.

"It was," he agreed affably.

She shot him a goaded glare and immediately became more irritated when she noted that he wasn't even looking at her. "I didn't *mean* to wreck your nice car," she said with dignity. "And if it comes to that, you didn't exactly leave Daisy in great shape, you know!"

"If I were you," he suggested, ignoring the larger part of her accusation, "I'd get another car."

"Well, you're not me. I've had Daisy since I was seventeen; she's a classic. She's also my good-luck charm."

"Judging by the number of dents in her that I can't claim credit for," Chase said dryly, "she doesn't seem to have been very lucky." He was completely unconscious of following Gypsy's lead in using the feminine pronoun to describe Daisy.

Uncomfortably aware of her accident-prone nature, she didn't dispute his point. And she was enormously relieved to see her house as they finally completed the long climb and the road leveled off. She pointed and Chase nodded, slowing the Mercedes for the turn into her driveway.

Her home for the next four months was a sprawling house, modern in design but not starkly so. Lots of glass, lots of cedar. It blended in nicely with the tall trees, and from the back it boasted a magnificent view of the Pacific. But the house next door was by far the more beautiful of the two. It *was* starkly modern, geometric in design, with an abundance of sharp angles and impossible curves. Cunningly wrought in glass, cedar, and stone, it was a jewel utterly perfect in its setting. And the landscaping around the house was among the most beautiful Gypsy had ever seen.

She usually didn't care too much for modern houses, but she loved that one. Glancing toward it as the Mercedes pulled into her driveway, she wondered for the hundredth time who lived there. She'd only seen a gardener who came every day to care for the trees and shrubs.

The thought slipped from her mind as Chase stopped his car just outside the garage. Reaching for the door handle, she said, "You'd better come in; it may take a while for me to find the insurance card."

He nodded and turned off the engine, his eyes fixed curiously on the somewhat battered trailer pulled over onto the grass beside the driveway. "What—" he began.

Gypsy slid from the car before explaining. "That," she told him cheerfully, "contains all my worldly possessions when I move. Aside from Corsair, that is; he rides in Daisy with me." She reflected for a moment as she watched Chase move around to her. "Although I don't suppose one could call a cat a possession."

"Not any cat I've ever heard of," Chase agreed, eyeing Corsair with disfavor. "They seem to be complete unto themselves." He accompanied Gypsy and friend up the walkway.

She fished her keys from a pocket and unlocked the heavy front door. Opening it and stepping inside, she murmured, "I suppose I should warn you."

"Warn me? About wha—" Beginning to follow her inside, Chase suddenly found himself pinned solidly against the doorjamb by two huge paws. Inches from his nose loomed a black and white face in which a grin of sorts displayed an impressive set of dental equipment. It was a Great Dane, and it looked as though it would have considered half a steer to be a tidy mouthful.

A calm Gypsy holding an equally calm Corsair studied Chase's still face for a long moment. "Meet Bucephalus," she invited politely. "He was named after Alexander the Great's horse."

"Obviously," Chase murmured carefully. "Two questions. Is it yours?"

"No; he belongs to the Robbins couple—the ones who live here. Second question?"

"Does he bite?"

"No." She considered briefly. "Except for people who rear-end cars. He makes an exception for them."

"Funny lady. Would you mind getting him down?"

"Down, Bucephalus."

The big dog immediately dropped to all fours, looking no less huge but considerably more friendly. His long tail waved happily and he tilted his chin up slightly in order to wash Corsair's face with a tongue the size of a hand towel. The cat suffered this indignity with flattened ears and silence.

Chase carefully shut the door, keeping a wary

eye on the dog. "Any more surprises?" he asked ruefully.

"I shouldn't think so. This way." She led him down the short carpeted hallway. A huge sunken den at the end of the hall boasted a brick fireplace, a beamed ceiling, and an open *L*-shaped staircase leading up to a loft. The furniture consisted of an off-white pit grouping with abundant cushions, a large projection television, and assorted tables and lamps.

Gypsy stepped down into the den, set Corsair on the deep-pile carpet, and immediately headed for a corner that was either an afterthought to the beautiful room, someone's idea of humor . . . or both.

Chase followed slowly, staring in astonishment. The corner was partitioned off from the room by an eight-foot-tall bookcase, clearly made from odd pieces of lumber and sagging decidedly in every shelf. It was crammed to capacity. Within the "room" was a battered desk that had seen more mileage than Daisy; it was cluttered with papers, a couple of dog-eared dictionaries, stacks of carbon paper, and a few more unidentifiable items. A ten-year-old manual typewriter sat squarely in the middle of the clutter.

"Your corner," Chase murmured finally.

"My corner," Gypsy confirmed absently, scrabbling through a desk drawer.

Chase wandered over to examine the bookshelf, uneasily aware that the giant Bucephalus was right beside him. Trying to ignore his escort, he scanned the titles of Gypsy's books, becoming more and more puzzled. "I've never seen so many books on crime and criminology in my life. Don't tell me you're also a cop?"

Still searching for the elusive insurance card, Gypsy answered vaguely, "No. Murder." She looked up a moment later to find him staring at her with a peculiar expression, and elaborated dryly, "Murder *mysteries.* I write murder mysteries."

"*You?* Murder mysteries?"

"I wouldn't laugh if I were you. I know ninety-eight ways to kill someone, and all of them are painful."

Chase absorbed that for a moment. "Do your victims lose their insurance cards?" he asked gravely.

"My victims are usually dead, so it doesn't matter. Damn. It's not here."

Chase was frowning. Then the frown abruptly cleared and he was staring at her in astonishment. "No wonder your name rang a bell! I've read some of your books."

"Did you enjoy them?" she asked him politely.

"They were brilliant," he replied slowly, still staring at her in surprise. "I couldn't put them down."

Accustomed to the astonished reaction to her authorship, Gypsy smiled faintly and began to search through the clutter on her desk. "Don't bother telling me that I don't look like a writer," she advised. "I've heard it many times. I'd like to know what a writer is supposed to look like," she added in a reflective voice.

Chase discovered that he had been absently petting Bucephalus and stopped, only to continue hastily when the dog growled deep in his throat. "Can't you tell this monster to lie down somewhere?"

"Tell him yourself. He knows the command."

"Lie down," Chase said experimentally, and was

immediately rewarded when the dog flopped down obediently. Stepping carefully around Bucephalus, Chase approached Gypsy and observed her unfruitful search. "Can't find it?"

Gypsy lifted a feather duster and peered beneath it. "It's here somewhere," she said irritably. "It has to be."

"You could offer me a cup of coffee while I wait," he said reproachfully.

"It isn't Tuesday."

Chase thought that one over for a moment. No matter how many times he ran it through his mind, her meaning didn't appear. "Is that supposed to make sense?"

She looked up from her search long enough to note his puzzled expression. "I only fix coffee on Tuesday," she explained.

"Why?" he asked blankly.

"It's a long story."

"Please. This is one answer I have to hear."

Gypsy pulled a squeaky swivel chair out and sat down, beginning to search through the center drawer for a second time. "When I was little," she told him patiently, "I became addicted to iced tea. My mother thought that it was unhealthy, that I needed to drink other things like milk. I hate milk," she added parenthetically.

"So anyway Mother decided to assign different drinks to the days of the week. That way, she could be sure that I was getting a healthy variety. By the time I got around to drinking coffee, the only day left for it was Tuesday. And today isn't Tuesday."

Chase shook his head bemusedly. "When you adopt a habit, it's your life, isn't it?"

"I suppose."

"Well, what's today's drink?" he asked, deciding to go with the tide.

"Is today Friday? Let's see. . . . Friday is wine. Or a reasonable facsimile thereof." She looked up with sudden mischief in her eyes. "Mother doesn't know about that. Poppy—my father—told me that I'd better save Friday for when I grew up. So I did. It's a good thing I listened to him. I like wine."

Staring at her in fascination, Chase murmured, "You seem to have . . . interesting parents."

"To say the least." Abruptly she asked, "What do you do for a living?"

Chase blinked, but quickly recovered. "I sell shoes," he replied blandly.

With sudden and disconcerting shrewdness, she said calmly, "If you're a salesman, I'll eat my next manuscript—page by page."

Chase wondered why he'd lied, then decided that it had probably been due to sheer bewilderment. "I'm an architect."

Gypsy made no comment on the lie, other than a brief look of amusement. "Now, *that* I believe. Residential or commercial?"

"Commercial. I've designed a few private homes though."

"Would you like some wine?" she asked suddenly.

After a moment Chase complained, "You take more conversational shortcuts than any person I've ever met."

"It saves time," she said solemnly.

He decided again to go with the tide. By this time he was beginning to feel like a piece of driftwood being battered against the shore. "Yes, I'd like some wine. Thank you."

Gypsy frowned. "I'd better see if I have any."

She rose from the chair and headed for the hallway, saying over her shoulder, "Go through the desk again, will you? I may have missed it."

It took Chase several seconds to realize that she meant the insurance card. With a shrug he sat down in the creaky chair and began searching through the desk.

He'd searched three drawers by the time Gypsy came back into the room carrying two glasses filled with white wine. "Find it?" she asked, handing him a glass.

"No. Tell me something." He waved a hand at the general clutter of her desk. "How can someone so obviously disorganized write such ruthlessly logical and neatly plotted books?"

"Luck, I guess."

Chase lifted an eyebrow at her as she rested a hip against the corner of the desk. "Luck. Right." He lifted his glass in a faint toast, but the expression on his face indicated that he was not toasting Gypsy's answer but rather some wry thought of his own.

"Tell you what." He sighed almost to himself. "Why don't you keep looking for the card? Maybe you'll have found it by the time I pick you up tonight."

"Pick me up? For what?"

"Dinner."

Two

"Dinner?" Gypsy leaned an elbow on her typewriter and stared at Chase. The reluctance in his voice had been so audible as to be ludicrous, and she fought an urge to giggle. "You don't really want to do that."

"No," he agreed amiably. After a moment he added cryptically, "I've always considered myself an intelligent man."

Was that supposed to make sense? she wondered. "Look, if you're feeling guilty because of what you did to Daisy—" she began, but he cut her off decisively.

"I'm not feeling guilty about Daisy; the accident was more your fault than mine. And taking women out to dinner because I feel guilty isn't one of my noble habits. Do you want to go or don't you?"

Gypsy sipped her wine to give herself time to

think. After hesitating, she asked cautiously, "Why are you asking me?"

He stared at her. "You want to hear my motives, I take it?"

"A girl likes to know where she stands."

"Well, my motives are the usual ones, I suppose. Companionship. Interest in a lovely woman. A dislike of eating alone. And," he added wryly, "I think that I should get to know my next-door neighbor."

Gypsy blinked. "You live . . . ?" She gestured slightly and sighed when he nodded. "You've been gone for two months."

Chase nodded again. "Back East working on a project."

"You didn't know Bucephalus," she pointed out.

"I hardly knew the Robbins couple. And I never saw that dog before today. They must have kept him hidden, although how to hide something that big . . . Are you going out with me?"

Gypsy hesitated again, and somewhere in the back of her mind her uncertainty was still nagging her. "Chase. . . ." She was searching for the right words. "If you want a companion across the dinner table, that's fine. If you want a neighbor you can borrow a cup of sugar from, that's fine. Anything more than that isn't fine. I don't want to get involved."

"I see." Chase set his wineglass on top of a dictionary, then took hers from her hand and set it down also. "That's an interesting point."

"What is?" she asked blankly.

"Whether we could become involved with each other. Would Bucephalus protect you?"

Gypsy had the detached feeling that there was

something here she was missing totally. Deciding that the simplest course would be to answer his question, she said, "I suppose he would. If I screamed or something."

"Don't scream." Chase rose to his feet and pulled her upright into his arms.

"What're you . . . ?" she sputtered, caught off guard.

"A little experiment," he murmured. "To see if we could become involved with each other." Before she could utter another word, his lips had unerringly found hers.

In that first instant Gypsy knew that she was in trouble. Definite trouble. A fiery tingle began in her middle and spread rapidly outward to the tips of her fingers and toes. It was totally unexpected and frighteningly seductive. And Gypsy couldn't seem to find a weapon to combat the stinging little fire.

Something had kicked her in the stomach; dizziness overwhelmed her, and shock sapped the strength from her knees. Her body seemed to disconnect itself from her mind, her arms lifting of their own volition to encircle his neck. She felt her lips part beneath the increasing pressure of his, and then even her mind was lost. Searing brands moved against her back, pulling her body inexorably against his, and the hollow ache in her middle responded instantly to the fierce desire she could feel in him.

Gypsy was aware of the hazy certainty that she should stop this. Yes. Stop it, she thought. But she couldn't even find the strength to open her eyes, realizing only then that they were closed.

Stop it. In a moment. . . .

The stinging little fire wasn't so little anymore. It was a writhing thing now, scorching nerve endings and boiling the blood in her veins. She could feel her heart pound with all the wild unreason of a captive beast, and it terrified her with its savage rhythm.

She was dimly aware of drawing a shuddering breath when Chase finally released her. Her hands fell limply to her sides and then reached back to clutch at the edge of the desk she was leaning weakly against. Wood. Solid wood, she assured herself. Reality.

She stared at him with stunned, disbelieving eyes, only partially aware that his breathing was as ragged as hers and that the jade eyes held the same expression of bemused shock as her own.

Chase lifted his wineglass and drained it very scientifically. "Scratch one casual friendship," he muttered hoarsely.

Gypsy immediately shook her head. "Oh, no," she began.

"I've been wanting to do that," he interrupted musingly, "ever since you told me about coffee on Tuesday."

She blinked and then fiercely gathered her scattered wits. "No, Chase," she said flatly. "No involvement."

"Too late."

Hanging on to the desk as if to a lifeline, she shook her head silently, ignoring the sneering little voice inside her head that was agreeing with his comment.

"I don't know about you, but I'm not strong enough to fight," he said wryly.

Gypsy silently ordered the little voice to shut

up and took hold of her willpower with both hands. "No involvement," she repeated slowly.

He gazed at her with a disconcerting speculation. "I'm reasonably sure it isn't me," he observed, "so what is it?"

For the first time her small work area was giving Gypsy a claustrophobic feeling, and she pushed away from the desk to wander out into the den. She sat down rather bonelessly on a handy chair and watched as Chase followed her into the main part of the room. Since he had a somewhat determined expression on his face, she searched hastily for words.

"Gypsy—"

"Chase, I— Oh, hell." She decided on honesty. "Chase, I've never . . . slept with a man before."

"You haven't?" Something unreadable flickered in his eyes.

"No."

"Why?"

She bit back a giggle, her sense of humor abruptly easing the tension in her body. "A girl used to have to explain why she did; now she has to explain why she doesn't."

"The times they are a changin'," he murmured.

"Uh-huh." She gave him a wry look. "Look, I've spent most of my life traveling, which isn't exactly conducive to lasting relationships. Summer flings and one-night stands hold no appeal for me. It's got nothing to do with morality, it's just me. In spite of my footloose life-style, I'm the home and hearth type at heart."

"A ring and a promise?"

Gypsy shook her head patiently. "That's just it: I don't want to get married."

Chase sank down in a chair across from hers

and peered at her bemusedly. "You've just done an about-face here, haven't you?"

"Not at all. I'm trying to make a point. The only relationship acceptable to me would be a lasting relationship with one man—which, to my mind, means marriage. But at this point in my life I don't want to get married. So . . . no relationship."

"No involvement," he murmured.

Gypsy felt an enormous sense of relief when he seemed to understand. She also felt oddly disappointed. The resulting confusion left her unusually nervous. What on earth was wrong with her? She had a book to write, and heaven knew that would occupy her for weeks. Why this sudden wish that she had not voiced her "no involvement" policy. Policy? That made her sound like a politician!

"You never gave me an answer."

"What?" She stared at him, trying in vain to read his expression. "Dinner? I . . . can't. I have a deadline, and I need to organize my notes and get to work."

"You have to eat."

"Yes, well. . . ." She produced a weak smile from somewhere. "If you'll take a close look at my typewriter, you'll probably find crumbs inside. I usually eat right over the keyboard."

"You'll get ulcers eating like that," he warned dryly.

Gypsy shrugged and murmured vaguely, "Deadlines, you know." She hoped that she'd given him the impression her deadline was considerably closer than it actually was. Little white lies never hurt anyone, she reasoned and, besides, she needed time to figure out what was wrong with her.

Along those lines she abruptly changed the subject. "Did you design your house?"

Chase didn't even blink; apparently he was getting accustomed to her conversational leaps. "Yes. Like it?"

"It's beautiful. I've never seen anything like it. Did you design it especially for yourself, or did you just decide afterward that it was for you?"

"It was mine all the way. Shall we talk of cabbages and kings now?" he added politely, doing a bit of conversational leaping of his own.

Gypsy signed. It was not, she reflected, going to be easy for her to hold her own with this man. He seemed to be extremely adaptable. As unusual as she obviously was in his experience, he had learned quickly how *not* to be thrown off balance by her. "I don't know what you mean."

"You know. Can you cook?" he asked abruptly.

He was using her own tactics on her, damn him! Gypsy sighed again and mentally threw up her hands in surrender. For the time being, at least. "No, I can't cook. Also I can't sew, and I hate washing dishes." If she'd hoped to discourage him with these admissions of unfemininity, she was defeated.

"Nobody's perfect. What's your favorite meal?"

"Spaghetti."

"My speciality. What time would you like to eat?"

Gypsy decided that either the wine, the kiss, or both had addled her wits; otherwise she'd be a lot sharper than she seemed to be at the moment. Was he or wasn't he riding roughshod over all her objections? "I'm working, I told you."

"You have to eat. I'll do the cooking. My place or yours?"

With some vague idea of having the home-team advantage, she said, "Mine. Can you really cook?" She was suddenly dimly astonished to realize that she'd just *let* him ride roughshod over all her objections.

"They teach you to at military schools," he answered absently, his mind obviously on something else.

"You went to military schools?"

"Grew up in them." Gypsy had his full attention now. "My father hoped I'd go on to West Point, but I had other plans."

She'd had little experience with father-son relationships, but she was apparently the type of person that others invariably confided in, so she'd heard many tragic stories resulting from conflicts over career choices. Chase certainly didn't look to be the victim of a tragedy, but her ready sympathy was nonetheless stirred.

"Was he . . . very upset?" she probed delicately.

"He wasn't happy," Chase replied wryly. "I told him I was getting even for all those lonely years spent in military schools."

"Oh, poor little boy!" she said involuntarily. To her surprise Chase flushed slightly. But there was a considering expression in his jade eyes.

"If I were an unscrupulous man, I'd take advantage of your obvious sympathy," he told her gravely. "However, since the last thing I want to do is to begin our . . . friendship with a lie, I'll confess that my childhood wasn't in the least deprived."

"It wasn't?"

"Hell, no." He smiled at her. "The schools

were good ones, I had plenty of friends, and Dad visited frequently. He always came and whisked me away to whatever post he happened to be at for holidays and vacations. I was a seasoned world traveler by the age of twelve."

Gypsy had to admit that it didn't sound sad, but she was still puzzled. Chase calmly enlightened her.

"My mother died when I was five, and Dad couldn't very well drag me all over the world with him. More often than not, he was assigned a post squarely in the middle of some revolution. So I went to boarding schools, where I learned to pick up my socks and cook spaghetti. Good enough?"

She nodded slowly. "Sorry to be nosy."

"Not at all. I'm glad you're interested. It'll be my turn to hear your life story tonight." He held up a hand when she would have spoken. "Fair trade. And I *have* to hear more about your parents. What time shall we have dinner?"

She stared at his politely inquiring face for a long moment. "About seven. I guess," she added rather hastily, deciding that she was giving in too damn quickly.

"Fine. I'll come over around six and bring the fixings with me." He rose to his feet and made a slight gesture when she would have got up. "Don't bother. I think I can find the door. See you at six. Oh, and keep looking for that insurance card, will you?"

Gypsy gazed after him, and she felt a sudden pang. Not a pang of uneasiness or uncertainty, but one of sheer panic.

I don't know about you, but I'm not strong enough to fight.

Reluctantly she allowed her mind to relive that . . . kiss. Kiss? God! Vesuvius erupting had nothing on that "kiss," Gypsy thought. She had never in her life been shaken like that. And Chase had made no secret of the fact that it had shaken him as well.

And that meant trouble with a capital everything.

She rubbed absently at the sudden gooseflesh on her arms, wondering at the inexplicable caprices of fate. Her life was going so smoothly! And she didn't want the status quo to change . . . not now. Her writing produced enough upheaval for any sane person; asking for more was like asking for a ringside seat at the hurricane of the century.

By the time Chase knocked on her door at six on the dot, Gypsy had come no nearer to an answer. She'd had several hours to think and in all that time, her thoughts had turned continually to that kiss.

She knew that her peculiar life-style and offbeat habits had caused her to miss a lot. She had friends, but not close ones. During high school and college, she'd indulged in the normal sexual experimentation, but a natural unconformity had kept her safe from peer pressure. And she hadn't cared for any man enough to attempt the serious relationship that her own private ideals demanded.

But she had convinced herself over the years that the only things she had missed by her celibacy had been vulnerability and potential heartache. And she knew from experience that it demanded a rare and extremely adaptable person to survive—happily—living with her. To date only Amy, her housekeeper and mother hen, had managed the feat.

Not even her loving and uncritical parents, unusual themselves, had been able to live with their daughter once she'd reached adulthood. And if *they* couldn't do it, what chance had the sane, normal man? Gypsy wondered.

So when she opened the door to let Chase in at six, she was staunchly determined to nip any romantic overtures in the bud. After which, according to all the books on etiquette, the noble warrior would retire from the field in dignified defeat.

The problem was . . . Chase apparently intended to retire from the field only if carried off on his shield.

"Did you find it?" he asked cheerfully.

Belatedly shutting the door behind him and hurrying down the hall to keep up with his tall form, Gypsy struggled briefly to figure out what he was talking about. "The insurance card? Yes, I found it." She followed him into the modern kitchen, reflecting absently that he looked *really* good in jeans. "It was in Corsair's envelope."

"Corsair's what?" He paused in unloading a bulging grocery bag onto the deep orange countertop, looking at her blankly.

Gypsy was staring at his T-shirt and trying not to giggle. Obviously he wasn't as conservative as she'd first thought. The T-shirt read: THIS IS A MOVING VIOLATION. Above the words was a picture of a leering man chasing an obviously delighted and sketchily dressed woman.

Trying to keep her voice steady, Gypsy finally

replied to his question. "Corsair's envelope. You know, where I keep his vet records."

"Oh. I won't ask what it was doing there." He went back to unloading the groceries.

"Uh . . ." She gestured slightly. "Nice shirt."

"Thank you. Is it too subtle, do you think?"

"Depends."

"On what?" He looked at her with innocent mischief in his eyes.

"On whether it's a declaration of intent."

"Bite your tongue." He looked wounded. "I would never be so crass."

Gypsy wasn't about to ask what the shirt was if it *wasn't* a declaration of intent. She decided to leave the question of subtlety up in the air for the time being.

Chase was looking her up and down, considering. "You look very nice," he commented, eyeing her neat jeans and short-sleeved knit top. "But what's this?" he asked, reaching out to pluck a pair of dark-rimmed glasses from the top of her head.

"They're working glasses." She reclaimed them and placed them back on top of her head. "To help prevent eyestrain, according to the doctor."

"Oh." Chase removed the glasses from the top of her head and placed them on her nose. He studied the effect for a moment while she frowned at him, then said, "They make you look very professorial."

She pushed them back up and said briefly, "They make me look like an owl. If you want me to help cook, by the way, the consequences will rest on your head."

Chase accepted the abrupt change of subject

without a blink. "You get to watch the master chef at work. Sit on that stool over there."

Gypsy debated about whether or not to dig in her heels. "Those military schools didn't help your personality," she offered finally in a deceptively mild voice.

"I take it you dislike being ordered around."

"Bingo."

"Will you *please* sit on that stool, Miss Taylor, so that I can demonstrate my culinary skill before your discerning eye?"

"Better," she approved, going over to sit on the high stool.

"Trying to reform a man is the first sign of possessiveness, you know." He was unloading the bag again.

"I've taught *manners* to quite a few children," she responded politely, refusing to be drawn.

"Really? How did that come about?" Chase was busily locating what he needed in cabinets and drawers. "I assumed you didn't have any siblings."

"You assumed correctly." Gypsy reflected wryly that he had a disconcerting habit of dangling a line her way and then abruptly cutting bait when she ignored it. "But I like kids, so I usually find a nursery school or kindergarten wherever I'm living and volunteer to help out a couple of days a week."

"So you like kids, eh?" He sent a speculative glance at her as he began to place hamburger in a pan for browning. "I'll bet you'd eventually like to have a houseful of your own."

"You'd lose the bet. I'd make a lousy mother; I'm not planning on having kids at all."

Chase halted his preparations long enough to

give her a surprised look. "Why do you think you'd make a lousy mother? Your 'gypsy' life-style?"

She shook her head. "I grew up that way, and it didn't bother me. No, it's my writing. Some authors work nine to five with nights and weekends off, just like an average job." She smiled wryly. "And then there's me. When I'm working, it's usually in twelve to fourteen-hour stretches. For weeks at a time. I lose pounds and sleep . . . and sometimes friends. I swear and throw things and pace the floor. Corsair, poor baby, has to remind me to feed him." Her smile unconsciously turned a bit wistful. "What kind of life would that be for kids?"

Chase was watching her with an expression that was curiously still. After a moment he shook his head as if to throw off a disturbing thought. When he spoke, it was about her work habits, and not about her decision not to have children. "Aren't you afraid of burning yourself out?"

"Not really." She spoke soberly. "Notice that I said *when* I'm working. I usually take a break of several weeks between books. I'm healthy and happy—so where's the harm?"

He shook his head again—this time in obvious impatience. "You need someone to take care of you."

"I *have* someone to take care of me—my housekeeper, Amy. The hamburger's burning."

Turning swiftly back to the stove, Chase swore softly. He repaired the results of his inattention silently, then said, "Tell me about your parents. Your mother first; I have to hear about the creator of coffee on Tuesday."

"You're hung up on that." Gypsy sighed. "Well,

Mother is an artist—very vague, very creative. She's also a spotless housekeeper, which drives both Poppy and me absolutely nuts; he and I share an extremely untidy nature." She sought about in her mind for a further description of her mother. "Mother is . . . Mother. She's hard to describe."

"An artist? Would I have heard of her?"

"Know anything about art?"

"Yes."

"Then you've heard of her. Rebecca Thorn."

Chase nearly got his thumb with the knife he was chopping onions with. "Good Lord! Of course I've heard of her." Staring at Gypsy, he nearly got his forefinger with the knife. "You come from a very illustrious family."

"You haven't heard the half of it."

"Your father too?"

"Uh-huh. You'd have to be a scientist to recognize his name though. He's a physicist. Disappears periodically and can't talk about his work." She reflected for a moment. "Poppy looks like the typical absentminded professor. He's soft-spoken, very distinguished, and wouldn't pick up a sock if it were made of solid gold."

She grinned suddenly. "It's amazing that he and Mother have lived together in perfect harmony for nearly thirty years. If I didn't know the story behind it, I'd wonder how Poppy ever managed to catch Mother."

"What *is* the story?"

"Never mind."

"Unfair! It'll drive me crazy."

"Sorry, but it's not my story. If they come over to visit, you can ask. They live in Portland."

"I thought they traveled?"

"Used to. Poppy still has to fly off somewhere occasionally, and Mother has her showings from time to time, but they're pretty settled now."

Cutting up ingredients for a salad, Chase glanced at her innocently. "They're so different, yet they get along perfectly?"

Gypsy missed the point. "Usually. Although they told me that there was a definite disagreement before I was born. Mother decided to go on tour when she was six months pregnant, and Poppy protested violently. You'd have to know Poppy to realize how astonishing that is. He never gets mad."

"What happened?"

"Well, Poppy said that he'd be damned if he'd have his child born in an elevator or the back room of some gallery—quite likely, given Mother's vagueness—and that she wasn't going to exhaust herself by trying to give showings in twelve cities in twelve days, or something equally ridiculous. So he planned a long, leisurely tour lasting three months and went with her, and the government was having kittens."

Chase blinked, digested the information for a moment, and then asked the obvious question. "Why?"

"Why was the government having kittens?" Gypsy looked vague. "Dunno exactly. Poppy was working on something for them, and they got very cranky when he took a sudden vacation. They couldn't do much about it, really, since genius doesn't punch a time-clock."

After staring at her for a moment, Chase asked politely, "And where were you born?"

She looked surprised. "In Phoenix. Mother woke up in the middle of the night having labor pains. She got up and called a cab; she knew that she wouldn't be able to wake Poppy—he sleeps like the dead—so she went on to the hospital alone. The problem was, she forgot to leave poor Poppy a note. He nearly had a heart attack when he woke up hours later and found her gone."

Chase had a fascinated expression on his face. "I see. So you were born in a hospital. Somehow that seems an anticlimax."

"Actually I was born in the cab. They made it to the hospital, and the cabbie ran inside to get a doctor. The doctor got back to the cab just in time to catch me. The cabbie—his name is Max—still sends me birthday cards every year."

Chase leaned back against the counter, crossed his arms over his chest, and shook his bowed head slowly. It took Gypsy a full minute to realize that he was laughing silently.

"What's so funny?"

He ignored the question. "Gypsy," he said unsteadily, "I have *got* to meet your parents."

Puzzled, she said, "They'll be here on Sunday for a visit; you can come over then." She had totally forgotten her intention of discouraging Chase's interest.

"Thanks, I'll do that." Still shaking his head, he went back to fixing the salad. A moment later he softly exclaimed, "Will you look at that?"

"What?" She slid off the stool and went over to peer around him.

"Your knife bit me." Chase quickly held his right hand over the sink, and a single drop of blood dripped from his index finger to splash onto the gleaming white porcelain. "Or the Robbinses' knife. Whichever—" He broke off abruptly as a muffled thump sounded behind him.

• • •

Gypsy opened her eyes to the vague realization that she was lying on the coolness of a tile floor. A pair of jade eyes, concerned, more than a little anxious, swam into view. She gazed up into them dreamily, wondering what she was doing on the floor and why Chase was supporting her head and shoulders. He looked terribly upset, she thought, and didn't understand why the thought warmed her oddly.

Then her memory abruptly threw itself into gear, and she closed her eyes with the swiftness born of past experience. "I hope you put a Band-Aid on it," she said huskily.

"I have a paper towel wrapped around it," he responded, a curious tremor in his deep voice. "Gypsy, why didn't you tell me you couldn't stand the sight of blood? God knows I wouldn't have thought it, considering the type of books you write."

"It's not something I normally announce to everybody and his grandmother," she said wryly, opening her eyes again. "Uh . . . I think I can get up now." She felt strangely reluctant to move, and grimly put that down to her sudden faint.

"Are you sure?" Chase didn't seem to be in any great hurry to release her. "Did you hit your head when you fell?"

"If I did, it obviously didn't hurt me. Help me up, will you, please?" She kept her voice carefully neutral.

Silently he did as she asked, steadying her with a hand on each shoulder until the last of the dizziness had passed. "Are you sure you're all right?"

"I'm fine." Gypsy made a production out of straightening her knit top. "Sorry if I startled you."

"*Startled* me?" Chase bit off each word with something just short of violence. "You scared the hell out of me. How on earth can you write such gory books when you can't stand the sight of blood?"

Patiently Gypsy replied, "I don't have to *see* the blood when I write—just the word."

He stared down at her for a long moment, shaking his head, until the bubbling sauce on the stove demanded his attention. He was still shaking his head when he turned away. "I hope you don't have any more surprises like that in store for me," he murmured. "I'd like to live to see forty."

Curious, Gypsy thought, then shrugged. Turning away, she caught sight of Corsair. The way he was sitting by one of the lower cabinets communicated dramatically. She frowned slightly as she got his cat food out and filled the empty bowl at his feet. "Sorry, cat," she murmured.

"What about Bucephalus?" Chase asked, obviously having observed the little scene.

"I fed him earlier."

"Oh." Leaping conversationally again, he said, "Tell me something. Why is it that the heroes in your books really aren't heroes at all? I mean, half the time, they're nearly as bad as the villains."

"Heroes don't exist," she told him flatly, going back to sit on her stool.

He tipped his head to one side and regarded her quizzically. "You're the last person in the world I'd expect to say something like that. Care to explain what you mean?"

"Just what I said. Heroes don't exist. Not the kind that people used to look up to and admire. The heroes available today are the ones created years ago out of pure fantasy."

"For instance?"

"You know. The larger-than-life heroes who were always fighting for truth, justice, and the American way. Superman. Zorro. The cowboys or marshalls in the white hats. A few swashbucklers. Knights on white chargers. They're all fiction . . . or just plain fantasy."

Chase set the bowl filled with tossed salad into the nearly barren refrigerator. "No modern-day heroes, huh?"

"Not that kind, no. The larger-than-life heroes are either long dead or else buried in the pages of fiction. It's a pity, too, because the world could use a few heroes."

Spreading French bread with garlic butter, Chase lifted a brow at her. "Those words carry the ring of disillusion," he said. "Don't tell me you're a romantic at heart."

Gypsy squirmed inwardly, but not outwardly. "I know that's a sin these days."

"No wonder you haven't gotten involved with anyone."

"You're twisting my meaning," she said impatiently. "I would never expect any man to measure up to fantasy heroes. That's as stupid as it is unreasonable. But there's a happy medium, you know. It's just that . . . romance is gone. I don't mean romance as in love or courtship. I mean *romance*. Adventure, ideals."

She ran a hand through her black curls and tried to sum up her meaning briefly, feeling somehow that it was important for him to understand what she meant. "Fighting for something *worth* fighting for."

Chase was silent for a long moment, his hands moving surely, and his eyes fixed on them. Then he looked over at Gypsy, and the jade eyes held a curiously shuttered expression. "Heroes."

"Heroes." She nodded. "Now, master chef—when do we eat?"

Three

Thinking back on it the next day, Gypsy had to admit—however reluctantly—that Chase was a marvelous companion. He'd kept her interested and amused for several hours, telling her all about what it was like to grow up in military schools—one prank after another, judging by some of the stunts he and friends had pulled—and how clients could easily drive an architect crazy.

And he asked questions. About the different places she'd lived, about her parents, about how she wrote her books. He plied her with an excellent red wine, pressed her to eat more spaghetti than Italy could have held, and then refused her virtuous offer of help in cleaning up the kitchen.

He left on the stroke of midnight . . . with a casual handshake and a cheerful good-bye.

Not *quite* what Gypsy had expected.

Rising on Saturday after an unusually restless night, she fiercely put him out of her mind.

She fixed herself a bowl of cereal for breakfast, absently noting that she was nearly out of milk. She fed Bucephalus and Corsair, unlatched the huge pet door leading from the kitchen out into the backyard, and rinsed her cereal bowl.

Saturday was juice, so she carried a large glassful out to her desk. Orange juice today; she usually alternated between orange, grape, or tomato juice. Wearing a pair of cutoff jeans and a bright green T-shirt, she sat down at her desk to work.

Two hours later Gypsy discovered that she'd been shuffling papers around on her desk, and had accomplished absolutely nothing.

Physical labor—that's what she needed. Working at a desk was fine, but working at a desk meant thinking, and she was thinking too damn much about Chase Mitchell.

Locating her gardening basket with some difficulty—why was it in the bathroom?—she went out into the front yard. There were several flower beds all bearing evidence that she'd indulged in physical labor quite often during the last two months.

Gypsy was a good gardener. And she had not merely the proverbial green thumb but a green *body*. Flowers that weren't even supposed to be blooming this time of year were waving colorful blossoms in the early-morning breeze. The half-dozen flower beds in the front yard were beautiful.

She glanced around, remembered where she'd left off, then dropped to her knees beside a flower bed ringing a large oak tree at the corner near Chase's property. She attacked a murderous weed energetically.

There was a sudden rustle in the tree above

her, and then a metallic sound as a bunch of keys fell practically in her lap. Gypsy stared at them for a long moment. Keys. *Not* acorns. She looked up slowly.

Chase was lying along a sturdy-looking lower limb, staring down at her. He was dressed casually in jeans and a green shirt, open at the throat, and the only way to describe his expression would be "hot and bothered."

"What are you doing?" she asked with admirable calm.

"Getting my car keys," he replied affably.

"Oh, is that where you keep them?"

"Only since I met your cat."

Gypsy's gaze followed his pointing finger and located Corsair, who was sitting farther out on the same limb. The cat's furry face was a study in innocence, and his bushy tail was waving gently from side to side.

Gypsy looked back at Chase in mute inquiry.

Chase crossed his hands over the limb and rested his chin on them, with all the air of a man making himself comfortable. "Your cat," he explained, "has somehow found a way into my house. Beats me where it is, but he's found it. He was sitting on my couch a little while ago—with my car keys in his mouth. I chased him three times around the living room and then lost him. The next thing I knew, he was sitting outside the window, on the sill. When I came out of the house, he climbed this tree. Ergo, I climbed up after him."

"Uh-huh." Gypsy glanced again at the innocent cat. "Why would Corsair steal your keys?"

"You don't believe me?"

"Forgive me. I've known Corsair a little longer."

"He stole my keys."

"Why would he do that?"

"How the hell should I know? Maybe he wanted to drive the car; God knows, he's arrogant enough."

"Don't insult Corsair, or I won't let you climb my tree anymore."

"Cute. That's cute."

"Chase, cats don't steal keys. And Corsair's never stolen anything." Gypsy exercised all her willpower to keep her amusement buried. She waved the trowel about. "What would he want with your keys?"

"He wanted to annoy me. I tell you, that cat doesn't like me!"

"Well, if you keep on calling him *that cat* in that tone of voice, I wouldn't be surprised if he actually did start disliking you. Besides, it's obvious that you know nothing about cats. *If* he disliked you, he'd shred your curtains or attack you when you weren't looking, or something like that. *Not* steal your keys."

"He stole my keys."

Gypsy stared up into stubborn jade eyes. "Of *course*, he did. He just sat down and decided very logically that since he didn't like you, he'd steal your car keys. Then he'd let you chase him three times around your living room. Then he'd let you chase him up a tree—"

"All right, all right!" Chase sighed in defeat. "Obviously I imagined the whole thing."

"Obviously." Gypsy went back to work with the trowel.

There were several rustling noises from above. Then a muffled "Damn!" Then a long silence. Gypsy kept working; another weed poked up an unwary head and she attacked it lethally.

"Want to give me a hand here?"

Gypsy murdered another weed. "A grown man can't get down from a tree by himself?" She had to swallow hard before the question would emerge without a hint of the laughter bubbling up inside of her.

"I'm not too proud to ask for help." There was a pause. "Help!"

She sat back on her heels and looked up at him. She was trying desperately to keep a straight face. "What do you want me to do? Climb up and get you down, or cushion your fall?"

There was a frantic gleam in the jade eyes. "Either way—when I get down, I'm going to murder you!"

"In that case, stay where you are."

"Gypsy—"

"All *right*! What's the problem?"

"I can't look over my shoulder to see where to place my feet. Every time I try, I lose my balance. And stop grinning, you little witch!"

"I'm not grinning. This isn't grinning." Gypsy struggled to wipe away the grin. "It's a twitch. I was born with it."

"Sure. Tell me where to put my feet."

Gypsy swallowed the instinctive quip. "Uh . . . slide back a little. Now a little to the right. No, *your* right! Now . . ."

A few moments later Chase was safely on the ground. Gypsy, who hadn't moved from her kneeling position, looked up at him innocently. "That'll teach you to climb trees. What would you have done if I hadn't been here?"

"Perished in agony. I thought you were supposed to be working."

"I told you I worked odd hours."

"What're you doing now?"

"What does it look like? I'm planting weeds."

"You have a sharp tongue, Gypsy mine."

She ignored the possessive addition to her name. "One of my many faults." She tossed him the keys. "Don't let me keep you," she added politely.

Deliberately misunderstanding her, he asked solemnly, "Would you keep me in comfort and security for the rest of my life? I have no objections to becoming a kept man."

The unexpected play on words knocked her off balance for a moment—but only for a moment. She and her father had played word games too many times for this one to throw her. "I won't be a keeper; the pay's not good enough."

"But there are benefits. Three square meals a day and a place to rest your weary head." He sat down cross-legged on the grass beside her, still grave.

"Not interested."

"A live-in proofreader."

"I can read."

"Typist?"

"I'll ignore that." Gypsy weeded industriously.

"That's not a weed," he observed, watching her. The word game was obviously over for the moment.

"It is too. It's just pretending to be a flower."

"What are you pretending to be?"

"A gardener. If you're not leaving, help weed."

"Yes, ma'am." Chase searched through the wicker garden basket, obviously in search of a tool with which to weed. "Why is there a dictionary in this basket?"

"Where do *you* keep dictionaries?"

"One would think I'd learn not to ask you reasonable questions."

"One would think."

"Do you do it deliberately?"

Gypsy gave him an innocent look. "Do what deliberately?"

"Uh-huh." He sighed. "There's a fork here; shall I use it to weed?"

"Be my guest."

"Would you like to have lunch?" he asked, using the fork enthusiastically to destroy a marigold in the prime of life.

Gypsy gently removed the fork from his grasp. "Not just after breakfast, no."

"Funny."

"Sorry." She hastily took the fork away from him a second time. "No more help, please. I don't want Mr. and Mrs. Robbins to come home to a bare lawn."

"Are you criticizing my gardening skills?" he asked, offended.

"Yes."

"Oh."

"No wonder you hire a gardener."

"You made your point. I didn't rub it in that I cook better than you."

"Not better. You cook—I don't. Period."

"Whatever." Chase sighed and got to his feet. "Well, since you won't let me weed, I'll be on my way. Do you need anything from town? I have to run some errands."

Gypsy paused in her work long enough to look up at him. "Now that you mention it—I could use a gallon of milk."

"Is Saturday milk day?" he asked interestedly.

"No, Monday is."

"You're going to drink a gallon of milk on Monday? It'll spoil if you don't."

"I use it for cereal. That doesn't count as a drink."

"Right." He nodded slowly. "Uh . . . what're you doing this afternoon?"

Glancing past his shoulder, Gypsy saw Corsair about to launch himself. "Step back!" she ordered briskly.

Instinctively Chase did so, and Corsair overshot him to land with a disgruntled expression in the grass beside Gypsy. The cat's face seemed to proclaim irritably that not even a cat could pause to correct his aim in midair.

"I told you he didn't like me."

Gypsy swatted the cat firmly. "Leave!"

Corsair stalked toward the house with offended dignity.

"Sorry," Gypsy murmured. "I can't understand it; Corsair likes everybody."

"Everybody but me."

"I may have misjudged you about the keys," Gypsy said slowly.

"Good of you to admit it."

"I'm nothing if not fair."

"I won't comment on that. You didn't answer my question. What're you going to be doing this afternoon?"

"I usually go for a walk on the beach, but I won't know for sure what I'll be doing until then."

"Don't believe in planning ahead, eh?"

"I treasure spontaneity."

"I'll keep that in mind. One gallon of milk coming up." Lifting one hand in a small salute, Chase headed across to his house.

Gypsy stared after him. It occurred to her

that anyone listening to one of their conversations—particularly if he or she came in on the middle of it—would be totally bewildered. Neither she nor Chase ever lost the thread. It was as if they were mentally attuned, on the same wavelength.

It was a disturbing thought.

She put more energy into her attack on the weeds, slaughtering without mercy while frowning at the thoughts that flitted through her mind.

She was in trouble. *Definite* trouble. Chase possessed a sharp intelligence, a highly-developed sense of the ridiculous, and an indefinable talent for holding her interest—no mean accomplishment, considering her wayward mind. He was also fatally charming.

Besides . . . she'd always had a thing about redheads.

Gypsy uprooted a marigold by mistake, and hastily replanted it. Damn! She was thinking about him too much. It didn't help to remind herself of that. Long hours at her typewriter had taught her that the mind was a peculiar instrument, given to absurd flights of fancy all mixed up with spans of rational thought.

If only there were a lever that she could switch from ABSURD to RATIONAL. But no such luck.

Her lever was stuck on ABSURD. Or something was. Why else was she kneeling here on the grass and wistfully contemplating a relationship with a man? Particularly *that* man?

"Face it," she told four marigolds and a rose. "You'd drive him crazy inside a week—once you really started to work. And he'd play merry hell with your concentration."

She worked vigorously with the trowel to loosen the soil around her audience. "And you don't want to get involved. You *don't.* Just think . . . you'd have to live in one house for *years.* And he'd expect you to learn how to cook—you know he would. And he wouldn't like whatisits in the refrigerator, or dirty clothes strewn through the house, or cat hair on the couch. Especially Corsair's hair.

"The smart thing to do would be to sink your scruples and settle for an affair," she told her audience, dirt flying like rain as she unconsciously dug a hole at the edge of the bed. "At least then you wouldn't have to go to court whenever he decided that enough was enough. You'd just politely help him pack his suitcases—or pack yours—and call it quits. Nice and civilized."

She frowned as a drop of moisture fell onto her hand. "Oh, for Pete's sake," she muttered angrily, swiping at a second tear with the back of one dirty hand. "It hasn't even *begun,* and already you're crying because it's over!"

Gypsy filled the minor excavation with dirt, dropped the trowel into her basket, and rose to her feet. She picked up the basket and stared down at the colorful flowers for a moment. Then she turned and made her way toward the house.

"Everybody talks to plants," she muttered aloud. "They make good listeners; they don't butt in with sensible suggestions, and they don't warn you when you're about to make an utter fool of yourself!"

Since Chase had arranged to have Daisy towed to a garage for repairs (Gypsy didn't hold out much hope), she was pretty much housebound. Chase hadn't specified any length of time for his "errands," but the morning dragged on with no sign of him, and Gypsy was bored.

She didn't feel like writing. Gardening had palled decidedly. She played fetch with Bucephalus for an hour, but then *he* got bored. She tried to teach Corsair to play the same game; for her pains, she got a stony glare from china-blue eyes and a swishing tail indicative of cold contempt.

"Why do I put up with you, cat?"

"Waurrr."

"Right. Go away."

She watched as Corsair headed for the shade of a nearby tree in the backyard, then glanced at her watch. Twelve o'clock. The morning was gone, and she hadn't accomplished a thing. Wonderful.

Gypsy walked across the lawn to the redwood railing placed about two feet inside the edge of the cliff. She leaned on the railing for a few moments, gazing out over the Pacific and thinking muddled thoughts. Maybe a walk on the beach would clear the cobwebs away.

She followed the railing to the zigzagging staircase leading down to the beach. On the way down, she absently glanced across to the twin staircase leading from Chase's backyard. The beach below was narrow as beaches go, but it was private for a quarter of a mile in either direction. North and south of the private stretch were various small towns, and, of course, other privately owned properties.

But only these two homes possessed the eagle's perch of the cliffs. In this area anyway.

Gypsy loved it.

Barefoot as usual, she walked out to the water's edge and stood listening to the roar of the surf. It was a comforting sound. A *comfortable* sound. Endlessly steady, endlessly consistent, though at the moment it possessed the disturbing trick of reminding one of one's own mortality.

Frowning, Gypsy turned and walked back a few feet toward the cliffs. She stopped at the large, water-smoothed rock jutting up out of the sand. It was a favorite "place of contemplation" for her, and she sat now in the small seatlike depression in its side.

Mortality.

It was one of those odd, off-center, out-of-sync moments. Gypsy wasn't generally given to soul-searching, but in that moment she searched. And she discovered one of life's truths: that complacency had a disconcerting habit of shattering suddenly and without warning.

How many times had she told herself that her life was perfect, that she had no need to change it? How many times had she asserted with utter confidence that she needed no one but herself to be happy?

Gypsy's frown, holding a hint of panic, deepened as she stared out over the ocean. Had she been wrong all these years? No. No, not wrong. Not *then*. She'd needed those years to work at her writing, to grow as a person.

But had she grown? Yes . . . and no. She'd certainly grown as a writer. And she was a well-rounded person; she had interests other than writing, and she got along well with other people. But she'd never opened herself up totally to another person.

For *person*, she thought wryly, read *man*. No relationships, other than the strictly casual. No vulnerability on that level. No chance of heartache. And . . . no growth?

She was more confused than ever. Who, she wondered despairingly, had conceived the unwritten rulebook on human relationships? Who had decreed long ago in some primal age that total growth as a human being was possible only by risking total vulnerability?

Reluctantly Gypsy turned from the philosophical and abstract to the concrete and specific. Chase.

She was reasonably certain that she didn't *need* Chase—or any other man—to be happy. At the same time she had no idea whether or not that mythical man could make her *happier.*

And for her—more so, she thought, than with most other women—any relationship would be a great risk. She already had one strike against her: She was difficult, if not impossible, to live with. And she wasn't even sure that she could live for more than a few months in one place.

And then there was—

Gypsy's thoughts broke off abruptly as a sound intruded on her consciousness. If she didn't know better . . . it sounded like hoofbeats. She got to her feet and stepped away from the rock, looking first to the south. Nope—nothing there. Definite hoofbeats, and they were getting louder. She turned toward the north.

The horse was coming up the middle of the narrow beach at a gallop. It was pure white and absolutely gorgeous. The black saddle and bridle stood out starkly, and the metal studs decorating the saddle glinted in the sunlight. And on the horse's back was a man.

In the brief moment granted her for reflection, Gypsy felt distinctly odd. It was as if she'd stepped into the pages of fiction . . . or into the world of film fantasy.

The rider was dressed all in white—pants, boots, gloves, and shirt. The shirt was the pirate-type, full sleeves caught in tight cuffs at the wrist and unbuttoned halfway down. And the rider wore a mask and a black kerchief affair which hid all his hair. Almost all. A copper gleam showed.

Gypsy took all that in in the space of seconds. And then horse and rider were beside her, and the totally unexpected happened. Gypsy would have sworn that it couldn't be done except by trained stuntpeople on a movie set. Forever afterward, she maintained that it was sheer luck, *not* careful planning, that brought it off.

The horse slid to a halt with beautiful precision, leaving the rider exactly abreast of Gypsy. Then the animal stood like a stone while the rider leaned over and down.

"Wha—" was all she managed to utter.

She was swept up with one strong arm, and ended up sitting across the rider's lap. Through the slits of his mask, darkened eyes gleamed with a hint of green for just a moment. And then he was kissing her.

Ravishment would have been in keeping with the image, she supposed dimly, but the rider didn't use an ounce of force. He didn't have to. He kissed her as if she were a cherished, treasured thing, and Gypsy would have been less than human— and less of a woman—to resist that.

She felt the silk beneath her fingers as her hands came to rest naturally—one touching his chest and the other gripping his upper arm. The dark gold hair at the opening of the shirt teased her thumb, and the hand at her waist burned oddly. The hard thighs beneath her were a potent seduction.

She felt the world spinning away, and released it gladly. Her lips parted, allowing—inviting—his exploring tongue. Fire raced through her veins and scorched her nerve endings. She felt the arm around her waist tighten, and then . . . the devastating kiss ended as abruptly as it had begun.

Gypsy was lowered back to the sand, green eyes glinted at her briefly, and then the horse leaped away.

Dazedly she stared after them. She took a couple of steps back and found her seat by touch alone, sinking down weakly. The horse and rider had disappeared. Without conscious thought she murmured, "Say, who was that masked man?"

Then she giggled. The giggle exploded into laughter a split second later. Gypsy laughed until her sides ached. Finally she wiped streaming eyes, and tried to gather her scattered wits. In a long and eventful life nothing quite so wild had ever happened to her.

A gleam from the sand at her feet caught her attention, and she bent down to see what it was. She held the object in her hand for a long moment, then her fingers closed around it and she laughed again.

Delighted laughter.

It occurred to Gypsy as she climbed the stairs to her backyard a few minutes later that Chase had somehow found the time to plan that little scene very carefully. Where had he got the horse? And how could he have been certain that she'd take a walk on the beach? The only thing she *didn't* wonder about was the point of it all.

Heroes.

She crossed the yard and entered the house through the kitchen, still giggling. Who would have thought the man would go to such absurd lengths to catch her attention? Why in heaven's name hadn't some woman latched onto him years ago?

Gypsy hastily brushed that last thought away.

There was a gallon of milk in her refrigerator, and no sign of the Mercedes next door. She smiled and went on through the house to her work area. After a moment's deliberation she placed the masked rider's souvenir on the middle shelf of her bookcase. She studied the effect for a moment, nodded to herself, and sat down at the desk.

This time she did accomplish some work. Her notes fell into place naturally, and she didn't foresee any major problem with the forthcoming book. Aside from pushing Corsair off the desk twice and firmly putting Bucephalus outside after he'd chewed on her ankle for the third time, she worked undisturbed.

"You should lock your doors. Anybody could come in."

It was Chase, back in his jeans and shirt of the morning, and carrying a bag from a hamburger place in town. Before she could say a word, he was going on cheerfully.

"Hamburgers; I didn't feel like cooking. Let's eat." He headed for the kitchen.

Gypsy rose from the desk, smiling to herself. So he was going to play innocent, eh? Well, she could play that game as well. It occurred to her wryly that Chase was rapidly on his way to becoming a fixture around the place . . . but she didn't have the heart to send him away.

At least that's what she told herself.

"How do you know I haven't already eaten?" she asked, following him into the kitchen. "It's past two o'clock."

"You've obviously been busy; I guessed that you'd forget about lunch. What's the drink for the day? I forgot to ask this morning."

"Juice. I'm having tomato."

"With hamburgers?"

"With anything. What would you like?"

"The same; I'm always open to new experiences."

Gypsy started to comment on his remark, then thought better of it. She poured the juice while he was setting out their lunch on the bar.

"Will you do something about this dog? I'm going to fall over him and break my neck."

"He's supposed to be outside. Why did you let him back in?"

"I don't argue with a dog that size."

"Right. Out, Bucephalus." She put the dog back out in the yard.

"Salt?" he asked politely, holding up a salt-shaker when they were seated.

"No, thank you," Gypsy tasted the hamburger thoughtfully. "I notice you ordered them both with everything."

"Certainly I did. That way, no one gets offended later."

"Later?"

"When we make mad passionate love together, of course."

"Is that what we're going to do?"

"Eventually."

"Oh."

"You could sound a little more enthusiastic," he reproved gravely.

"Sorry. It's just that I've never heard something like that announced quite so calmly. Or so arbitrarily."

"My military upbringing, I suppose."

"Better learn to rise above it."

"What?"

"Your military upbringing. We've agreed that I don't like to be ordered around."

"I didn't order you around. I just stated a fact."

"That we're going to make mad passionate love together."

"That's right."

"Best laid schemes, and all that."

"Ever hear the one about the dropping of water on stone?"

"Are you trying to say—"

"I'll wear down your resistance eventually."

"I wouldn't be so sure, if I were you."

"But you're not me, Gypsy mine."

"I'm not *yours* either."

"We'll be each other's—how's that?"

"The last thing I need in my life is a man who accuses my cat of leading him up a tree."

"Let's forget about that, shall we?"

"Put down that catsup bottle!" Gypsy giggled in spite of herself. "I'll never forget. That's another of my faults, by the way."

"You seem to have a regular catalog of faults."

"Precisely. Sorry for the disappointment, but I'm sure you can find somebody else to while away your vacation with."

"One of *my* faults, Gypsy mine, is that once I set my mind on something, I never give up."

Four

Gypsy thought about that calm statement during the remainder of the day. As a declaration of intent, she decided, it lacked something. And what it lacked was a simple *definition* of intent. Just exactly what had he set his mind on? Her, apparently. But what exactly did he—

Oh, never mind! she told herself irritably. It wasn't going to do her a bit of good to keep wondering about it.

And in the meantime Chase was making his presence felt. Not in a big way; he left right after lunch, politely saying that he didn't want to interrupt her work. But he came back. He came back four times to be precise—between three and six P.M. Each time, he stuck his head around the corner of her work area and apologized solemnly for bothering her. And each time he asked to borrow something. A cup of sugar, a stick of butter, two cups of milk, and a bud vase, respectively.

It was the bud vase that piqued Gypsy's curiosity.

"What's he up to, Herman?" she asked her typewriter after Chase had vanished for the fourth time. Herman didn't deign to reply. Herman did, however, repeat a word three times. At least she *blamed* Herman for the mistake.

She was still glowering at Herman ten minutes later, when Chase returned. He came over to the desk this time, decisively removed the sheet of paper from Herman, and then looked down at Gypsy with a theatrical leer.

"Are you coming willingly, or will I be forced to kidnap you?"

"Coming where?" she asked blankly.

"Into my parlor, of course. My house, if you want to be formal."

"Why should I come to your house?"

"You're invited to dinner."

"Invited or commanded to attend?"

"Invited. Forcefully."

"And if I politely refuse?"

"I'll throw you over my shoulder and kidnap you. Of course, if I'm forced to those lengths, no telling when I'll release you. Much better if you come of your own free will." His voice was grave.

Gypsy sighed mournfully, unable to resist the nonsense. "I suppose I'd better come willingly, then. Do I have your word of honor as a gentleman that I can come home whenever I want?"

He placed a hand on his chest and bowed with a certain flair. "My word of honor as a gentleman."

Since he was still leering, Gypsy looked at him suspiciously, but rose to her feet. "Is this a dress-up party, or come-as-you-are?"

"Definitely come-as-you-are. We'll have a dress-up party later. Better put some shoes on though."

Gypsy silently found some sandals. Corsair was sleeping on one of them and wasn't happy at the disturbance, but she ignored the feline mutters of discontent. Chase was waiting for her in the hall.

He led her out the front door and across the expanse of green lawn to his house. Since the two properties were separated by only a low hedge, broken in several places, it was a short walk. He opened one of the double doors and ushered her inside.

It was Gypsy's first look inside the house that she had admired so much from the outside. Immediately and whole-heartedly she fell in love with it.

The front doors opened into a huge, open area. The sunken room was carpeted in a deep rust-colored pile, and both the light-colored paneling and the open, beamed ceiling added to the spaciousness. The furniture—a pit grouping and various tables—was modern. There were plump cushions in a deep ivory color, and colorful throw pillows for a pleasant contrast. A combination bookshelf and entertainment center ran along one wall, containing innumerable books, an extensive stereo system, and a large-screen television set.

If the remainder of the house looked like this . . . Gypsy took a deep breath, dimly aware of Chase's gaze on her. "Did you do the decorating?" she asked finally.

"All the way. Would you like the nickel tour?"

"Please."

The remainder of the house looked *better*. There were three bedrooms, two baths, a large study, a formal dining room in an Oriental motif, a combination kitchen and breakfast nook that Julia Child would have killed for, and a Jacuzzi.

The Jacuzzi occupied a place in half of the redwood deck in back, which stretched from the glass doors opening into the breakfast nook to the identical glass doors opening into the master bedroom. The deck was enclosed by glass around the Jacuzzi, and houseplants abounded, giving the illusion of a jungle scene.

Gypsy stared around her for a moment and sought for a safe topic. "I thought you weren't good with plants," she managed finally.

"I'm not. But for some reason, houseplants do well for me. This concludes the nickel tour, ma'am. Now, if you'll come back to the dining room with me, dinner will be served."

She preceded him silently, speaking only when they'd reached the dining room. Gazing at the table laid out formally and intimately for two, she murmured, "Now I know why you wanted the bud vase."

Chase seated her ceremoniously and in grand silence, then disappeared into the kitchen.

Gypsy stared after him for a moment, then looked back at the bud vase. After a moment she reached out and gently touched the single peach blossom it contained. Idly she wondered why he'd chosen that particular flower. Did it have some special meaning? She didn't know.

What she *did* know was that, like a person going down for the third time in a deep river, there was little hope of saving her now.

Gypsy had never in her life had pheasant under glass, vichyssoise, or anything else Chase served her that night. She enjoyed it all, but the picture they must have presented sitting at the formal table wearing jeans and casual tops caused her to giggle from time to time.

Or maybe the giggles were caused by Chase's "juice surprise."

"What is this?"

"Juice, I told you. Different kinds."

"Chase, there's more in this than juice."

"So I stretched a point a little. So what?"

"You're disrupting the habit of a lifetime, that's so what."

"It's time to broaden your horizons."

"You sound like a travel ad."

"Sorry."

"This is very good, you know."

"I'm glad you like it. It's—"

"No, don't tell me what it is," she warned hastily.

"Why not?"

"Because if it's snails, I don't want to know about it."

"It isn't snails."

"Good. Don't tell me what it *is*."

"Whatever madam desires. Would madam like more—uh—juice?"

"Chase, are you trying to get me drunk?"

He looked scandalized. "How you could ever suspect—"

"Easily," she interrupted, peering at him owlishly.

"A *baby* has more kick than this stuff," he maintained staunchly.

"Strong baby. Shall I sit here in royal detachment while you clear the table? I'll help if you like, but I hope your china's insured."

"You stay put. I'll clear the table and bring in dessert." He began to do so efficiently.

"What's for dessert?"

"Baked Alaska."

"I'll take a wild guess," she said drily, "that you're a gourmet cook."

"Something like that."

"So tell me, master chef, to what do I owe the honor?"

"Honor?" He placed a delicious looking dessert in front of her.

"Of having you cook for me."

"I'm trying to seduce you, of course."

Gypsy was vaguely glad that she'd swallowed the first bite before he answered her question. Otherwise, she'd have choked. "I see." She touched her napkin delicately to her lips—mainly to hide the fact that they were twitching. "The way to a woman's heart, and all that?"

Very seriously he responded, "Well, I thought that either the food would get you . . . or the juice would."

She stared at his deadpan expression. How *could* the man look so ridiculously serious? After a moment she began eating again. "I'll say this for you—the approach is certainly original. I don't think I've ever heard the brutal truth used to such good effect."

"Not *brutal*!" he protested, wounded.

She gave him a look.

Chase sighed sadly. "It isn't working, is it?"

"No." She didn't mince words. She also didn't tell him just how well his strategy was working. His straightforward approach was certainly startling, novel in her experience, and if she didn't get out of his house very quickly, she was going to make a total fool of herself.

"Aren't you tired of a predictable life?" he asked persuasively. "Wouldn't you like change, excitement, adventure?"

"Sounds like you're inviting me on a safari," she observed, eyes firmly on her dessert.

Chase gave up—for the moment, at least. Dessert was finished in silence, and then he sent her into the living room with her juice. Gypsy didn't protest, and she didn't try to leave. The juice was beginning to have the inevitable effect on her.

But the inevitable effect on Gypsy was a bit different from what Chase had probably hoped for. Except that she didn't believe Chase had hoped for seduction at all. She had the definite feeling that he'd wanted to keep her off-balance more than anything else. However, visions of seduction or whatever notwithstanding, Chase would probably get more than he bargained for.

The juice really didn't have much of a kick. But then . . . it didn't take much for Gypsy. It didn't take much, that is, to release the reckless mischief she normally kept tightly reined.

She was going to teach him a lesson, Gypsy decided.

When Chase came into the living room after clearing up in the kitchen, Gypsy was prowling the room like a caged tigress. The empty juice glass had been placed neatly in the center of the chrome and glass coffee table.

"Gypsy?"

She whirled around and flung herself into his arms. "I thought you said that we were going to make mad passionate love together?" she questioned throatily, gazing up into startled jade eyes.

Chase had automatically caught her, and now stared down at her as though he'd caught a bundle of dynamite with a lighted fuse. "I did say that, didn't I?" he mumbled.

"Yes. So what are we waiting for?"

"Sobriety," he answered involuntarily.

Gypsy fiercely disentangled herself and stepped back, regaining her balance by sheer luck. "Did you or did you not intend to get me drunk and take advantage of me?" she demanded accusingly.

"Yes—no! Dammit, don't put words in my mouth!"

"You're rejecting me!" she announced in a hurt tone, doing a sudden and bewildering about-face.

"*No*, I'm not rejecting you! Gypsy—"

"Don't . . . you . . . touch . . . me!" she warned awfully when he stepped toward her. "You had your chance, buster, and you blew it!"

For a long moment Chase looked about as bewildered as a man could look. Then the bewilderment slowly cleared, and a whimsical expression replaced it. "Do you like playing with fire, Gypsy mine?"

Damn, but he's quick! she thought wryly. Deciding that there was no graceful way out of the situation, she merely shrugged with a faint smile.

"I could read a great deal into that shrug," he told her.

"Don't imagine things. Thank you for the excellent dinner, master chef, and I think I'd better be going now."

"You're welcome, and I'll walk you to your door."

His easy acceptance bothered Gypsy for some reason. It might have had something to do with the unexplained gleam in his jade eyes. Or it might have had something to do with the fact that he'd twice announced his intention of attempting to seduce her today—and no attempt had yet been made.

The walk across to her front door was accomplished in silence, with Gypsy growing more nervous with every step. Along with the nervousness was a sudden, heart-pounding awareness of the man at her side, and she realized dimly that every muscle in her body was tense.

It was neither dark nor light outside; it was that odd twilight hour. Daylight was colors, darkness was stark black and white, but twilight was elusive shades of gray.

When they reached the front porch, Chase caught her arm and turned her to face him. Gypsy looked up at him instinctively, wary and uneasy. Her heart had recaptured its captive-beast rhythm, and she felt suddenly adrift in a dangerous and unpredictable sea.

"May I kiss you good night?" he asked softly, his hands coming to rest on her shoulders.

Gypsy wanted to say no, sharply and without mincing words. But she wasn't very surprised to find herself nodding silently.

His hands lifted to cup her face, his head bending until their lips touched with the lightness of a sigh. There was no pressure, no demand. Just warmth and sweetness, and a gentleness that was incredibly moving.

Gypsy felt herself relaxing, felt her body mold itself bonelessly to his. Her arms moved of their own volition to slide around his waist even as she became aware of his hands moving slowly down her back.

If this was seduction, she thought dimly, then why on earth was she fighting it? It was a drugging, insidious thing, sapping her willpower and causing her to forget why she should have been protesting.

A tremor like the soft flutter of a butterfly's wings began somewhere deep inside her body. It spread outward slowly, growing in strength, until she felt that her whole body was shaking with it.

When Chase finally drew away, Gypsy had the disturbing impression that she had lost something. She didn't know what it was. But the tremor was still there, and she was having trouble breathing.

The man was a warlock, she thought.

"Good night, Gypsy mine," he murmured huskily, reaching over to open the door for her.

Gypsy forced her arms to release him. "Good night," she managed weakly, sliding past him to enter the house. She hesitated for a moment, glancing back over her shoulder at him, then softly closed the door.

She went into the den and sat down on the couch, curling up in one corner and staring at the blank television screen. For a long time she sat without moving. Corsair came to sit beside her, his rough purr like the rumble of a small engine. Gypsy stroked him absently. Bucephalus came and lay down on the carpet by the couch.

Gypsy smiled wryly. "What are you two trying to do—comfort me?" she asked. A canine tail thumped the floor, and feline eyes blinked at her. "Thanks, guys, but I think it's beyond your power."

She sat for a while longer, listening to silence and the whispering voices of reason. But it was the gentle murmurs of desire that tormented her. She finally got up and went to take a long hot bath, hoping that the steam would carry away her problems.

It didn't.

She let Corsair and Bucephalus outside for a few minutes, then called them back in and latched the pet door. She wandered around downstairs for a while, until disgust with her own restlessness drove her to bed. It was midnight by the time she crawled between the sheets, and Gypsy lay there for a while and stared at the ceiling. She finally reached and turned out the lamp on her nightstand, absently moving Corsair off her foot and patting Bucephalus where he lay beside the bed.

Ten minutes later the phone rang. She picked up the receiver without bothering to turn the lamp back on, wondering who could be calling her at that hour. "Hello?"

"Will you dream about me tonight?" a deep, muffled masculine voice asked softly.

Gypsy's first impulse was to hang up. The last thing she needed tonight was a semi-obscene phone caller. But something about that voice nagged at her. It *could* be Chase, she decided finally. Besides, who *else* could it possibly be? So why not play along?

"Of course, I will," she murmured seductively.

"Sweet dreams?"

"As sweet as honey."

"I could make them even sweeter," he drawled.

"Promises, promises."

"Just give me the chance."

"A man should always . . . make his own opportunities."

"And what should a woman do?"

"She waits."

"An old-fashioned lady, I see."

"In . . . some ways." Gypsy was thoroughly enjoying the suggestive conversation.

He chuckled softly. "Sweet dreams. . . ."

Gypsy listened bemusedly to the dial tone for a moment, then cradled the receiver gently. " 'Curiouser and curiouser,' " she murmured to herself. She smiled into the darkness for a while.

Then she fell asleep.

Gypsy slept six hours—no more, no less. It was a peculiarly exact habit in a quite definitely inexact person. But apparently her biological clock was set for precisely six hours of sleep and not a second more. And during those six hours, Armageddon could have occurred without disturbing Gypsy.

She dressed and went through her morning routine. She fed the animals and herself, unlatched the pet door, and checked the weather (rainy). Sunday was "dealer's choice" when it came to the day's drink. She decided on iced tea and made a pitcherful.

Since her parents were coming to visit, she unlocked the front door—heaven only knew what she'd be doing by the time they arrived, so they usually just walked right in.

Then she carried a glass of tea to her desk, put a sheet of paper into Herman, and got down to work.

The morning advanced steadily as she worked. The rain stopped and the sun came out. Her canine and feline companions checked on progress from time to time and then disappeared. Gypsy refilled her glass once.

With utter concentration and not a little willpower, she'd managed to put Chase out of her mind while she worked. And she was glad about that; not even friendship would be possible between them if thoughts of him disrupted her work, and Gypsy knew it. As impossible as she was to live with while she was writing, she was even worse when something prevented her from writing.

Around ten A.M. she heard the sound of a car in her driveway, but continued to work without a pause. If it was her parents, they'd come inside; anyone else would knock.

A few moments later her father came in. He was a tall man, slender and distinguished. His hair was black, save for wings of silver framing his lean face. Mild blue eyes gazed peacefully out from beneath straight brows. And lines of struggle coexisted peacefully with lines of humor on his face.

An interesting face for any artist—and Gypsy's mother had painted it more than once.

Gypsy lifted an absent cheek for his kiss. "Hi, Poppy," she said vaguely.

"Hello, darling." Her father saluted the cheek, and then rested his hip against the corner of her desk. Conversationally he added, "There's a man up a tree in your front yard."

"Oh?" She briskly corrected a misspelled word. "That's Chase."

"An admirer, darling?"

"Neighbor." Gypsy finished a paragraph and briefly debated over the next one before beginning to type again. "Did you ask him why he was in the tree?"

"I didn't want to pry," her sire murmured.

Gypsy acknowledged the gentle remark with a faint twinkle as she pulled the completed page from Herman. "I suppose Corsair stole his car keys again," she explained cheerfully.

Allen Taylor didn't even blink. "When did Corsair start stealing keys?"

"Yesterday. Where's Mother?"

"Helping Chase, I assume. She went to see if he needed help."

"Oh. Half a minute, Poppy; let me finish this page and I'll be through for the day." Gypsy was trying desperately not to think about Chase's first meeting with her mother. But . . . oh, she wished she could be a butterfly poised on a flower out there. . . .

Just as she was pulling the last sheet out of Herman, her father spoke again. He'd wandered over to her bookcase, and now held the masked rider's souvenir in his hand.

"What's this?"

"What does it look like? It's a silver bullet obviously."

"Silver plated," her father corrected gravely.

"It's the thought that counts," Gypsy reproved.

"Oh. Where did you get it?"

"That's obvious too."

"I see." He placed the souvenir back on the shelf.

Gypsy's father was very good at not asking nosy questions.

They had just stepped into the living room when her mother and Chase came inside. And Chase looked so utterly bemused and fascinated that Gypsy wanted to burst out laughing.

Many mothers and daughters look like sisters; Gypsy and her mother looked like twins. The same height, roughly the same weight, the same short black curls and wide gray eyes. They were even dressed similarly in jeans and blue knit pullovers. It was an odd thing, but even if they were in different parts of the country, nine times out of ten Gypsy and her mother would wear at least the same colors on any given day.

Rebecca Taylor, née Thorn, looked eighteen. The only thing that set her apart from her daughter in looks was a single silver curl at her left temple. Her voice was different, slower and richer with age, but her conversation made Gypsy's sound positively rational by comparison. And she never missed a thing.

"Hi, Mother." Gypsy hugged her mother briefly. "I see you've met Chase."

"Yes. Gypsy, you need to talk to Corsair. Stealing keys is a very irritating habit."

"I will, Mother." Gypsy swallowed a laugh as she glanced at Chase. "Poppy—Chase Mitchell. Chase, my father, Allen Taylor."

Still bemused, Chase nearly forgot to shake hands.

It was a fun day. Gypsy's parents had the knack of setting anyone at ease immediately, and they both obviously liked Chase. As for Chase, he'd apparently decided to go with the tide. Although he still tended to blink whenever he looked at Rebecca—particularly whenever she and Gypsy were standing near each other—he was quickly back on balance again.

Rebecca commandeered the kitchen to cook lunch, towing Chase along behind her when Gypsy helpfully mentioned his culinary skill. Allen and Gypsy were almost immediately ordered to make a trip to the store when the cupboard was found to be bare. Corsair and Bucephalus got into the act, mainly by being constantly chased from the kitchen by Rebecca.

When Gypsy looked back on the day, she remembered snippets of conversations, frozen stills from the action.

"Why didn't you tell me that your mother was also your twin? I made a total fool of myself in that tree!"

"There are no fools in my mother's orbit—just interesting people."

"I wish I could believe that."

"Believe it. My mother *expects* to find strange men in trees."

"A sane man would run like a thief in the night."

"Are you sane?"

"Apparently not."

"He's a redhead."

"Yes, Mother."

"Temper?"

"So far, no. But give him time; I only met him Friday."

"I like his eyes. Would he sit for me?"

"Like a shot, I imagine. He likes your work."

"He cooks well."

"Yes, Mother. Military schools."

"Really? That explains it."

"Explains what?"

"He stands and moves like a soldier. Precise."

"I haven't noticed."

"Of course not, darling."

"Mother. . . ."

"I like your Chase, darling."

"He's not mine, Poppy."

"Better tell him that."

"I have. The man's deaf."

"The man has good taste."

"You're prejudiced."

"Slightly. Not that it matters."

"Gypsy, Corsair's sitting in the sink."

"Check his water dish, Mother."

"Chase, why do you keep letting Bucephalus inside?"

"Sorry, Rebecca, but he knocks."

"Do you let in every salesperson who knocks?"

"Only the ones with good legs."

"Chauvinist."

"Dyed-in-the-wool."

"Chase, what were you talking to Mother about? You look strange."

"I feel strange. She just told me the story of how Allen managed to catch her. No wonder you wouldn't tell me."

"Well, it's their story. Don't take it too much to heart, by the way."

"You mean, don't let it give me ideas?"

"Something like that."

"I wouldn't dare. You look like her, but you're not Rebecca. You'd come after me with a gun."

"I'm glad you realize that."

"Military schools don't produce idiots."

By the time Gypsy tumbled into bed that night, she was still laughing softly. The little party had broken up only an hour before, with Chase saying good night along with Rebecca and Allen.

Gypsy pushed Corsair off her foot and turned off the lamp, settling down to sleep.

The phone rang. Gypsy reached for it automatically. "Hello?"

"Did you dream about me last night?"

She smiled into the darkness. "I told you I would."

"Reality's better than dreams."

"Oh, really?"

"I could show you."

"I don't know who you are," she told him serenely.

"I could show you that too."

"It's better this way. Ships passing in the night, unseen."

"But lovers have to meet."

"It would destroy the mystery."

" 'But love is such a mystery,' " he quoted softly.

Gypsy found herself automatically quoting the last line of the verse. "And would you be 'such a constant lover'?"

"Eternally, love. Eternally. Sleep well."

Gypsy cradled the receiver slowly, gently. She plumped up her pillow and lay back, thinking whimsical thoughts. About a white horse and a masked rider. About an inept gardener and a marvelous cook. About a late-night caller who quoted obscure poetry and called her love.

About a lover.

Five

The old saying about time passing on winged feet had never meant anything to Gypsy until that next week. The days flew by.

Chase was in, out, and around. Going up the tree after Corsair became a morning ritual; no matter where Chase hid his keys (even under his pillow one night, he said), the cat always found them. Chase began to talk darkly about felines murdered in the night.

He didn't interfere unduly with Gypsy's work, although he insisted on making sure that she ate at regular intervals. So he either cooked, carted in a bag of "take-out" something, or took her out somewhere. He kept her laughing, continued his talk of seduction . . . and never once tried to follow through.

He kissed her occasionally, but Gypsy was never quite sure what kind of kiss it would be or where it would land. A gentle kiss on her forehead, a playful kiss on her nose . . . or a hungry kiss that left her lips throbbing and her knees weak.

Always prone to talk to herself, Gypsy was fast approaching the point of answering herself as well.

And Chase was obviously having problems of his own. He stalked in late Tuesday afternoon, tightly reining the first sign of temper Gypsy had ever seen in him. With what looked like heroic patience he announced, "There's a white cat in my bedroom closet that has chosen to have three kittens in a box containing my new dinner jacket."

Looking up from the page she'd been proofing, Gypsy blinked at him in bewilderment. "Well, what do you want me to do about it?" she asked reasonably.

Chase hung on to control. "Corsair," he explained through gritted teeth, "is standing guard at the closet door, and won't let me near them."

Frowning, Gypsy said reproachfully, "You aren't supposed to disturb newborn kittens."

Chase looked toward the heavens imploringly. Gypsy went on in a puzzled voice. "Why wasn't your dinner jacket hanging up? It should have been, you know."

"I didn't get the chance to hang it up. It was delivered yesterday; I just checked to make sure it was my order and left the open box in the bottom of the closet." He stared at her. "I thought you only had one cat."

"I do. She must be Corsair's girlfriend. I knew he had one around here, but I've never seen her."

"Couldn't we transfer the family over here?"

"With Bucephalus around? She'd only move them back, Chase. Cats are particular."

"Would you like me to tell you how much her nest is worth?" Chase asked politely.

Gypsy wasn't listening. "Chase, does she have blue eyes?"

He blinked. "I don't know. Corsair won't let me close enough to turn on the closet light, and it's dim in there. Why?"

"Well, if she's solid white and has blue eyes, she's probably deaf. I'll bet that's why Corsair's protecting her."

"Deaf?"

"It's fairly common. Some kind of genetic defect, I think."

He stared at her.

"There's cat food in the kitchen," Gypsy murmured, trying not to laugh. "Help yourself."

"Gee, thanks." He left.

Chase apparently became accustomed to his new pets. He gave Gypsy periodic reports and complained of being unable to sleep at night because of squeaks and rustles in his closet. He also made a sort of peace with Corsair, since it was impossible to get to his closet through a hostile cat. But the morning key-ritual continued.

And Gypsy's "night lover" continued to call. More obscure poems were quoted, and the conversations became more and more suggestive. She looked forward to the telephone calls each night and found that she was sleeping better than ever before. The calls were . . . a nice way to end the day, Gypsy thought.

Whenever he thought she'd been working too hard, Chase pulled Gypsy away from her typewriter. For a meal. For a walk on the beach. She didn't protest because she wasn't far enough into her story to become obsessed by it. But she knew that, sooner or later, Chase would discover a witch with a capital *B* sitting at the desk where his laughing companion had sat just the day before. She didn't look forward to that day.

In the meantime he kept coming up with things for them to do together. On Thursday afternoon he announced his latest plan.

"It's a masquerade party. In Portland."

"Are you serious? I thought those things went out with hoop skirts."

"I'm serious. It's for charity. So be a good girl and rent a costume tomorrow."

"I'm without a car, remember."

"I'll loan you mine."

"Like to live dangerously, don't you?"

"Always."

Gypsy reflected. "A masquerade. What kind of costume should I get? Or does it matter?"

"It matters. Old West."

"It'd serve you right if I went dressed as Calamity Jane."

"Don't do that. Your gun and my sword would get all tangled up when we dance."

"Your what?"

"Sword."

"What Old West character wore a sword?"

"Wait and see."

"Beast. Just for that, I'll come as a saloon girl."

"With feathers?"

"And sequins."

"Oh, good."

"You'll have to fight the other cowboys off me with a stick," she warned him gravely.

"I'll use my sword. I've always wanted to challenge somebody to a duel."

"Murder?"

"An affair of honor," he corrected nobly.

"Only if he's bigger than you. Otherwise it's murder. And you're talking to someone who knows murder."

Chase perched on the corner of her desk, obviously willing to stay and talk for a while. "So tell me, what's the perfect murder weapon?"

"No such animal." She chewed on a knuckle thoughtfully, her chair leaning backward until it was in imminent danger of going over. "I've always wanted to use the jawbone of an ass as a murder weapon. Interesting, huh?"

"I think that's been done."

"Not recently."

"You'd know better than me."

"Naturally."

"What's your plot in this book?"

"I don't talk about them until they're finished."

"That's cruel. You know I'm a mystery buff."

"No exceptions."

"Orders from the muse?"

"I suppose."

"I'll rig a Chinese water torture."

"Go feed your cats."

"That's 'the unkindest cut of all.' "

Gypsy drove Chase's car—*very* carefully—into Portland on Friday to get a costume. She toyed with the idea of finding the briefest saloon-girl costume possible, but discarded the notion.

She wanted something else.

She found the something else in the first costume-rental shop listed in the Yellow Pages. So far, Chase had seen her in nothing but shorts or jeans, and she wanted to wear something feminine.

And what could be more feminine than a long dress with a hoop skirt?

Gypsy didn't question her desire to look feminine. She wasn't questioning anything these days. And that was a bad sign. But she didn't want to question *that* either.

The boxes were loaded into the trunk of the Mercedes, and Gypsy left the rental shop. She ran a few errands in Portland, and then headed back toward the coast. It was late afternoon when she arrived back home.

She parked Chase's car in his driveway and collected the boxes from the trunk, absently putting the keys in the pocket of her jeans. Chase was nowhere to be seen; she shrugged, then carried the boxes across to her house.

She hung the costume in her bedroom, put away the few odds and ends she'd bought, and then settled down in the living room with the book of poetry she'd found in a used bookstore. Obscure poems and poets. Her "night lover" had her on her mettle, and she wanted to refresh her memory. She ended up going through two more books from her shelves, discovering a treasure-trove in Donne and Shakespeare.

"What *are* you doing?"

"Reading poetry. You did say that the masquerade is tomorrow night, didn't you?" She looked up from her cross-legged position on the floor to peer at Chase over the tops of her study glasses.

"Tomorrow night it is." He slid his hands into the pockets of his jeans and leaned against the bookcase, gazing down at her with a smile that looked as if it were trying hard to hide. "Do your murderers read poetry to their victims at the eleventh hour?" he asked gravely.

Gypsy pushed the glasses back up her nose. "Are you kidding?" She narrowed her eyes expressively. "My murderers stalk their victims on cloven hooves."

"Mmm. Then why are you reading poetry?"

"I like poetry, peasant."

"I beg your pardon, I'm sure."

Gypsy pulled off the glasses and waved them magnanimously. "You're forgiven."

"Thank you. There's another pair on top of your head."

"What?"

"Another pair of glasses."

That explained his trying-not-to-smile expression, Gypsy thought. She pulled off the second pair and set them absently on the bottom shelf of the bookcase.

"Does it take two pairs for you to read poetry?" he asked politely.

"Never mind."

He went on conversationally. "I've counted eight pairs of glasses scattered throughout this house. All in strange places. Like the pair I found in the refrigerator yesterday."

"I wonder why I put them in there?" Gypsy murmured, more to herself than to him.

"I haven't the faintest idea, and I don't think I want to know."

"Smart man."

"But what I *would* like to know"—he pointed at the corner of her desk, where a new acquisition was sitting—"is why you got *that* during your trip into Portland."

That was a statue of an eleven-inch-tall Buddha with a clock in its stomach. A broken clock.

Gypsy ran her fingers through her black curls

and gave him a harassed look. "I asked myself that. *What do you want with a Buddha with a clock in his tummy?* No answer. I must have been possessed. There was a garage sale, and somehow or other . . . Anyway I paid five bucks for it." She shook her head darkly.

Chase reached down and pulled her to her feet. He removed the glasses from her hand and tossed them lightly onto the desk. Then he caught her in a tight bear hug. "Gypsy," he said whimsically, "I can't tell you what a delight you are to me."

She pulled back far enough to look up at him blankly. "Because I bought a Buddha?"

He laughed. "No, because you're you. I thought we'd cook out tonight; how do you like your steaks?"

"Cooked." Gypsy made no effort to disentangle herself from his embrace.

"There goes that sharp tongue again, Gypsy mine. You shouldn't sass your elders; you're liable to get paddled."

"Are you my elder? I didn't know."

"I'm thirty-two, brat."

"Methuselah."

He swatted her jean-clad bottom lightly. "How do you like your steak?"

"Well done. And stop hitting me!"

"It'll teach you not to sass me." Chase was unrepentant.

"I'll sic Bucephalus on you!" she threatened.

"I've been slipping him snacks for days now; that dog loves me like a brother."

Gypsy pushed against his chest, curiously pleased when she couldn't budge him. "Leave! People over thirty can't be trusted."

"That slogan went out of style years ago."

"Only because the people saying it reached thirty."

"Are you sassing me again?" he demanded.

"For all I'm worth."

He bent his head and kissed her suddenly. But it wasn't a gentle kiss. It was demanding, probing, possessive, and just short of violent. He kissed her as though he wanted—needed—to brand her as his for all time. The kiss lasted for brief seconds only, but Gypsy felt as though every nerve in her body had been lanced with sheer electricity.

Chase stared down at her. "Are you through sassing?" he asked hoarsely.

Gypsy nodded mutely, wondering dimly when she was going to start breathing again.

"Good." He lowered her gently to her former position on the floor. "You finish reading your poetry. I'll yell when I get the grill going."

She nodded again, and watched him turn away. When he'd gone, she gazed blindly down until a line of Donne's jumped out at her from the open book before her on the carpet. "Take me to you, imprison me. . . ."

Why did it suddenly make her ache inside?

He called again that night, and their conversation took a turning point. No longer seductively suggestive, it was filled with gentle whimsy.

It was somehow easier to open up to a husky voice on the telephone, easier to admit to and show vulnerability. Alone in her bedroom, lying in the darkness, she could be the sensitive woman who mourned the loss of heroes. . . .

"I've missed you," he breathed softly. "The

sound of your voice haunts me, and yet I can't hear enough of it."

"You don't know me," she murmured in reply.

" 'Twice or thrice had I loved thee, before I knew thy face or name,' " he quoted tenderly.

Gypsy smiled into the darkness. He'd read Donne as well. "You don't know me," she repeated.

"Then tell me what I should know."

"I don't . . ." Her voice trailed away.

"Do you love rainbows?" he asked gently.

She smiled. "Yes."

"And the sound of rain in the morning?"

"Yes."

"Do you wish on stars?"

"I do now," she whispered, tears springing to her eyes.

"Then I know all that I should know," he said.

"Do you believe in unicorns?" she asked him.

"I do now," he replied.

"And life on other worlds?"

"Yes."

"And . . . heroes?"

"And heroes."

"I don't think you're real," she told him with a shaky laugh.

"I'm real, my love. Flesh and bone, heart and mind . . . and soul. And my soul aches for you."

Gypsy felt her heart stop for a moment and then pound on. What could she say to that? What could she possibly say?

But he didn't expect a response.

"Sleep well, my love. And dream of me."

She did.

It took Gypsy two hours to get into her costume late the next afternoon. She wasn't really accustomed to dresses of any kind, and even less to dresses fastened with tiny hooks and eyes, and beneath which were rather puzzling under- garments.

She had decided to stretch a point with the costume; otherwise, she'd have had to wear some- thing like calico if she wanted to be authentic. And since she had a hunch about Chase's costume, she felt free to stretch a point. Besides—*Old West* covered a lot of territory.

Gypsy giggled over the shiftlike garment and the frilly bloomers, but the corset presented a problem. She had a small waist, but she'd been astonished at how much smaller it appeared after the assistant at the costume shop had laced her up in the corset. Being Gypsy, she'd had the cor- set included without a single thought as to who would lace her up at home.

She finally put it on backward, laced it up, and then spent a few comical moments holding her breath and tugging. With the strings finally tied in a fierce knot, she collapsed on her bed, flushed and breathless.

No wonder the pictures of women in that era always looked so stiff, she thought. And no won- der genteel ladies were constantly swooning.

But once the dress was on, Gypsy understood why women had sacrificed comfort for the dic- tates of fashion.

The dress was black silk, and it rustled softly whenever she moved. Worn over a wide hoop— Gypsy had giggled for ten minutes after seeing herself in shift, bloomers, corset, and hoop—it was low-cut and off-the-shoulder. The corset nipped in her waist to a tiny span, and lifted her breasts until it seemed that a deep breath would get her arrested. She wasn't worried though; she could barely breathe anyway.

The dress was wicked for any era, and instantly branded her a scarlet woman in the era it pretended to belong to. The colorful splash of fake emeralds at her throat and dangling from her ears, however, loudly announced that she—or rather, her character—possessed wealth, and wealth could open doors even for scarlet women.

Gypsy had worked long and hard with her makeup, but was still faintly surprised to find that she had actually achieved a seductive look. The emeralds lent her gray eyes a green gleam, and the careful shading she'd done gave them a catlike slant. And the scrap of black silk that would serve as a mask only emphasized the seductive look.

"I look like a hussy," she told Corsair, who was sitting companionably at the foot of her bed, watching her. He'd stopped constantly guarding his family since Chase had proved to be reasonable.

"Is this what's called playing with fire, cat?" she asked him wryly.

Corsair yawned.

"Don't let me keep you awake," she begged politely.

By the time Chase knocked on the front door, Gypsy had donned the floor-length cloak and fastened it securely to hide the low neckline of her dress. Not that she was nervous about the cleavage, but there was no need to startle the man right off the bat, she decided mischievously.

Gypsy opened the door and gazed silently from the black-booted heels to the top of a Spanish-style hat. Her hunch had been right on target: He was dressed as Zorro.

"Are you going to run around tonight slashing Z's in the woodwork?" she asked him solemnly.

"Only if someone maligns your honor," he replied with equal solemnity and a deep bow.

She started to warn him that just about anyone would malign her honor once they got a good look at her dress, but decided to await developments.

"Black suits you," he noted critically, head to one side as he studied her masked face. "As a matter of fact, you look beautiful. Why are your eyes green?"

Gypsy flicked a dangling earring with one finger. "It's the emeralds. And thank you."

"You're welcome. It's a long drive to Portland, so we'd better get started. Just as soon as you tell me where you left my car keys."

"Car keys. . . ."

It took Gypsy half an hour to locate the keys; she'd left them in the pocket of her jeans and had forgotten to return them to Chase. He waited patiently while she searched, but every time she passed him, he fingered the hilt of his sword and gave her a threatening look.

The sixty-some-odd-mile journey to Portland took less than an hour.

"Do you know what the speed limit is?"

"Of course, I know."

"No wonder you killed Daisy."

"Funny. Besides, it's this damn sword; it keeps stabbing me in the foot."

"You're supposed to be wearing it on your *left* hip."

"Why?"

"You're right-handed."

"Oh. Remind me to change it around when we get there."

"Right. Are you sure you'll be able to dance in that thing?"

"Of course I will." There was a pause. "The couples dancing near us'll have to watch their step though."

The masquerade was being held in a huge recreation center on the outskirts of Portland. The charity involved was one for needy children. From the looks of the size of the crowd that had turned out, whatever goal had been set for this fund-raising event, it had been reached easily. Costumes were varied and ranged from the sublime to the ridiculous. Royalty from the Court of St. James vied with those of other European countries, and clashed with various fuzzy creatures from recent movies and assorted fairy-tale and nursery-rhyme characters. There was even one giant of a man who was dressed as Paul Bunyan, and kept wandering around asking if anybody'd seen his ox.

Refreshments had been set out along one wall, and the buzz and laughter of a hundred conversations filled the tremendous room. A small band of musicians tuned their instruments screechily in one corner.

Gypsy winced at a particularly discordant clash as Chase, standing behind her, removed her cloak and handed it over to the cloakroom attendant. "Are we supposed to be able to dance to that?" she asked wryly, turning to face him.

Chase's mouth fell open.

Suddenly remembering her dress, Gypsy fought to hide her smile. "Didn't know I was so well blessed, did you?" she asked him gravely.

His eyes lifted to her face, and he laughed. "Gypsy, you say the damnedest things!"

"What's a little bluntness between friends?"

"Oh, I wholeheartedly approve. Of the bluntness—and the dress. Shall we check out the refreshments?"

"Yes. I'm dying of thirst, but I won't be able to eat anything."

"Why not?" He took her arm and began leading her toward the refreshments.

"I'll tell you about it someday." Her voice was rueful.

He looked at her curiously. "Now you've got me wondering."

Gypsy thought of her afternoon's struggle, and her lips twitched. "Never mind."

"Gypsy . . ."

"Hang onto your sword, will you? You just stabbed that Louis in the shin."

"I wondered why he was glaring at me." Chase handed her a cup of punch with his free hand. "And don't try to weasel out of it; why can't you eat something?"

Gypsy glanced furtively around to make sure no one was close enough to overhear. "It's my corset," she told him in a stage whisper.

"Your what?"

"My corset. I can barely breathe, much less eat." Gypsy thoroughly enjoyed the struggle going on on his face.

After a moment he set his own cup of punch on the table, released his death grip on the hilt of his sword, and solemnly measured the span of her waist with both hands. "Yep. It's definitely smaller."

"Looks great to me," announced a strange masculine voice over Chase's left shoulder.

Chase turned suddenly, stabbing another Louis (or was it the same one?) in the shin as he greeted the tall man who'd come up behind him. "Jake, the last I heard, you were building something in Texas."

"Surprise! I finished building it."

Introduced to Jake Thomas a moment later, Gypsy's first impression was that Chase's builder friend was an absolute nut. He was big and rawboned, his size and obviously cheerful personality perfectly suited to his lumberjack costume. It took Gypsy only a moment to realize that he was the Paul Bunyan in search of his ox.

"You're the one who writes those mysteries Chase is always raving about, aren't you?" Jake asked Gypsy after the introduction.

Gypsy looked up at Chase in surprise, only to find him gazing studiously into space. "Well, I write mysteries," she answered Jake.

"You don't look it," Jake told her gravely, and at her expressive grimace, added, "You've heard that before, I take it?"

"Innumerable times."

A black cat wandered up just then, holding on to her long tail to avoid having it stepped on. She was about Gypsy's size, with a petite figure and blond hair escaping from beneath her ear cap. And she had large blue eyes that looked dumb but were obviously lying.

"Jake, how dare you leave me in the clutches of that King George? He kept bumping me with his stomach and stepping on my tail."

Laughing, Jake introduced Gypsy to his fiancée, Sarah Foxx. Chase she obviously knew, since she stood on tiptoe to kiss his cheek lightly.

"You write mysteries?" Sarah asked in surprise, studying Gypsy. "You—"

"—don't look like it," the other three chorused.

"I seem to be redundant," Sarah observed wryly.

"That's all right," Gypsy told her. "I'm getting used to it."

"I'll bet." Sarah gave her a friendly grin. "That's the price you and I pay for looking as if we can't string two words together."

Gypsy looked interested. "What do you do?"

"I'm a psychologist."

Gypsy felt an immediate affinity for the other woman. "Isn't it terrible? That nature played this awful trick and made us look dumb, I mean?"

"Yes, but it has its advantages. People are always bending over backward to do things for us because we look so helpless."

"There is that," Gypsy agreed thoughtfully.

Chase sighed in manful long-suffering. "Don't you two start talking about the failings of mankind, or Jake and I won't get to dance."

Sarah looked solemnly at him and said, totally deadpan, "You and Jake can dance if you like. It might look a little odd, but if *you* don't mind . . ."

"Cute, that's cute." Chase took a giggling Gypsy firmly by the arm. "Dance with me, Gypsy mine, before Sarah puts us both on her couch."

The musicians had struck up a waltz, and he swept her regally out onto the floor. One *ouch!* and two muffled *dammit*'s followed them.

"Chase, you're going to have to take off that sword."

"Zorro without his sword? Don't be ridiculous."

"They'll throw us out."

"They can't afford to refund our money."

"You're making enemies."

"We're supposed to be dancing in romantic silence here."

"How can we dance in romantic silence with curses following us all around the floor? See? You just stuck Louis again."

"He'll learn to keep out of my way."

"Chase—"

"All right, shrew! I'll take it off and let the cloakroom attendant keep an eye on it. But you're coming with me. I don't want anyone stealing you away from me."

"Who'd want to do that?"

"Louis. Revenge."

"Thanks a lot."

"You're welcome."

Six

Louis obviously wasn't in the market for revenge that night. As a matter of fact, he kept a respectful distance from Gypsy and Chase—sword or no sword. A couple of braver souls attempted to cut in on Chase, but retreated in some confusion when Zorro sneered at them.

Between dances Gypsy and Chase stood talking to Jake and Sarah. The two couples were apparently on the same wavelength; there was none of the normal awkwardness or guardedness of new acquaintances. By evening's end Gypsy knew that she had two new friends.

She was also a bit unnerved to realize that her response to Chase during the evening had been very much like Sarah's to Jake; teasing, playful, bantering. It shouldn't have surprised her, since the same type of thing had gone on since the day she'd met him. But it did surprise her.

It surprised her because she had never looked

at their relationship objectively—from the outside, so to speak. But in comparing them to the other couple, the similarities were startling. It was as though she and Chase were lovers of long standing. Companionable, playful, teasing, they reacted to each other with the certain knowledge of two people who were very close.

It gave Gypsy food for thought.

The party broke up around midnight, with invitations extended and accepted for a barbecue at Chase's house on Sunday afternoon, and the two couples went their separate ways: Sarah and Jake to the apartment they shared in Portland, and Gypsy and Chase toward the coast.

It was silent in the car for most of the trip, a companionable silence that neither chose to break. Gypsy was occupied by various thoughts and by the rumbling in her stomach; she had eaten nothing since breakfast, and was by now heartily cursing the binding, uncomfortable corset. She was also beginning to wonder how on earth she was going to get out of the thing; she'd never been very good with knots. And along the same lines was her dress; the tiny hooks and eyes had been nearly impossible to fasten, and she wasn't at all sure that she could *un*fasten them without tearing the rented costume.

A solution occurred to her, and Gypsy considered it idly. Dangerous. Definitely dangerous. Playing with fire for sure. She wondered why she wasn't at all concerned any longer about burning her fingers. It might have had something to do with the kiss Chase had bestowed during the unmasking at the party. It had been a definitely fiery kiss—a first cousin to Vesuvius. Her lips were still tingling.

And after that . . . why worry about burning her fingers?

Chase parked the Mercedes in his driveway, and they walked across to Gypsy's door. She located her key in the string purse dangling from her wrist, and Chase unlocked the door.

"Is the evening over, or are you going to ask me in?" he inquired politely.

"The evening is young. Besides, I have a favor to ask. Come in, please."

"A favor?" Chase followed her into the dimly lighted den, his cloak and mask landing beside Gypsy's on one of the chairs. "Your wish is, of course, my command."

"I'm so glad. It's a . . . delicate favor."

"So much the better." Just as she turned to face him he caught her in his arms. A faint, lazy smile lifted the corners of his mouth. "Gentlemanly courtesy aside, though, I'm afraid I have other things on my mind right now."

"Chase—"

He kissed her, and Gypsy promptly forgot all about the favor. She might have been vague, but she wasn't stupid; what woman would pass up an opportunity to revisit Vesuvius? She felt his hands lifting, the fingers threading through her black curls, and her own arms lifted to slide round his waist. His lips toyed with hers for a brief moment; gentle, sensitive. And then he abruptly accepted the unconscious invitation of her parting lips, deepening the kiss in a sudden surge of curiously yearning hunger.

Gypsy abandoned herself to sensation. A part of her stood back and watched, both disturbed and fascinated by the woman who gave herself up totally to addictive sensations. She felt one of his hands move to caress the side of her neck lightly, his thumb rhythmically brushing her jawline; his free hand slid slowly down her back, over bare flesh that tingled at the touch. The warmth of his mouth seduced, impelled, made her forget everything except the need to have more of this. . . .

The phone rang.

Gypsy wanted to ignore it. She *tried* to ignore it. But it was ringing persistently, and finally Chase raised his head with a groan.

"Oh, Lord! And we were doing so well too!"

She stared up at him, dazed, for a long moment, then firmly got a grip on herself. A warlock. He was definitely a warlock. She moved toward the phone as he reluctantly released her. Clearing her throat as she lifted the receiver, Gypsy managed a weak "Hello?"

"You've been out!" a wounded male voice accused sadly.

Gypsy slammed the phone down so hard and fast that she nearly caught her fingers beneath it. "Oh, God . . ." she whispered to herself, appalled. A stranger? Some nut had been calling her, and she'd—

"Who was that?" Chase had come up behind her and began to nuzzle the side of her neck.

"Uh . . . wrong number." She was glad he couldn't see her face; it probably scaled the limits of human shock.

He chuckled softly. "You obviously have no patience with wrong numbers; somebody's ears are still ringing."

Apparently not; the phone began ringing again.

Gypsy didn't move, she just stared at it silently.

"Persistent devil." Chase made a move toward the phone. "Want me to . . . ?"

"No!" Hastily Gypsy picked up the receiver, trying to ignore Chase's startled look. "Hello?"

"Darling, why did you—"

"I can't talk now," she interrupted hurriedly, and hung up before another word could be uttered. There was a dead silence from behind her. She decided not to turn around.

"Should I ask?" he inquired finally in a mild voice.

"No." Gypsy sought hastily for something to divert his mind. Although why she should feel so guilty . . . ! And who the *hell* had been calling her all this time? she wondered. "Uh . . . Chase, about that favor . . . ?"

"I'd forgotten. Other things on my mind, I'm afraid." His voice was disconcertingly formal. "What is it?"

Gypsy mentally flipped a coin. She lost. Or won. Or maybe, she thought miserably, it didn't matter either way. She arranged her face and turned to gaze up at him. "Would you please help me get these clothes off?" she requested baldly.

It diverted his mind.

Chase blinked at least three times, and Gypsy could definitely see some sort of struggle going on beneath his tightly held expression. And then he relaxed, and she knew that she had won after all. A jade twinkle was born in his eyes.

"I thought we were doing well," he murmured.

Gypsy fixed him with a plaintive look. "I don't think I can get them off by myself. The dress has tiny hooks and eyes, and the corset . . . well, I tied the strings in a knot. And I'm not very good with knots," she added seriously.

He sat down on the arm of the couch and

folded his arms across his chest, bowing his head and laughing silently.

"It's very uncomfortable!" she told him severely.

"Sorry." He wiped his eyes with one hand. "It's just . . . dammit, Gypsy—Cyrano de Bergerac couldn't romance you with a straight face!"

"Oh, really?" She lifted a haughty brow at him.

"Really." He pulled her into his lap, and both of them watched, totally deadpan, as her hoop skirt shot into the air and poised there like a quivering curtain.

She turned her head to stare at him. "You may have a point."

"Yes."

"This never happens to heroines in the movies."

"Uh-huh." Chase looked as though his expressionless face was the result of enormous effort and clenched teeth.

"They *never* get stuck in their dresses," Gypsy persisted solemnly.

"God forbid."

"Or lose control of their hoops."

He choked.

"Or have to put their corsets on backward."

Chase bit his bottom lip with all the determination of a straight man.

"Or ask a man, with absolutely no delicacy, to take their clothes off." Gypsy reflected a moment, then amended gravely, "Except a certain kind of heroine, of course."

"Of course," Chase agreed unsteadily.

There was a moment of silence, broken only by a peculiar sound. Gypsy looked down at her tightly corseted stomach disgustedly. "Or have stomachs that growl like volcanos," she finished mournfully.

It was too much for Chase. He collapsed backward on the couch, pulling Gypsy with him, unheeding and uncaring that her hoop was doing a fan dance in the air above them. He was laughing too hard to notice. So was Gypsy.

She finally struggled up, fighting her hoop every step of the way and sending Chase into fresh paroxysms of mirth. Sitting on the edge of the couch and clutching the hoop to keep it grounded, she requested breathlessly, "Please unfasten this damn dress—it hurts to laugh!"

Gaining a finger-and-toe-hold on his amusement, Chase rose on an elbow and began working with the tiny fastenings of her dress. They were undone much faster than they'd been done, and she was soon rising to her feet and wrestling yards of material up over her head. When she emerged, flushed and panting, she tossed the dress carelessly onto a chair and looked at Chase.

No man had ever beheld a woman stripping with more appreciation, she decided wryly. Chase was all but rolling on the couch, and if a man could die laughing, he was clearly about to.

She posed prettily, one hand holding the bare hoop and the other patting tousled curls in vain. The vision of herself in shift, bloomers, corset, and hoop obviously affected Chase just as it had her.

"I thought all men liked to see women in their underwear," she said provocatively.

Chase gathered breath for one sentence. "Take it off," he gasped. "Take it *all* off!"

Gypsy placed hands at hips and affected a

Mae West drawl. "You think I do this for free, buster? There's a cover charge, you know."

He laughed harder.

Uncaring of the ludicrous embellishments of fake emeralds dangling from her ears and around her neck, and delicate black high-heeled slippers, Gypsy discarded—with some difficulty—the hoop and went over to sit on the couch beside Chase. He'd struggled to a sitting position and was once more wiping his eyes.

"Pity you left your sword in the car," she said, struggling with the stubborn knot on her corset.

"Sorry," he murmured unsteadily. "I didn't know you'd need it."

Gypsy sighed, kicked off her slippers, and sat back, giving Chase a pleading look. "D'you mind? If I don't take a deep breath in the next few seconds, I'm going to be the first woman of the twentieth century to suffocate because of a corset."

Not bothering to hide his grin, Chase reached for the stubborn knot. "In the twentieth century?" he queried gravely.

"You can't make me believe that nobody ever died in one of these things. The lengths women go to for fashion!"

"You should try wearing a sword," he said.

"No, thanks. Besides, swords were for self-defense, not fashion. How could a woman defend herself with a corset?"

"It obviously gave her an edge in defending her honor," he pointed out, tugging at the stubborn knot. "I don't understand how the population of the world managed to increase during this stage of fashion."

"Carefully," she murmured. "Ouch!"

"Sorry. Maybe we'll need the sword after all. Could you inhale a little?"

Gypsy gave him a look reserved for those persons one step below the moron level in intelligence. "Are you kidding?"

"Cyrano would definitely find it an uphill struggle," Chase murmured wryly. "What are those things called?" He gestured.

"Bloomers."

There was a moment of silence, then Chase said carefully, "I see."

Gypsy crossed her ankles and linked her fingers together behind her neck, affecting a pose of comfort. "If my father were to walk in right now . . ."

"Yes?" Chase asked politely.

"Well, think about the picture we're presenting. Here I am in a very undressed state, with a man dressed all in black and bending over me in a very suggestive and villainous pose. . . ."

"Do you want to sleep in your corset?"

"I was just making conversation. It's not easy to sit here calmly and watch you trying to take my clothes off, you know."

"And you not even struggling! What's the world coming to?" he said in a shocked voice.

"Terrible, isn't it?"

"Definitely." He sighed. "I'm going to have to cut the strings."

"Oh, no, you don't! This thing's rented."

"What could a couple of strings cost?" he asked reasonably.

"It's the principle of the thing. Could you just try a little while longer? Please?"

"You like watching me suffer," he accused wryly.

"Are you suffering?" she asked interestedly.

"I'm dying by inches. I've been struggling to keep my hands to myself all night, and now here I am. You're at my mercy, dressed in a corset, bloomers, and some kind of top that I can see right through—"

"Keep your eyes on the corset," Gypsy muttered, embarrassed for the first time.

The jade eyes gleamed with mischief—and something else. "You're blushing," he announced, chuckling.

"I am not. If my face is red, it's due to lack of oxygen. I'm telling you—this thing's killing me!"

"Then you'll have to let me cut— There! That's got it. Now you can breathe again."

Gypsy took a deep, ecstatic breath while he removed the corset and tossed it on top of the dress and hoop. "Air!" she murmured blissfully. "Both lungs full. If you ever take me to another masquerade," she added flatly, "I'll go as a writer."

"I'll remember that." Chase's mind didn't seem to be on what he was saying. His left hand was resting on her flat stomach, separated from her skin only by the almost transparent linen of her shift. His jade eyes, darkening almost to black were gazing into hers.

Suddenly wordless, Gypsy watched as he leaned toward her slowly. She wondered dimly at the abrupt cessation of laughter, of humor. And marveled at how quickly her heart had leaped to a reckless rhythm. And then all academic wonderings ceased, faded into nothingness.

His lips touched hers lightly, and Gypsy was just about to abandon reason willingly when she felt him shaking with silent laughter. He lifted his head, then dropped it again abruptly, resting his forehead against her stomach.

"Poor Cyrano," he murmured helplessly. "Oh, poor Cyrano!"

Gypsy was bewildered for a moment, but then she both felt and heard her empty stomach rumbling. So much for the fires of ardor! she thought. "Sorry," Gypsy said with a sigh. "I haven't eaten since breakfast."

"So I gathered." He rose to his feet, still chuckling, and offered her a hand. "Come on, Pauline."

"As in *The Perils of*?" she inquired dryly, accepting the helping hand.

"Well, you've got to admit that you're batting a thousand," he pointed out ruefully. "I don't know what you've got in the fridge, but—"

"Tons of stuff," she interrupted, leading the way to the kitchen without a thought of her decidedly strange hostess outfit. "I called a takeout place this afternoon with a huge order; I had a feeling I'd be starving by the time we got back. Chinese food."

"At two A.M.?" Chase protested weakly.

"When do *you* eat Chinese food?" she asked politely, busily removing various boxes and cartons from the refrigerator.

He sighed. "Another stupid question."

"Can you get that pitcher of tea?"

"Tea on Sat— No, it's Sunday, isn't it? And here I thought you were breaking with tradition willingly."

"Have an egg roll."

"Might as well." He sighed again. "My plans for the evening seem to be all shot to hell."

"Sorry."

"You sound it. Pass the soy sauce, please."

Half an hour later, Chase finally spoke again,

diverting Gypsy's thoughts from her stomach and lungs—both full and content for the first time in hours.

"Gypsy?"

"Mmmm?" She bit into her third egg roll with relish.

"Could you at least button the top button?"

Startled, she instinctively looked down to see that her shift was displaying more of her charms than her dress had. Before she could say anything, he was going on conversationally.

"It's not that I hate looking, you understand. But since the end result of this Chinese culinary retribution is bound to be acute indigestion, I don't think I really need to add skyrocketing blood pressure to my sleepless night."

Gypsy hastily buttoned the top button. "Sorry."

"Think nothing of it," he begged politely. Five minutes later he rose abruptly and left the kitchen without a word. When he returned, he was carrying her black cloak, which he dropped around her shoulders. "Not enough coverage," he said gruffly.

She fastened the cloak, hoping that he didn't think she'd been deliberately teasing him. "Chase, I'm sorry. I didn't mean—"

"I know," he said with a sigh, resuming his seat. "If I've learned anything about you, Gypsy mine, it's that the obvious answer is never the correct one."

"Is that good or bad?"

"I'll answer that question when *I* find out the answer."

Gypsy followed him to the front door some time later, feeling curiously vulnerable and not sure why. She held on to the cloak and gazed up at him as he opened the door, wondering if he was disappointed at the unplanned turn the evening had taken. She couldn't tell from his expression.

"Remember the barbecue tomorrow—I mean, today. Jake and Sarah will be at my place around three."

She nodded. "I'll remember."

It's been . . . an unusual evening, Gypsy mine." He grinned suddenly. "I don't think I ever enjoyed an evening half as much in my life. Has anyone ever told you that you're something different?"

"No." The relief in her voice was obvious even to her.

"An oversight, I'm sure." He bent his head to kiss her quickly, adding in a whisper, "And you look cute as hell in bloomers." With a cheerful wave he vanished into the night.

Gypsy slowly closed and locked the door, smiling to herself. She went through the house to the kitchen. She cleaned up in her usual manner, dropping cartons into the trash can and anything not made of paper into the sink. She let Bucephalus and Corsair in from the backyard, fed them (ignoring Corsair's irritated grumbles at being left outside for so long), and went up to bed.

"You hung up on me," he told her sadly.

Gypsy rubbed sleep-blurred eyes and stared at her bedside clock. She'd been in bed half an hour. "Who *are* you?" she demanded, by now more angry and frustrated than horrified.

"I'm yours, my love—"

"Stop it!" she snapped.

"You're angry with me?"

"What do you think?" she asked witheringly.

"Some *nut* calls me every night, and I'm supposed to be entranced?"

"Last night you—"

"Last night," she interrupted, "I thought I knew who you were."

"But you know who I am," he murmured whimsically. "We meet every night in your dreams."

"Quit it!"

"You belong to me."

"I'm calling the police."

"Mine."

She hung up. Hard.

The phone rang. And rang. Gypsy finally picked it up with a rueful sense of great-oaks-from-little-acorns-grow. Why had she ever started this?

" 'The day breaks not, it is my heart,' " he whispered.

"Stop quoting Donne, dammit," she ordered.

"So cruel. . . ."

Gypsy could feel herself weakening. Whoever he was, this man had seen the vulnerable side of her. And she wondered dimly why she was so sure that he had shown her a side of himself that no one else had ever seen. It had to be Chase. But how *could* it be? Nothing made sense!

"Stop calling me," she heard herself pleading.

"Would you ask me to stop breathing? It's the same, my love. The very same. I'd die. I love you."

"Don't love me. I . . . I'm in love with someone else." She cradled the receiver gently.

In the darkness of her bedroom Gypsy slid from the bed and dressed in jeans and a sweat shirt. She barely heard the phone begin to ring again as she left the room.

With Bucephalus as escort she went through the house to the kitchen, and then out into the yard. She crossed to the stairway down to the beach. Moments later she was sitting in her favorite seat and gazing out over a moonlit ocean, the big dog at her feet. She listened to the muted roar of the surf; she looked up to count the stars, wishing on a few; she might even have cried a little bit.

She thought about loving Chase.

Gypsy wasn't quite herself at the barbecue later that day. She might have been developing a cold after sitting on a windy beach for the better part of a cool June night. Or it might have been lack of sleep. Or it might have been a last defensive gesture in a battle lost for good.

Whatever it was, Chase and her two new friends obviously noticed.

Being Gypsy, she couldn't pretend that everything was fine. She couldn't hide her almost nervous silences in response to Chase's teasing. She couldn't recapture the light bantering of the past days. And she couldn't help but stiffen at his lightest touch.

As the barbecue progressed his jade eyes began to follow her with an anxious, puzzled expression, and he asked her more than once what was wrong. She always answered with a meaningless smile and a swift change of subject.

By the time Gypsy picked her way through the meal of excellent barbecued ribs, baked potatoes, rolls, and crispy salad, Sarah had obviously seen enough. Laughing, she ordered the men (who had cooked) to do the cleaning up, seized Gypsy's arm in a companionable grip, and led her across the yard to the railing at the cliff.

"If you'll forgive an old, outworn cliché," she told the other woman ruefully, "the atmosphere between you and Chase is thick enough to cut with a blunt knife. You two have a fight? Or am I being incurably nosy?"

Having seen more than enough of the ocean the night before, Gypsy turned her back on the view and leaned against the railing. She smiled slightly and murmured, "No to both questions."

Sarah was silent for a moment. "Forgive me if I'm probing—a psychologist's stock-in-trade, I'm afraid—but can I help?"

"Is your couch free?" Gypsy managed lightly.

"For a friend in need? Always." Sarah leaned back against the railing and pulled a pack of cigarettes and a lighter from the pocket of the man's shirt she was wearing over a halter top. "Dreadful habit. Want one?"

"Thanks." Gypsy accepted a light.

"I didn't think you smoked," Sarah said.

"I quit three years ago."

"Uh-huh. But now . . . ?"

"Am I on your couch?" When Sarah nodded with a smile, Gypsy murmured, "I need a temporary crutch, I suppose." She blew a smoke ring and concentrated on it.

"Why?"

"To keep from falling flat on my face. Although I think it's too late to prevent that."

"Falling as in 'in love'?"

"Are you that perceptive or am I that obvious?" Gypsy asked wryly.

"A little of both. You watch him when he isn't

watching you. And another woman always knows."
She paused. "You're scared." It was a statement.

"Terrified," Gypsy admitted almost inaudibly.

"Why? Chase is a wonderful man." She smiled
when Gypsy looked at her. "I've known him longer
than I've known Jake; he introduced us."

Gypsy wondered suddenly—an inescapable
feminine wondering—and Sarah obviously understood; her smile widened.

"No, there was nothing serious between Chase
and me. Just friendship. He's been searching ever
since I've known him. Last night I realized that he
wasn't searching any longer."

Gypsy fixed all her concentration on grinding
the stub of her cigarette beneath one sandal.

Sarah went on slowly, thoughtfully. "He's been
lonely, I think. His upbringing . . . well, he missed
a lot. Don't get me wrong—Chase and his father
have a very good relationship. But he missed being
part of a family. He missed the carefree, irrespon-
sible years. I don't think he's ever done a reckless
thing in his life."

Gypsy, thinking of a masked rider on the
beach, smiled in spite of herself.

Sarah was obviously observing her closely. "Or
maybe I'm wrong about that. You've been good for
him, Gypsy."

Gypsy moved involuntarily, not quite sure that
she wanted to hear this; not quite sure she could
stand to hear it.

"You've unlocked a part of his personality."
Sarah's voice was quiet and certain. "He was so
relaxed last night, so cheerful and humorous. I've
never seen him like that before. And he looked at
you as if you were the pot of gold at the end of the
rainbow."

"Please . . ." Gypsy murmured.

"What is it? What's the problem?"

"Me," Gypsy said starkly. "I'm the problem. I'm afraid—very much afraid—that I'll ruin things between us."

"How?"

"My writing." Gypsy showed Sarah a twisted smile. "He doesn't understand—and I don't think you will." She fumbled for an explanation. "Sometimes I get . . . obsessed. The story fills my mind until there's no room for anything else. For days or weeks at a time." She laughed shortly. "A friend with a couple of psychology courses under his belt told me once that I had a split personality."

"No," Sarah disagreed dryly. "Just an extremely creative mind. One out of every ten writers goes through roughly the same thing." She smiled when Gypsy gave her a look of surprise. "Creative minds fascinate scientists and shrinks; research has been done, believe me. You're not alone."

It was strangely reassuring, Gypsy thought. "But can Chase adapt to those kinds of mood swings? Sarah, I'm an absolute shrew! My own parents couldn't live with me once I started writing. And I'm no bargain when I'm *not* obsessed! I can't cook, I hate housework, I'm untidy to a fault—totally disorganized."

"Has any of this bothered Chase so far?" Sarah asked reasonably.

"No. But we're not living together."

"I'll bet he's around a lot though."

"Yes, but it's not the same."

"True." Sarah lifted a quizzical brow. "You won't thank me for pointing out that you're crossing your bridges before you come to them."

Gypsy sighed. "Meaning that all these rocks I'm throwing in my path may turn out to be more imagined than real, and why don't I give it a chance?"

"Something like that."

"Let's drag out another cliché. I'm afraid of getting hurt."

"Welcome to the human race." Sarah's voice was as sober as Gypsy's had been.

"Close my eyes and jump, huh?"

"Either that—or don't take the chance. And spend the rest of your life wondering if it would have been worth it." After a moment of silence Sarah added softly, "Some smart fellow once said something about it being better to have loved and lost. . . . I have a sneaking suspicion that he knew what he was talking about. But I don't think you'll lose."

"Why not?"

"Because I think you'll find that Chase is as adaptable as a stray cat. I think you'll find that he'll treasure the laughter *and* the fights, that he may even make it easier for you. I know he'll try."

"And I couldn't ask for more than that," Gypsy said softly.

The two women smiled at each other, and Gypsy added wryly, "Keep a couple of hours of couch time open, will you, friend? I just may need them."

Sarah laughed. "I'll do that. But I don't think you'll need them. Shall we join the menfolk, friend? Jake should be swearing a blue streak by now; he hates cleaning up as much as you do."

"*Nobody* hates it as much as I do."

"Better hang on to Chase, then. With him it's sheer habit."

"Military schools have their uses."

And on that light note they joined the men.

Seven

Gypsy relaxed a bit during the next few hours. She was still thoughtful, introspective, but able to respond naturally to Chase. And she no longer stiffened when he touched her. Chase was patently relieved, although obviously still puzzled.

A late afternoon shower sent them inside around five, where they sprawled in various positions in the den and commenced a spirited game of charades. Sarah was the hands-down winner with her comical silent rendition of "My Old Kentucky Home" and received a standing ovation from the others. A fire was kindled in the fireplace as the rain continued outside, and Sarah and Jake went happily to raid Chase's kitchen for popcorn.

Gypsy sat silently on the couch, trying not to think too much about the jade eyes gazing up at her. Chase was lying on the couch with his head in her lap, and she could feel the steady beat of his heart beneath the hand resting on his chest. She stared into the fire.

"All day long," Chase said in a musing voice, "I've had this weird feeling, Gypsy mine."

Reluctant to meet his eyes, Gypsy nonetheless looked down. "About what?" she asked lightly.

"It's hard to explain." Chase toyed absently with her fingers. "As if . . . Juliet was about to shove Romeo off the balcony. As if Cleopatra told Marc Antony to walk the plank of her barge. As if Lois Lane asked Superman to take a flying leap."

Gypsy couldn't help but smile.

"As if you were trying to find some way of saying good-bye to me, Gypsy mine," he finished quietly.

She felt the utter stillness of the room, the level, searching gaze of his eyes, and her smile died. She shook her head slowly. "No."

He lifted her hand to cradle it against his cheek. "I'm glad." His voice was husky. A faint twinkle lighted the darkness of his eyes. "Besides—I wouldn't let you run me off with a loaded gun. Don't you know that by now?"

"Masterful," she murmured in response, her free hand unconsciously stroking his thick copper hair.

"Always." He pressed his lips briefly to the palm of her hand. "Which reminds me, about that phone call last night . . ."

Gypsy's faint smile remained. This was one subject she had been prepared for. "What about it?"

"That's just it: what about it? Why do I get the feeling I have a rival for your affections?"

"Sheer imagination."

"Will you tell me who it was?" He wouldn't be put off.

"Can't. I don't know myself." Her smile widened at his skeptical look. "I swear. It was my—uh—mystery lover. He calls every night." She carefully studied Chase's blank look; if he was acting, he deserved an Oscar, she thought wryly.

"Have you called the police?" he demanded.

"No." Gypsy wasn't about to explain *that*.

"Gypsy—"

"He's harmless, Chase. Besides . . . I like him."

Chase stared at her. "Maybe *I* should start calling you," he muttered.

"Maybe you should. And muffle your voice a bit."

"What? Why?" He looked thoroughly bewildered.

"Never mind." Gypsy looked up as Sarah and Jake entered with the popcorn. "Oh, good. Popcorn!"

Both the rain and the other couple had gone by eleven that night, after a late supper of leftover barbecue and a shoot-'em-up western on television. After Sarah and Jake had driven off, Gypsy felt more than a little let down when Chase solemnly offered to walk her home. She wondered irritably if he was trying to drive her crazy, then thought of the night before with a smothered giggle. Well, maybe he had cause!

As soon as they stepped out onto the porch, Chase stopped her with a frown. "You'll get your feet wet." As though she were contemplating a walk across crushed glass, he added, "Sandals are no protection." He swung her easily into his arms and started across the darkened lawn.

Gypsy linked her fingers together at the nape

of his neck. "Let me guess." Her voice was grave. "Sir Walter Raleigh? The White Knight?"

"The former."

"No cape to lay across a puddle?" she asked in a wounded voice.

"No puddle," he pointed out. "And the cape's rented."

"Details, details," she said airily.

"Don't pick on me when I'm trying to be heroic," he complained mildly.

"Sorry. Shall I change the subject, Walter?" She felt his arms tighten, and added hastily, "I'll change the subject. I've been meaning to ask you what you named your cat."

"She's not my cat, she's Corsair's cat. And he can have her back whenever he wants her."

"Uh-huh. The mailman told me Friday that you'd been asking around to see if she has a home hereabouts. And you ran an ad in the paper too."

"Busybody," Chase muttered.

Gypsy ignored the interruption. "So you found out that she's homeless?"

He sighed. "Not anymore."

"I thought so. What did you name her?"

If a man could squirm while walking and carrying a grown although pint-size woman, Chase squirmed. "Cat."

"Try again," she requested solemnly.

He sighed again. "Angel. Dammit."

Gypsy bit back a giggle. "Those blue eyes get 'em every time," she said soulfully.

Not really uncomfortable, Chase laughed softly. "Corsair's obviously been talking to her; she thinks she's a queen. I've moved the family into one of the spare bedrooms, and she keeps trying to move them back. One of us is going to give up sooner or later."

"Bet I know which one."

Chase dipped her threateningly over a very wet hedge. "And just which one do you bet it'll be?" he asked politely.

"Angel, of course." Gypsy giggled. "I have every faith in your perseverance, Walter."

"Smart lady." He stepped onto her front porch and set her gently on her feet. But he didn't release her. "Busy tomorrow?"

Gypsy managed to nod firmly, even though she couldn't seem to make her fingers remove themselves from his neck. "I have to work. I've fallen behind."

"My fault?" he asked wryly.

"No. The first half of a book is always slow." She hesitated, wanting to warn him of what would surely come, but dimly aware that it was something he'd have to find out for himself.

"You'd better get some sleep, then." One finger lightly touched the faint purple shadows beneath her eyes. "You look tired."

"I'm not." Gypsy felt heat sweep up her throat at the hasty reply. But the truth was that she *didn't* feel tired. She felt on edge, restless, and sleep was the last thing on her mind.

Unfortunately Chase apparently wasn't picking up undercurrents tonight.

"Good night, Gypsy mine."

He kissed her. On the nose.

Leaning back against the closed front door after he'd gone, she automatically turned the deadbolt and fastened the night latch.

Dammit.

She frowned as Bucephalus came into the

hallway and wagged a long tail at her. "Out?" she queried dryly. Bucephalus woofed softly.

Sighing, Gypsy went through the house to the kitchen, letting him out and Corsair in. "You're wet, cat," she muttered. She looked at the few dishes in the sink, mentally flipped a coin, and turned away from them. She dried Corsair and fed him, then let Bucephalus back in and dried and fed him. Gypsy ignored the dishes. Again.

Restlessly she took a long shower, changing the water from hot to cold halfway through and musing irritably over the untruth of certain remedies. She killed time by washing her hair, then stood naked in front of the vanity in the bathroom as she dried it with her dryer.

She stood there for a long moment after the buzz of the dryer died into silence, staring into her own eyes. Resolutely she mentally flipped another coin.

The gown was in the bottom drawer of her dresser—just where Rebecca had placed it on one of her visits.

"You might need it, darling."

"I have the only mother on the West Coast who advises her daughter to go out and seduce a man."

"Surely not. Look at the statistics."

Silently Gypsy slipped the gown over her head. It was white silk, nearly transparent, and as form-fitting as a loving hand. Delicate lace straps were almost an afterthought to hold up the plunging **V** neckline. The silk was gathered slightly just beneath the **V**, then fell in a cascade of filmy material to her feet.

The matching peignoir was long-sleeved, made

of see-through lace to the waist and silk from waist to floor. It tied in a little satin bow just at the *V* of the gown.

Gypsy slipped on the high-heeled mules and studied herself in the dresser mirror, a bit startled. Normally she wore a T-shirt to bed; seductive silk nightgowns had never been a part of her wardrobe. This one suited her, however. The stark whiteness emphasized her creamy tan and raven's-wing hair, and turned her eyes almost silver. Almost.

She scrabbled through three drawers to find the bottle of Christmas perfume never opened, locating it finally and using only a drop at the gown's *V* neckline.

"I'm going to feel like an absolute fool if this doesn't work out," she muttered to herself, leaving her bedroom after a hurried glance at the clock. It was just after midnight, and she didn't want to be around if her "night lover" decided to call tonight.

She left the pets in the kitchen, closing the back door behind her but not locking it. Who knew when she'd be back? She stood on the porch for a few moments, gazing over at Chase's house; only a few dim lights were on. Gypsy stepped off the porch . . . and her courage deserted her.

Only half aware that her high heels were sinking into the wet ground with every step, Gypsy began to pace back and forth. She held up the long skirt as she walked, absently addressing whatever shrub or flowering plant happened to be handy.

"*Now* what? Do I go over and ask to borrow a cup of sugar? In this outfit? Not exactly subtle, Gypsy. Why don't you just hit the man over the head with a two-by-four?"

She frowned fiercely at an inoffensive holly bush. "So what if he rejects you? You're a big girl—relatively speaking. You can handle it. The world won't come crashing down around your ears if the man laughs at you. Will it?"

Since the holly bush remained mute, she paced on. A rosebush listened meekly to her next strictures.

"You're a grown woman, dammit! Why don't you act like one? You're only *technically* innocent, after all. You've probably seen things he's never seen! Why, you spent an entire summer observing the D.C. plainclothes cops, and if *that* didn't show you life, I don't know what would!"

The rose didn't venture a response, so Gypsy started to turn away. But she nearly fell. Regaining her balance, she looked down slowly. She was standing completely flat-footed: both heels had sunk completely into the wet earth.

Using words her mother had never taught her, Gypsy stepped out of the shoes. Still holding her skirt up, she bent over, wrestled the shoes from the clinging ground, and flung them angrily toward the house.

"A grown woman," she muttered derisively. "Just call me Pauline!"

Courage totally gone and ruefully aware that she couldn't pull off a seduction even if somebody drew her a diagram, Gypsy abandoned the idea. It would have to be up to Chase, she decided. And if she'd said "No involvement!" one time too many, then that, as the man said, was that.

Miserably wide-awake, Gypsy finally headed for the stairs leading down to the beach. Why waste her outfit? Let the moon have a thrill.

It was unusually warm for early June, and

she briefly debated a moonlight swim before discarding the notion. It wasn't all that warm. And she didn't feel like swimming. She felt like sitting on her rock and crying for an hour or two. Or three.

Blind to everything except inner misery, she made for her rock as soon as the stairs had been successfully negotiated. But normal vision took over when she reached the rock. There was a white towel lying on it.

Gypsy picked up the towel slowly, blankly. Had someone left it here, or—Chase! Swimming alone? She turned quickly toward the roaring ocean, a sudden fear filling her sickeningly. It drained away in waves of relief as she saw him.

The huge orange moon, hanging low in the sky, silhouetted his head and shoulders as he moved toward the beach. Gypsy watched, hypnotized by the unforgettable sight of him rising from the ocean as raw as nature had made him.

He was all wild, primitive grace, curiously restrained power, she thought. His wet flesh glistened in the moonlight; rippling muscles were highlighted, shadowed. It was as if the Creator had begun with a jungle cat and then decided to mold a man instead from the living flesh. He was bold and strong and male, Gypsy felt—a living portrait of what a man could be. And Gypsy's heart nearly stopped beating.

She fixed her eyes on his shadowed face as he stopped before her, automatically handing him the towel with nerveless fingers. "You shouldn't swim alone," she said, wondering at the calm tone.

"I know." His voice was husky. He slowly knotted the towel around his lean waist.

Gypsy tried in vain to read his expression; the moon behind him prevented it. "Why did you?"

"I flipped a coin. Swimming won over a cold shower."

"They don't work, you know." She laughed shakily. "Cold showers, I mean."

"Have you tried?" he murmured, one hand lifting to brush a curl from her forehead.

She nodded. "Tonight. It didn't help."

His hand moved slowly downward, the knuckles lightly brushing along the plunging *V* of her gown until he was toying with the little satin bow. "And . . . you were coming to me, Gypsy mine?"

Gypsy swallowed hard, mentally burning her bridges. "I—I was. But I lost my courage."

"Why?"

He was nearer now, and she could see the cat-like gleam of his jade eyes in the shadowy face. What was he thinking? "Because . . . I was afraid. Afraid you'd laugh at me."

"*With* you, yes. At you, never." His voice matched the muted roar of the ocean in its infinite certainty. His fingers abandoned the bow to slide slowly around her waist, his free hand lifting to cradle her neck. "You're so lovely. I thought I'd dreamed you. And now I'm afraid I'll wake up."

Gypsy felt damp, hair-roughened flesh against her palms, aware only then that she'd lifted her hands to touch his muscular chest. The pounding of the surf entered her bloodstream; the moonlight blinded her to reason. "If you wake up," she breathed, "wake me up too."

Chase made a soft, rough sound deep in his throat, bending his head to kiss her with a curiously fervent hunger. She could feel the restraint in his taut muscles, the fierce desire he couldn't hide, and a fire ignited somewhere deep in her inner being. Her arms slid up around his neck as Chase crushed her against his hard length, and Gypsy gloried in the strength of his embrace.

She met the seductive invasion of his tongue fiercely, her fingers thrusting through his thick hair and her body molding itself to his. Hunger ate at her like a starving beast, stronger than anything she'd ever known before.

In a single blinding moment of understanding, of clarity, she realized why she was taking this chance, why she was willing to risk pain. It was simply because she had no choice. This—whatever it was—was stronger, far stronger, than she was.

Chase lifted his head at last, breathing roughly, harshly. She could feel his heart pounding against her with the same untamed rhythm of her own. Staring up at him with dazed eyes, she realized that she was trembling, and that he was too.

"Let me love you, Gypsy mine," he pleaded thickly. "I need you so badly, so desperately . . ."

It wasn't in Gypsy to refuse, to protest. It just wasn't in her, she realized. She tightened her arms around his neck, rising up on tiptoe to press shaking lips to his, telling him huskily, "I thought you'd never ask. . . ."

He kissed her swiftly and then swung her up easily into his arms, heading across to the stairs leading up to his backyard. Surprisingly he chuckled softly. "I wouldn't dare try making love to you on the beach, sweetheart," he murmured whimsically. "One of us would be bound to get bitten by a sand crab . . . or something."

Gypsy found herself smiling. "Just call me Pauline."

"I'd rather call you mine." His arms tightened as

he climbed the stairs, her slight weight obviously not bothering him in the least. "Fair warning. . . . I'm playing for keeps." He stopped at the top of the stairs, looking down at her as if waiting for her to change her mind . . . or to commit herself.

She fought back a sudden unease. "Can we talk about that tomorrow?" she asked softly, her lips feathering along his jawline.

"I'm not sure." His voice had grown hoarse. "I think I should have it in writing with you, sweetheart. You're so . . . damn . . . elusive!"

"Not really," she murmured, fascinated by the salty taste of his skin. "But if you keep standing here, it's going to start raining or something, and ruin the mood. . . ."

Rather hastily Chase headed for the deck. "You're so right, Pauline!"

Gypsy laughed, but her laugh faded away as he carried her through the glassed-in half of the deck to the sliding glass doors leading to his bedroom. The doors were open, and he brushed aside the gauzy drapes and carried her inside.

His bedroom was lighted only by a dim lamp on the nightstand. The covers were thrown back on the king-size bed, evidence of his inability to sleep. The room was definitely a man's room: solid, heavy oak furniture, earth tones—a place for everything and everything in its place. But there was a curious sensitivity in the unusual seascapes on the walls; they were lonely, bleak, riveting in their otherworldly aloneness.

Gypsy noticed little of the room; her full attention was focused on Chase. She could see his face clearly now in the lamplight, and the undisguised need gleaming in his jade eyes held her spellbound. She'd never seen such a look in a man's eyes before, and it made her suddenly, achingly aware of the hollow emptiness inside herself.

He set her gently on her feet beside the bed, his fingers lifting to fumble at the little satin bow. "Gypsy . . . I want you to be sure," he said roughly, as if the words were forced from him.

Shrugging off the lacy peignoir, she said unsteadily, "The only thing I'm sure of is that I'm glad I found you on the beach tonight."

His eyes darkening almost to black, Chase bent his head to touch his lips to hers as if she were something infinitely precious. His hands brushed the lacy straps of her gown off her shoulders, and Gypsy felt the cool slide of silk against her flesh as the gown fell to the deep pile of the carpeted floor. Her arms slid up around his neck, the searing shock of flesh meeting flesh sending tremors through her body as he crushed her against him.

His hands moved up and down her spine, pressing her even nearer, his mouth exploring hers as if he could never get enough of her. Tongues clashed in near-violent hunger as Gypsy matched his need with her own. She lost herself in that moment, something primitive possessing her with the strength of a fury.

Gypsy felt she wasn't close enough to him, could never be close enough, and the realization was maddening. She fumbled with the towel at his waist, flung it aside, just before he lifted her into his arms, placed her gently on the bed and came down beside her. Gypsy looked up at him, her eyes heavy with desire, watching as his gaze moved slowly over her body.

"So perfect," he murmured huskily. "So tiny

and perfect. . . ." He bent his head, capturing the hardened tip of one breast with fervent lips.

Her senses spiraled crazily as his hands and lips explored. She was floating, being pulled inexorably in a single direction, and the current was too strong to resist. She felt the sensual abrasiveness of his hands, the heated touch of his mouth, and moved restlessly in a vain effort to ease the tormenting ache inside her.

"Gypsy. . . ." He rained kisses over her face, her throat; he took her hand and placed it on his chest. "Touch me, sweetheart. I need your touch. . . ."

Eagerly, driven by curiosity, by a starving sense of not knowing enough of him, she touched, explored. She felt the thick mat of dark gold hair curling on his chest, the muscles bunching and rippling with every move. Her fingers molded wide shoulders, traced along his spine, slid around to marvel at his flat, taut belly.

"I didn't know," she whispered, almost to herself.

"What?" he breathed, his mouth slowly trailing fire along a path leading him downward. The sensitive skin of her lower stomach quivered at the touch.

Gypsy gripped his shoulders fiercely, biting back a soft moan. "That a man could be so beautiful," she gasped.

"*You're* beautiful," he rasped softly, his fingers probing gently, erotically, until they found the heated center of her desire. "So sweet, Gypsy mine. . . ."

She was only dimly aware of her nails digging into his flesh, her eyes wide and startled at sensations she'd never experienced before. A strange tension grew within her, winding tighter and tighter until there was no bearing it. "Chase . . ." she pleaded hurriedly, desperate to reach some unknown place, frantic to tap the critical mass building inside her frail body.

"Yes, darling. . . ." He rose above her, his breathing as rough and shallow as hers, eyes blazing darkly out of a taut face. With almost superhuman control he moved gently, sensitively.

Gypsy knew that he was being careful, trying not to hurt her. But the primitive fury possessing her burst its bounds, escaping with the exploding suddenness of a Pacific storm. She took fire in his arms, as wild as all unreason, giving of herself with passionate, innocent simplicity. She drew him deep inside herself fiercely, caught him in the silken trap of woman unleashed, held him with every fiber of her being. He was hers. For one brief, eternal moment he was hers, and she branded him. . . .

Gypsy barely stirred when Chase drew the sheet over their cooling bodies. Nothing short of a massive earthquake would have budged her from his side, and she didn't care how obvious that fact was to him. She felt drained, contented, and very much at peace.

"Gypsy?" He was raised on one elbow, gazing down at her with a sort of wonder in his eyes.

She looked up at him, smiling, much the same wonder shining in her eyes. Without thought she lifted a hand to touch his cheek, her smile turning misty when he held the hand with his own and gently kissed the palm.

"Rockets," he murmured whimsically, smiling crookedly at her. "And bells . . . and shooting stars . . . and earthquakes."

"You're welcome," she told him solemnly, reaching for humor because she felt the moment was almost unbearably sweet.

Chuckling, he drew her even closer, arranging her at his side and wrapping his arms around her. "You're quite a lady, Gypsy mine."

She decided that his shoulder had been expressly designed for pillowing her head. "Well . . . I wasn't such a total slouch as a seductress after all, was I?"

"Honey," he laughed softly, "you've been seducing me since the day we met."

"Have I? Then why did you keep on talking about seducing *me*?"

"Encouraging you. I thought it was time you— uh—spread your wings."

"That was big of you."

"I thought so. After all—I'm a great supporter of the quest for human knowledge. And experience."

"Will you give me a reference?"

"Not a chance. We'll keep all your experience in the family."

"In the family?"

"No summer flings, Gypsy mine. I warned you. For keeps."

Gypsy was silent for a long moment. It warmed her that Chase should be so set on making a commitment, but it also disturbed her.

"Gypsy?" There was a thread of anxiety in his deep voice.

"You don't know what I'm like," she said softly. "You really don't know, Chase. I'm afraid . . . afraid I'll ruin things."

"Your writing?"

She nodded mutely, staring across the lamplit room at one of the lonely seascapes and wondering suddenly if there was a very lonely man behind Chase's cheerful facade.

"We can work it out, honey," he told her in a voice of quiet certainty. "I know we can. If you'll just give us a chance."

"How will you feel," she persisted tonelessly, "when I start ignoring you—maybe for days at a time? When I can't stand to be touched or bothered in any way? When I snap at you for no good reason? When I work around the clock?"

"We'll work it out," he repeated quietly.

"But what if we can't?" Her voice sounded afraid of itself.

"If we both make an effort, there's nothing we can't do. I promise you, sweetheart."

"I need time," she whispered. "Time to be sure." After a moment she felt his lips moving against her forehead.

"Then we'll take all the time you need." His hands began wandering beneath the covers, and he abruptly lightened the mood. "Meanwhile back at the farm . . ."

"Chase . . ." She swallowed a giggle, wondering how he could have her near tears one moment and giggling the next.

"I'm hooked on you, Gypsy mine; you'll just have to accept that."

"Take your hand off my derriere, sir!" she commanded with injured dignity. "Or I shall retaliate!"

"Please do," he invited politely.

Luckily she just happened to discover his weakness. She tickled him and was immediately rewarded when he choked back a laugh.

"Gypsy—"

"Ha! You're ticklish! I knew there was a chink in the armor."

"I'm bigger than you, sweetheart," he warned, struggling to keep her hands away from ticklish places.

"Not if you're ticklish." Gypsy feinted and lunged with happy abandon, breaking through his defenses from time to time. "If you're ticklish, you're at my mercy!"

"Stop that, you witch!" He choked, making a vain attempt to pin her down to the bed. "I'll tickle you until you can't breathe," he promised threateningly.

"Go ahead." Gypsy launched another sneak attack, smiling with evil enjoyment. "I'm not ticklish."

"What?" He looked horrified. "Not at all?"

"Well . . . there is *one* place."

"I'll find it," he vowed determinedly, hastily blocking her newest line of attack. "If it takes me the rest of my life!"

"Until then—" She commenced a two-handed, hell-for-leather attack.

"Gypsy!"

Eight

"Chase, you can't *do* that in a Jacuzzi."

"Says who?"

"Me. We'll drown."

"It's a chance in a million. I'm willing to risk it; how about you?"

"I have to get out. It's nearly noon. We've wasted the entire morning."

"Wasted?"

"Well . . ."

"You look so lovely . . . like Circe, rising from—"

"I hope you've got your legends mixed up," she interrupted tartly.

Chase was suspiciously innocent. "Why?"

"Circe turned men into swine, *that's* why."

"Sorry. Who do I mean?"

"I haven't the faintest idea."

"Helen of Troy?"

" 'The face that launched a thousand ships'? I don't look that good, pal."

"You launched my ship," he pointed out.

"It's not hard to launch a leaky canoe."

"I'll get you for that!"

"Chase! Stop it this instant! I'll tickle you! I swear, I—"

There was a long silence, broken only by the bubbling water, and then Gypsy's voice, bemused and breathless.

"Well, what do you know . . . you *can* do that in a Jacuzzi."

Chase headed into Portland after lunch to return their costumes, leaving Gypsy hard at work behind the typewriter. Half expecting to be dreamy-eyed and thoughtful after their first night together, she was more than a little surprised to find that she was able to keep her mind on writing. In fact, she turned out page after page that more than satisfied her own critical standards.

It was enough to spark a faint hope. If, somehow, Chase stirred her to write *better*, then perhaps the obsessions were a thing of the past. At least she could hope they were.

Daisy was delivered around four, and Gypsy was walking in a slow circle around the car when Chase pulled into the drive and began unloading the Mercedes.

"Groceries," he announced cheerfully. "Both our cupboards are bare. I see Daisy arrived safe and sound."

Gypsy automatically accepted the bag he handed to her. "Chase, you had her painted. And *all* the dents are out—not just the ones from the Mercedes."

"Looks pretty good, doesn't she?" Chase studied the little blue car critically. "I told them to reapply the daisy decals."

Still staring at him, Gypsy protested, "But she's got a whole new interior. New carpet, newly upholstered seats. Chase, the insurance didn't pay for all of that."

"Daisy deserves the best." He kissed Gypsy on the nose and headed for the house.

"Why?" Gypsy asked blankly, following behind. "And why haven't you had the dent taken out of the Mercedes? It's a *sin* to drive a dented Mercedes."

"The dent is a memento," he told her gravely, unloading the groceries in the kitchen. "And Daisy deserves the best because she introduced us. We probably wouldn't have met otherwise; until you came along, I never paid attention to neighbors."

"Oh." Gypsy thought that over for a while.

"I hope you like lobster."

"Love it. You're *never* going to get the dent taken out?"

"That Mercedes will go to its grave with the dent."

Gypsy helped Chase put away groceries. "I bet Freud could have had a field day with that," she murmured finally.

"I wouldn't doubt it. Through for the day?"

She blinked, remembered her writing, and nodded. "With the book. But I got a set of galleys in the mail, and I have to proof them. They have to go back in the mail tomorrow."

"Without fail?"

"Without fail."

"How long will it take you to proof them?"

"Couple of hours. Give or take."

"Ah! Then we'll have plenty of time."

"Time for what?" she asked innocently.

"To cook lobster, of course," he replied, totally deadpan.

"Let a girl down, why don't you."

"Never."

"Besides, I don't cook. Remember?"

"I'll cook. You'll keep me company. What is this?" He was holding up a covered plastic bowl taken from the refrigerator.

Gypsy crossed her arms and leaned back against the counter. "I don't remember what it started out to be. Now it's a whatisit."

"Come again?"

"A whatisit." She smiled gently at his bafflement.

"Is it alive?" he wondered, prudently not lifting the lid to find out.

"Probably." Gypsy choked back a giggle. "I warned you that I wasn't a housekeeper."

"I seem to remember that you did." Chase stared at the mysterious bowl for a moment, then placed it back in the refrigerator.

"Lack of courage?" she queried mockingly.

"Common sense. No telling how long that thing's been growing in there; it might bite by now."

"Superman would have looked."

"Superman would have thrown it into outer space."

Gypsy sighed mournfully. "They just don't make heroes like they used to."

"Pity, isn't it?" He lifted an eyebrow at her.

She crossed the room suddenly and wrapped her arms around his waist, hugging fiercely.

"Hey!" He was surprised, but clearly pleased. "What did I do?"

"You made Daisy beautiful." She hugged

harder, rubbing her cheek against his chest. "Thank you."

"Superman would have gotten you a new Daisy," he said gruffly, returning the hug with interest.

"Superman wouldn't have known I wanted *my* Daisy. You did."

"I won out over Superman?" he asked hopefully.

"Hands down. Let Lois have him."

Chase turned her face up gently, gazing down into misty gray eyes. "I think the lobster will wait awhile," he murmured.

"Lobsters are tactful souls. . . ."

Gypsy didn't get around to proofing the galleys until nearly midnight. And she only managed to get started then because she flatly refused to share Chase's shower.

"You'll be sorry. . . ."

"And you're a menace!" Gypsy carelessly discarded the caftan she'd been wearing all evening and climbed into bed. Ignoring her audience, she pulled the covers up, arranged them neatly, and drew the galleys forward. "I absolutely *have* to read these. Go take your shower."

There was a moment of silence, and then Chase said in a laughing voice, "I'd much rather watch you."

Gypsy was hanging half out of bed, fumbling beneath it and muttering to herself. "Ah!" She righted herself, rescued the sliding galleys, and held up a pair of her reading glasses in one triumphant hand. "I knew they were there somewhere."

"You keep a pair under the bed?" Chase asked politely.

"Where do—"

"I know," he interrupted ruefully. "Where do *I* keep glasses?"

"Am I in a rut?" she wondered innocently.

"No, sweetheart." He bent over the bed to kiss her lightly. "You're the last person in the *world* who could ever be in a rut."

"Close the door," she called after him, polishing her glasses on the sheet. "I don't need steamy galleys."

"If it's *steamy* you want—"

"Don't say it!"

The closing bathroom door cut off his laugh.

Smiling to herself, Gypsy began to read the galleys. She was vaguely aware of the shower going on in the bathroom, but concentrated completely on the job at hand. Until the phone rang.

Gypsy quickly picked up the receiver, only half her mind on the action. "Hello?"

"You were gone again last night."

She cast a baffled, harrassed look toward the bathroom door. Dammit, it *had* to be Chase. "I told you to stop calling me!" she said fiercely.

" 'I am two fools, I know, for loving, and for saying so,' " he breathed sadly.

He was quoting Donne again.

Gypsy pushed the glasses to the top of her head and tried to think. "Don't call me again— and I mean it this time!"

"I dream of you," he whispered. "I dream of a voice like honey, of sweetness and gentleness. I believe in unicorns and heroes, and I wish on stars."

"Quit it," she said weakly.

"I created a dream-love, and she's you. She's the first flower of spring, the first star at night, the sun's first ray in the morning. She's a song I can't forget, a light in the darkness, and I love her."

"*Please*, quit it," Gypsy moaned desperately.

"Dream of me, love." The phone clicked softly.

Gypsy cradled the receiver. She nudged Corsair off her foot, not even noticing when he immediately resumed his favorite sleeping place. Undecided, she looked toward the bathroom door, then shook her head.

"No," she murmured to Corsair, or to Bucephalus beside the bed. "If I went and looked, he'd be there. And I don't think I could take it." She gazed into Corsair's china-blue eyes bemusedly. "I might well be in love with two men—and one of them's faceless, nameless, and probably a nut!"

When Chase came out of the bathroom a few minutes later, she was chewing on the earpiece of her glasses and staring into space.

Chase, a towel knotted around his waist, came over to the bed. He picked up Corsair, got Bucephalus by the collar, and escorted both to the door, shutting them out in the hall. When he turned around, he looked at Gypsy for a moment, then asked politely, "You'd rather they slept in here?"

"Hmmm?" She blinked at him.

"The pets." He crossed to sit on the foot of the bed, adding, "You were frowning at me."

"Cheshire cat," she murmured absently.

It was his turn to blink. "Earth to Gypsy?"

She stirred, finally giving him her full attention. "I wasn't frowning at you—I was just frowning."

"Why?"

Gypsy looked at him for a moment. "Seemed the thing to do."

Chase gave up. He shed the towel and climbed

into bed beside her. "About finished up?" he asked
seductively.

"About at the end of my rope," she confided
seriously.

He propped himself up on an elbow and stared
at her for a long moment. "You're just full of
cryptic comments tonight, Gypsy mine."

"Uh-huh." Gypsy dumped the galleys on the
floor beside the bed, dropping her glasses on top
of them. "I'll do these in the morning. *Early* in the
morning before the mailman comes. Don't let me
forget."

"Perish the thought. . . ."

The galleys were late.

The next few days were interesting to say the
least. Nights were alternately spent in Chase's
house or Gypsy's, although days were generally
spent at Gypsy's since she flatly refused to "clutter
up" Chase's lovely den or study with her stuff.

She worked during the day; her story was still
shaping without an obsessive urge to work constantly. Chase made several trips into Portland,
where his office was located; he was officially on
vacation, but since his was a one-man office, and
since he was designing a house for Jake and Sarah,
the trips were necessary.

But he was usually somewhere nearby. Gypsy
would look up occasionally to see him stretched
out on the couch reading, or hear him whistling
in the kitchen. And he always made sure she ate
regularly.

"I'll gain ten pounds if this keeps up!"

"Ten pounds on you would just be necessary
ballast."

"Funny man. That 'ballast' won't be able to fit into my jeans."

"Have another roll."

With Chase, every day—and certainly every night—became an adventure. Gypsy never knew what he'd do next.

"What *is* that?"

"The mating call of whales."

"Really? I didn't even know you had an aquarium."

"Cute. It's a record. To set the mood."

"And I thought we were doing so well."

"Change is the spice of life, Gypsy mine."

"Right. Where's the water bed?"

"Damn. Knew I forgot something."

Gypsy discovered that it was definitely nice to have a man around. She was as mechanically inept as she was forgetful, her usual method of fixing anything being a few swift kicks or thumps.

"Chase, where are you?"

"In the kitchen feeding your pets."

She headed for the kitchen, announcing without preamble, "Herman's *e* is sticking, and it's driving me crazy. Can you do anything?"

Chase nearly lost a finger since he was giving Bucephalus a steak bone and looked up at the crucial moment. He stared at Gypsy for a second, then apparently deduced that Herman was the typewriter. "I'll certainly try," he told her, accepting named typewriters without a blink.

Ten minutes later Gypsy was happily typing again. "My hero," she murmured absently as Chase straightened from his leaning position against the desk. He touched her cheek lightly and said, "That's all I ever wanted to be, sweetheart."

Gypsy looked up only when he'd left the room.

She stared after him for a long time, eyes distant and thoughtful. Then she bent her head and went back to work.

Chase came in late one afternoon to find her pounding the keys furiously and wearing a fierce grimace that didn't invite interruption.

"Gypsy—"

"Hush!" she said distractedly, hammering away at her top speed, which was pretty impressive. "Someone's about to get killed."

It was half an hour before her assault on Herman ceased. Gypsy straightened and rubbed the small of her back absently, reading over what she'd written. Only then did she become aware of a presence. She looked up to find Chase leaning against the bookcase and watching her with a faint smile.

"Hello," she said in surprise. "How long have you been there?"

"A few minutes. I tried to interrupt you, and you told me to hush."

"Oh, I'm sorry," she muttered, horrified.

He chuckled softly. "Don't be. I knew it was the wrong time but, to be honest, I wanted to find out what you'd do. And if that was the worst, we're home free, sweetheart."

Gypsy pushed her glasses up on top of her head, never noticing that the pair already there fell to the floor behind her. She looked curiously at his trying-hard-to-hide grin. "We'll have to wait and see, won't we?" she murmured in response to his comment.

"If you say so. What would you like for dinner?"

Gypsy's "night lover" continued to call whenever she and Chase were spending the night in

her house. Chase was always around, but never
in the room, and her suspicions were growing by
leaps and bounds. It was much easier, she admitted to herself ruefully, to believe that it was Chase;
otherwise, she was quite definitely in love with
two separate men . . . and *there* was a wonderfully
cheering thought!

A few days later, suddenly and with no warning,
her book became an obsession. It wasn't too bad
at first; Chase found wonderfully unique ways of
getting her away from the typewriter for a break
or a meal or sleep—and all without causing her to
lose her temper once.

"Gypsy?"

"Not now."

"You have to help me—it's desperately important!"

"What then?"

"My zipper's stuck."

"Chase!"

"It got you away from the typewriter."

"I know, but really!"

"Now that you're *here*—"

"You're incorrigible!"

Or:

"Gypsy?"

"*What?*"

"You have to help me."

"What's desperately important now?"

"I have to get my car keys."

"Chase, you've been up that tree every morning for weeks; you should know the way by now."

"Corsair went up a different tree. Sneaky
cat."

"I'll bet you told him to."

"How could I? He doesn't listen to me. Come

now, Gypsy mine, just a moment of your time. I don't ask for much, after all."

"Stop sounding pitiful; it won't wash."

"It was worth a try."

He found her outside one morning, sitting cross-legged on the ground and methodically pulling up handfuls of grass.

"Why are you mangling the lawn?" he asked sweetly, sinking down beside her.

Gypsy was fixedly watching her hands. "I've painted myself into a corner, dammit," she muttered irritably. "And now I don't see . . ."

"Let the paint dry and repaint the room," he advised cheerfully, obviously without the least idea of what she was talking about.

She froze, lifting startled eyes to his. "Wait a minute. That just might work. I could— And then—" She reached over to hug him exuberantly. "You did it! Thank you!"

Chase followed her into the house, murmuring, "Great. What did I do?"

Chase managed to get her away from the typewriter all day the following Sunday by inviting her parents to have dinner and spend the afternoon at his house. Gypsy was inclined to be temperish about it at first; in fact, it was the first time she really snapped at him—and it upset her more than it did Chase.

"*Why* did you do that? I can't stop working for a whole day! I'll never get this book finished, dammit, and it's all your fault!"

"Gypsy—"

"You've messed up my whole life!"

"Have I?" he asked softly.

She stared at him and her anger vanished.

Quickly she rose from her chair and went over to him, wrapping her arms around his waist. "Why do you put up with me?" she asked shakily.

"Well, you're just an occasional shrew," he told her conversationally. "And I always did prefer tangy to sweet."

"Chase—"

"Cheer up. You haven't seen *my* worst side yet."

"Do you have one? I was thinking of having you canonized."

"Saint Chase?" He tried the title on for size. "Doesn't sound right, somehow. We'll have to think it over. Come along now, Gypsy mine; we're going to prepare a feast for your parents."

"We?"

"This time you get to help."

"Help do what? Kill us all? Face it, pal—I have absolutely no aptitude for cookery."

"You can slice things, can't you?"

"You're going to let me have a knife?"

"On second thought I'll do the slicing. You can set the table and keep me company."

"As I asked once before, is your china insured?"

"Since the day after I met you."

The entire day was fun laced with nonsense, and Gypsy thoroughly enjoyed it. She always enjoyed her parents' visits, but Chase's presence made it even better. He got along very well with both of them, accepting Gypsy's definitely unusual parents with clear enjoyment.

And they just as clearly approved of him:

"Mother, what were you and Chase in a huddle about?"

"Nothing important, darling. Are you working on a book? You don't look as tired as usual."

Knowing her mother, Gypsy accepted the change of subject. "Chase makes me rest."

"Your father is just the same with me. When's the wedding?"

"Are you and Poppy getting married again, Mother?"

"Gypsy . . ."

"He hasn't asked, Mother."

"Nonsense, darling. He doesn't have to."

"Etiquette demands it."

"Write a new rule. Ask him."

"I'm an old-fashioned kind of girl."

"Stubborn. Just like your father."

"Poppy, where are you going with that ladder?"

"Corsair stole *my* car keys. He's on the roof; Chase is going up after him."

"Oh. Chase had a ladder all this time? I'll get him for that; I've been helping him out of trees all week."

"Corsair?"

"Chase."

"Oh, I like him, darling."

"Corsair?"

"You're worse than your mother. Chase, of course."

"Stop smiling at me, Poppy."

"I like smiling at you; fathers do that, you know."

"Yes, but it's *that* kind of smile. A definitely parental Father-always-knows-kid-and-don't-try-to-hide-it kind of smile. Unnerving."

"You're misreading my expression. This is my I-want-to-dandle-a-grandchild-on-my-knee-one-day smile."

"Poppy——"

"I'll take the ladder to Chase."

"Do that."

"Did you get Corsair off the roof?"

"After a merry chase, yes. Your cat has a devious mind."

"I've been meaning to tell you. If you'd only stop playing his game, he'd stop too. He never would have gone up a tree a second time if you'd only ignored him the first time."

"I needed my keys."

"He would have dropped them. Eventually."

"Uh-huh."

Days passed and Gypsy became more and more wrapped up in her book. The clutter on her desk, composed of notes on odd sheets of paper, reference books, and assorted alien objects like the Buddha, grew until it was nearly impossible to find her or Herman in the middle of it. Chase pulled her from the muddle for meals but otherwise left her strictly alone.

Gypsy made a tremendous effort and firmly stopped working at midnight every night. She'd never held herself to any kind of fixed schedule before, and was agreeably surprised to find that it didn't seem to be interfering with her creativity. If anything, it helped; she always stopped before she got too tired now.

Besides . . . she cherished the nights with Chase. He showed her an enchantment she had never before known, and she loved him more with every day that passed. Neither of them ever put their feelings into so many words, and she had a suspicion that Chase wouldn't say a word until she did. He'd said that he was "playing for keeps" and was leaving the rest up to her.

But Gypsy still wasn't ready to commit herself fully. She was still uneasy, still worried that his patience would run out.

And it did.

As the book neared its completion Gypsy warned him that the midnight halts were at an end. The last few days of a book were written in a white-hot headlong rush, interrupted by nothing except a catnap when the typewriter keys blurred before her eyes. At that point Gypsy was driven by the need to just *finish* the thing, and there was nothing else she could do.

It went on for three days. Gypsy ate little and rarely left her desk. She catnapped on the couch at odd hours, then took showers to refresh her mind before going immediately back to work. She was dimly aware of Chase, but not distracted by his presence. As for Chase, he was always around but didn't intrude.

Three days. At two A.M. on the fourth day, the headlong rush came to a crashing halt.

Gypsy found herself jerked suddenly to her feet, banging both knees against the desk's center drawer, and quite thoroughly and ruthlessly kissed.

"Do I have your attention now?" Chase demanded hoarsely.

She blinked up at him, a bit startled by the suddenly unleashed primitive man. Clearing her throat carefully, Gypsy barely managed a one-word response. "Yes."

"Good!" He lifted the glasses from her nose, dropped them on the foot-high clutter on the desk, and then threw Gypsy over his shoulder with one easy, lithe, far from gentle move.

"Chase!" Dangling helplessly, she realized that he was carrying her into the bedroom.

"*Don't* have me canonized!" he snapped.

"Chase, what're you—" She bounced once on the bed, looking up with wide eyes as he joined her with a force that stole her breath. "Chase?"

He kissed her with a roughness just this side of savagery, a bruising impatience that stripped away all the civilized layers of the mating game. His hunger was voracious, insatiable. Restraint was gone, gentleness was gone; there was only this crucial need, this desperate hunger.

Gypsy had believed that she could never be surprised by his lovemaking, but she discovered her mistake. And after the first moment of shock, she responded with a mindless need to match his own wild hunger.

It was silent and raw and indescribably powerful. They loved and fought like wild things compelled to mate once and die, their movements swift and hurried and uncontrolled. Something primal drove them relentlessly, pushing them higher and higher, until they soared over the brink in a heart-stopping, mind-shattering release. . . .

Floating in a dreamy haze, Gypsy was lying on her back close beside Chase. She felt his arm, heavy across her middle, heard his rough breathing gradually steady. She wanted to smile all over. Eyes closed, she felt rather than saw Chase raise himself on an elbow, felt his gaze.

"Honestly," she murmured in an injured tone, "you could have just asked, pal. I mean—I think they used to call it ravishment."

"Gypsy . . ."

Startled by his hesitant, anxious voice, her eyes snapped open. She looked up at him, searching his concerned face and darkened eyes, realizing in slow astonishment that he was really worried. She wasn't about to let *that* go on.

Sliding her arms up around his neck, she allowed her inner smile to show through. "You should get creative more often."

The jade eyes lightened, but he still looked anxious. "You really don't mind?" he asked in a low voice. "I didn't mean to be so rough, honey."

Gypsy rather pointedly traced a long scratch on his shoulder with one finger. "We both got a little carried away. Let's get carried away again . . . real soon."

He chuckled softly, apparently realizing that she wasn't the slightest bit upset by ravishment. "You should be mad, Gypsy mine; I interrupted your work."

"With a vengeance," she agreed dryly. "But I forgive you. I only had a few pages left to do anyway."

"To finish the book?" When she nodded, he said ruefully, "That close to the end and I stopped you. . . . You should be furious."

"No, but I am *curious*. What finally pushed you over the edge? I mean, you've been Saint Chase for weeks."

"I'm not quite sure." He paused, then went on firmly, "Yes, I am sure, dammit. I was jealous."

"Jealous?" Gypsy was startled. "Of what?"

"The book. The typewriter. The desk. Everything standing between you and me. I was lying here in bed—alone, I might add—and suddenly decided that enough was enough."

Gypsy frowned uneasily, and he immediately understood her worry.

"Honey, I really don't think that your writing

will get between us. It only happened tonight because . . . because you're still so *new* to me." His voice deepened, roughened. "You're like a treasure I stumbled on by accident—I want to keep you to myself for a while. I want to—to hoard my riches until I'm sure I won't lose them."

She tried to speak past the lump in her throat, but found it impossible.

"Still . . ." He was suddenly rueful, obviously trying to lighten the atmosphere. "The White Knight wouldn't have approved."

Tightening her arms around his neck, Gypsy swallowed the lump and said huskily, "The White Knight doesn't know what he's missing. And neither does his lady."

"Hey . . ." He smiled down at her. "I win out over the White Knight too?"

"He's not even in the same race."

Chase kissed her gently, murmuring, "You're running out of heroes, Gypsy mine."

"I hadn't noticed. . . ."

Nine

Due to one thing or another—and Chase fit into both categories—Gypsy didn't finish her book until late the next day. As always, the book was too fresh in her mind for her to be objective about it. She only knew that she was satisfied.

She woke the next morning with the disquieting sensation that something was wrong, and it took only seconds for her to realize what it was. Chase wasn't in bed with her. She listened to the silent house for a moment, then slid out of bed and put on one of his T-shirts. By this time both their wardrobes were pretty equally divided between the two houses.

She padded soundlessly through the house until she reached the doorway of the living room. There she stopped, leaning against the wall and watching him with quiet eyes.

He was sitting at her desk, the chair pushed back to accommodate his long legs. Dressed only in cutoff jeans, hair still tousled from sleep, his head was bent over the last few pages of Gypsy's manuscript. He'd obviously been there for some time.

When he'd read the last page, Chase turned it facedown with the others in a stack on the corner of the desk, his expression thoughtful. He looked up suddenly a moment later, as though sensing her presence. Gazing at her, he murmured, "I think it's the best thing you've ever written."

Gypsy came across to him, sinking down on the carpet at his feet with her folded hands resting across his thigh. "Why?" she asked, her voice as soft as his in the early-morning hush.

Chase reached out to stroke her tumbled curls absently, frowning slightly in thought. "Certain things haven't changed—from your other books, I mean. It's ruthlessly logical, neatly plotted, with unexpected twists and turns. But your *characters* are different. Especially the hero." Chase smiled suddenly. "He's the type you want to stand up and cheer for. Not an *anti*hero like the others, but a human hero with strengths and weaknesses. He's smart but not cynical, idealistic without being a fool. And he has a fiendish sense of humor. You'll have to make him a continuing character, sweetheart—readers will love him."

Gypsy smiled, more than content with the critique. "I'm glad you think it's good."

"It's more than good, Gypsy mine. It's terrific. A sure bestseller." He leaned forward to kiss her lightly, remaining in that position as he gazed into her eyes and asked casually, "Want to go to Virginia with me?"

"Virginia?" She was still smiling. "What's in Virginia?"

He seemed to hesitate for an instant. "A project they want me to do."

Her smile faded slightly. "They?"

"The city fathers in Richmond. The project I worked on for two months was for them. Now they want a big shopping mall."

Dimly Gypsy realized that it would be a professional feather in Chase's cap. "When do you have to be there?"

"I'm supposed to meet with them Friday afternoon."

"That's tomorrow," she said slowly. "How long—I mean, will you have to be there for months?"

"Not at this early stage. We'll be talking about budgets and designs—that sort of thing. Guidelines have to be ironed out before they commit themselves, and before I commit myself. It'll take days. Weeks, if they're as slow as last time."

He was still smiling, but there was a curiously blank look in his eyes, as if he were deliberately hiding his thoughts. "Come with me?"

"I can't."

"Jake and Sarah'll watch the houses for us." He was still casual.

She shook her head. "That's not it. The book's finished, Chase, but the manuscript isn't. I have days of retyping to do."

"I see." His eyes remained blank. "Can't type in Richmond, I guess?"

Gypsy felt strangely shaken by his light tone, disturbed by the shuttered gaze. "Would it be worth the bother to carry all my stuff out there?" she asked uncertainly. "You said it might just be days, and—"

"You're right, of course." He sat back, looking down at her with a glinting smile. "Then I go alone." Softly he added, "You're still not sure about us, are you, Gypsy?"

Before she could answer, he rose to his feet and pulled her gently to hers. "I'll catch an afternoon plane today; I'll need time to check out the proposed site tomorrow before the meeting. And since I have a few things to take care of in Portland before I leave— I'd better get a move on, I guess. Want to help me pack?"

"You're leaving right away?" she asked weakly.

"After breakfast. I'll cook if you'll pack for me. Deal?"

Two hours later he was gone, leaving Gypsy at the door with a light kiss and a cheerful wave.

His eyes had still been blank.

"Well, dammit. . . ." Gypsy muttered miserably to herself, watching the Mercedes disappear from sight.

Days passed, while Gypsy worked to retype her manuscript. She worked long hours, but not because the story drove her; she worked because something else was driving her.

Chase called every evening around eight to report progress (none, from the sound of it). He was casual, cheerful. He didn't once call her Gypsy mine or sweetheart or honey. He didn't talk about heroes.

So Gypsy threw herself into her work. She worked so fiercely that the manuscript was retyped and on its way to her editor by the middle of that week. And then she was at loose ends, struggling to find things to do. She gardened. She washed Daisy three times in two days. She used the key Chase had left her to let herself into his house and take care of Angel and the kittens. She watched television. She read poetry.

Poetry. If it hadn't been for her "night lover," Gypsy didn't know what she would have done. He called every night around midnight. Gypsy always listened intently, trying to pin down the voice, trying to convince herself it was Chase. But she just wasn't sure. And she was too fearful of a negative answer to ask if it was him.

" 'Come live with me and be my love,' " he invited softly one night.

Lying in bed in darkness, Gypsy smiled to herself. "Will you show me 'golden sands and crystal brooks'?" she murmured.

"I'll show you . . . the ones inside myself," he vowed. "I'll show you all the things you have to *believe* in before you can see them. Will you let me do that, love?"

She laughed unsteadily. "You haven't shown me *you.*"

"I'm one of those things that has to be believed first, love. If you believe in me, then I'm real."

"Like unicorns?" she whispered.

"Like unicorns. And heroes."

Gypsy tried desperately to deny the emotions welling up inside of her. "I can't believe in you," she told him shakily. "I—"

"You must believe in me, love. Without you I can't exist."

"Don't say that. . . ."

"Dream of me, love."

Gypsy found herself pacing the next night. Pacing restlessly, endlessly. She had talked to Chase only an hour before; a casual, meaningless conversation. Why was he doing this to her? He was deliberately holding back a part of himself, and—

She stopped dead in the center of the room, her lips twisting suddenly as the realization slammed at her. "Idiot!" she breathed softly to her usual audience of Corsair and Bucephalus. "Of course, that's what he's doing. He's showing you what it's like, you fool! You've spent weeks huddled inside your own stupid uncertainties, while he waited patiently for you to—to grow up."

What was she *really* afraid of? Gypsy asked herself. Not that they couldn't live together—they could. Not that her writing would come between them—because, dammit, she wouldn't let it.

"Drag out the cliché, Gypsy," she told herself softly. "You're really afraid of getting hurt. You told yourself for years that you didn't want to get involved, and when it finally happened, it scared you to death. For the first time in your life, you let someone close enough to see you. And now . . . ?"

Facing the fear squarely for the first time, she realized slowly, gladly, that it was fading into nothingness. Chase would never hurt her—not intentionally. And being seen by him was a very special thing indeed. She only hoped that it wasn't too late to tell him.

Gypsy's heart thudded abruptly as a sudden painful question presented itself. It pounded in her head, slammed at walls already crumbling, leaving panic in its wake.

What if she lost him?

Not the vague, elusive worry of "someday," but the concrete realization that life was uncertain at best. What if he never came back? What if she never saw him again, was never given the chance to say . . .

One glance at the clock and Gypsy was sitting on the edge of her bed and reaching for the phone. It was midnight in the East; he'd be at his hotel. She placed the call and listened as his phone rang, her only thought that "tomorrow" was sometimes too late.

"Hello?"

"I miss you," she said starkly.

"Do you?" He was guarded, his voice still and waiting.

"Chase . . ."

"You sound upset." It was a question.

"I'm lonely." She laughed shakily. "For the first time in my life, I'm lonely. Are you— When are you coming home?"

He sighed. "Looks like another few days."

Gypsy closed her eyes, knuckles showing white as she gripped the receiver. "I don't think I can wait that long."

"Gypsy?"

"Nothing's right." Her voice was hurried, half blocked by the lump in her throat. "Nothing's the same. The house seems empty. . . . Bucephalus isn't eating. . . . I can't find my glasses. . . . The Buddha fell off my desk, and he's shattered, just shattered. . . . Corsair goes from room to room, and he can't seem to find what he's looking for—"

"Gypsy—"

"Angel moved her kittens back to your bedroom," she went on disjointedly. "And some kind of bug's attacking the roses. I washed dishes last night because I didn't want to be messy, and I picked up all the clothes on the floor. . . . It rained all day. . . . My bed's so big . . . so empty. . . ."

"I'm catching the first plane home," he told her, his voice oddly unsteady.

"But your work—"

"Never mind my work. You're more important. I'll be home tomorrow, honey."

"I'll be waiting," she promised huskily.

"Good night, Gypsy mine."

"Good night."

Gypsy cradled the receiver gently, staring across the room blindly.

"You're more important."

Her mind flashed back to an earlier inner resolution not to let her writing come between them, and she felt a sort of wonder. Somehow, without her being consciously aware of it, the two most important things in her life had softly changed places. From now on, she knew, nothing would ever be as important as Chase.

As for her writing . . . Gypsy shook her head ruefully. It had been right there in front of her all the time, and she'd never seen it. But Chase had. He'd told her that her fictional hero was "the kind you want to stand up and cheer for," and she hadn't realized the importance of that.

She could imagine heroes now. Human heroes; fallible, but heroes nonetheless. And Chase had given her that. Chase and her "night lover."

Gypsy frowned suddenly. It was Chase. Period. She'd go on playing the game as long as he did, and just stop questioning. And one day, when they were old and gray and rocking side by side on a vine-covered porch, she'd ask him. And if he didn't say yes . . . she'd hit him with her cane.

"Do you believe in unicorns, love."

"Yes," she whispered.

"And heroes?"

"And heroes."

"And . . . me?"

"And you." Her voice was tender.

"We'll find those 'golden sands and crystal brooks,' " he told her with impossible sweetness. "We'll follow rainbows until we find the pot of gold. And when it storms outside, when the world goes crazy, we'll have each other."

"Never alone," she murmured wonderingly.

"Never alone. Sweet dreams, love. . . ."

Gypsy was restless, on edge. She was bursting to tell Chase how she felt, and the morning dragged by with no sign of him. She washed Daisy again and cultivated two flower beds, and *still* he didn't come.

She wandered around the house, trying to rehearse what she wanted to say. But she knew ruefully that—rehearsals notwithstanding—heaven only knew what would come out of her mouth when the moment came.

It was after two when she finally left the house, wandering out to the edge of the cliffs and sitting down on the grass at the top of the steps. She stared out over the ocean, her mind empty of everything except the wish that he would come to her.

She didn't hear him coming, but was instantly aware when he knelt on the grass just behind her.

"Gypsy?"

She twisted around abruptly, her arms going around his neck with blind certainty. She felt his arms holding her tightly, felt the smooth material of his shirt and the heavy beat of his heart beneath her cheek.

"I've found a new kind of hero," she told him breathlessly. "A kind I never knew existed."

"What kind?" he asked gently, holding her as if he would never let her go.

"He makes me laugh. And he doesn't mind that I'm messy and can't cook. He fixes Herman and helps me find my glasses and cooks marvelous meals for me. He makes me stop work to help him down from trees, even though he's got a ladder. He does impossible things in Jacuzzis and plays music made by whales, and thinks I'm a treasure he stumbled on by accident. He puts up with a huge dog and an invasion of cats, and keeps a dent in his Mercedes. And he's so very patient with me. . . ."

"Gypsy . . ." Chase turned her face up with gentle hands, looking down at her with glowing jade eyes.

"I love you," she told him fiercely. "I love you so much, and if you can only put up with me—"

"Put up with you?" His voice was an unsteady rasp. "God, Gypsy, don't you realize what you mean to me?" He rubbed his forehead against hers in a rough movement. "When we first met, I didn't know whether to kiss you or have you committed. Within six hours I knew that I wanted you committed—to me. For the rest of our lives. I love you, sweetheart."

"Chase . . ." Gypsy closed her eyes blissfully as his lips met hers. She was dimly aware of movement but was not troubled by it, responding with all the love inside herself to the sweetness of his kiss. When her lashes finally drifted open again, she discovered that she was lying on her back in the soft grass, with Chase lying close beside her.

His lips were feathering lightly along her jawline, teasing the corner of her mouth.

"Why did you leave me?" she asked huskily, knowing the answer but needing to hear it from him. "Why were you so—so indifferent?"

"I was gambling, Gypsy mine," he murmured, lifting his head to gaze into her eyes. "You still weren't sure about us, and I was going crazy trying to think of some way of proving to you that we belonged together. So I decided to leave, suddenly and with little warning. I hoped you'd miss me. But driving away that morning was the hardest thing I've ever done in my life. These last days have been hell," he finished roughly.

Gypsy touched his cheek, a gentle apology for the pain of his uncertainty, and her senses flared when he turned his head to softly kiss her palm.

"Everything happened so fast that morning," she said. "You didn't give me a chance to stop and think; you were just gone."

His smile was twisted wryly. "If I'd given you a chance to think, honey, I would have given myself one as well. And I never would have gone. It was like taking bad-tasting medicine; I had to get it over with quickly."

"And . . . the project in Richmond?" she asked softly.

"Oh, it was real. They called me a couple of weeks before I left. The project's on, by the way. There are still a few details to be hammered out, but the contract's being drawn up now. Would you like to spend the winter in Richmond, Gypsy mine?"

"I've never been to Richmond." She smiled up at him, and then the smile turned wondering. "I just can't believe it," she said almost to herself. "I'm so hopeless to live with, and yet you—"

"Honey . . ." He shook his head with a faint smile, and went on slowly. "You brought something different into my life, something special. There aren't enough hours in the day for me now, because every one brings something new and exciting. Don't you realize how fascinating you are just to *watch*?"

He kissed her lightly on the nose, one finger tracing the curve of her cheek. "The way you blink like a startled kitten when you're surprised. The way you absentmindedly put on one pair of glasses while another's on the top of your head. The way you explain something totally ridiculous with all the reasonableness in the world.

"You accept the absurd without a blink and make the commonplace seem fascinating. You have a mind as sharp as a razor, and yet you can never find whatever you're looking for. You have a penchant for naming objects and talking to them— and about them—as if they were people. You're prone to collect strange things like Buddhas, and the urge to collect them honestly bewilders you." He smiled tenderly at her. "And when I'm with you, I feel as if I'm on the world's biggest roller coaster—exhilarated and breathless."

Gypsy tried to think straight. "But I can't cook, and I'm not a housekeeper."

He kissed her suddenly, as if he couldn't help himself, and she realized that he was laughing silently.

"How you do harp on that," he chided gently. "Do you think I give a damn that you don't cook and aren't a housekeeper? So what? I couldn't write a book if you took me through it sentence by sentence. I couldn't create a hero you'd want to stand up and cheer for—"

"Yes, you could," she interrupted breathlessly, the emotions inside of her threatening to burst their fragile human shell.

Chase hugged her silently, a suspicious shine in the jade eyes. "The point is," he went on huskily, "that I don't have to 'put up' with you at all, honey. I love everything about you. You're beautiful inside and out. Warm and giving, humorous and ridiculous, and passionate. You fill my days with laughter and my nights with magic. From the moment I saw compassion in your lovely eyes for the lonely little boy I might have been, I knew that I'd found the woman I've been looking for all my life. The treasure I stumbled on by accident . . ."

"I love you, Chase," she told him shakily. "I was so empty when you left, so alone. I realized then that if I never wrote another word, it wouldn't bother me—but if I never saw you again, I'd die. I was so stupid, so stupid not to see it sooner!"

"My love," he murmured, kissing her.

Long moments passed, the silence broken only by the muted roar of the ocean, the soft twittering of birds, and murmurs of love.

"I really hate to break the mood," Gypsy said at last, her voice grave, "but I think we'd better get up."

"Why?" he lifted a brow at her. "No neighbors."

"Neighbors are closer than you think." Gypsy made a slight, restless movement. "Uh . . . I believe you put me down on an ant's nest."

Chase began to laugh helplessly.

She grinned up at him. "Just call me Pauline!"

Still laughing, Chase got to his feet and helped her up. "I believe I've mentioned it before, sweetheart, but even Cyrano would have a hell of a time trying to romance you!"

"Are you glad you've got me instead?" she asked politely.

"I can't believe my luck." He began enthusiastically brushing her down to remove possible ants.

"Chase?"

"What?"

"I was lying on my back. Not my front."

"So you were, so you were." He grinned at her, linking his hands together at the small of her back as they stood close together.

"You're impossible!" she told him severely.

"Can I help it if I can't keep my hands off you?" he asked, wounded.

"Dignity," she said austerely, "should be our uniform of the day."

"That uniform won't fit either one of us."

"We must strive to cultivate dignity," she insisted solemnly.

"Why?"

"Because we're grown-up adult people, that's why."

"Are we?" Chase frowned thoughtfully. "I don't think so."

"We'd better be, if we're going to get married. Are we going to get married?"

"Of course we are."

"I wondered. You never said."

"I was waiting for you to ask me."

Gypsy thought of her mother's advice, and bit back a giggle. "Never let it be said that I didn't do what was expected of me. Shall I make an honest man out of you? I think I shall. Will you marry me?"

"You're supposed to get down on your knees and swear undying love," he pointed out critically.

"Can't I stand and swear undying love?" she asked anxiously. "The ants, you know."

"I'm willing to stretch a point," he allowed graciously.

"Thank you." Gypsy tightened her arms around his neck and looked up at him soulfully. "My darling, you're everything I didn't dare hope to find, everything I looked for in my dreams." The light mockery fell away from her slowly as she gazed at the lean face that meant so much to her.

"I can face the worst of life with you beside me, and enjoy the best of life as I never would without you. I'd do anything for you, pay any price for your love. I'd willingly give up everything that ever mattered to me if you asked it of me. I'd follow you through the fires of hell itself." Her voice became suddenly unsteady, but not uncertain. "I'll love you until I die . . . and after. Will you marry me, my love?"

Chase drew a deep, shuddering breath, his arms tightening fiercely around her. "Yes, please," he said simply.

Gypsy swallowed the lump in her throat and smiled tremulously up at him. "Now we're be-trothed," she said gravely.

"And a very short betrothal it'll be, love," he told her firmly. "I hope you hadn't planned on a big wedding."

"What? With my *Perils of Pauline* luck?" Gypsy was honestly horrified. "I wouldn't dare! I'd trip over my train, or drop the flowers—or the ring—"

Chase was laughing. "You probably would, Gypsy mine. So we'll have a nice quiet wedding as soon as it can be arranged. Would your parents mind if we were married at the office of a justice of the peace?" A whimsical expression crossed his face as he thought of Gypsy's parents. "Stupid question," he murmured.

Gypsy was grinning up at him. "My parents wouldn't mind if we were married in the middle of Portland during rush hour—just as long as it's legal."

"Mmmm." Chase lifted an eyebrow. "Dad won't be able to get leave to return to the States for the wedding, so you'd better be prepared for a second ceremony—in Switzerland."

"Switzerland?" she mumbled.

"Uh-huh. Nice place for a honeymoon, don't you think? I can watch you wrap Dad around your little finger, and then we can spend a few weeks seeing all the places the tourists miss. We'll even rent a chalet—that way we won't have to bother about DO NOT DISTURB signs. How does that sound?"

Gypsy frowned at him. "Why do I suddenly get the feeling that you've had this arranged for quite a while?"

Chase looked thoughtful, the jade laughter in his eyes giving him away. "I couldn't say—unless it's because you know me so well, sweetheart."

"Chase!"

He chuckled softly. "Guilty—and I don't regret it a bit. Actually I called Dad during one of those hellish nights in Richmond and told him that I was bringing my bride to the Alps as soon as possible, and would he please rent a chalet for us?" Chase looked reflective. "I'm sure I sounded a little wild. Anyway Dad can't wait to meet you."

Gypsy realized that her mouth was open, and hastily closed it. "Oh, Lord," she murmured.

"He already knows you from your books," Chase was going on cheerfully. "We share an addiction for mysteries. As a matter of fact, we both agree that you're number one; we each have your books hardbound, and guard them jealously."

"You never told me that," she mumbled, suddenly remembering Jake's comment about Chase's "raving" over her books.

"You never asked." He kissed her nose; it seemed to be a favorite spot for him. "How many children shall we have, Gypsy mine?"

She blinked. "You like your questions loaded, don't you?"

"Never answer a question with a question," he chided gravely. "I was thinking of three. That's a nice, uneven number. However, I absolutely *insist* on being consulted over the names. Otherwise, our children will end up with names like Vladimir or Shadwell or Zenobia or Radinka. Or Bucephalus."

"I didn't name him!" Gypsy objected, trying not to laugh.

"I have my suspicions about that," Chase told her darkly.

Gypsy giggled, and then sobered. "Three," she murmured, and then looked up at Chase with sudden vulnerability and uncertainty in her eyes. "Our children. . . . Darling, I'd love to be a mother, but do you think—"

He laid a gentle finger across her lips, cutting off doubts. "Our children will cherish their mother all the days of their lives," he assured her huskily. "They'll come to her with their laughter and their tears, because she'll laugh with them and cry with them. She'll be the type of mother who'll gather all the neighborhood kids at her house for an impromptu party or a picnic, and she'll never run out of games or stories. It'll be a disorganized home, filled with laughter and love, and innumerable pets—and I wouldn't miss it for the world!"

Afer a moment of drowning in the warm jade depths of his eyes, Gypsy murmured softly, "In that case, three won't be enough."

He kissed her nose again. "I'm open to negotiations, darling."

"Why don't we try out that Jacuzzi of yours again?" she suggested solemnly. "It should be a good place to . . . negotiate."

"Great minds. We could—"

"So here you are! I turn my back for an instant, and just look at the trouble you've gotten into!"

The authoritative voice—rather like the screech of a disturbed crow—caused Chase and Gypsy to step hurriedly apart, their expressions those of guilty children caught with their entire arms in a cookie jar. They turned toward the house, Gypsy with resignation and Chase with astonishment.

"Is *that* Amy?" he asked Gypsy in a comical aside.

"Uh-huh." Gypsy didn't dare look at Chase for fear of coming unglued. "Hi, Amy," she said in a stronger voice. "You turned your back for more than an instant, you turned it for *weeks*. Of course, I got into trouble." Chase poked her with an elbow, and she continued obediently, "Amy, this is Chase. The trouble I got into."

After a rather desperate look at Gypsy, Chase produced a winning smile. "Hello, Amy. It's nice to meet you finally, after—"

"You have a last name?" Amy demanded tersely, never one to possess scruples about interrupting other people in the middle of their sentences.

"Mitchell," Chase supplied in a failing voice.

Gypsy was coming unglued.

Amy was six feet tall in flat shoes (which she normally wore) and built like a fullback. She had long hair worn in a no-nonsense bun and as red as a fire engine, snapping blue eyes, and the kind of face artists drew on Vikings. That face had character; it also had the trick of looking like a scientist's face in the act of dispassionately studying the latest bug under a microscope.

She might have been any age between forty-five and sixty-five, and looked about as capable as a human being could look without resembling a computer. She had no waist, and there was more of her going than coming, all of it tightly bound in gasping blue jeans and a peasant blouse. And her voice would easily wither a Bengal tiger in his tracks.

"So you're Mitchell. Rebecca told me about you." She looked Chase up and down with cold suspicion.

Recovering from that inspection—when Amy looked at you, he decided, your bones felt scoured—Chase hastily decided on a strategy. Exposure to Gypsy and her parents had taught him nothing if not that unpredictability was "a consummation devoutly to be wished." So he decided on a fast charge through forward enemy positions.

Stepping forward, he caught Amy around her nonexistent waist with both arms, planted a kiss squarely on her compressed lips, and said in a conspiratorial whisper, "You'll have to excuse us for a while, Amy; Gypsy and I are going to negotiate in a Jacuzzi."

He released her and turned to pick up a laughing Gypsy and toss her lightly over his shoulder.

When he turned back, he saw that Amy's face had altered slightly. There was the faintest hint of a possibility that there *might* have been a twitch of her lips which an optimistic man would have called the beginnings of a smile.

"Negotiate what?" she asked. (Mildly for her, Chase decided, although a grizzly bear would have happily claimed it as a lethal growl.)

"Important things," Chase told her solemnly. "Like the number of children, and names for same . . . and cabbages and kings. You will excuse us?" he added politely.

"Certainly." Her voice was as polite as his, and her deadpan expression would have moved a marble statue to tears. "Supper's at seven—don't be late."

"We wouldn't think of it," Chase assured her, carrying his future bride over his shoulder and striding toward the deck at the rear of his house.

As he went up the steps to the deck Chase swatted a conveniently placed derriere, and said despairingly, "I was expecting a *motherly* sort of woman!"

"I know you were!" Gypsy was laughing so hard, she could barely speak. "Oh, God! Your expression was priceless!"

"Why didn't you warn me, you heartless little witch?" he demanded, setting her on her feet beside the Jacuzzi. The gleam in his eyes belied his fierce frown.

"And miss that little scene?" Gypsy choked. "I wish Poppy could have seen it; he'd have dined out on that for a month! Oh, darling, you were perfect—Amy loves you already."

"How could you tell?" Chase asked wryly, and then a sudden thought apparently occurred to him. "Gypsy . . . is Amy going to live with us?"

"Of course she is, darling," his future bride told him serenely.

Chase raised his eyes toward heaven with the look of a man whose cup was full. More than full. Running over.

"Don't worry." Gypsy patted his cheek gently. "If you're good, she'll only come after you with her broom once a week or so."

"Gypsy?"

"What is it, darling?"

"You're kidding?"

"No, darling."

"Gypsy?"

"Yes, darling?"

"I'll never survive it."

"Of course you will, darling." She smiled up at him sunnily. "My hero can adapt to anything. That's one of the reasons I love him."

"News for you, sweetheart," he murmured, kissing her nose. "Your hero has feet of clay."

Gypsy smiled very tenderly. "That's another of the reasons I love him."

"My Gypsy," he whispered. "My love."

They were late for supper. But Amy didn't fuss.

Ten

The shrill demand of the telephone finally roused Gypsy, and she felt a distinct inclination to swear sleepily. They'd flown half around the world the day before, from Geneva, Switzerland, to Portland, Oregon, with only brief layovers. Gypsy wasn't even sure what *month* it was—never mind the day. She was suffering from lack of sleep, a horrendous jet lag, and the irritating conviction that she'd forgotten *something* in Geneva.

And now the phone. It was only a little after eight A.M.—the birds weren't even up, for Pete's sake!

Gypsy half climbed over Chase to reach the phone; he was dead to the world and didn't move. She fumbled for the receiver and managed finally to lift it to her ear, murmuring, "What?"

"You've been gone," a soft, muffled masculine voice told her sadly. "For weeks . . . and you didn't tell me. . . ."

Gypsy slammed the receiver down and sat bolt upright in bed, staring at the phone as if it had just this moment come to life. Now, *that* was a hell of a thing to wake up to in her condition! She had to ask Chase. She had to know.

Chase stirred and looked up at her with sleep-blurred eyes. "You look like a house fell on you," he observed, muffling a yawn with one hand. "Who was that on the phone?"

Shock tactics, she decided, might have some effect.

She snatched the sheet up to cover her breasts and stared at Chase in patent horror. "We have to get a divorce. Immediately," she announced in a very firm voice.

Chase raised himself on his elbow and stared at her with sleepy courtesy. "We just got *married* a few weeks ago," he pointed out patiently. "Are you tired of me already?"

Gypsy struggled hard to maintain her expression of shocked indignation. "I've married the wrong man! I fell in love with a voice over the telephone, and now I find out that it wasn't you at all. Get out of my bed!"

Chase was soothing. "You probably had a bad dream. Jet lag will do that to you. Lie down, sweetheart."

"I want a divorce."

"I won't let you divorce me. I like being married. Besides, my father would stand me in front of a firing squad if I lost you. He's telling half of Geneva about his daughter-in-law, the famous writer."

"Well, if that's the only reason you want to hang on to me, I'll go and see a lawyer today!"

"It's Saturday."

"Is it? Monday, then."

Chase pulled her down beside him and arranged them both comfortably. "Not a chance. Amy loves me. And Corsair's coming around. You'd never find anyone as adaptable as me. Besides, we've already arranged to house-sit in Richmond for the winter."

With an inward sigh Gypsy abandoned her ploy to find out if Chase was really her "night lover." "Did we say hello to Jake and Sarah last night?" she asked suddenly. "I seem to remember something about it."

Chase laughed. "Well, sort of. I was carrying you, and you waved at them and asked how they liked my Jacuzzi. I think you were sound asleep at the time."

Gypsy frowned. "Were they over here, then? Shouldn't they have been at your place?"

"Our place," Chase corrected. "And they were over here keeping Amy company until we arrived. Jake's determined to win her over," he added with a chuckle. "He says he wants the friendship of any woman who can defeat him at arm wrestling."

Gypsy accepted this information without a blink. "Oh." She yawned suddenly and changed the subject again. In an injured tone she said, "It's inhuman to drag a person halfway around the world. If man had been meant to fly—"

"He'd have wings?" Chase finished politely.

"No. He'd have a cushion tied to his rump to make up for airport lounges," she corrected disgustedly. "I seem to have spent eons in them, and my rump *hurts*!"

Chase patted it consolingly. "You'll recover. And, besides, whose fault was it that we made the trip in one fell swoop?"

"Mine, and don't rub it in." Gypsy sighed. "Can I help it if I wanted to get the whole thing over with as quickly as possible?"

"No, but you could have warned me before we went over that you had a phobia about flying."

"It isn't a phobia, it's just an uneasiness," she defended stoutly.

"Uh-huh." Chase grinned at her. "Tell me what the Swiss Alps look like from the air."

"I can't."

"Why not, sweetheart?"

"Because I had my eyes closed, and you know it, dammit!"

Chase laughed at her expression. "Seriously, honey, we should have taken Dad's suggestion: gone overland to Bordeaux and then taken a ship."

"Across the Atlantic?" Her tone was horrified.

They'd had this same discussion in Geneva, and Chase laughed as much now as he had then. "It beats me how you're willing to fly over an ocean, although you hate flying—but you aren't willing to sail across an ocean, although you love swimming."

"A plane's faster," Gypsy said definitely.

"So?"

"So don't make me explain my little irrational fears. I warned you long ago that I was no bargain, but you just wouldn't listen. So now you have an irrational wife."

"I have a wonderful wife," Chase corrected comfortably. "And I have Dad's stamp of approval to verify it. I thought he was going to cry when you hugged him that last time at the airport. You definitely made a conquest there."

Gypsy smiled. "I love your dad. He reminds

me of Poppy—very quiet, but with a deadly sense of humor."

"Mmmm. I think you've about got him talked into settling in Portland when he retires. You can work on him some more when he comes over for Christmas."

"It'd be nice to have both families nearby," she agreed, then frowned as part of his remark set up a train of thought. "Christmas. That reminds me—before we left for Geneva, I saw you and Mother come in here with a package all wrapped up. It looked like a painting. Somehow or another, I forgot to ask you about it."

Chase laughed silently. "That's my Gypsy—give her enough time, and she'll get around to it eventually!"

Gypsy raised up on an elbow and stared down at him severely. "Stop avoiding the subject. What have you and my mother been up to?"

"That question sounds vaguely indecent," he murmured.

"Chase!"

"I have a shrewish wife," he told the ceiling, then relented as the gleam in her eyes threatened grievous bodily harm. "Take a look behind you, shrew," he invited. "On the wall—where you were too much asleep last night to notice it."

Gypsy twisted around to look. Then she sat up and looked a while longer. Then she looked at Chase as he sat up beside her.

He smiled. "Rebecca painted it for me. Although she said she didn't know why I wanted it—since I was bound to end up with the original. I asked her to paint it that Sunday I invited them for lunch. And we left it here because I knew we'd spend our first night back in this room."

After a moment he added softly, "I didn't know she'd put me in it."

Gypsy looked at the painting again. Her first thought was that Rebecca must have seen the seascapes in Chase's bedroom and, with her usual perception, decided to paint another seascape which would blend in . . . and yet stand out. Because this painting wasn't bleak or lonely.

The central figure was Gypsy. She was wearing the silk nightgown and leaning back against the rock jutting up behind her, staring out to sea. Above her were storm clouds, curiously shaped, as if Nature had been in a teasing mood that day, bent on luring mortals out to sea. The clouds were wispy, insubstantial; their dreamy visions seen only by those who cared to see. There was a unicorn leaping from one cloud, a castle topped another; a rainbow cast its hazy colors over the ghost-ship sailing beneath it, a ghostly pirate at its wheel. There was Apollo, driving his sun behind dark clouds; there was a masked figure on a white steed; there was a knight climbing toward his cloud-castle.

And there was Chase—real, substantial. The view caught him from the waist up, half hidden by the rock Gypsy was leaning against. And Chase wasn't looking out to sea at the siren-visions of clouds. He was looking at Gypsy, and his face was soft with yearning.

Gypsy took a deep breath, realizing only then that she'd suspended breathing for what seemed like eternal seconds. "I never stop wondering at Mother's perception," she murmured almost inaudibly. She looked again at the cloud-heroes, seeing in each one an elusive resemblance to Chase.

"She saw it, Chase—she saw it all. I was looking at visions of heroes and seeing you without realizing it."

"And I was looking at you," Chase murmured, bending his head to kiss her bare shoulder.

"I'm so glad you're a patient hero," she whispered, smiling up at him as he lowered them both back to the comfortable pillows.

Chase grinned faintly. "An original hero, anyway. What other man would have scoured Geneva—of all places!—to find a Buddha with a clock in his middle?"

Gypsy giggled helplessly. "Did you see your dad's face when we carried it in? And when you told him very seriously that your watch had stopped?"

"He looked even more peculiar when we opened the other boxes," Chase noted ruefully. "Such odd souvenirs for a honeymoon: an abstract wooden sculpture of a knight on horseback, a bogus nineteenth-century sword—complete with scabbard, a hideous little genie-type lamp covered with tarnish. . . . You'd do great on a scavenger hunt, sweetheart."

"*You're* the one who fell in love with the sword," Gypsy pointed out calmly.

"A memento of our courtship," Chase said soulfully.

"Right. Just don't try to dance while wearing it."

"As long as you don't try to conjure a genie from that lamp."

"Why not?" she asked in mock disappointment.

"I shudder to think what'd pop out."

Gypsy sighed. "You're probably right."

"And speaking of being right"—he patted her

gently—"I've been meaning to tell you that the Swiss cooking did wonders in adding that extra ballast you needed."

"Uh-huh." Gypsy twisted slightly for a view of her blanket-covered posterior. "Too much ballast, if you ask me. Just look! I'm getting broad in the beam!"

He choked on a laugh. "Your beam looks great to me."

"Flatterer."

"The choice of words was yours." He drew her a bit closer. "Besides, you still weigh no more than a midget. I'll have to fatten you up some more before we go to work on Radinka or Shadwell."

Gypsy started laughing. "You're hung up on those names! I thought you just used them as a terrifying example of the names I'd come up with on my own."

Sheepishly Chase murmured, "They kinda grow on you though."

"No, Chase," she told him firmly.

"I suppose not. Still—"

"No."

"No?"

"Definitely no. I'd be a widow as soon as the kids realized what you'd done to them."

He sighed. "My first opportunity to come up with some really creative names," he mourned sadly.

"Exercise your creative powers by naming Angel's kittens. Or you can name the Mercedes. Or we'll get a dog—"

"We already have one," Chase told her casually.

Gypsy lifted her head to stare down at him. "We do?"

"Uh-huh. Bucephalus."

"But he belongs to the Robbinses—"

"Not anymore. Remember when we called before the wedding to explain about Amy being in sole charge of the house while we were gone?" When Gypsy nodded, he went on. "You had to leave the room because Rebecca wanted to talk to you about flowers or something. Anyway, I was talking to Tim. It seems he's been offered a two-year position, which could turn out to be permanent, in London starting next year. Bucephalus would have to spend six months in quarantine, and he'd be miserable. So Tim offered to give him to us. I accepted—for both of us."

Gypsy smiled. "That's wonderful. Now we have a head start on our family."

Chase began to nuzzle her throat. "Mmmm. Would you care to start working toward the rest of our family, Gypsy mine?"

"I thought you'd never ask," she murmured, feeling that delicious tremor stir to life inside her. Then she smiled, and said almost to herself, "Gypsy mine; you've called me that from the first. Were you that sure of me, darling?"

"Not sure. Hopeful." Chase pulled her easily over on top of him and smiled up at her whimsically. "I've never been one to search for rainbows, but you were my dream." He hesitated, then added very softly, " 'So if I dream I have you, I have you.' "

A thousand and one thoughts tumbled through Gypsy's mind.

"What is it, love?" Chase asked gently. "You're giving me a very peculiar look."

Gypsy carefully searched her memory of events. She was almost sure— Yes, she *was* sure! Her "night lover" had called only twice when Chase was actually in the room, and on both occasions, she'd hung up on him before he could say more than a few words. What if . . . what if she *hadn't* been so quick to hang up? Would she have discovered that it had been a tape-recorded message? Held up to the phone by a helpful friend, perhaps?

"You're staring at me, love. Somewhat fiercely, I might add."

"Chase . . ."

"Yes, love?"

"You just quoted Donne."

"Did I, love?" He was smiling slightly, the jade eyes veiled by sleepy lids. "The man obviously had a way with words."

"Chase."

"Hmmm?"

"It was you. It *was* you . . . wasn't it?"

"What was me, love?"

Gypsy tried to ignore wandering hands. "The phone calls. It had to be you. Wasn't it you?"

"I don't know what you're talking about, love."

"Chase, you *have* to tell me! I'll go nuts, and—" A startled giggle suddenly escaped her.

Jade eyes gleamed up at her, filled with laughter. "Ah-ha! I finally found your ticklish spot. You're at my mercy now, love."

Gypsy choked back another giggle, trying to ward off his tickling hand. "Chase! Stop that! And tell me it was you, dammit! Darling, I have to *know*!"

"What was that, love? Didn't quite catch it."

"Chase!" she wailed.

He smiled.

THE EDITOR'S CORNER

As Mrs. Denise L. Miller, Warner Robbins, Georgia, wrote to us about LOVESWEPT heroes, "they should be ruled dangerous to the readers' hearts and minds. I for one have fallen in love with quite a few of the leading men. . . ." What a wonderful comment! And we're so pleased to bring you four more love stories next month with irresistibly lovable heroes, the kind who put us in mind of yet another quote. This one comes from that famous lady, Mae West: "It's not the men in your life that count, it's the life in your men!" So, here's a brief description of the LOVESWEPT romances you have to look forward to next month, described chiefly by their lively and lovable heroes.

First, Nancy Holder gives us one of the most charming of lovers in **THE GREATEST SHOW ON EARTH**, LOVESWEPT #47. Evan Kessel is like no bank loan officer I ever met! He's tall, tanned, has seal-black hair, blue eyes . . . and a secret little boy wish to run away and join the circus. You guessed it, I'll bet—heroine Melinda Franklin owns a wonderful old-time circus. But poor Evan! He has to do his courting over the blaring of Guido Zamboni's calliope and the antics of two chimps named Marcel and Marceau. And when Melinda throws herself at him, it is only from the bar of a flying trapeze. **THE GREATEST SHOW ON EARTH** is a deliciously romantic confection!

(continued)

Speaking of chimps, when patent attorney Laurel Brett Fortier meets her new client, a toy inventor named Thane Prescott, he's wearing a gorilla suit! Now Thane is a little offbeat to be sure, but not so bizarre a man that he chooses to dress in costume . . . it's just that the zipper is stuck. And he can't get out of the suit even when he's preparing to meet Laurel's very stuffy, very conservative family—her father the judge and her brothers the lawyers. What a clash of lifestyles and what merriment ensues as true love blossoms . . . even to the squawking of handsome Thane's foul-mouthed parrot in Sara Orwig's wonderfully humorous **BEWARE THE WIZARD**, LOVESWEPT #48.

When opportunity and Jessica Winslow knocked, Ethan Jamieson seized the moment . . . and the lady in his arms. Never one to miss an opportunity in business or romance, this sensitive entrepreneur knew he'd found a neighbor to share his life forever. But there were misunderstandings galore to overcome. First, he thought Jess was a snoopy opportunist; then Jess thought he was an unscrupulous materialist. Sorting it all out makes for a touching and delightful romance. We're very, very pleased to be able to present yet another talented new author to you. Kathleen Downes makes a most memorable debut with **THE MAN NEXT DOOR**, LOVESWEPT #49.

Brent Taylor is one of Noelle Berry McCue's most delectable heroes. A foreign correspondent who has faced death in every corner of the earth where there's been a dangerous assignment to cover, Brent captivated his foster sister's heart when Joy was just seventeen. **IN SEARCH OF JOY** opens with the heroine a much more mature woman, but still mad about the dashing Brent who has come home at last. We feel sure that this poignant love story, LOVESWEPT #50, will captivate you.

As always, we send you our heartfelt thanks for the wonderful response you've given to each and every one of the LOVESWEPT authors and those of us on the staff.

With every good wish,

Sincerely,

Carolyn Nichols

Carolyn Nichols
  Editor
LOVESWEPT
Bantam Books, Inc.
666 Fifth Avenue
New York, NY 10103

LOVESWEPT

Love Stories you'll never forget by authors you'll always remember

☐	21603	**Heaven's Price** #1 Sandra Brown	$1.95
☐	21604	**Surrender** #2 Helen Mittermeyer	$1.95
☐	21600	**The Joining Stone** #3 Noelle Berry McCue	$1.95
☐	21601	**Silver Miracles** #4 Fayrene Preston	$1.95
☐	21605	**Matching Wits** #5 Carla Neggers	$1.95
☐	21606	**A Love for All Time** #6 Dorothy Garlock	$1.95
☐	21607	**A Tryst With Mr. Lincoln?** #7 Billie Green	$1.95
☐	21602	**Temptation's Sting** #8 Helen Conrad	$1.95
☐	21608	**December 32nd . . . And Always** #9 Marie Michael	$1.95
☐	21609	**Hard Drivin' Man** #10 Nancy Carlson	$1.95
☐	21610	**Beloved Intruder** #11 Noelle Berry McCue	$1.95
☐	21611	**Hunter's Payne** #12 Joan J. Domning	$1.95
☐	21618	**Tiger Lady** #13 Joan Domning	$1.95
☐	21613	**Stormy Vows** #14 Iris Johansen	$1.95
☐	21614	**Brief Delight** #15 Helen Mittermeyer	$1.95
☐	21616	**A Very Reluctant Knight** #16 Billie Green	$1.95
☐	21617	**Tempest at Sea** #17 Iris Johansen	$1.95
☐	21619	**Autumn Flames** #18 Sara Orwig	$1.95
☐	21620	**Pfarr Lake Affair** #19 Joan Domning	$1.95
☐	21621	**Heart on a String** #20 Carla Neggers	$1.95
☐	21622	**The Seduction of Jason** #21 Fayrene Preston	$1.95
☐	21623	**Breakfast In Bed** #22 Sandra Brown	$1.95
☐	21624	**Taking Savannah** #23 Becky Combs	$1.95
☐	21625	**The Reluctant Lark** #24 Iris Johansen	$1.95

Prices and availability subject to change without notice.

LOVESWEPT

Love Stories you'll never forget by authors you'll always remember

☐	21630	**Lightning That Lingers #25** Sharon & Tom Curtis	$1.95
☐	21631	**Once In a Blue Moon #26** Millie J. Green	$1.95
☐	21632	**The Bronzed Hawk #27** Iris Johansen	$1.95
☐	21637	**Love, Catch a Wild Bird #28** Anne Reisser	$1.95
☐	21626	**The Lady and the Unicorn #29** Iris Johansen	$1.95
☐	21628	**Winner Take All #30** Nancy Holder	$1.95
☐	21635	**The Golden Valkyrie #31** Iris Johansen	$1.95
☐	21638	**C.J.'s Fate #32** Kay Hooper	$1.95
☐	21639	**The Planting Season #33** Dorothy Garlock	$1.95
☐	21629	**For Love of Sami #34** Fayrene Preston	$1.95
☐	21627	**The Trustworthy Redhead #35** Iris Johansen	$1.95
☐	21636	**A Touch of Magic #36** Carla Neggers	$1.95
☐	21641	**Irresistible Forces #37** Marie Michael	$1.95
☐	21642	**Temporary Forces #38** Billie Green	$1.95
☐	21646	**Kirsten's Inheritance #39** Joan Domning	$1.95
☐	21645	**Return to Santa Flores #40** Iris Johansen	$1.95
☐	21656	**The Sophisticated Mountain Gal #41** Joan Bramesch	$1.95
☐	21655	**Heat Wave #42** Sara Orwig	$1.95
☐	21649	**To See the Daisies . . . First #43** Billie Green	$1.95
☐	21648	**No Red Roses #44** Iris Johansen	$1.95
☐	21644	**That Old Feeling #45** Fayrene Preston	$1.95
☐	21650	**Something Different #46** Kay Hooper	$1.95

Prices and availability subject to change without notice.

Buy them at your local bookstore or use this handy coupon for ordering:

Bantam Books, Inc., Dept. SW, 414 East Golf Road, Des Plaines, Ill. 60016

Please send me the books I have checked above. I am enclosing $_____
(please add $1.25 to cover postage and handling). Send check or money order
—no cash or C.O.D.'s please.

Mr/Mrs/Miss _____

Address_____

City_____ State/Zip_____

SW2—5/84

Please allow four to six weeks for delivery. This offer expires 11/84.

SPECIAL
MONEY SAVING
OFFER

Now you can have an up-to-date listing of Bantam's hundreds of titles plus take advantage of our unique and exciting bonus book offer. A special offer which gives you the opportunity to purchase a Bantam book for only 50¢. Here's how!

By ordering any five books at the regular price per order, you can also choose any other single book listed (up to a $4.95 value) for just 50¢. Some restrictions do apply, but for further details why not send for Bantam's listing of titles today!

Just send us your name and address plus 50¢ to defray the postage and handling costs.

Nowhere to Run

HER ARMS FELT as though they were going
to fall off. The burning pinpricks of pain were
so bad she almost wished they would. She flexed
her fingers, her wrists, her shoulders—to get
the blood moving again.

Now what?

She couldn't go back to Saint Toby's.
They'd just bring her straight back here, and
this time make sure she was tied securely.

And she couldn't just go to a different village and try to make a new life. It wasn't like she
was a boy with a trade, or even one who could
be apprenticed. A very young girl child might
be taken in on mercy, but she was too old by at
least half.

Wrapping her sore arms around herself for
warmth, Alys stooped down to ease her legs. She
was no longer tied to the stake, but she had not
really escaped for she had nowhere else to go.

That was when the dragon came. . . .

Dragon's Bait

Books by Vivian Vande Velde

Wizard at Work

Heir Apparent

Being Dead

Alison, Who Went Away

Magic Can Be Murder

The Rumpelstiltskin Problem

There's a Dead Person Following My Sister Around

Never Trust a Dead Man

A Coming Evil

Ghost of a Hanged Man

Smart Dog

Curses, Inc. and Other Stories

Companions of the Night

Tales from the Brothers Grimm and the Sisters Weird

User Unfriendly

A Well-Timed Enchantment

A Hidden Magic

Vivian Vande Velde

Dragon's Bait

Magic Carpet Books
Harcourt, Inc.
Orlando Austin New York San Diego Toronto London

www.HarcourtBooks.com

First Magic Carpet Books edition 2003
First published 1992

Magic Carpet Books is a trademark of Harcourt, Inc., registered in the United States of America and/or other jurisdictions.

The Library of Congress has cataloged the hardcover edition as follows:
Vande Velde, Vivian.
Dragon's bait/Vivian Vande Velde.
p. cm.
Summary: Wrongly condemned for witchcraft, fifteen-year-old Alys is tempted to take revenge on her accusers when the dragon to which she has been sacrificed turns out to be an ally.
[1. Dragons—Fiction. 2. Revenge—Fiction. 3. Fantasy.] I. Title.
PZ7.V2773Dr 1992
[Fic]—dc20   92-3761
ISBN 0-15-200726-1
ISBN 0-15-216663-7 pb

Text set in Fournier
Designed by Cathy Riggs

H G F E D C B A

Printed in the United States of America

To the members of my writers group,
without whom nothing would get done

Dragon's Bait

Chapter 1

THE DAY ALYS was accused of being a witch started out like any other.

She woke to the gray light of dawn and to the sound of her father coughing. Did he sound any better than he had the morning before? *Yes,* she told herself—*just a little bit, but definitely better.* And though she'd thought that every morning since late winter when he'd been so sick she'd been afraid he'd die, and though here it was with the wheat already harvested and the leaves beginning to turn, and he still too frail to run the tin shop by himself—that did nothing to lessen her conviction. He definitely sounded better.

Of course, it wasn't normal for a girl to help in her father's business. A man without sons was expected to take in apprentices, not teach his trade to a fifteen-year-old daughter. But her father had had no need for an apprentice before he got sick, and now there was nothing extra with which to afford one. Without the goat cheese that Vleeter and his wife had given them and the bread that the widow Margaret had periodically left at their doorstep, they might well have starved during those long, long days when he'd been too sick to work at all. So now he was teaching her how to draw out tin into wire, how to pour it to fashion buttons, how to cut and join. She was slow, just learning, and he was slow, having to rest frequently. Between the two of them they could craft just barely enough tin to keep themselves alive.

Until the day Alys was accused of being a witch.

It started in the late afternoon, when a man she didn't know came into the shop.

Saint-Toby's-by-the-Mountain was small enough that everybody knew everybody, so it wasn't often that she saw a stranger. She put down the shears with which she'd been cutting a sheet of tin and said, because her father had gone into the house to lie down, "Yes? May I help you?" It wasn't fair to judge someone by the way he looked, she knew, but there was something decidedly unpleasant about this man, about the way he didn't seem to fit together properly. The toothy smile didn't go with the cold eyes; the head, shaved in the manner of a man of the Church, didn't go with the long, elegant, beringed fingers; the clothes were much too fine for Saint Toby's—even for someone simply passing through Saint Toby's.

"You are Alys, the tinsmith's daughter?" the man asked, though his gaze was roving all over the shop and he must see who she was even if— she could tell—he disapproved.

Beyond him, she saw a flitter of movement by the door and recognized their neighbor, the wheelwright Gower. Now what was he doing? His shop had been closed all day, which was unusual, Gower being an ambitious man. He was so ambitious he had even made offers to buy their land so he could expand his own shop. His wife, Una, and their daughter, Etta, had refused to talk to Alys ever since her father had refused to sell. Leave it to Gower to show up at the first sign of trouble. "I'm Alys," she said.

"I am Inquisitor Atherton of Griswold,"

the stranger said, naming the town on the other side of the mountain. Alys's attention leaped back from Gower, but before she could say anything, he continued, "You have been accused of witchcraft, and it is my duty to prove that." The already insincere smile broadened. "Or disprove it, if the evidence so warrants."

"Witchcraft?" Alys had no idea what to say. "Who . . . I mean what . . . I mean . . ."

"You will come with me," the Inquisitor told her.

Alys knew she wasn't a witch and reasoned that she would therefore be proven innocent. Still, fear began to overcome confusion as Inquisitor Atherton took firm hold of her arm. Her voice shook. "But my father's aslee—"

The Inquisitor's fingers dug into her arm as he repeated, "You will come with me."

That was when she knew, deep in her heart—though she wouldn't admit it—that he would never find her innocent, no matter what. "Father!" she cried.

The Inquisitor pulled her out into the street. People were gathering to see what the stranger was up to. But out of all those faces, Inquisitor Atherton picked Gower. "Go fetch the father."

"Gower," Alys said, finally realizing.

And lest she have any lingering doubts, the Inquisitor was pulling her next door, to the storeroom behind the wheelwright's shop. "This will be our court," the Inquisitor said. "Gather those who would testify."

The room filled quickly. "What'd she *do*?" she heard several of the children ask. But the parents only told them "Hush," and looked at Alys with fear, while the whispered word "witch" played over the crowd so that she could never tell who had spoken it. She had known these people all her fifteen years. Surely they couldn't be afraid of *her*? But standing there among wheel rims and spokes of various sizes, with Inquisitor Atherton's grip bruising her arm, she couldn't be sure.

Her father came rushing in. Alys's heart sank, for she was alarmed by how pale he was. But Atherton wouldn't let her go and he wouldn't let her father approach.

"Stand there," the Inquisitor commanded her father. "Let it begin."

Let what begin? Alys wanted to ask, but she only had time to draw breath.

"I saw her"—Una's loud voice cut through

the murmuring of the crowd and everyone turned to face her—"in the street in front of Goodwife Margaret's cottage. I saw her look around to see if anybody was watching, but she didn't see me because I was bending over in my garden. She made a sign, and then she spat on the ground, and the next day Margaret's goat went dry and it's been dry ever since."

"I never—," Alys started.

"Be silent!" the Inquisitor warned.

"I will not," Alys protested. "What she's just said simply isn't true." She took a step toward Una, and Una threw her arms up in an exaggerated gesture as though to protect herself.

"Don't let her make the Sign against me!" Una cried, hiding her face.

"That's the most ridiculous—"

Before Alys could finish, Atherton grabbed her by the arm and dragged her away from Una. "We need a rope to bind her," he said. "And keep the father back."

"Don't hurt him!" Alys cried, seeing Gower shove her father, who'd been struggling to get to her. Atherton twisted her arms behind her back, and she felt rope being wrapped around her wrists.

Once she was tied, Atherton spun her around to face him. "Another attempt to harm the witnesses will be dealt with severely."

"But I didn't, and my father's sick, and—"

He put his finger close to her face. "Speak out of turn again, and *that* will be dealt with severely."

Alys jerked away from his finger but didn't dare answer. She looked at her father and tried to tell him with her expression not to worry, but she was too worried herself to be convincing.

It was Margaret who stepped forward, though she was almost half Atherton's height and probably twice his age. "Well, if she can't talk, I will," Margaret said. "What Una said is total nonsense."

"Has your goat gone dry?" the Inquisitor asked.

"Yes, but—"

"And it was a good milker before?"

"Yes, but—"

"Next!"

"I seen her," Gower said before Margaret could protest again. Everyone turned to look at him. "I seen her this past Midsummer's Eve. I just come back from fixing Barlow's cart wheel.

They had me to supper and I stayed late." He turned to Farmer Barlow. "You remember?"

Barlow was watching the Inquisitor and looking nervous about being involved. "I remember you coming."

"The moon had risen," Gower continued, "and I seen her plain as day in the meadow beyond Barlow's pasture. *What's she doing there?* I said to myself. She had her arms out like this and she was just turning round and round, like she was dancing real slow. I stood a moment, just wondering what she was doing. And then..."

"Then?" the Inquisitor said.

"She took her clothes off."

Horrified, Alys protested, "I never—"

The Inquisitor raised his hand as though to slap her. "Gag her," he commanded.

"No, wait," Alys gasped. "Please. I promise to be quiet."

Atherton changed his upraised hand to a gesture of warning. He turned back to Gower. "Then what?"

"She danced faster and faster, in a frenzy. A lewd, devilish dance. And then I could hear the sound of pipes playing high and sweet almost beyond hearing. Fairy music, I reckoned. Not something a man who believes in the good word of God should listen to. Nor see, neither."

Atherton turned to Farmer Barlow. "And you, have you heard or seen something a man who believes in the good word of God shouldn't?"

Barlow's gaze shifted nervously from Atherton to Gower to Alys, back to Atherton, as though searching for the safest answer. "I ain't seen nothing," he said, licking his lips. "But then, that meadow's to the back of the house."

"I've seen something," Etta said, "something half the people in Saint Toby's saw and heard."

"And what's that, my daughter?" the Inquisitor said, sweet and gentle.

"She went to the carpenter's shop, to have a stool made. After it was done, she and apprentice Radley had a big argument about the price. We all heard her. 'That's too much,' she said. 'I could make a better one than that,' she said, 'in fact from now on I will.' Several of us were gathered around the door to see. She pushed past me on the way out, but then I saw her turn back. And the moment she did, the *moment* she did,

Radley's chisel slipped and he gouged his hand something terrible so that he was hardly able to work for almost half the rest of the month."

"Is Radley, the carpenter's apprentice, here?" Atherton asked. "Step forward and tell us: Is this how it happened?"

Radley shuffled his feet and wouldn't look up, neither at Atherton nor at Alys. Tilden, the master carpenter, stood silent, next to him. "It's true," Radley mumbled.

"Who witnessed this argument and the aftermath?" Atherton demanded.

Hands raised, some reluctantly, some eagerly.

"What else?" Atherton asked.

And so it went.

Alys watched as one by one the friends who tried to defend her were bullied or frightened into backing down.

If only fat, jovial Father Joseph were still here, Alys thought. 'And did she dance naked even though it rained?' he would have asked. 'And isn't Goodwife Margaret's goat almost as old as Goodwife Margaret herself? And how often has apprentice Radley struck his thumb with a hammer and asked his master for the rest of the day off, and was young Alys there every time?' He might have dramatically clapped his hand to his brow and said, 'Last Sunday I forgot the words to my sermon. Maybe I've been bewitched, too.' Everyone would have seen how foolish the accusations were. Everyone would have noticed that Gower Prescottson and his wife, Una, and his daughter, Etta, were the only ones claiming to have actually seen her dance or spit or make the evil eye. Everyone would have laughed with Father Joseph.

But Father Joseph was dead, killed by the coughing sickness which had ravaged Saint Toby's this past winter, the same sickness that had left her father frail and bent over at the least exertion, so that now he could do nothing but put his thin hands over his face and rock back and forth where he stood.

Instead of Father Joseph, there was only Inquisitor Atherton. And Alys could see that he never laughed. Instead, he smiled. He smiled while Gower and his family told lies about her. He smiled while the confused villagers made vague comments about her. He smiled as they went from saying that she couldn't have done those awful things to saying that they didn't know anything about whether she'd done those awful things to saying that she may well have done those awful things.

It was only when the villagers were totally confused that he finally told her she could speak.

"I'm innocent," she started, "I—"

"Only the Blessed Virgin is innocent," Inquisitor Atherton bellowed. "Born into this world without blemish on her soul. How dare you compare yourself to the Mother of Our Lord?"

She heard her father groan. "But," she stammered, "but..."

"Do we burn her at the stake now?" Etta asked, unable to mask her enthusiasm. "Or do we throw her into the water first?" Water was sure proof. If the accused floated, that meant she was a witch and she was taken out and burned. If she sank and drowned, that meant she hadn't been guilty after all, and the village elder would apologize to any surviving members of the family.

Gower gave his daughter a dirty look. The last thing he needed at this point was a chance for Alys's name to be cleared.

But in any case Inquisitor Atherton was shaking his head. "We can solve two problems at once. A dragon has been terrorizing Griswold and the other villages on the north side of the mountain. It is a *small* dragon, as dragons go, contenting itself so far mostly with sheep and the occasional dog. Perhaps a *small* token of our respect will keep it from bothering the villagers themselves."

"Dragon?" Alys breathed. Her knees almost gave out under her. *I will not,* she commanded herself, *I will not give them the satisfaction.*

"Only a small one," Inquisitor Atherton repeated. With a smile.

In the end it was Alys's father whose knees buckled. Without uttering a sound, he clutched at his heart, then dropped to the floor and lay completely still. Nobody moved: perhaps because they were so surprised, but then again perhaps because he was father to a convicted witch.

Alys tore away from the two farm lads who had assigned themselves to guard her. Her hands were still bound behind her back, but escape was not what she had on her mind. "Father," she cried, throwing herself to the floor beside him. "Father!" But his chest no longer moved up and down with breath.

I will not beg for my life, she told herself, *and I will not let them see me cry.*

"Look at her," she heard some of them murmur. "Her heart is made of ice."

And others: "It's made of stone."

And again: "She's given it to Satan."

Someone jerked up on the rope that bound her wrists, dragging her up onto her feet. She forced her face to hide the pain. Instead she concentrated on the crucifix that hung on Inquisitor Atherton's chest, all gold and gems though she had never heard that Griswold was a rich town. She thought once again of Father Joseph, who had worn a cross his own father, a casket maker, had carved from wood.

"Get a cart to transport her," Inquisitor Atherton commanded. "We'll bury the old man when we get back."

And once more he smiled at her.

Chapter 2

IT WAS DUSK by the time Atherton called a halt to the parade that had followed out of Saint Toby's to the place where Alys was to meet her judgment.

It was also raining.

But despite the dark and the churned-up mud, Alys could see clear evidence of the dragon. First of all it looked like dragon country: fertile farms scattered about, a large nearby lake, a series of peaks and plateaus separated by deep valleys and crevasses and thick woodlands that would confound pursuit by those forced to go on foot rather than by wing. Alys had heard it all in ballads, and although she had never seen a dragon, had never met anyone who had personally seen a dragon, had never heard of a dragon in these parts in her lifetime, she recognized the signs: the trampled farms closest to the foot of the mountain, the scorched trees, the deep grooves—no doubt left by dragon claws—in a rocky outcrop by the lake. The cart horses kept tossing their heads and making nervous *huff* sounds and showing the whites around their eyes, as though something that only they could see or hear or smell spooked them.

Her mind shied away from the thoughts that crowded her. She tried to regain the image of her and her father. She pictured their heads together, with sunlight streaming through the shop window as he patiently explained tin craft to her as thoroughly as if she'd been born a boy and could really be his apprentice.

I will not give them the satisfaction, Alys repeated over and over, so afraid she could hardly think. But the repetition had kept her back straight during the journey as she'd sat in the cramped cart, which smelled of stale turnips. It had helped her to focus beyond the gawking faces and the jabbing fingers. And if her teeth and bones felt all rattled loose from the ride, surely the people who had walked, slogging those last miles through mud, were hardly to be envied.

They dug a hole, deep to go beneath the shifting mud, then set up a rough-hewn pole, tamping down the dirt to hold it fast. Gower pulled her from the cart, using more force than was needed considering she didn't resist. They never untied her arms, but ran another rope through the bindings and then around the pole.

"Iron's surer," Gower complained.

"Fey creatures have an aversion to iron," Inquisitor Atherton said. "We don't want to frighten the dragon away." Then he stood before her and bellowed, "Do not, therefore, let sin rule your mortal body and make you obey its lusts. No more shall you offer your body to sin as a weapon of evil. Rather, offer yourself to God as one who has come back from the dead to life, and offer your body to God as a weapon for justice. Then sin will no longer have power over you."

It was bad enough they were going to kill her; she wasn't going to let him twist Scripture to fit her. She spat at him, remembering what they had said about Margaret's goat. The action lost some of its effectiveness since he was already soaked with the rain and she couldn't even tell if she had hit him.

But Atherton could afford to be magnanimous. "Repent," he told her, "and save your immortal soul."

She stared beyond his right shoulder, to a place in her mind where dust motes played in the sunlight and her father's big but gentle hands guided hers over a piece of tin that would eventually become a cup.

Atherton was willing to be magnanimous, but he wasn't willing to get wet for nothing. He instructed them to stick some of the flaming torches into the ground so that the dragon wouldn't have any trouble finding her. Then he sketched the sign of the cross in her general direction and turned his back on her.

The villagers followed him, returning down the slope lest the dragon come and make a meal of them all. She could hear the creak of the cart and a snatch or two of excited chatter, and then the rain swallowed up the sounds as thoroughly as the shadows had swallowed the people themselves. The torches sputtered and smoked in the dampness.

I should have left them with a nice curse, Alys thought. *Something to keep them up nights, shivering in their beds.* But Alys didn't know any curses, and anyway it was too late now.

She found a position where she could lean against the pole without any of the rough places sticking into her back.

At least she was alone, and for a while that was a comfort. But she could no longer form the picture of her father's workshop. Pieces of it kept slipping away, like shards of tin falling to the floor. And when she'd concentrate on those elusive parts, force them into being, other things would dissolve until eventually she couldn't even picture her father's face.

Then, with no one there as witness, she finally cried.

EVENTUALLY THE RAIN stopped. Clouds like tattered rags raced across the face of the almost-full moon. Alys was certain the rope around the pole was loose enough that she could slide down to rest her legs, but she wasn't sure she could get back up. The pole had been shaped so quickly, so roughly, that it was likely to snag the bindings, and that would be a terrible way to die:

caught in a half-crouch, her bottom all muddy from sitting on the wet ground.

How would the dragon kill her? Perhaps she would be less afraid if she figured out just what to expect.

A blast of flame? *Not likely,* she decided. In the stories, dragons frequently asked for young maidens. If they simply incinerated their victims, why worry about age or gender or lack of . . . Alys's stomach tightened. Despite what Inquisitor Atherton had shouted at her about sin and lust and Satan ruling her body, she *was* a maiden. In the village of Saint Toby's, there were girls who had been born the same year as she who were already married; two of them— Nola, whose father had gone to sea and never returned, and Aldercy, who was wed to Barlow's second-youngest son—already had babies. But Alys had never had much use for the village boys, who had all seemed coarse and pushy and who never dreamed of anything beyond Saint-Toby's-by-the-Mountain and one day running their own fathers' shops. Alys had always thought . . . she'd thought . . .

What difference did it make what she had thought? Here she was tied to a pole as dragon's bait, and if the dragon ever got around to coming, it would kill her in some fashion that probably would not be with a blast of flame.

Which undoubtedly would have been the quickest.

In all likelihood it would eat her. The call for maidens could conceivably have something to do with the quality of taste. All she had to worry about was whether it would start to eat her right away, while she was still breathing and screaming and knowing what was going on, or kill her first, perhaps with a swift flick of those claws, which had cut through the stone by the lake, or maybe by biting off…

This wasn't helping. This was making things worse.

It would probably be fast, she tried to convince herself. *I won't cry again.* It wasn't enough that Gower and his horrid family and Atherton and all the rest couldn't see her, would never know: She wasn't going to cry again.

It *would* be fast. She'd seen the claw marks on the stone, the trees knocked out of the way of the creature's passing. It had a wingspan hundreds of feet across, and it was incredibly strong. It would be fast.

In the distance a wolf howled.

Alys shivered, a combination of the cold breeze through her rain-soaked clothes and the thought that a wolf wouldn't be fast.

The moon was no longer directly overhead. It wasn't exactly sinking below the horizon, but what if the dragon didn't come? What if she remained here for days, starving, fevered from the chill she was surely already catching? And what of wolves?

She twisted her arms and realized the rope that held her wrists was looser than she had anticipated. She tried to think back, to remember all the way to this afternoon and to who had tied her.

Perryn the wood-gatherer. Ah yes. Not that he was of a kinder disposition than the others, but he never could get anything right.

Alys folded her thumbs and little fingers in, trying to make her hands as narrow as possible. The twine rubbed painfully against her flesh as she tugged.

She yanked and nothing happened.

She pulled with steady pressure and felt the rope ease down over her right hand. Again she tugged.

This time her right hand came loose. She shook the tangle of knots off her left wrist, and that rope, still entwined with the rope that went around the pole, dropped in a heap to the mud at the foot of the pole.

Her arms felt as though they were going to fall off. The burning pinpricks of pain were so bad she almost wished they would. She flexed her fingers, her wrists, her shoulders—to get the blood moving again.

Now what?

She couldn't go back to Saint Toby's. They'd just bring her straight back here, and this time make sure she was tied securely. And even, she thought, *even* if they did take her escape as proof that she was innocent and forgave her, how could *she* ever forgive *them,* live with *them,* see *them* every day for the rest of her life knowing what they had thought, what they had caused to happen to her father, what they had wanted to do to her, what they still might do?

And she couldn't just go to a different village and try to make a new life. It wasn't like she was a boy with a trade, or even one who could be apprenticed. A very young girl child might be taken in on mercy, but she was too old by at least half.

Wrapping her sore arms around herself for warmth, Alys stooped down to ease her legs. She was no longer tied to the stake, but she had not really escaped for she had nowhere else to go.

That was when the dragon came.

Chapter 3

HER FIRST INCLINATION was to hope the dragon hadn't seen the torches and that she'd have time to run under cover of the nearby trees. It was hard to judge how high the creature was flying—above the treetops, below the almost-full moon—without knowing how big it was. And it *was* big, whatever the distance worked out to be. Its enormous wings carried it halfway across the sky with one powerful beat. The thing was close enough that she could see it had a mane, which she had never heard mentioned in any of the legends, but far enough away that she couldn't make out the individual scales.

Then she realized the dragon *hadn't* seen her, and that if she stayed still for a few moments longer, she was free. But she was soaked to the skin and cold, and she hadn't eaten since early morning—and here it was, almost dawn of the following day—and she was an orphan with nowhere, absolutely nowhere, to go. And she remembered the wolves.

Her choices, as she saw them, were to die quick or to die slow.

She chose quick.

Standing, she flung a rock with all her might. "You stupid dragon!" she screamed. "Come and get me!"

Her muscles, cramped and strained from being tied so long, rebelled. The rock arced and plummeted to the ground far short of the dragon. But her movement, or her shout, attracted its attention.

Probably the wrong choice, she thought, as the creature wheeled gracefully and glided back toward her. She closed her eyes and braced herself.

She felt the wind of its wings as it passed overhead, circling, perhaps suspecting a trap. Then it settled to the ground before her. She braced herself . . . braced herself . . . braced . . .

She opened her eyes just the tiniest bit, sure

that what she'd see would be her last sight: a tongue of flame about to engulf her, or great slathery jaws opened wide to tear her, or sharp claws about to rake the life out of her.

What she saw was the dragon's kneecap.

Momentarily she reclosed her eyes. She had expected the creature to tower over her; she just hadn't realized that it would tower over her even before its legs ended.

She swallowed and opened her eyes again. She tipped her head back, back, back.

The dragon watched her from that impossible height.

"Well, kill me," she whispered.

Still the dragon just stood there, pale in the light of the moon and torches, its wispy mane fluttering in the soft breeze, its eyes too far up for Alys to see more than a dark hint. It didn't smell of sulfur, which was something the balladeers almost always said, or of blood or carrion, which was something else she'd expected. More like damp meadow grass on a spring day.

Alys thought back to this past winter when so many people had gotten sick, which made her think of her father, who had survived, which made her think of him collapsing in Gower's storeroom, his hand to his chest. She kicked the dragon, hard.

The impact made her toes sting.

The dragon tipped its head slightly to one side as though considering. Something.

So, this wasn't going to be quick after all: The dragon was going to play with her. She should have chosen the wolves while she'd had the chance. But, from some unexpected place within, a giggle bubbled up. "Now, dear," she said, "don't play with your food." She covered her face with her hands and sank to the ground. She had so wanted to be brave, even if she was the only one who'd know it, and here she was laughing and sobbing at the same time, facing her death with her rear end in the mud after all.

With her eyes scrunched closed behind her hands, she was aware of the dragon moving. *This is it,* she thought. But still she jumped as something brushed her hand. *I'm sorry,* she thought desperately to God, not for being a witch, which they both knew she wasn't, but for anything else—she was too scared to think of specifics—the impatiences, the missed opportunities to go out of her way to be kind, the times

she'd daydreamed during Mass, the...the...
what? Her mind shut down, refusing to come up
with anything. And what was this stupid dragon
doing?

Just as she was trying to get up the courage
to open her eyes, she realized that hands were
pulling at her hands, uncovering her face.

Hands—not claws.

Alys gasped, opening her eyes and dropping
her hands all at the same moment.

A young man, looking maybe two years
older than she, crouched before her, his hands
still on hers even now as they rested in her lap.

There was no sign of the dragon.

For the briefest moment she wondered if he
were some sort of dragon-slaying prince who'd
killed— No, there'd been no time for that—
who'd frightened away...But there'd been no
sound....

She looked again, and didn't know how she
could have ever mistaken him, however briefly,
for human.

The thing that was most obviously wrong
were the eyes. And she thought that before she
even noticed the color, which was that of the
amethyst gem in the crucifix Inquisitor Atherton

wore. *"It's a small dragon,"* Alys recalled Atherton saying. No wonder. If this human manifestation was any indication, the dragon wasn't fully adult yet. It gave her a perverse pleasure to think of the villagers of Saint Toby's having to contend with him when he reached his full size. Even if she wouldn't be alive to see it.

By the light of the torches she saw that his hair was the color the mane had been, palest gold, and it hung almost to his waist. Alys jerked her gaze back up to the face, for she had suddenly— finally—noticed that he wore no clothes.

For the first time, the purple eyes flickered with emotion: amusement. He had seen her discomfort, and recognized the cause.

"I didn't know," she said, to say anything, and looked away and simultaneously tried to pull her hands from his, "that dragons could take on human shape." She was surprised that her voice worked. His hands felt like human hands—the texture, the warmth, everything was just as it should be, but . . .

He refused to release her hands until she looked at him again. He smiled, but this time the amusement didn't reach his eyes. "It's not often," he said in a voice that was soft and husky, but well within the norms for a human of his—apparent—age and build, "that I find a damsel flinging rocks at me." He paused as though considering and slowly added, "It happened once with a knight, but I'd already eaten his horse and most of his weapons. The squire, too, as I recall." He tipped his head slightly as though waiting for a response, the same gesture he had made while in dragon shape.

"I see," Alys said.

He raised his eyebrows doubtfully.

Alys stared at her hands in her lap. Dragon or human, he certainly appeared human, and it was disconcerting to have him crouched before her with nothing on.

The dragon-youth sighed and sat down on the cold ground, his right leg folded under him, the left up so that he could rest his elbow on his knee, which afforded some modesty, if she didn't think about it. "Humans," he sighed in a tone that reminded Alys that—whatever was the dragon equivalent to seventeen years old— dragons lived for hundreds of years. "Sometimes I forget."

Alys glanced up and then away. Up long enough that she saw him nod toward the pole to which she'd been tied.

"That yours?"

She nodded, never looking up.

"You had time to get away."

She met his eyes then. Defiantly. "You didn't see me."

That stirred something deep beneath those cut-glass eyes, but it was already gone before he spoke. "Of course I saw you. I wasn't interested until you began to act out of the ordinary."

His superior attitude annoyed her despite her still very real fear. "People staked out on hillsides is ordinary?"

He flashed his cold grin. "It is for me."

She sucked in a breath, reminded of her earlier concern. "Why is it . . . ?" She hesitated, not sure she wanted to know.

"What?"

Maybe she was worrying needlessly. "Can all dragons change to human shape?"

He paused, as though considering how much to tell her. "No," he said, just at the point she realized she couldn't believe him, whatever he answered. "Only gold-colored dragons have magic." He repeated her own words to her: "'Why is it...?'"

She looked down again.

He forced her chin up.

In a very small voice, never meeting his eyes, terrified of the answer that she had so glibly dismissed earlier, she asked, "Why is it dragons ask for maidens?"

The dragon-youth released her, his hand shaking. Startled, she looked up and saw that he was silently laughing. "Dragons don't ask for maidens," he said. "Dragons are offered maidens."

Alys shook her head to show she didn't understand.

"Is a king likely to be a maiden? Or a village headman? It's the men who make the laws that decree that maidens be offered."

Alys thought of all the lovely old songs, the grieving kings, the valiant knights. "That's a lie," she whispered.

"Perhaps." She saw a glint in his eyes. "I *do* lie."

"Yes," she snapped at him, suddenly more angry than afraid, "just like the old riddle: Everything I say is a lie. But if that's true, then it's not a lie, so that makes it not true, which means it's a lie, which—"

The dragon swept to his feet, and Alys kept her gaze firmly on his face. "I didn't say *everything* I said was a lie. And I hate riddles. The last time a knight challenged me to a riddling contest, I lost. And then I ate him anyway. Why"— he leaned down with his hands on his knees to put his face on a level with hers—"didn't you run away when you had the chance, before I saw you?"

"You—" Alys had started to say, "You said you saw me all along," but she stopped just short of it.

Maybe he read her thought in her eyes.

She looked at her hands in her lap.

"Why didn't you run away?"

"To where?" she shouted. "I have nowhere to go. They killed my father. They convicted me of being a witch. I'm cold and wet and hungry." She gave a ragged sigh and lowered her voice. "And I have nowhere to go."

The dragon sat down again. "*Are* you a witch?"

"No."

"What are you going to do about it?"

"There's nothing I can do. Except enjoy the thought of you flying over Saint Toby's village and breathing fire and roasting them all, every single one of them, down to the last baby."

The dragon raised his brows.

"Well," she said, "maybe not the babies."

The dragon grinned and stood again.

Alys refused to look up.

The dragon gave an awful cry, like a huge bird of prey.

Alys jerked her head up and saw that he'd resumed his dragon form. Now she'd made him angry, failed whatever test it was he'd set, or simply no longer amused him. The great wings flapped with a sound like sails snapping in the wind, and she threw her hands up to protect her face.

The claws grasped her forearms and she gritted her teeth. But the talons didn't sink into her flesh, they raised her from the ground. Her arms felt as if they would be pulled from their sockets, reawakening the pain that had just begun to subside. Alys opened her eyes and saw that she was already dangling high, high up above the trees. She screamed in terror at the thought that he would drop her and she would plummet long moments before hitting the ground, or that he wouldn't drop her at all but was carrying her to his lair. She screamed again and again, too frightened to close her eyes against the stinging wind and the lurching countryside.

And then he did let her go.

The rushing air tore the scream from her throat, but she didn't fall for long. And the ground she hit was soft, bouncy. A haystack, she realized from the smell of it, and the prickliness, before the fog of terror cleared from her eyes.

She lay there flat on her stomach waiting, waiting, her heart beating so loudly she could hear nothing else.

A half-lifetime later she finally raised her head, saw that she was alone. "Where are you?" she screamed into the night. "What are you doing to me?"

The night didn't answer.

She lowered her face into the crook of her arm and rocked back and forth. Despite everything that had happened—because of everything that had happened—she drifted off to sleep.

Something dropped beside her.

She gasped, sitting up.

It was a rough-spun peasant dress and a sturdy pair of shoes that she had felt land next to her. The dragon, once again human-shaped, was crouched beside her, this time wearing clothes—a peasant's shirt and breeches. He nodded his head to where she had been lying. "I thought you were crying."

"No," she said. "I don't cry, ever."

His face showed nothing.

"Where'd you get these?"

He gestured off into the pink-edged dark. "Farmhouse."

"You didn't...kill the people? Did you?"

He paused, with that expression of his that said he was weighing his answer. "They'd run off. Abandoned the place."

She sighed in relief. "Really?"

He shrugged, with a condescending smile. "Perhaps. You better get out of your wet clothes."

"Turn around," she commanded.

He did, but she could see his shoulders shaking once more with silent laughter.

Chapter 4

ALYS FINISHED LACING the bodice of her borrowed dress and looked up to find the young man who was a dragon unabashedly regarding her. No telling, from that bland expression, if he'd turned a moment before she had, or if he'd been watching all along. Warmth flooded her cheeks, from anger and embarrassment. The suspicion that he could see her blush, even in the dim predawn light, made her angrier yet and even more embarrassed. He sat too close to her, but perched on the top of the haystack, she had nowhere to go. She lowered her gaze to avoid his face. Except for the color of the eyes, everything was just too right.

And nothing was right at all.

She concentrated on her anger, to give her

voice the bite it needed. "That's very rude, you know."

For a long moment he said nothing, as though in the interim he'd forgotten how to speak. Finally he said, "What is?"

"Watching me get dressed. People don't do that."

"Don't they?" he asked with just enough balance between polite inquiry and irony to show that he knew the truth of it.

"*Nice* people don't." He looked momentarily startled, as though taken aback that she could have ever confused him with someone who could be nice. His expression shifted to amusement. Before he could start laughing outright, Alys said, "And I don't like the way you sit so close to me, either." She regretted the words immediately for they gave him yet another advantage over her.

So she wasn't completely surprised when he seized her arm. But she wasn't expecting him to tug. Together they skittered and wobbled down the side of the haystack, sending flurries of hay flying till she landed in a heap, half on top of him, though she'd been sliding down haystacks for as far back into her childhood as she could remember.

Once she managed to figure out which end was up, Alys jerked her arm to break the dragon-youth's grip. He held on just long enough so that, when he did let go, she tipped over. She fell flat on her back, and more hay showered on her. Furious, she leaped to her feet and ineffectually brushed at the hay that was in her hair and clothes. Unsure how much of her discomfort was actually premeditated on his part, she snapped, "Thank you."

Still sitting at the foot of the haystack, he looked up at her but said nothing.

Surely it couldn't be that easy. "For everything," she added.

Still nothing.

So Alys turned and took a step away.

And a second.

And a third.

She braced herself for him to grab her from behind, knowing that he could move with uncanny speed and silence. She took another step, her shoulders involuntarily hunched in anticipation, cringing from the thought that he could transform himself as silently as he could move, and that it might not be with hands that he'd choose to catch hold of her.

She managed one more step.

When she turned, he was sitting as before, watching her. Her voice quivered. "Why are you doing this?"

He put on an expression that was a bit too much of wide-eyed innocence.

"What do you want from me?" she demanded.

Still he gave her nothing, as though waiting for her to choose the direction the conversation must take.

She returned to the haystack and sank down beside him. "I don't trust you."

Finally he reacted: He laughed, soft and throaty. "All for the best."

Trying to undermine her confidence, was he? In an attempt to appear equally mysterious and dangerous, she said, "And you shouldn't trust me."

He arched his eyebrows.

Alys worked to keep her chin level. "Just so we both know."

He inclined his head solemnly, though she suspected he didn't take her seriously. "Just so we both know," he repeated, his voice, as ever, telling her nothing.

"What do you want?"

He paused, perhaps considering what he could say that she would believe, perhaps working on regaining his sincere look. "To help you."

"To help me . . . ?" If he had hoped to find something she would believe, he had failed. "That's very kind of you," she said bitterly, for she no longer believed in kindness. "And you're willing to do this . . . why? Because you're fond of helping others?"

"I'm fond of revenge," the dragon answered.

Alys sat back on her heels, considering. She had a fleeting image of her father clutching his chest, sinking, ever sinking, to the floor of Gower's storeroom. *Revenge*. Never once had the word actually formed in her mind, but now that the dragon had said it, she recognized the thought that had been with her all day. She remembered what she'd said, about roasting the village, babies and all. "You'd burn their fields, demolish their houses, devour the survivors?"

"Yours for the asking," the dragon said. He gave her his chilliest smile and advised, "Don't ask."

So there *was* a catch. "Why?"

"Revenge," the dragon said, "is sweetest when it's slow enough that the one doing it can see the results, and the one to whom it's done knows from where it comes."

She thought of Gower, and his wife, Una, and their daughter, Etta. And she thought of Inquisitor Atherton, and she nodded.

"Do you want my help?" the dragon asked.

She knew exactly what he was doing, forcing her to put it into words, to admit to it, to take responsibility for it. "Yes," she said, savoring the sound of the word.

There was a flicker of something across his face, something too fast, or too far removed from any human emotion, for her to recognize. Again she was left with the feeling of having just passed—or failed—some test. His voice gave no indication which. "Who do you most want to see suffer?"

"Gower," she said, almost before he'd finished the question. And again, more calmly, "Gower."

"Then, of course," said the dragon, "we'll have to do him last."

So she told him all of it. The lies spoken. The lies implied. Her father's death.

The dragon-youth listened to everything, never asking questions, never bringing her back to the main point when her story wandered to Father Joseph sprinkling holy water on the fields every spring or to her mother who'd died two days after Alys was born.

I'll tell him everything, Alys thought, *and when I'm done, he'll tell me what to do.*

But when she was done, the dragon only said, "We will go indoors now, since your human body is more fragile than mine." He was on his feet before she saw him start to move, as though he'd only been waiting for the sound of her voice to stop. As though he hadn't been listening to the words.

And was the reference to her fragile body a subtle threat, she wondered, masquerading as concern? Or concern, perhaps, masquerading as threat? She wasn't comfortable with either idea. Nor with the thought of being confined with him, trapped by walls.

Not that she was in any less danger out here.

Now would be a good time to run, to break away from him and hide. Without checking to see if she followed, he was already headed for the farmhouse to which this haystack no doubt belonged. But ... *was* he that confident that she would come, or was it just that he didn't care one way or the other? He had made no move to stop her before, after pulling her down the haystack. *Didn't* it make any difference? Was it all the same to him?

And her situation was certainly no better now than it had been on the hillside when she had first gotten loose from her bonds, before she had ever seen him. She had nowhere to run then, and she had nowhere to run now. Except that now she had told him her life story, and he had indicated—hadn't he?—that he would help.

He'd entered the cottage with never a backward look for her. He must have lit a fire earlier while getting the clothes, for cheery firelight spilled out of the doorway. She could make out that this side of the cottage—the front—was singed, and the door hung loose on one twisted hinge. Beyond, what had to have been the barn was a burned-out shell. If there had been anybody still alive in either building, surely they'd have been up by now, and out here to inquire about the presence of strangers in their haystack.

Of course, the fact that there was nobody alive didn't mean there was nobody in the cottage.

At the last moment Alys balked yet again, unwilling to confront proof that the dragon had lied to her in this. But if she had a chance—*if* she had a chance—it wasn't out here. Slowly she entered.

There were no bodies after all. Or at least none lying out in the open. In the light from the fire in the hearth, Alys could see that the contents of the cottage were strewn about, but it was impossible to tell whether that was from the owners trying to decide what to take in a hurry as they fled, or from looters, or from the dragon searching for clothes and not knowing enough of humans to guess where they'd be kept. Presumably a dragon would have no trouble lighting a fire.

Somehow he was behind her, close enough that when he spoke his breath stirred the hair that had come loose against her neck. "If you want," he offered, "I could fetch you something to eat."

She jumped and whirled to face him. "No," she answered so quickly that he smiled.

Annoyed, she turned her back on him and began searching for food. "See," she meant the set of her shoulders to tell him, "I'm not afraid of you." And when was he going to do something or say something about all that she had told him? She found a sack with three wrinkled apples left over from last autumn; and, though it was almost time for this year's crop, they looked like the most delicious things she'd ever seen.

"Do you—" She started to turn around, saw that he was just removing his shirt, and hastily kept on turning. She bit her lip, her heart pounding. "What are you doing?" she asked in a panic.

He didn't answer and didn't answer, and still she wouldn't look. Then she heard a sound that could only be a huge mass of talons and scales and tail settling down on the packed-dirt floor. She turned and found the dragon curled up like a cat, his tail around him and his chin resting on his paws, never mind that he took up almost the entire room.

"What if the owners come back?" she asked.

The dragon, who'd already closed his eyes, reopened them and looked at her, unblinking.

"What if the people from Saint Toby's return to make sure I'm dead?"

From outside she could hear the first twitterings of birds rousing themselves for day, though it was still dark out. The dragon closed his eyes again, ignoring her.

"I've told you everything about me," she cried, "all my secret dreams, everything I ever hoped for, all my fears and inner thoughts. I hate it when you act as though I'm not here."

He looked up at her with a flash of annoyance but still said nothing.

Alys opened her mouth, but then closed it as things became clearer. "You can't talk when you're not in human form, can you?" She sighed. "You should have said so before."

The dragon jumped to his feet, transforming so quickly that he had lunged and grabbed her arm before she realized that it was his hand and not a claw that held her. "Of course I can talk when I'm not in human form." His fingers dug into her arm. "I can talk the language of whatever beast I'm in the shape of: When I'm a horse, I talk horse. When I'm a hawk, I talk hawk. *When I'm a human, I talk human.*"

Wincing from the pain and the intensity, Alys objected, "Humans aren't beasts."

"*THEY ARE TO DRAGONS,*" he shouted. "And only a human would be arrogant enough to argue about it."

"Arrogant?" Alys was too angry to be concerned about him standing there naked, holding her close. "*Arrogant? You're* calling *me* 'arrogant'?"

The dragon put his face close to hers. His voice suddenly soft and dangerous, he warned, "Be careful you don't become more trouble than you're worth."

As far as she could tell, she was already more trouble than she was worth. She tugged to snatch her arm away and realized he'd only let go of her before because he'd been good and ready to let go; if it was a contest of strength, he wouldn't even be aware of the force she exerted against him. Her anger cooled to an icy lump in her chest. "I'm sorry," she said quietly.

There was nothing in his face to indicate what he thought of that, whether he was disgusted by her fear or if, like Inquisitor Atherton, he took pleasure in it.

"I'm sorry," she repeated, softer yet.

He took a step back from her, giving himself room to return into dragon shape, and she decided that meant he wasn't going to kill her after all.

"Wait." As soon as she said it, she realized that he could kill her just as well in either shape. Still, maybe she should act as though she assumed the best, just in case he hadn't made up his mind. She said, "If we're going to be working together, I can't very well call you, 'Hey, you, dragon.'"

He narrowed his purple eyes at her and must have weighed considerations about which she wasn't even aware. "You may call me Selendrile," he said with just the slightest hint of sibilance. A moment later he'd resumed dragon shape and once again settled on the floor.

"Selendrile," she repeated, tasting the sound of it. "I'm Alys."

The dragon opened his eyes just long enough to look bored, then went to sleep.

Chapter 5

BY THE TIME Alys woke up, it was dark again. There was still, or again, a fire in the hearth. The dragon—Selendrile—was awake and in human form and crouched beside her, close enough to touch. She flinched, thinking he'd been about to shake her awake and that if she didn't look alert fast enough he might yet. But then she realized he was too still; she hadn't caught him between motions after all. He was simply there watching her, with that appraising expression that made him look as though he'd been either trying to read her mind or speculating how she'd taste.

She scrambled to her feet. He stayed where he was, only tipping his head back slightly to continue watching her. "Don't do that," she demanded, recalling—even as she said it—having heard the younger children at Saint Toby's say much the same thing, in much the same tone. "Stop looking at me."

He looked neither amused nor annoyed. Nor about to comply.

She swept past him so she wouldn't have to admit to either of them that her words had no effect on what he did or did not do. Her stomach felt as though it were twisted in a knot, she was so hungry; and despite the fact that she had searched earlier and found only the three apples, scouring the cottage for food would take her mind off both Selendrile and the thought of how long it had been since her last meal.

She paused in midstride, seeing a large wooden bowl on the table, filled almost to the top with a thick stew. She suddenly realized that the warm smell of it—potatoes and chicken and barley—filled the small cottage, and her stomach clenched even tighter as her mouth began to water. "What's this?" she asked softly.

"It's called stew," the dragon said. "Assorted grains and vegetables and some meat, heated to the point where no one can tell which is which."

Alys turned to see if he was being sarcastic or if he really thought he was telling her something she didn't know. She couldn't be sure. "I meant, where'd it come from?"

Selendrile gave a slight tip to his head. "I got it from a farmhouse on the outskirts of town."

"*Got* it?" she asked.

"Stole it," he corrected readily enough. "I didn't know how long your human form could go without nourishment. You seemed to be too weak to rouse yourself and I thought you might be dying."

Again the not-so-subtle hint that she could never keep up with him. His speculation on her mortality was spoken in the same tone he'd used to describe the contents of the stew.

"I was just tired," Alys said, annoyed, and somewhat chilled despite the fire. "I hadn't slept at all last night. Don't dragons sleep?" She knew they did; she'd seen him at it. Except that apparently he'd kept at it for a much shorter time than she had. He'd waited for her long enough to consider the possibility that she wouldn't get up, to fetch nourishment, bring it back here, and be crouched for who-knew-how-long staring at her until she'd opened her eyes.

Selendrile didn't answer, as though he couldn't be bothered with affirming something he knew she already knew.

Alys wondered whether—if she *had* died—he'd have eaten her, and if that was why he'd been waiting so patiently by her side. "Thank you," she said, sitting down at the table. "For the food."

Again he didn't answer.

"Are you going to eat some with me?"

"I've already fed."

And looking down into those cold amethyst eyes she had no idea if he'd eaten some of the stew or the person who'd prepared it. She forced down a mouthful that seemed intent on lodging itself in her throat. *He's never going to let you live,* a small part of her warned. *He'll help you get revenge on Atherton and Gower just for the pure spiteful fun of it. And then he'll rip your throat out, and enjoy it twice as much for having first tricked you into trusting him.*

Alys swallowed another lump of stew. *No,* she told herself, *I'll take his help, but if it comes to that, I'll kill him before he kills me. He's just a—IT's just a—dragon. It's not a real person.*

She took another swallow. Even if she was

in too much turmoil to taste anything, the food would keep her from starving. It would give her the strength she would need later. She said, "Have you considered what we talked about yesterday?"

Selendrile finally shifted position and sat on the floor, but still said nothing.

"About a plan?" she prompted.

"It's your revenge," he pointed out. "Surely you don't expect me to tell you what to do."

That was exactly what she'd expected.

Alys sighed. "Do you have any suggestions?"

She thought she caught a flicker of what may have been disappointment on his face. "You want to do Gower last," he reminded her.

"Yes."

"Then it would seem to make sense to do his family directly before him."

"So Atherton first, since he's in Griswold?"

The dragon-youth inclined his head.

"What exactly are we going to do to him?"

Selendrile only continued to watch her.

Alys shook her head. It was one thing to know she wanted Atherton to pay for what he'd done to her and her father; it was quite another to come up with a plan. "Maybe I shouldn't rush into this. We can go to Griswold, see what the town is like, decide on what to do there."

Selendrile asked, "Where do humans live when they're in a town they don't know, while they're trying to decide what to do?"

"An inn, I guess," Alys said. "If they have gold or silver to pay."

Selendrile smiled, faint and chilly, and Alys shivered.

His amusement shifted to something darker, a mood for which she had no name. "I think," he told her, "you'll have to go as a boy."

"What?" she squeaked. "I'd never pa—"

"For your own protection," he interrupted. "The other choice is to go as a married couple, though that has the disadvantage of Atherton recognizing you as soon as he sees you."

Alys found it hard to catch a breath despite the knowledge that he was watching her and was aware of her every movement. *A married couple?*

He took her silence as agreement. "We'll go as brothers. Pick a name."

Alys clenched her teeth, knowing that he was right, that a woman couldn't take a room by herself at a respectable inn, that he didn't need to bring her all the way to Griswold if he intended her harm. Still—soft-spoken and almost tame as he seemed at the moment—she could never be *sure* what he was thinking, could never trust him completely. She could never allow herself to forget that one of them would most probably end up killing the other. "Jocko," she said, picking the name out of the air.

Selendrile turned his back to her and, sitting cross-legged, gathered up his long fair hair at the nape of his neck. "If you can braid this or tie it up somehow to look more in the fashion of your countrymen, we'll attract less attention."

There was no chance Selendrile would *ever* not attract attention. Or was this another twist in the game, offering up trust—or the semblance of it—by turning his back to her while she sat in a kitchen full of knives?

Alys picked up the piece of twine that had tied the apple sack, and then, to shake him, to reveal as a lie his pose of complacent indifference, she reached for one of the knives. But he didn't scramble to his feet, or tense up, or give any indication that he was even aware that she held a weapon. The knife was badly made, wobbling in its wooden handle, but she managed to saw the twine into manageable lengths, watching him all the while. Not foolhardy, after all, but only unobservant. Still holding the knife, she approached his unprotected back, knowing this was stupid, that he could whirl around at the last moment with that deadly speed of his and turn the blade on her, and she would never have the chance to protest it had only been a test.

Alys knelt behind him. And only then made the decision that it *was* a test. She'd do his hair, and then afterward show him the knife she'd silently laid on the floor, show him the danger he'd never known he was in.

Alys ran her fingers through his hair to separate it into strands for braiding. When she was finished, she pulled the braids back and fastened them behind. "There," she said.

Selendrile turned before she had a chance to pick up the knife, but his purple eyes locked onto hers, never glancing to either side or down to the floor. "Turn around," he told her.

"Why?"

"So I can cut off your hair." With his eyes

never flickering away from hers, he picked up the knife she had finally convinced herself he couldn't have seen.

She stiffened. "Why can't we just braid it like yours?"

"Because there can't be a hint of a question in anybody's mind. The moment someone suspects you're a girl, the clothes won't work. You don't want Atherton to recognize you right away. You want him to feel there's something familiar about you so that he thinks about you after you're gone, after you've destroyed him. You want him to realize who you are only when you're not there anymore."

"That's what I want, is it?" she asked, unable to look away from the blade in his hand.

He used the knife to indicate she put her back to him, to take her turn in this game of trust and nerve.

She sat down, and he swept her hair back over her shoulders. His fingers were light and gentle as they brushed against her cheek, her neck. But the knife tugged mercilessly as he hacked away long strands of hair.

It'll grow back, she thought as big chunks of

it dropped all around her. And even if it didn't, this would still be worth it, to get revenge on Atherton. And then Una and Etta, Gower's family. And then Gower himself.

Anything would be worth that.

Chapter 6

ALYS ASSUMED THAT they would set out for Griswold immediately, so she was surprised when—after she thought they were all set—Selendrile said, "Wait here."

"For what?"

"You said we'd need gold and silver."

"Ah," Alys said, "of which you have..."

He gave a perfectly charming smile. "Much."

"Much." Alys sighed. "I can imagine. Wouldn't it be faster if I went with you?"

He shook his head.

"Once it's really dark, they'll close and lock the town gates."

Again he shook his head.

"You don't trust me," she said.

He just smiled.

By the time he came back, clutching a leather bag of coins, and by the time she re-braided his hair and by the time they'd walked to Griswold, the sky had turned from gray to black. Now here they were, standing with only the moon to light them, trying to convince the night watch that they were, in fact, harmless and should be allowed to enter.

The guard who had the lantern leaned down from his vantage on top of the wall, holding the light out to get a better look at them. But since he was up about eight feet higher than they were, they got a better look at him than he got at them.

Alys thought he looked cranky and sus-picious.

The other guard seemed to be the first man's superior; the one with the lantern had fetched him when Alys and Selendrile had knocked on the wooden gate, demanding en-trance and refusing to go away and come back in the morning. Alys couldn't see him, but he *sounded* cranky and suspicious. He said, "How do we know you ain't that witch?"

Selendrile, who'd been looking down to

avoid the glare of the light in his eyes, jerked his head up, but appeared more amused than startled.

Word of her couldn't have traveled this far this fast, could it? "What witch?" Alys asked.

"That old witch lives behind one of them waterfalls up to the glen." The guard jerked his head in the general direction of the mountain.

Alys realized she'd been holding her breath. She shook her head to indicate she didn't know what he was talking about.

"Sold her soul to the devil for the witch-power," he explained. "And never did use it for nothing but mischief and sorrow all her life. But now she's old and close to dying, she's looking to buy someone else's soul to take her place. Been bothering decent, law-abiding folk."

Alys continued to shake her head.

Selendrile finally spoke up. "No witches here," he said in a tone that gave away the fact that he was suspiciously close to laughing.

Alys added: "Does either of us look like an old witch?"

The guards were unimpressed with irony or logic. "Gate opens at dawn. Come back then."

If she weren't disguised as a boy in tunic,

breeches, and cap, she could have started crying, loudly, to see if that would help, but under the circumstances it probably wouldn't. The first guard straightened, pulling the lantern up with him. Seeing the light move away, Alys yelled up, "It was the dragon's fault." She was aware of Selendrile watching her, but she was watching the light. It stopped moving, returned to the wall.

"Dragon?" the guard said.

Alys decided to put a little quiver into her voice after all. "It killed our parents, ravaged our fields. We didn't dare stay another night. We were afraid it might come back." She pointed vaguely in the direction from which they'd come, then snuffled loudly, rubbing her sleeve arm over her nose.

The guard's voice became more gentle. "How old are you lads?"

"Twelve," she said, because there was no way she could pass as a fifteen-year-old boy and because she figured the younger the guards thought them, the more sympathetic they would be. Then, indicating Selendrile, she said, "And seventeen," which was what he looked like. *Seventeen, going on three hundred.*

The guards muttered together.

"All right," the senior one finally said.

There was another delay, then the creak of rope and wood as the latch was raised, and the gate swung open.

The guard stood in the middle of the open space, glowering at them over his crossbow sights.

Alys forced down a swallow.

"Move, move," he told them from between clenched teeth.

Selendrile gave her a shove just strong enough that she staggered forward a couple of paces. Her first thought was that he was offering her up as the target, but he came with her, and the guard continued to aim at the spot where they *had* stood, all the while anxiously peering into the shadows beyond the walls.

The heavy gate thudded back into place, maneuvered by the guard who'd been holding the lantern. Once the latch was secured, the other lowered his crossbow, apparently satisfied that no one was coming in with them. A lot of good gate or wall would do to keep Selendrile or his real kin out.

"You got people in Griswold?" the guard asked.

"No," Alys said. "But we do have a few copper pieces for lodging." She wanted him to know they weren't going to make a nuisance of themselves begging, without indicating they had enough that it'd be worth his while to rob them.

But now that she and Selendrile were in, the guards lost interest. The first was already scrambling up to resume his position on the wall. "The Green Barrel's probably your best bet, then," the other said, waving airily in an arc that indicated three-fourths of the town. "There's probably cleaner and definitely cheaper, but at least you won't wake up in the morning to find your throats slit."

While Alys paused to sort that out, Selendrile took her arm and started pulling her in the general direction the guard had indicated.

The inhabitants of Saint Toby's would be mostly home and in bed by this hour, but Griswold was a lot bigger, if no grander, and there were still lights on in many of the buildings and people out on the streets. For Alys it was a strange sensation, being in a town big enough to get lost in, being surrounded by people she hadn't known all her life. By the time she and

Selendrile finally found themselves in front of the Green Barrel Inn, her heart was beating too hard and fast for her to ask Selendrile to wait while she caught her breath.

He swept her past the painted rain barrel that gave the place its name and in through the open front door.

This is where we get set upon by thieves and cutthroats, Alys thought, *just waiting for an innocent victim to blunder in.* Unless, of course, anybody took more than the hastiest glance at Selendrile, in which case they were sure to see beyond his human disguise to the monster beneath, and that would start a commotion of a different sort.

But nobody at the dozen or so tables in the place looked at them with anything that even the wary Alys could call more than indifferent curiosity. From across the room came a skinny little man who was no taller than Alys, wiping his hands on his apron and smiling. His gaze flickered from Alys to Selendrile and he looked neither murderous nor about to panic. "May I help you?" he asked instead. Asked Selendrile, who appeared the older.

How can he look at him and not see? Alys

wondered. She said: "My brother and I, we're looking for a room."

The innkeeper shifted his gaze back to her and raised his brows skeptically.

"Our parents were killed in a dragon raid," she said. "It knocked down our house, burned our fields. We've come to Griswold looking for work."

One of the people at the nearest table asked, "You Upton's boys then?"

It was too dangerous; if somebody here knew this man Upton, somebody else might know his sons. "No," Alys admitted. "We're from the other side of Saint Toby's village. But there wasn't any work to be had there. We've got enough money for the night"—Selendrile had brought enough money to buy the place, but she certainly wasn't going to announce that—"or we could work for our keep."

The innkeeper hesitated and Alys nudged Selendrile. The gold was useless—there was no way a pair of orphaned peasants could come by gold—but she'd had him put a few of the silver and copper pieces in his pocket. Now he took one of these out and held it to the innkeeper.

"This'll get you your lodgings and a bit of

supper if you haven't eaten yet," the man said. "Breakfast comes with the room. Odelia," he called to a girl who was cleaning one of the tables. She looked just like him except for the fact that she had more hair and was obviously a couple of years younger than Alys. "You and your sister get a room set up."

"This way, please," the little girl said. She led them through the kitchen, where she introduced them as paying customers to another girl. This older one put down the spoon she was using to stir a kettle of soup and gave Selendrile a long, studied stare.

Here it comes, Alys thought.

With admirable calm, the older sister said, "We need to get straw for the bedding." She flung her arm around her sister's shoulders, but Alys saw her fingers dig into Odelia's upper arm, and the younger girl's confused expression as her sister hustled her outdoors. *Run, run,* every instinct warned Alys. *They're going to raise an alarm.* Selendrile was looking around the kitchen, oblivious to it all, peeking into the corners, looking under the counters. "We've got to get out of here," Alys warned him in a frantic whisper.

"We just got here," Selendrile pointed out, picking up a clay pot lid as though he'd never seen one before.

The two girls returned, carrying armloads of straw. Alys caught the hurried glance Odelia gave Selendrile before she lowered her gaze. "This way," she murmured.

But that wasn't fear which was causing her cheeks to redden. Alys glanced at the older sister, who was staring at Selendrile again.

Oh, heaven help me—they're flirting with him, she realized.

The two sisters led them to an upstairs room and began stuffing the straw into the mattress.

Alys tugged on Selendrile's arm. "There's only one sleeping pallet," she hissed at him.

He'd been looking out the window at the people in the street below, and he turned to her with a blank expression that could have been either lack of understanding or his usual give-nothing expression.

"What's that?" the older girl asked, straightening.

"There's only one sleeping pallet," Alys repeated.

"There's hardly room for two."

"Yes," Alys said, finding her patience wearing thin at the smug tone, "but there are two of us."

"But this one's wide enough for two," said the younger girl, Odelia, "and you *are* brothers." Both girls seemed on the verge of a giggling fit.

"Of course we're brothers"—Alys was balanced between annoyance and panic—"but we need two sleeping pallets."

Selendrile came up behind her and flung his arm around her shoulders in imitation of the older sister's protective gesture. Somehow Alys kept from jumping out of her skin. Selendrile told the girls, "My brother kicks and snores terribly."

This time the girls did burst out laughing, but, leaving, they promised to bring up more bedding.

Alys sat on the sleeping pallet and rested her head in her hands and waited for the thudding of her heart to slow down. "I think I'll stay here until I've calmed back down," she muttered between her fingers. "Barricade the door for a year or two, will you?"

Selendrile stooped down beside her, his leg

brushing against her arm. This time Alys *did* jump. But there was no way to move back to put more distance between them, not without scrambling over the mattress. "Staying in the room makes no sense," he said. "We've got to go out and mingle with the townspeople."

Alys sighed.

The worst part of it was knowing he was right.

Chapter 7

THE THING WAS, Alys thought, Selendrile made a passable human.

No, that was being unfairly snide.

He made a very good human.

At first, when they'd just come down into the inn's common room, she had been able to watch him watching others, his responses a half-heartbeat too slow as he gauged others' reactions. Made judgments. Learned. Soon he no longer glanced at her to see what emotions his expression should indicate. He didn't wait for her to answer when somebody asked him a question. It was together that they wove their story of how their farm had been destroyed by a dragon and how, with no family surviving, they had made their way to Griswold. When somebody asked why they hadn't gone to Saint Toby's, which was closer, Alys gave the same answer she had to the guards, "No work," but Selendrile added, "Well, that and..." And he let his voice drift off, so that everybody looked at Alys, as the more talkative brother, to finish the thought.

"That and...," Alys repeated, wondering what, if anything, Selendrile had in mind. He sat chin in hand, elbow on table, and in the flickering light of candles and hearth, his purple eyes appeared soft and gentle though she knew they were really hard and cold. She had taken note of the way the women in the room watched him, as though pretty eyes and a sweet smile were any indication of what a person was. She decided he *didn't* have anything in mind but was only trying to make things more difficult in order to watch her squirm. "Saint Toby's is not a nice place," she said with a sigh, which seemed to her to be appropriately vague and totally dull, but suddenly everyone, even Odelia's older sister, was waiting for her next words.

Alys rolled the cup of ale that had come with their dinner between her palms. Didn't anyone notice that Selendrile hadn't taken a bite of his meal, had never once sipped from his cup? "The thing is—"

"And this is very hard to talk about . . . ," Selendrile interrupted, which might have passed among the listeners as explanation for her hesitation, but put her no closer to what to say.

Still, she looked at him appraisingly. If he wasn't determined to see her make a fool of herself, what was he up to? Alys realized she'd been so intent on explaining themselves, on fitting in, that she'd come close to losing sight of their purpose here. Explaining how Atherton had falsely condemned her would do no good. The people here had no more reason to believe her than her own townsfolk, especially if they'd been recently harassed by a witch of their own. On the other hand, if she couldn't get the Inquisitor in trouble by accusing him of what he'd done, she might get him in trouble by accusing him of something he hadn't done. "The thing is," she said, "someone stole things from the chapel in Saint Toby's."

It seemed to her that stealing from the Church had to be the worst of crimes, and from the expressions of the people around her, they agreed. Except for Selendrile. She couldn't tell what he thought.

"The poor box was ripped out of the wall," she continued, "the silver candlesticks snatched right off the altar."

"Who would do such a thing?" someone asked in a voice of awed horror.

"Inquisitor Atherton—"

Selendrile gave her a swift kick under the table. While Alys tried to be unobtrusive about rubbing her ankle, he said, "Inquisitor Atherton came to Saint Toby's to see about some girl who was accused of witchcraft."

"Not," Alys stressed, "that there was any real—"

Selendrile sat abruptly back in his chair, dragging his hands across the table so that he struck his cup and sent it spinning into her lap. "Sorry," he said blandly as she jumped to her feet and wiped ineffectively at the wetness.

And what was that look supposed to mean?

"Anyway," he finished her story for her, "what with all the commotion of the theft and the witch trial, nobody from Saint Toby's was in a hospitable mood. We were rushed out of there so fast we didn't have a chance to tell them about the dragon. And then, coming here, we had no way of knowing if we'd left the thieves behind us in Saint Toby's or if they were about to waylay us on the road."

One of the townsmen shook his head. "Leave it to Atherton to get caught up in a witch trial while thieves are happily stealing the shirt off your back."

This seemed a fine opening to Alys, but Selendrile tipped his head at her the way he'd first done when he'd been in dragon shape. "My brother and I have had a very long, hard day." His voice had just the right edge of weariness to it so that Alys could have sworn that he'd just lost his parents and everything he had in the world in the past two days.

The crowd parted for them, though Alys could hear the background murmur of people saying, "Terrible thing," and "What's the world coming to?"

She waited until they were back up in their room before turning on him. "What was that for?" she demanded, hands on wet hips and aware of how she stank of ale.

He flashed one of his colder smiles. "I didn't want you accusing him."

"I thought that was the whole point."

"Better to play naive and let people draw their own conclusions." He held his arms out straight and slowly turned.

Checking to see if the room was big enough for him to resume dragon shape, she realized. It wasn't. Which was probably a good thing; she doubted the floor would have held his weight.

He sat down on one of the sleeping pallets and looked up at her as he took off his boots. "What do people say when they're about to go to sleep together?"

"We are *not* about to go to sleep together," she informed him in a voice that was too loud, suddenly aware of how close the narrow room forced the two pallets to be.

"Well, I'm planning to go to sleep." He took off his shirt. "Of course, you're welcome to stay awake if you choose."

"Stay away from me," she warned, as furious as afraid. "Just stay over there away from me."

He managed the same innocent look he'd done downstairs for the women of Griswold.

But she knew better.

She turned her back so she wouldn't have to

look at him and lay down in her damp, smelly clothes, as close to the far wall as she could get. "They say 'good night,'" she told him.

But he was too busy laughing to answer.

It was midday when Alys woke up, and Selendrile was gone. *Wonderful,* she grumbled to herself, and went downstairs without waiting for him.

Her meal was the same as last night, except this time the soup was served cold and the bread warm. "So where's that handsome brother of yours?" asked the woman who was working in the kitchen. *The mother of the two girls?* Alys wondered, unable to decide whether the woman had been one of those present last night, or whether Selendrile's reputation had already begun to spread.

Alys shrugged and took her bowl out into the common room. Only a few people were here this early. She recognized a couple of faces, and smiled and nodded back at the greetings she got, but chose a table by herself.

What am I doing? she asked herself. She couldn't just continue to blunder around, hoping that things would fall into place and that

Selendrile would pull through and help her when she needed it. She forced herself to think of Atherton—though her mind had a tendency to shy away from the turmoil of angry feelings he stirred up. Assuming the best about him, he might have been unaware that Gower and his family were lying to get her father's shop and land. Assuming the best, he might have been so eager to solve Griswold's dragon problem that when he'd found a maiden to offer to the dragon he hadn't cared.

Alys tried to focus her feelings of rage. All right. She and Selendrile had made up their own lies, had said that someone had stolen from the little chapel in Saint Toby's at just the time Inquisitor Atherton had been there. Would the people of Griswold draw the conclusion that Atherton himself had been the thief? Possible, she decided, but not definite. Would they believe it if she and Selendrile could get some of Selendrile's gold into Atherton's possession? She thought back to the faces of the townsfolk last night, when she had first mentioned the Inquisitor's name. She hadn't been concentrating, because Selendrile had been attacking her with foot and ale. Still, she didn't think she'd seen any smiles, any softening of their expressions the way she'd have seen if somebody had mentioned Father Joseph's name in Saint Toby's. And at least one in their audience had complained about Atherton's preoccupation with witch trials. Surely he couldn't be popular. Not with his high-handed manner and the amount of satisfaction he obviously got from condemning people to death. She remembered the large gemmed crucifix that would be as showy and out of place in this town of simple homespun and rough-carved furniture as it had been in her own village. Surely the people here must resent him, and surely resentment was the first step toward convicting him.

The second step was hers.

The second step was confronting Atherton.

Chapter 8

ATHERTON'S HOUSE was behind the church, off the main street. Alys knocked, knowing that if he wasn't home, her plans would be delayed even more, but the idea of seeing him again— of letting him see her—was almost enough to send her back to the Green Barrel to wait for Selendrile. She braced herself, but still wasn't prepared.

The Inquisitor himself flung open the door without her having heard footsteps approach. "What is it?" he asked, standing close enough to spit on. He hadn't changed at all. Which, after two days, shouldn't have surprised her. But the knowledge that he had condemned an innocent victim to be devoured had left no physical trace on his face. His pale brown eyes regarded her

85

coldly. Surely she hadn't changed either, and he would see through her silly disguise.

She tugged her cap lower over her forehead. "I...I..."

"*What is it?*" he repeated, patience gone in the span of two stammers.

He didn't know her after all. Her plan, such as it was, was safe. So far. It wasn't much to go on, but it was all she had.

She found speaking easier if she didn't look at him, and she lowered her gaze to the dusty street. "I come from Tierbo," she said, trying to match the regional accent to disguise her voice. "There's a man there what got himself possessed. Done speak in voices, he does, and throw fits. He got a gleam in his right eye what ain't normal and his left eye's all clouded over and turned up in his head like. My da says, 'Better get the priest,' he says, 'before somebody gets hurt.' Will ya come?"

"Tierbo," Atherton repeated. It was a seaport, a good three days away.

"My da says give this to you, for your church here." She reached into the bag of silver Selendrile had brought and grabbed a fistful of the coins. When she looked up from handing it over, she knew she had him. "There be more," she said, "what they were still collecting when I left."

Atherton nodded slowly. "Tonight's the vigil of Saint Emmett, Griswold's patron saint. Be here first thing tomorrow morning, and look you don't keep me waiting."

Now that she had started, Alys wasn't willing to delay. She saw Atherton start to move his arm—he had it up against the doorway as though to block her lest she try to forge ahead into his room. In another moment he would slam the door shut, dismissing her. She said, "Right, that's what my da said."

She watched him weigh his choices. He tightened his grip on the door, but asked, "*What* did he say?"

"Not to keep him waiting. He's in a terrible rush, the possessed man's that violent. That's why Da sent my brother over to Wendbury, to ask the priest there to come, too—see?— figurin' someone's got to get there first." The implication she hoped he'd come away with was that only the first would get the extra money.

Atherton considered. Then, as though doing her a favor, "All right, all right," he said. "If the man's that bad off, we'll set out tonight. Meet me here directly after the vigil service." Alys was nodding, but he repeated, "Directly. I'll have my things packed and a horse ready to go, and I want no nonsense from you."

"No nonsense," Alys agreed.

Atherton looked doubtful, but he said nothing more. He just—finally—slammed the door in her face.

ALYS SPENT THE REST of the afternoon wandering about the town of Griswold, hoping to find Selendrile and meanwhile talking to the merchants about what work was available, lest anyone become suspicious. Nobody had seen Selendrile since last night, but she did get three job offers.

As evening set in, her mood shifted from annoyance to anger to worry.

Then, as she passed a dark, narrow alleyway, she heard someone say, *"Psst."*

Hoping that it had nothing to do with her, Alys ducked her head and walked faster.

"Psst! Little boy."

Alys glanced into the darkness only long

enough to see that there were far too many shadows. But apparently that was long enough. She heard a quick, startled laugh. Then the voice—a woman's—called, "Little girl disguised as a boy."

It was no use pretending she didn't hear or that it wasn't true. From the corner of the alley with the darkest shadows she caught a movement—a gnarled white hand beckoning. Alys looked around to make sure nobody on the street was watching and stepped into the alley.

Part of the shadows resolved themselves into the shape of an old woman with a shawl over her head. "Well, well, my sweet one," the woman said. But despite her gentle words, Alys flinched when she raised her hand to brush Alys's cheek. "What's such a pretty child doing dressed in nasty boys' clothes and with her lovely hair all cut off? Are you in trouble?" The woman smiled gleefully. "You *are*." She tapped the side of her own nose with a crooked finger. "I can *smell* people in trouble. You've gone and gotten yourself in bad company, haven't you?"

Not as bad as this, Alys wanted to say, but the words caught in her throat, and Alys was afraid that might be because they were untrue. She took a step away and felt the rough wall at her back, snagging her clothes and hair.

"You better get out," the old woman warned, "before you get in too deep."

"Yes," Alys said, easing toward the mouth of the alley, toward the open street. "Thank you for your advice."

"Advice is free," the woman said. "Would you like my help?"

Alys shook her head and the woman laughed. Alys felt the edge of the corner building, realized she was back on the street. Was the woman going to follow her? Prevent her from leaving? Yell out the truth about Alys to all the world?

But the woman did nothing, yelled nothing, only continued to laugh. "I'll be here if you change your mind," she called after Alys. "Here or in the glen behind the waterfall. I may well be your only chance—if you don't wait too long."

Alys ran the rest of the way back to the Green Barrel Inn, but she didn't go there directly, just in case she was being followed. She ran past it and circled to the right, then the left, temporarily lost herself, and only then approached the inn. At the door she stopped and looked back.

Silly, she told herself for the nagging feeling that the witch was watching her from the evening darkness. The witch was too old to run, and besides, Alys would have heard her. Still, it was a relief to enter the Green Barrel's brightly lit common room, especially when she saw Selendrile. He was sitting at a table by the fire, where the flames cast their glow on the long blond hair he'd gathered at the nape of his neck. For a moment she forgot how annoyed she was at him, until she noticed his impatient look, as though *he'd* spent all afternoon looking for *her.*

Which she didn't believe for a moment.

She sat down next to him before speaking so that not everybody in the room would overhear their business. "Where have you been?" she demanded.

He smiled, as though to say she didn't really want to know.

Which she didn't. "Don't do that again. I was worried."

"About me?" His tone was insincere, which made her answer: "About the plan," though she hadn't liked the thought he could be hurt or in trouble. He sat back on the bench and smiled. "What about the plan?" he asked.

She couldn't answer, because the cook came out then, carrying bowls of smoked-mutton stew, which she set before them on the table.

"None for me, thank you," Selendrile said, never looking at her.

"You don't eat enough," the cook scolded him, "that's your problem."

At which point he did look at her.

Any appetite that Alys may have had dissolved in that look. "Let's go to our room," she said, scrambling to get to her feet, to get away. "Come on, Selendrile."

He got up slowly, with a smile for the cook, which she no doubt took as charming.

In their room, Alys talked fast to get his mind away from the path she was sure it was taking. "I went to see Atherton," she said, and saw a shadow of surprise. "I told him I was from Tierbo and that we needed him there for an exorcism. He agreed to come. I'm supposed to meet him after the vigil service tonight to take him there."

"When is a vigil service?" he asked.

She suddenly wondered if he knew *what* a

vigil service was. Or an exorcism, for that matter. "Sundown. Which means it already started, so we'll have to hurry. My plan, since you weren't there to help, was to put the rest of the gold that you brought into his saddlebags, and then somehow get people to notice. I hoped that they'd think he'd been stealing from them, maybe." It sounded so lame, so ridiculous.

Instead of saying that, he pulled a large leather bag out from under his bedding.

So that's what he'd been doing, at least part of the day. It was more gold, much more. He'd also brought a pair of silver candlesticks, a delicately engraved silver goblet studded with emeralds, and a little golden plate—which, if it wasn't a paten meant to hold the Eucharist during Mass, certainly could pass as one. She tried not to gawk like a peasant at court, but judging from his half smile she hadn't quite pulled it off. "I take it these are from your...ah..."

"Hoard."

"...hoard," she repeated, wondering why she felt guilty saying it if he didn't. "Good." *Good?* He'd stolen these things, how could she be saying "good" about that? "I can put part of this in his saddlebags and then make a little slit, so some of it spills out on the street while everybody's watching him leave for Tierbo. I saw that his house has a small upper window. I couldn't fit through, but if you could get in and hide the rest of this in Atherton's room, it'll seem as though he's been stealing for a long time."

He nodded, following her reasoning. "If you can toss the bag up into the room, I can turn into a bird, fly in the window, change back to human, hide the things, resume bird shape..." He considered. "Of course, if I walk into the church without any clothes, somebody's sure to notice. *You* always do."

Alys felt her cheeks get warm.

Selendrile smiled that dragon smile, which always made her afraid she was missing something obvious.

She said, "I'll bring your clothes and hide them behind the church. Join me as soon as you can."

He nodded and Alys tried to think if they were forgetting anything. "All right," she said slowly. She put her back to him before he could get his shirt up over his head.

Chapter 9

LIGHT FROM THE CANDLES streamed out of the church windows into the street behind the church, where Alys stood in the shadows. Anybody watching would be able to see her clearly, and the only thing that gave her the courage to step out of the shadows was the knowledge that the streets were nearly deserted—just about all the townspeople would be at the vigil service.

A huge black shadow flapped against a nearby wall, silent warning that someone was approaching.

The witch, Alys thought, realizing at the same moment that there was no place to hide the two sacks of gold she was holding. The witch had *said* she could smell people in trouble, and of course she wouldn't be at the service. Too late, Alys realized she had been so intent on telling Selendrile about the Inquisitor, she hadn't mentioned the witch at all.

But it was a trick of candlelight and nerves. The shadow got smaller and smaller, and where shadow was finally met by substance, it was only a raven that had nearly caused her to panic. Selendrile: She could tell by the way he cocked his head at her. He had settled on one of the church's gargoyle waterspouts, which just went to show how useful those figures were at protecting the building from evil spirits.

Grimly Alys moved beneath the window of Atherton's house. What if he'd closed the shutters against the night air?

But he hadn't.

Taking a deep breath, she flung the sack full of money.

It struck the wall not even halfway up and fell to the ground with a clunk and a jangle.

Alys kept her back to the raven, sure that Selendrile would find a way to look superior and smug, even in bird form. She retrieved the bag, threw it again. Missed again. She hoped the service was a nice long one. How would she explain herself, standing in the dark, hurling a bagful of money at the Inquisitor's wall? For that matter, what would she do if the bag burst open and scattered coins all over the street?

Atherton's horse was nearby, readied and tethered, brought earlier by one of the boys from the public stable so that Atherton could leave immediately after the service. Alys had the sinking sensation that she'd never get to that part of the plan. The horse watched her and the raven warily.

On the fifth try, Alys got the sack through the window, and Selendrile dove in after it.

Gingerly, Alys approached the horse. "Easy, easy," she whispered, though it had already calmed down now that Selendrile was indoors. She got the silver candlesticks out of her own sack, then pulled everything out of the Inquisitor's saddlebags. Using one of the candlesticks, she poked a hole through the leather at the seam, then repacked the bag, starting with handfuls of gold.

With the coins in there, not all of the Inquisitor's clothes would fit. Now what? She pushed damp hair off her sweaty forehead and forced herself to remain calm. Selendrile wasn't here to give her advice, so she'd better come up with a plan on her own. She set aside a bulky cape and managed to jam in the rest. Giving the horse one final pat, she scooped up both the bundle of Selendrile's clothes and Atherton's cloak. The first she left against the back wall of the church, as planned, the other in the wooden poor box just inside the front door.

The vigil service was almost over. She arrived just in time for the final benediction. Moments later, Selendrile slipped in beside her, and there was a murmur of disapproval from the surrounding people.

Oh no, she thought, assuming the townsfolk were upset because she had come in late and Selendrile had not quite made it at all. She opened her mouth to apologize, but already others had started talking—whispering, because of the place, but very intense, very upset.

"What happened?" at least three different voices asked. But nobody was even looking at her for an explanation. She heard Saint Emmett's name mentioned, and the word "relic," and the fact that Father Donato and Inquisitor Atherton had been as obviously surprised as everybody else. There were two priests in Griswold, Alys surmised, since Inquisitor Atherton was called away so often to deal with witches and dragons and demons, and somebody had to carry on the daily routine. But the single word she heard most often was "gone."

Trying to make sense of the jumble of voices, she let herself be carried along with the flow of people leaving the church, though it separated her from Selendrile. "Excuse me," she said at a point where only two people were talking at the same time, "something's missing?"

Closest to her was a man about her father's age and build, a cloth merchant who just this afternoon had offered to hire her to clean his shop and run errands. "That's right," he said, "you're new here and wouldn't know. The chalice is gone—the one Saint Emmett brought back from his pilgrimage to the Holy Land."

"They had to do the service without a chalice?" Alys asked.

"It was a gift to Saint Emmett from the bishop of Jerusalem," somebody explained. And somebody else: "Father Donato only uses it on special occasions on account of it's a relic, and because it's so precious since it's made of silver and emeralds."

On the verge of expressing her sympathy,

Alys felt the words drain out of her. Silver and emeralds?

"Oh my," said Selendrile, suddenly right beside her. "Then it's not likely to have been mislaid."

Alys was ready to strangle him for not having told her when he'd had the chance. How *could* he have taken the risk of stealing Griswold's chalice right out from under everybody's noses? But apparently the townsfolk read her furious expression as shock and dismay, for nobody asked her what was wrong.

Selendrile looked at her calmly and evenly, then raised his eyebrows expectantly.

Then, with an expression of chagrin since she was obviously not jumping in and playing her part as he expected, he said, "Just like at Saint Toby's."

The murmur of voices intensified. Was everyone who'd been in the church crowded around them in the square?

Slowly and deliberately Selendrile said, "Maybe it wasn't somebody from Saint Toby's who stole those candlesticks after all. There must be a thief going from town to town stealing from churches. We *were* lucky not to get set upon on the road. Did anyone see any strangers loitering about the church?"

In Alys's opinion he'd gone and convicted them. But nobody pointed out that *they* were strangers. "Maybe," Alys said, sure that the crime was written plain on her face, "we should tell Father Donato and Inquisitor Atherton that there was a similar theft at Saint Toby's church."

The crowd surged around the corner toward Atherton's house. Atherton was standing outside, one hand on the tether of his readied mount. Straightaway, Alys's gaze went to the saddlebag. If she'd made the hole too large, people would see that it had been made intentionally. If she'd made it too small, the coins wouldn't fall through and all that she'd have accomplished would have been to enrich her enemy. She forced herself to look away from the bag and now saw that Father Donato was out here, too. By the look of them, he and Inquisitor Atherton had been arguing.

Selendrile caught her arm as though the crowd's jostling had caused him to lose his balance, but Alys had been looking at him and knew that wasn't the case. "Stay back," he hissed into her ear. He made his way forward as

Atherton cast an annoyed glance at all the noisy people.

"Quiet!" the Inquisitor bellowed.

The townspeople stilled, so Alys could hear Father Donato say in his thin and whiny voice, "But why *must* you go now, when the church has been burglarized and we don't know how, and the villains might strike again?"

Atherton was aware of how many waited for his answer. "I already told you, I'm urgently needed in Tierbo for an exorcism."

"But surely tomorrow is soon en—"

"The boy they sent said it couldn't wait. In fact, he's supposed to be here now"—Alys ducked to avoid the searching gaze that passed over the crowd—"and if he doesn't hurry, I may be forced to leave without him. As for the burglar, just put three trustworthy men inside the church, lock the doors, then post three more men outside. I'm confident you can handle everything until I return."

Alys wasn't confident Father Donato could handle anything. He seemed a mild little man on the verge of being overwhelmed by life.

By this time, Selendrile had made it to the

edge of the crowd. People were calling out to Atherton, telling him about the theft of the silver candlesticks from Saint Toby's church, urging Selendrile to step forward and speak up, demanding attention in a confusion of voices that even Alys, knowing what they were saying, couldn't sort out.

Atherton's horse became suddenly skittish. It snorted and sidestepped and threw its head back in wide-eyed terror. Alys recognized that reaction from the cart horses that had brought her to the hill where she'd been staked out as dragon's bait. She glanced again at the saddlebag. The horse was shying away from Selendrile, but since the dragon-youth stood so close to everybody else, anyone would have assumed the size and noise of the crowd was the problem.

Atherton dragged on the bridle but to no effect. Finally he said, "I've got to get away before this foul beast steps on someone. Just set up guards to watch the church, and guards to watch the guards, and I'll be back as soon as I can." He swung up into the saddle and dragged hard to the right, which was toward the crowd in the street, which was exactly where the horse didn't want to go. The horse reared, then landed back on all fours with what was probably bone-jarring force.

Alys, who was looking for it, saw a coin fall to the packed earth.

As Atherton guided the horse into the street, Selendrile swooped in and picked up the coin. "Inquisitor," he called.

The horse reared again, and the saddlebag lost another coin. Atherton craned around to see what was the matter.

"You dropped this." Selendrile held up the coin so that it sparkled goldenly in the light of the nearby torches.

"Not mine," Atherton said, obviously annoyed with the interruption, the horse, and the world.

"Not mine either," Selendrile said. He held the coin up as though to let its owner claim it.

"There's another one." Alys pointed. "Under the horse."

Atherton's head swung round at the sound of her voice, and she stepped behind a wide woman lest he recognize her too early.

Someone else from the crowd retrieved the second coin.

"It's not mine," Atherton snapped when the man held it out to him. He sounded ill-tempered to have to admit it. "Now move out of my way. I have work to do."

Selendrile moved in closer. "Well, maybe you should hold it in safekeeping until the owner shows up."

At his approach, the horse reared again. This time several coins were jostled loose.

"They're coming from your saddlebag," someone pointed out.

"Nonsense," Atherton answered.

Another coin dropped onto the little pile, and the sound of it was clear in the silence that had settled over the crowd.

Father Donato came forward, wringing his hands in agitation. He licked his lips several times before he could bring himself to say what the townsfolk were already muttering amongst themselves. His voice was so soft, Alys could barely hear. "Perhaps we should take a look in that bag," he said, "just to... take a look."

Furious, Atherton swung off his horse. But as soon as he'd untied the bag and started to hand it to Father Donato, the entire bottom ripped out. Gold and silver coins poured onto the street, along with the silver candlesticks, the golden plate, and Saint Emmett's chalice.

"I—I—" Atherton moved from shock to suspicion in the interval between two breaths. "Somebody put these things here."

"Obviously," said the man who had tried to give Atherton the second coin. "Which just leaves us with the question of why you were so anxious to leave."

"Oh dear," Father Donato said, looking as though he were about to wring his hands off. "Oh dear, oh dear."

Atherton scowled. Although his words answered the townsman, he was looking at Father Donato. "I've been called to Tierbo for an exorcism, you silly little man."

"Tierbo's a seaport," someone pointed out. "Lots of smugglers, lots of opportunities to sell stolen goods."

"I did not steal these things," Atherton shouted.

"Oh dear, oh dear," Father Donato repeated.

Atherton grabbed him by the shoulders. "There was some boy, sent to call me to Tierbo.

That's where I'm going, and all we need to do is find him—"

That sounded like Alys's signal; she poked her head out from behind the wide lady.

"There!" Atherton cried. "There he is!"

Alys looked behind her and to both sides.

"You! You, boy!"

Alys stood there, as though waiting, like everybody else.

Atherton let go of Father Donato and pushed through the crowd to her. "Are you a simpleton, boy? I'm talking to you."

Again Alys looked to either side.

"Tell them about the man with the voices. Tell them that it wasn't my idea to go to Tierbo but that you summoned me."

"What?" Alys said.

He grabbed her by the front of her shirt, which she hadn't anticipated.

"Let go," she cried, twisting. The last thing she needed was for him to realize she was a girl. "I've never seen you before."

"You were here this afternoon!" Apparently he was too frantic to notice anything amiss. "Tell them you were here."

"The boy was with me," the cloth merchant said, "talking about working for me."

"He came to my shop, too," someone from behind called out.

"And mine." That person added, "And he sure don't come from Tierbo."

"Terrible thing," Father Donato said in his nervous little whisper-squeak, "terrible. Nothing like this has ever happened before. We'd better take a look in your rooms, Inquisitor Atherton."

"There's nothing amiss there," Atherton answered. Then he swung back to Alys and stuck his finger practically into her nose. Very quietly, very firmly, he said, "You were here."

"He can't have nothing to do with the thievin'," someone pointed out. "*He's* the one *told us* about the thievin'."

Two of the townsmen took Atherton by the arms and marched him back to his house, with Father Donato as the reluctant leader.

Too many people jammed into the house, so that Alys and Selendrile couldn't even see into the doorway, but it didn't take long before they heard someone cry out that there was a large leather bag full of gold in Atherton's clothes chest.

Selendrile motioned with his head for Alys to move away from all the people. At the next street, he turned to look back. "Well," he said, "what do you think? You don't look as pleased as I would have thought."

Alys had to stop to consider and realized she didn't feel as pleased as she would have thought. "I'm sorry Father Donato had to get involved," she said. "He seemed like a sweet man."

"Ah," Selendrile said.

She looked up at him sharply, trying to decide what that was supposed to mean.

"Maybe it'll be better with Gower," he said.

"Maybe," Alys agreed.

Chapter 10

IN THE DARK ALLEY behind the church, Selendrile resumed dragon shape so the two of them could leave Griswold without having to wait for the gate to open in the morning.

"Try not to pull my arms out of my sockets this time," Alys grumbled. With her back to him, she couldn't tell whether he'd already changed into a dragon and couldn't answer or if—still human—he simply chose not to.

In another moment she felt his talons wrap around her waist, enclosing her. She felt a twinge of panic and dug her fingers tighter into the bundle of his clothes, but she didn't have time to shut her eyes before her feet left the ground.

With slow, powerful beats of his wings, Selendrile carried her up, higher than the town walls, higher than the trees, higher than the church steeple. At first she was disoriented, looking down on everything from the air, trying to make sense of half-familiar streets and buildings dimly lit by candles and torches and hearth fires, till her eyes began to cross and dizziness bubbled up in the space behind her eyes. *As soon as my stomach catches up to the rest of me, I'm going to be in serious trouble,* she thought.

But in another moment they'd left the town behind and were in the countryside and higher yet. Now the ground was too far away and too unreal to be frightening. Selendrile stretched his wings to catch an updraft, and fields and woods unrolled beneath them as he glided effortlessly on air currents. His grip around her waist was firm without being painful, and steady enough that she didn't worry about slipping loose. At the speed they were traveling, the rush of the wind past her ears was deafening. Still, by the time she saw that Selendrile was getting closer to the ground, she suddenly realized how disappointed she was at that thought. She laughed out loud at herself, and the sound was strange to her ears and, a moment later, was left miles behind.

With her feet once more on the ground,

Alys again found herself dizzy, but this time it was a giddy, pleasant sensation. She let Selendrile's clothes drop to the ground so that she could hold her arms out and spin around, with her face up to the stars, wishing she could hug them to herself. "That was wonderful!" she announced. "I love flying!"

She let herself fall to the ground and lay on her back watching the sky spin above her.

When things were finally standing still in their proper places again, she pointed up to a dark wisp of cloud shrouding the moon. "Next time"—she giggled—"if there is a next time—wouldn't it be fun to fly through a cloud—like diving into a big pile of unspun wool?"

Selendrile sat down beside her to pull on his boots. "You can't feel them."

Alys rolled over and propped herself up on an elbow. "What do you mean? Are they too high up for you to reach?"

He shook his head. "I can reach them. But they don't feel like anything. Well," he amended, "some of them are a bit damp. What's the second part of your plan?"

Slowly Alys sat up. The silhouettes of the hills to her left were suddenly familiar, and she realized Selendrile had brought them to land just a short walk from the village of Saint Toby's. She rubbed her chilled arms. "I don't think," she admitted, "I'll be able to use the same disguise as I did in Griswold. I've lived with these people all my life, and men's breeches and a hat aren't going to fool anybody."

"All right," Selendrile said equably.

She sat looking at him, and he sat looking at her.

"Well?" she finally asked.

He sighed. "Assuming we can work around people recognizing you, what would you like to see done?"

Alys considered. "Gower wanted my father's land so that he could expand his own shop. His wheelworking is very important to him. I think I'd like to see him lose his shop, ruin his reputation."

"Easy to do. What about the daughter?"

Alys remembered the glee with which Etta had embellished the false accusations her parents had made, and how she'd suggested burning Alys at the stake. She felt a tightness in her chest and was suddenly finding it difficult to breathe. "I want her to be accused of the same thing I was, to know that she's innocent and to have nobody believe her. I want her to be just as scared as I was."

Selendrile smiled. "And the mother?"

Alys jumped to her feet. "I don't know," she cried. "It's not going to work anyway. They'll recognize me as soon as they see me. Why are you doing this?"

The dragon-youth looked at her calmly, and whether he was considering the nature of clouds or thinking that he could have saved himself a lot of trouble by eating her on the mountain that first night, Alys couldn't guess.

He said, "It's not that late. I'll go to the village now and tell Gower that I need a wheel for a farm cart. Then, tomorrow, we'll both go to the village." He kept on talking though she had started to shake her head. "We'll place a bandage around your head and face so that nobody can get a proper look at you, and tell them your jaw is broken so you can't talk. I'll tell them you were injured when the wheel we bought from Gower broke. That way we've already started to chip away at his reputation *and* we'll say that we have nowhere to stay so Gower—feeling guilty—will have to put us up."

"Gower has never felt guilty about anything in his life," Alys said.

Selendrile shrugged, an indication, Alys supposed, that they'd worry about that when they came to it.

Alys once again tipped her face up to the night sky, annoyed that he could take all this so lightly. "The rest of it could work," she conceded.

When he didn't answer, she looked and saw that he'd never waited for her decision but had already started walking toward the road that led to Saint Toby's. Alys had to run to catch up. "Am I supposed to wait here, or what?" she demanded.

"Your decision," he said. "Though I'd have thought you'd be interested." He was making it sound as though she'd been wheedling not to go.

"That's not— Oh, never mind." With his longer stride, it took all her breath just to keep up without looking like a silly little puppy.

"Through the woods here." She pointed to where the road began the final curve before the village.

They stayed to the perimeter of Barlow's pasture so that the trees would hide them from anyone looking out a cottage window, for the moon was full and the night was bright. Then they cut across the corner of Wilfred's wheat field and so came upon Saint Toby's from behind.

"This is as far as I dare go," Alys whispered, crouching between rows of black currant bushes to make herself as small as possible. Selendrile stooped down also, resting his hands on her shoulders to look beyond her to where she pointed. "That's Gower's house, the one with the wagon wheel by the right-hand corner." Candlelight peeked out through the chinks by the window, though it must be getting close to bedtime. Next door, dark, was the house in which she'd been born and had lived all her fifteen years. Loneliness—the yearning for her father, for things to go back to the way they had been—swept over her. The house was close enough that—except for the fear of being seen—Alys could have run up and touched it in the time she would need to count to twenty.

Selendrile showed no inclination to move, so Alys said, "If you're going to be telling them that you're—we're—from one of the farms between here and Griswold, you'd better circle round to the front and approach openly."

He gave her a cold look, which could have meant that he'd thought of that already, or that she was being too loud, or any of a dozen other things. Without acknowledging her suggestion, without even standing, he moved back and disappeared between the bushes. Only he could have made such a move look graceful. If she had tried it, she'd have pitched forward onto her face.

Eventually Alys gave up trying to catch some telltale movement or rustle to betray his passage, and she sat down to wait, trusting that there was no reason for him to abandon her here. She propped her chin up on her hands and enjoyed the quiet of the night and the reassuringly familiar smell of good farming earth. She found her head beginning to nod when suddenly she caught sight of Selendrile approaching Gower's house, walking next to Gower's wife. Presumably Una had been out late visiting one of the households on the edge of the village when Selendrile had entered, and she must have offered to guide him to her husband's wheelwright's shop. But to Alys's dismay, she realized that while she could see well enough, she could hear absolutely nothing.

All unsuspecting, Una led the dragon-youth

to her door. She turned back to say something to him—Alys could see the flash of her smile in the moonlight—then she went in while Selendrile waited outside, never glancing in Alys's direction. Gower came out, and in an agony of frustration she watched the two of them talk. Gower kept shaking his head, but after a few moments, he entered his shop, and Selendrile sat down on the ground, leaning his back against the wall. That had to mean everything was going smoothly. Didn't it?

The back window opened, and daughter Etta dumped out a panful of water before securing the shutters again.

Una came out of the house carrying a steaming bowl, presumably left over from supper, and handed it to Selendrile.

Hmph! thought Alys, who had never gotten a free meal from Una despite the nearly dozen wheels she and her father had paid Gower to make.

Una went back inside and Selendrile tossed pieces of whatever it was Una had given him out into the street, where a suspicious, but apparently half-starving, dog gobbled them up, coming closer and closer, but warily.

You'll be HIS dinner next, Alys mentally warned the dog.

Una came back out, fanning herself with her hand as though the house was too warm, which Alys didn't believe for a moment. She'd seen the way the women of Griswold had looked at Selendrile, and even from this far away she could recognize that Una was giving him the same look. Maybe if Alys hadn't known what he was, he'd have had the same effect on her. But, she told herself, she wouldn't have been so obvious about it.

Gower came out of the shop, rolling a wheel before him. Selendrile returned the bowl to Una, no doubt with his usual charming smile. Alys could see him pay Gower, then lift the wheel up onto his back and start off down the road to the outskirts of the village.

Alys crawled along the row between the bushes, then cut off through the wood to meet him just beyond where the road curved.

Either he heard her coming despite the fact that she had deliberately moved as quietly as possible, or being a great hulking dragon had given him steady nerves, for he didn't flinch when she jumped out of the dark at him.

"I couldn't hear a thing," she told him. "What did he say?"

Selendrile positioned himself so that he was facing in the direction of Saint Toby's. He set the wheel down on its edge and looked at her over the top. "The shop closes at sundown and I have a lot of nerve interrupting a hardworking man's rest."

Alys glanced meaningfully at the wheel. "Obviously something changed his mind."

"The wife."

Alys snorted. "I can imagine."

Selendrile seemed to shift intent between the breath he took and the words. "Is there something specific you want to argue about, or are you just being generally unpleasant?"

Alys squirmed, but couldn't bring herself to apologize. "They didn't seem to suspect anything?"

"No."

"Una seemed in a rare talkative mood. What did she say?"

He looked beyond her as though to make sure no one from the village had followed. "*All of it?*" He sighed.

She tried to stifle a smile. "Just the important parts."

"There weren't any important parts."

This time Alys laughed, and Selendrile's attention shot back to her. "She was flirting with you," Alys explained, lest he think she was laughing at him. "She liked you."

Selendrile considered. His expression never changing from thoughtful innocence, he looked back toward Saint Toby's and said, "Maybe we can use that against her."

Chapter 11

ALYS FELT AS THOUGH she'd slept only moments when Selendrile shook her awake.

"What? What is it?" She was alert enough to know that she wasn't alert enough to cope if something had gone wrong. And something *had* gone wrong, or else why was Selendrile getting her up while it was still dark out?

Not that he seemed anxious or afraid, she realized as he pulled her up to a sitting position.

But then again, when had he ever?

Only slightly less groggy now, she asked, "Has something happened?"

By the way he paused to consider she could tell that nothing had, at least not in the sense she had meant.

"I broke the wheel," he said, "so that it would look as though the wood had been stressed then patched while Gower was making it."

"Yes," Alys said, for this was what they had decided earlier. "Fine. Good night."

He held on to her arm so that she couldn't lie back down. "It's almost dawn. And I brought these." He dropped a handful of rags onto her lap.

It took a moment for her to realize that what in the dim light looked like black patches was in fact blood. She flinched and his grip tightened. "I'm awake," she assured him. **If** she was going to claim to be injured, it only made sense to have bandages that supported that claim. Still, she didn't ask where the blood had come from; and he didn't say. He just sat there looking at her.

The blood was still wet, though it had gone cold and sticky. Gingerly she draped one of the cloths over her head and around her chin, inwardly cringing at the touch of it against her cheek.

"Tighter," Selendrile advised. "You don't want it to sag, or they'll see that there's unbroken skin beneath." He took over, then sat back and evaluated his handiwork. He must have been satisfied, though she'd never have guessed from his face, because he picked up another cloth and began to wrap it around the knuckles of her right hand.

From between teeth which were clenched together from the tightness of his knot, Alys said, "I can't talk." Even she couldn't make out her words.

"What?"

Alys loosened the head cloth. "It's too tight. I can't talk."

Selendrile pulled it up tight again. "You don't need to be able to talk. You only need to be able to breathe. You *can* breathe, can't you?"

"Just barely." The words sounded garbled to her, and Alys doubted whether he'd understood. But apparently the fact that she was neither turning purple nor falling over onto her side and twitching satisfied him that she was getting enough air.

"If you talk," Selendrile said, "somebody might recognize your voice."

Alys sighed, knowing he was right.

"If you sigh around other people as much as

you sigh around me, somebody's bound to recognize that, too."

THEY REACHED the outskirts of Saint Toby's as the edge of the sky began to turn pink. Some of the villagers would be just getting up, Alys knew, though nobody was out and about yet.

Selendrile was dragging the damaged wheel and she was trying to remember to favor her right leg, which was supposed to be injured, in case anybody was watching. In front of Gower's home, she leaned against the wheel as though for support while Selendrile banged on the door, much louder than necessary to rouse just Gower's household. "Wheelwright!" he bellowed.

The door flung open, and there was Gower, holding a candle to see what the commotion was, looking as furious as a water-doused cat. At the sight of him, Alys's knees got weak and she was glad she had the wheel to support her after all.

"What's all this?" he demanded, looking straight at her.

She realized that she was breathing loudly, stopped, remembered that she was supposed to be hurt and that great wheezing breaths might be mistaken for exhaustion as well as panic, and resumed with a ragged intake of air.

"That wheel you sold us broke," Selendrile said, still overly loud. "My brother Jocko, here, has been injured."

Behind Gower, Etta and Una hovered in the doorway.

"My wheels don't break," Gower said.

Alys heard another villager's door open nearby and saw Gower's glance shift to the left.

"The wheel broke," Selendrile shouted. "Just look at my poor brother. This town was closer than our farm, so we came back here."

Yet another door opened a crack.

"Just"—Gower held his hands out, indicating there was no need for excitement in front of witnesses—"come inside."

Selendrile threw his arm around Alys as though she couldn't make it alone.

Gower shoved his daughter in the direction of the wheel. "Get that thing indoors," he commanded between clenched teeth.

Alys let Selendrile half drag, half carry her across the floor of the living area to the bed. Gower looked pretty sour about that, but Una lit a candle from the low-burning night-fire and brought it over.

Compassionate soul that she was, Etta made a disgusted face and put her back to them to get breakfast started.

With an expression that matched her daughter's, Una nodded toward Alys's head and said, "That probably needs a fresh bandage."

"No!" Alys mumble-cried. She couldn't be sure anybody could understand her, and she flinched away.

"No," Selendrile said quietly. "We had a terrible time getting the bleeding to stop. It's probably best to leave the wound alone."

For all that she'd gotten closer than her daughter had, Una looked relieved. "If you think that's best," she murmured.

Oh, for heaven's sake, Alys thought at the worshipful expression on the older woman's face.

"Never saw anything like this happen to one of my wheels before," Gower said, examining the wheel by the light of the fire.

"Well," Selendrile said charitably, "it can't be helped now. We're just lucky we weren't both killed when the cart tipped into the ditch."

"Oh my!" Una said breathlessly, never glancing away from Selendrile, not even to the wheel.

Slowly Selendrile looked up from Alys, flat on her back on Gower and Una's bed, and met Una's gaze. Even from this awkward position Alys could see his smile was dazzling. She groaned and burrowed deeper into the mattress.

"I'll make a new wheel for you," Gower said, heading for the workshop.

After he was gone, Selendrile said, "I should be going."

"What?" Alys cried, her voice muffled by the bandages.

"Must you leave?" Una asked.

Selendrile took Una's hand and held it gently between his own. With a look so sincere Alys wanted to choke, he said, "After the accident, Jocko and I just left the cart upturned in the ditch by the road, with the ox tethered so it could graze a bit without wandering off. I need to return it to the farm and make sure everything's all right there. Could you please watch over my brother until this evening?"

"Certainly," Una said, which Alys knew only meant that she wanted to see Selendrile again.

Between clenched teeth, Alys hissed, "Don't you dare leave me behind."

"What did he say?" Una was gazing at Selendrile in a dreamy sort of way.

"He said you're much too kind," Selendrile said, still looking deep into Una's eyes. "And you are. You're very kind."

Una modestly looked away. "I do what I can," she whispered.

Alys was tempted to demand, "Since when?" Instead she waited for Selendrile to once again lean over her.

"I'll be back as soon as I can, Jocko." He gently patted her shoulder.

With her supposed "good" hand, she grabbed a handful of shirt and, as distinctly as possible, whispered, "I'll get you for this."

"What did he say?" Una asked.

"I don't know." Selendrile turned and gazed at her sincerely. "After that knock on the head, he hasn't been making much sense lately. I think you just need to leave him alone all day—let him rest."

"Don't do this to me," Alys begged.

Without a word, he straightened, kissed Una's hand, and left.

Chapter 12

WHY WAS HE always doing this to her? Alys
wondered: helping her, guiding her, tricking her
into trusting him—*liking* him even—though
all her instincts warned against either, and then
repeatedly tossing her out on her own, forcing
her to plot and make decisions and confront her
enemies all by herself?

She burrowed deeper into the bedding and
lowered her eyelids so that they were open only
the slightest crack, pretending sleep. Una still
stood by the door, shifting her gaze from her
hand to the path Selendrile had taken. Wherever
she looked, she wore an expression that reminded Alys of the large moist eyes of particularly loyal and brainless cows. Alys thought of
the dog Selendrile had been feeding last night.

At least *it* had had the sense to be afraid. And at least *it* was getting food out of the relationship.

As though suddenly aware of what she was doing, Una cast quick looks at Alys and beyond, presumably to Etta, who was noisily setting out the breakfast meal. Apparently satisfied that no one had been watching, Una moved out of Alys's range of vision to help Etta.

"Here," she heard Una say, "go put this by him."

"But he's disgusting," Etta protested. "He's all bloody and"—Alys could just picture the wince—"dirty."

"Hush your mouth and do as I say."

Etta sneered, "*You* do it then if you're so taken by him and his brother." Then, "All right, *all right, ALL RIGHT,*" she squealed in a tone that made Alys suspect Una was twisting her ear.

Through the quivery slits between her eyelashes, Alys watched Etta gingerly approach. She stopped while still at least six feet away, then put the steaming wooden bowl on the floor and eased it somewhat closer to the bed with her foot, slopping grayish gruel over the edges.

Alys grumbled and snorted sleepily and Etta scampered away.

Eating in front of anyone was too dangerous: She'd have to loosen the bandages and they would easily see that she wasn't nearly so badly hurt as they'd been led to believe. With nothing better to do while she pretended to sleep, Alys actually did fall asleep.

When she awoke, she was alone. She could hear Gower in his shop next door hammering, a sound she had heard all her life. There was no sign of Etta, but Alys could hear Una talking outside, complaining to someone about the heat this summer. As far back as Alys could remember, Una had always complained; the weather was always too hot for her—or too cold, or too dry, or too windy, or too changeable. Possibly because she was just waking up, a wisp of laughter floated into Alys's memory. She thought of her friend Risa, who had died after stepping on a rusty nail the summer she was eight. Risa had been able to do a wonderful imitation of Una: "It's too ... it's too ... it's too *perfect*, for my taste," Risa would say, tossing her hair.

From the direction of the stream where the village women washed their clothes, Alys could very faintly hear singing, a sweet high voice that could only be Aldercy, who—until she'd put aside girlish interests and girlhood friends to get married—had been Alys's friend.

Without warning, Alys's eyes were suddenly full of tears. *Things weren't horrible in Saint Toby's before,* she thought. *I want to go back, I want to go back.* She wiped her nose roughly to bring herself to her senses. Her father was dead; there was no going back. Instead, she got up and fetched the bowl Etta had set out for her. She probably shouldn't have had the strength to do it on her own, but not eating could result in real weakness. She loosened the bandages. Though the meal was cold and congealed into thick lumps, she ate it in quick mouthfuls lest someone enter and find her at it.

Finished, she tied up the bandages again, lay back down, and hoped that whatever Selendrile was up to, he'd be quick at it.

Lying on the straw mattress, waiting, she thought about the years during which she had grown up in Saint Toby's, playing with her friends: the hoop games they had made with old wheels, the games of jackstraws, and the straw dolls they used to make. And with that she suddenly knew how to trap Etta. Everybody knew that village girls weren't the only ones to make straw dolls. Witches did, too, except theirs were made in the image of a particular person. Then, when the right spell was spoken, whatever the witch did to the doll would happen to the real person. Alys got up again.

Working hurriedly, she pulled a handful of straw from the mattress and fashioned a doll, folding the straw in half and tying off the head, then braiding arms and legs. She found a rag, which she wrapped around the figure for clothes, then pulled a tin button off Etta's feast-day dress. For a long moment she held the button, knowing that it was her father's hands which had poured the metal, then shaped it. She was torn between the desire to keep it and the knowledge that putting tin on the doll would make people think it had been imaged after the tinsmith's daughter.

"I'll make them sorry, Papa," she whispered, though her father had never been the kind of man to seek revenge on anyone.

Alys fastened the button to the doll, then got

a stick from the woodpile by the hearth and fastened the doll to the stick. Hopefully, when the villagers saw this, they would think that Etta had compelled them to condemn her, to leave her tied up on the mountain for the dragon.

Seeing the completed doll in her own image, Alys felt strangely unsettled. Although she knew she had no witch's power, she whispered out loud—three times, since that was the way with spells—"Not Alys. Not Alys. Not Alys," just to be safe. Then she hid the doll under Etta's mattress and lay down. She'd worry later about how to bring it to everyone's attention.

Eventually she fell asleep again.

Eventually she woke up again.

Slowly the day passed, and when Selendrile finally returned, it was already late evening.

"Welcome back." Una scrambled up from the table where she and her family were having supper to greet him. She wiped her hands on her apron. "I hope you found everything in order back at your farm." Gower glanced up to scowl at Selendrile; Etta never stopped shoveling food into her mouth, as though afraid somebody'd eat her portion if she let her attention wander.

Alys groaned and stretched as though Una's greeting had awakened her.

"Everything's as it should be." Selendrile took Una's hand in his and smiled into her eyes.

Una blushed and acted surprised, as though she hadn't wiped her hands hoping for just this.

"And how's my little brother?" Selendrile knelt beside Alys's bed.

"I hate you," she murmured into his ear. "Without you, the plan's going all wrong."

"What?" Una asked.

"He said better, thank you, but he feels weak from lying down for so long." Selendrile grabbed her by her unbandaged arm and pulled her to her feet. "There," he said chipperly, "how's that?"

She glared at him. "Now I'm supposed to be able to walk?" she asked.

"You want to go for a walk?" Selendrile said. "I'm not sure that's for the best."

She started to sit back down, but he held her where she was.

"Well, if you insist. But slowly." He smiled and nodded to the others and led her toward the door.

"What are you doing?" she demanded.

"You're doing fine," he assured her.

She sighed and didn't try to get any more out of him until they were outside. They walked very slowly, with her leaning heavily on his shoulder because many of the villagers were out, pointing at her and saying, "There's the poor boy hurt when Gower's wheel failed."

Alys loosened the bandage slightly. "We're going too far," she warned. "If we talk quietly, nobody'll hear us. If I'm supposed to be half dying, I shouldn't be able to walk this far."

Smiling and nodding at someone across the way, Selendrile said, "We can always say you overextended yourself. I'll carry you back."

"You will not," Alys told him.

He smiled but didn't answer till they were beyond the last cottage. "So," he said, "what have you done all day?"

"What have *I* done?" Alys pulled away from his encircling arm and sat on a log by the side of the road. "What have *you* done?"

Selendrile shrugged. "Nothing. I've just been waiting for evening."

"*What?*"

"Nothing. I've just been w—"

"Why?"

He paused to look at her before answering. "Evenings are more romantic."

"*What?*"

He sighed, sounding annoyed, either at her limited range of questions or at her tone. "Humans find moonlight romantic, right? You want me to flirt with Una, right? Why are you getting all upset when I'm doing exactly what you told me to do?"

"I never told you..." Alys rested her head in her hand, exasperated at the loss of a whole day.

"Besides," he added, "we don't want to arouse suspicion by working too fast."

"All right," she said.

"Besides—"

"*All right.*" She pulled the bandage entirely away from her face so she could speak properly. "I've been thinking more about the plan. We want everyone to believe Gower is making bad wheels, so we started with the wheel he made for us. Can you damage some of the ones he's made for other people?"

"Me?" Selendrile asked.

"Maybe by turning into a mouse and gnawing at a spoke here and there? Just a little bit, as though Gower gouged the wood while working it and didn't bother starting over?"

Slowly he nodded.

"As for Una...Eventually what we want is for her to leave Gower for you." Selendrile didn't react. "Slowly, over the next two or three days, we want her to fall in love with you, make a fool of herself in front of the other villagers."

His voice giving away nothing of what he thought, he asked, "Somebody falling in love with me would look foolish to the villagers?"

"No." Even in the moonlight she found herself distracted by the purple of his eyes. She looked away, suddenly confused. "No. I just mean...a married woman, with a daughter your age..." He arched his eyebrows. "...the age you seem..." She forced herself to meet his eyes again. "It'll look foolish for Una."

"Ah," he said.

"So that when you ask her to run away with you, to meet you in Griswold, and then you never show up there, she'll be too ashamed to come back to Saint Toby's because everyone will know where she went and why."

Once more Selendrile nodded.

"As for Etta, I made a straw image of myself

and hid it in her things. Now all we have to do is get people to look—just like we did with Atherton. I thought maybe you can turn yourself into a crow and follow her around—witches always have crows."

Selendrile didn't look convinced about that one.

"And every time she has an argument with one of her friends—she's always having arguments—we can do something to the friend."

"Something like what?"

"I don't know. It didn't take much for them to believe *I* was a witch."

"Cause them to fall down stairs?" Selendrile suggested. He looked interested again. Maybe too interested. "Have their geese or chickens disappear? Perhaps burn down a few houses? Something like that?"

Alys squirmed. "Something like that."

"I see."

"We'll discuss it beforehand, for each person."

"Certainly," he said with a smoothness she didn't like at all.

"Maybe," Alys started, "you—"

Selendrile lunged at her.

Alys didn't have time to gasp before he had one hand on her shoulder and the other . . . Suddenly she realized what he was doing: shoving the bloodied bandage up by her jaw. In another moment, even as she scrambled to tighten the cloth back around her head, she heard the sound of approaching footsteps and the jangle of metal.

The bandage wasn't as secure as it should have been when a man came around the corner from the direction of Saint Toby's. Alys tried to disguise her sigh of relief. The man was a stranger—obviously a wandering peddler: He had pots and crocks and assorted other merchandise lashed to his back and chest and belt.

"Hello, my friends, hello," he said in a loud, squeaky voice that hurt Alys's ears. He flashed a smile that showed good strong teeth despite the shabbiness of his clothes and the fact that he was dirty and had a patch over his right eye. He pointed at Alys. "You must be that young lad I heard tell about what got hurt in that farm-cart accident."

Alys nodded, holding the bandage with her hand, unsure whether it might come loose.

"I just been in town a few hours, but already I heard all about it from everybody. Everybody's talking. Terrible thing, terrible thing. I told that woman, the wheelwright's wife, I got just the thing for you, but she wouldn't let me in the house, more's the shame, but now, just as I'm leaving, here you are."

Here I am, Alys thought. Trust it to her luck that the man wasn't going to spend the night at Saint Toby's like any normal peddler but would set out again this late.

The man was disentangling himself from the various bags and harness that held his wares. "I have," he repeated, "just the thing."

"That's very kind of you," Alys mumbled into the bandage, "but really we don't have any money anyway——"

"No, no, I'll have it in a moment." With his one pale brown eye, he looked up from pawing through the contents of his bags. "Silver it is," he said. "Where am I going to sell silver in villages like this? But it has healing properties. That'll make it worth more, you say?" He waggled a dirty finger at her. "But it's not for sale. It's for giving. An old woman without enough money to put beans in her soup gave it to me when I caught the flux last winter. She said, 'I'll give you this-here bracelet, like someone gave it to me, and someone before that gave it to her, and when you're through with it you must give it away, too.'" He went back to looking through his bag. "That's where the magic is, don't you know, in the giving it away."

Alys glanced at Selendrile, who shrugged.

"Here it is." The peddler pulled something out of his bag with a flourish, but Alys couldn't get a good look at it. "Hmmm," he said, "it should probably go on your injured arm. You"—he indicated Selendrile—"hold the lad's arm out straight, and I'll put it on."

It seemed the fastest way to get rid of him. Alys gave a nod to Selendrile, who helped support her arm as though it were sore.

After seeing all the real silver that she had in the past couple of days, Alys caught one glimpse of the peddler's so-called silver bracelet and knew it was too dull, too heavy to be real. If he thought he was going to talk her into—

But before Alys could finish the thought, the peddler shoved her so that she fell off the log, causing the bandage to drop away from her face entirely.

She didn't have time to worry about that, for in the same instant he snapped the bracelet around Selendrile's arm and Selendrile cried out as though the metal burned. But before he could seize the bracelet off, the peddler swung one of his huge pots and cracked Selendrile across the side of the head with it.

Selendrile collapsed to the ground just as Alys sprang to her feet and leaped at the man. He hit her in the stomach with his elbow; then, when she doubled over, he ran into her so that they fell to the ground, him on top of her.

She tried to rake her fingers across his face, but he turned so that she only ripped off the eye patch before he had both her hands pinned to the ground on either side of her head. Two perfectly whole and healthy pale brown eyes looked down at her, and then the peddler smiled.

"Atherton!" she gasped.

Chapter 13

ATHERTON FLIPPED her facedown into the
dirt and dragged her hands behind her back.

"Selendrile!" she cried as the Inquisitor
twisted rope around her wrists. "Selendrile!"

But when Atherton finally got up, removing
his knee from the small of her back, she was
able to see the dragon-youth still sprawled motionless on the ground.

Backing away from her, his eyes shifting
warily from her to Selendrile, Atherton approached his dropped peddler's pack. *Be pretending,* she thought at Selendrile as Atherton
fished out another metal band, this one attached
to a short length of chain. *Grab him as soon as he
comes near.*

But Selendrile made no move as Atherton used the bands and chain to shackle his arms behind his back. Only when the dragon-youth was safely bound did Atherton nudge him onto his side. "Get up," he commanded. When a rough shake got no reaction, he slapped him hard enough that Alys winced.

Selendrile groaned and stirred, and Atherton sidled away from him.

"Coward," Alys jeered.

Atherton jerked her to her feet and shoved her at Selendrile. "Get him up and get him to cooperate, or I'll kill him here and now." Atherton pulled a short, broad dagger from his belt. He held it under her chin so that the point pressed against her skin just short of cutting. "Don't assume that as a man of the Church I'll stay my hand from doing it. I know what that creature is—spawn of Satan, evil incarnate. And your association with...*it*...proves that you are the same."

Alys didn't pause to try to reason out how Atherton could know that Selendrile wasn't what he appeared. "You're more evil—"

He slapped her, hard. All her fifteen years, no one had ever hit her before. Even during the trial, even with all the roughness edged with the threat of death, no one had struck her.

Be careful, she warned herself. Atherton seemed dangerously close to mindless violence. At least for the moment he apparently wanted them alive, and she had to take care not to change that.

With a deep breath she knelt beside Selendrile. What was she supposed to do, with her hands tied behind her back? She nudged him with her knee. "Selendrile. We're in trouble. Get up."

Again he groaned, then he caught his breath as though in pain. Still, she couldn't see any blood where Atherton had hit him. Maybe he wasn't too badly hurt after all.

"Selendrile," she repeated.

He opened his eyes slowly, gingerly.

"It's Atherton," she told him. "Atherton's here."

Selendrile winced, then kept his eyes closed.

Alys heard Atherton take a step closer. "Selendrile, get up," she begged, knowing that Atherton would consider driving the dagger into his heart as an act of faith in God. "I can't help you. He's tied my hands, too."

Selendrile forced himself to sit up, though he swayed dizzily.

Alys followed his gaze and saw Atherton pouring liquid from a vial into his hand. *Now what?* She jerked as he spattered it onto their up-turned faces, but it didn't hurt. *Water,* she realized; and, a moment later, *Holy water.* If he was expecting that they would go up in flames or that their skin would peel off, he must have been disappointed. But no, he seemed satisfied that they'd both flinched, as though this proved more than that they'd been startled.

Do something, she mentally urged Selendrile, wondering why he was so sluggish, why he didn't transform into something big and powerful and fierce.

Atherton put the vial back into his pack and once again waved the dagger. "Up, both of you."

"Can't you see he's hurt?" Alys said. "With that blow to his head, he won't be able to make it back to Saint Toby's without help."

Atherton snorted. *"Blow to his head,"* he sneered. "It's the iron shackles. Iron to bind the fey. He won't be able to take on other shapes until I remove the iron."

Alys looked to Selendrile to see if this was true. His teeth were clenched with what might have been pain or loathing or both, and his breathing was still ragged. She saw that his face was pale and damp with sweat. The last of her hope seeped out of her. "You should have told me," she said softly.

He looked at her but said nothing.

Atherton said, "Now *get up.*"

Alys scrambled to her feet. Selendrile followed more slowly, still looking unsteady.

"And as for Saint Toby's," Atherton said, "I don't care one whit about that foul little place or anybody in it. We're going back to Griswold, where you'll publicly admit what you did and why. You'll bare your black little soul for everyone, and then they'll know how they wronged me. Then they'll see what you are. Then you'll know what it's like . . ." He'd grabbed the collar of her shirt and raised his hand, the one with the knife in it.

He'd forgotten he held it, she was sure, and he was only intending to hit her, but instead he was going to kill her and her arms were tied behind her and there was nothing she could do to protect herself. She shrank away as far as she could, which wasn't far enough, from the knife, from the crazed look in his eyes.

Atherton didn't strike. He only repeated, "Then you'll know what it's like."

She didn't say that she already knew what it was like. "I'll tell them nothing," she said. "If you're going to kill us anyway, why should I cooperate?"

"For a fast death by fire," he told her, "rather than by knives, inch by inch for days and days. And days." He was breathing as unsteadily as Selendrile. "For this favor, you will tell them everything, and you will buy back my soul."

For a moment she thought he meant that her admission of guilt would buy back his honor, his reputation.

But then in one giddy realization she knew what he really meant.

And how he'd escaped the angry mob in Griswold.

And where he'd learned what Selendrile really was, and how iron would bind him.

"The witch in the glen," she whispered. "You sold your soul to her to get revenge on me."

"And when we get back there, you'll tell her that you'll take my place." Atherton flung her away from him so that, without her arms to balance herself, she fell down on one knee on the road. "Move," he snarled, indicating the direction toward Griswold.

WITH ATHERTON WALKING behind them, Alys didn't even try to squirm loose of the rope. What good would it do when, in the moonlight, he could see every move?

Beside her, Selendrile was shivering, and several times Atherton prodded him to get him moving faster. Once he stumbled and fell, and Atherton dragged him back to his feet by the hair. The second time, Atherton began screaming at him and strode forward so purposefully, with his dagger ready, that Alys threw herself to her knees behind him to protect his back. "Get up," she begged.

Selendrile leaned against her, and she thought he was too weak to go any farther. But possibly he drew strength from her, for he managed to stagger to his feet before Atherton could separate them.

The Inquisitor pulled her up by her shirt.

"Harm him and I'll never admit to anything," she warned.

Atherton just smiled at her, as coldly as Selendrile had ever done.

She thought he meant to walk all the way to Griswold that very night, but he stopped when they reached the hilltop where Alys had been condemned to die.

"We'll rest here," Atherton smirked, standing before the pole to which she'd been tied. "For old times' sake." He tucked his dagger into its sheath on his belt. Then, before she knew what was happening, he hooked his leg around hers and sent her sprawling.

From the ground, she saw him yank up on the chain that connected Selendrile's shackles, twisting the iron into his flesh. Selendrile gasped in pain and his knees buckled. Atherton yanked again, forcing him to fall into a sitting position, his back almost against the pole.

And suddenly, as Atherton reached into the leather pouch on his belt, Alys knew what he was doing.

He was counting on the dragon-youth being too overwhelmed with pain to resist being secured to the pole, but he'd made a mistake knocking her down where she stood rather than commanding her to move away and to keep her back to them. As soon as he unlocked the left shackle, Alys leaped to her feet and ran at him, head lowered like a goat.

With his own head bent down, concentrating on watching Selendrile, Atherton didn't see her till the last moment. He had time to turn to take the blow on his upper arm rather than his chest, but all three of them went sprawling in a tangle of arms and legs.

Having the use of both arms, Atherton recovered first and pulled himself to his knees. But rather than lashing out at either of them or going for his dagger, he did the worst possible thing: He hurled the key into the surrounding forest.

In another moment Selendrile whipped the loose chain around the Inquisitor's neck. The iron must have cut deeply into his own wrist and hands, but he tightened the chain and kept it up and kept it up until Alys, lying on her stomach with her face lifted up from the grass, realized that he wasn't going to let go. Certainly she had seen people die before, even her own father not four days since. But she'd never seen someone being killed before. "Selendrile," she said as Atherton's fingers scrabbled, weaker and weaker now, at the chain. "Selendrile!"

He looked up at her. His purple eyes met hers. Held hers. And still he didn't release the chain.

What had she done? As foul as Atherton was, she couldn't just stand by and watch him die. "Stop it," she told Selendrile. She scrambled to her feet, but by then Atherton's eyes rolled upward and he went limp against Selendrile.

Slumped over like that, he looked too much like her own father in Gower's storeroom.

"Stop!"

Still Selendrile didn't let go and didn't let go, and when he did, finally, it was only after giving the chain a final vicious tug, and—even if the Inquisitor hadn't been dead before—Alys heard his neck snap.

Now, slowly, Selendrile stood, too. The eyes that had looked so cool, so emotionless during the killing, now smoldered. "Stop?" he said. "Now? Isn't this what you wanted? Isn't this what you asked me to do?" He grabbed her by the shoulders and shook her.

"Yes," she said softly, and wondered: *What have I done?* Fly over the village, she'd told him, breathing fire and roasting them all, down to the last baby. She swallowed. "It's exactly what I asked you to do."

He seemed to suddenly feel the drag of the chain on his wrist and he let her go. Moving slowly, he got the dagger from Atherton's belt, holding it carefully by the wooden handle. Just how angry was he? Alys asked herself, warily watching his approach, afraid of him once more. She had talked herself into believing that— deep down—he was like her, thought like her, felt like her. She held her breath. But he only turned her around and cut through the rope that held her. Then, letting the dagger drop, he staggered several steps away before sitting down heavily on the ground. Too hurt to move? But he was running his left hand through the grass.

A moment later she realized he was searching for the key. Iron to bind the fey, Atherton had said. His death hadn't changed that. "You're not looking far enough." She carefully avoided looking at the body. "He threw it into the trees."

He glanced up at her but said nothing.

Alys went to the line of trees, where the

branches blocked the moonlight, and she had to get down on her hands and knees to feel the ground. She found little stones, and leaves and twigs from autumns gone by, but no key.

Perhaps it had landed farther away than she'd thought. She crawled farther, and farther, past the point where it could conceivably have reached, to the left and right of where she'd seen it fly, and still no sign of it.

She looked up through the trees back into the clearing. Annoyed, she saw that Selendrile was sitting exactly where she had left him, which just went to show that the key couldn't be *that* important to him. "Well," she said, wiping her gritty hands on her breeches, "we'll wait until morning, see if it's any easier to find in the daylight. If not, we'll have to think of some story to tell the blacksmith in Griswold, and have him cut the shackles off."

By this time, she'd made it back to him, and he looked up at her with that same calm expression he'd had while killing Atherton. "By morning I'll be dead."

She would have accused him of exaggerating, except that his level tone was like ice down her back. *Iron to bind the fey.* She had seen that it was poisoning him and she had refused to acknowledge it. She knelt down in front of him. His wrists were bruised and raw, though she could see from his still-bound right wrist that the iron band was loose enough that it could twist around freely. Not loose enough to slip over his hand though. The mechanism could tighten by pushing, but needed a key to loosen. "Maybe if we ripped your shirt—or Atherton's—and wrapped the fabric around the iron to protect the skin—we'll start out for Griswold immediately—or Saint Toby's, that's closer, although I don't know what we'll tell them—or—"

"Alys," he said, and it was the first time he'd ever called her by her real name. It made her stop, wait, while he closed his eyes and took a deep breath. "I can't change back into a dragon while I'm bound by the iron."

"Yes," she said.

"And I have to be a dragon come dawn or I'll die."

"Why?"

"*Why?*" He sighed, sounding more tired than exasperated. "Why can't you soar on the wind? Why can't you breathe underwater? Why can't you shed your skin and turn into a butterfly?"

She didn't understand. But she believed.

"All right," she said. He couldn't die now. Not after all this. "The night's not even half gone. We'll walk back to Saint Toby's..." She drifted off because he was shaking his head, and in fact she could see it as well as he: He'd scarcely made it here; there was no way he could walk all the way back to Saint Toby's. "All right," she said again. "*I'll* go. I'll *run* back to Saint Toby's. I'll get one of my father's metal-cutting tools and run back here with it. I'll—"

"There's not enough time," Selendrile interrupted her.

He might have been right. Or not. She couldn't be sure. "Well, what *should* we do?" she demanded.

Selendrile shook his head. "I don't know." His voice was soft, hopeless. "I've run out of plans."

"I'll go to Saint Toby's, then. You can keep looking for the key." He started to protest and she talked over his objections. "You *might* find it. Maybe. It's better than doing nothing."

There was just a flicker of fear in the set of his mouth, and then he lowered his eyes, accepting her judgment. And that was when she knew that he didn't believe that she'd be back, or at least not in time; but he was too proud to ask her not to let him die alone.

"I'm not going to abandon you," she promised him. "I'll be back, and I'll be back in time." She threw her arms around him and gave him a quick kiss, too quick for him to be able to respond, even if dragons knew how. But he caught her hand in his, which was, she knew, as close as he'd come to asking her to stay. She wanted to linger, to reassure him, but knew she might need the time that it would take. She pulled away. "I'm sure I can be back," she told him.

But she wasn't sure.

# Chapter 14

ALYS RAN WHERE the path permitted, and
fretted when tree roots or knife-pricks of exhaustion forced her to slow. Feebleminded,
that's what she was. Selendrile had admitted
from the first that he was a liar, and if she'd
stopped to think about it she'd have known that
the greater part of lying was not telling everything. How could she have assumed that he'd
freely share his limitations? She'd had to guess
that he couldn't speak except when he was in
human form; how then could it have escaped
her notice that he was always somewhere else
during daylight hours?

It wasn't fair if he died because she hadn't
been paying attention.

Especially now, having Atherton's death on his soul.

If he *had* a soul.

"He didn't mean it," she said out loud, meaning the words for God. "He doesn't think the way people do, and anyway he did it for me."

Speaking took the last of her breath and she had to stop, hands braced against her knees, panting. She thought, for the first time, about what it meant to be without a soul. Not petty and cruel, which Atherton had always been, but actually lacking a soul. Certainly Atherton's dead body didn't look significantly different from her father's. Would it? *Could* a soul be bought or traded, like woven baskets or salted fish? The more Alys thought about it, the less she believed so. And yet . . . and yet, she thought, she herself had come dangerously close—not to selling her soul, but to giving it away, to throwing it away—in her search for revenge. And she hadn't needed the help of the witch in the glen to do it.

"He's sorry," Alys gasped to God. "I know he is. *I'm* sorry. Please don't let him die."

Surely the fact that Atherton had been planning to let Selendrile die should count for something.

As soon as she caught her breath, she once again began running.

When she—finally—approached the last curve before Saint Toby's, she tried to gauge how long she'd been and how much time was left. But she couldn't be sure. There was no sign of the sky becoming lighter in the east, which would have meant there definitely wasn't time to get back. But this way it was an agonizing case of maybe she could, and maybe she couldn't.

The village was still, no candles burning, the houses black blocks beneath the moon. She slowed to a walk, which was quieter than running, and approached the door to the tin shop. Saint Toby's was too small for locks, but there was a latch on the door to keep it from blowing open. Alys lifted the wooden beam out of the slot and gently lowered it.

The door creaked as she pushed, and she paused, thinking her heart would stop from the fear of getting caught. She fought her instinct to bolt, to hide in the surrounding darkness of the trees. Surely the noise seemed louder to her than it really was. From all around her in the village she heard nothing out of the ordinary, nothing to suggest anyone had heard or was watching. She stepped into the shop and slowly, slowly leaned against the door, pushing it shut as the hinges again screeched.

She blinked, waiting for her eyes to adjust to the darkness.

They didn't.

There was a window on the far wall, she knew even though she couldn't see it. Even the little bit of light she'd get from opening the shutters would be enough for her to find her way around this shop, which had always been a part of her life. But it was different, it didn't feel the same knowing that her father would never be back. She'd find a tool with which to cut Selendrile's one remaining shackle and be out of here in the time it would take to say two *Pater Nosters*.

Carefully she slid her feet across the packed-dirt floor so that she wouldn't trip over anything that wasn't where she remembered. On the third slide, her foot struck something— a table leg?—which had no business being there. Instinctively she straightened her arms in front of her. But it wasn't a table leg; it was a wagon wheel resting upright. And as her left hand caught it in time to keep it from tipping over, her right hand upset a metal bucket that was hanging from a nail on the wall. She lunged for the falling bucket, caught it at the same instant the wheel fell over onto her foot, dropped the bucket—which clattered against the wall, the wheel, and the floor, all the while emptying itself of what had to be half the world's supply of nails—then she lost her balance and fell down, knocking over two boards and a broom.

Alys sat on the floor where she'd landed, holding her breath, waiting for someone to come in and kill her.

Nothing, nobody stirred.

A wheel. It was a wheel she'd tumbled over. Gower hadn't wasted a moment taking over her father's shop.

Once she stopped shaking, she got to her hands and knees very slowly and crawled to the door. She opened it a crack and peeked out into the street. Much good stealth would do now that the door had once again shrieked on its hinges, announcing her intent.

As far as she could see, nobody was coming.

Alys took a deep breath and stood.

The open door illuminated the shop somewhat. And anyway, she couldn't very well flee, knowing that that would condemn Selendrile to death. Unless, of course, he'd somehow found the key—which she didn't believe for a moment. She picked her way across the rubble she'd made on the floor and headed toward the cabinet where her father had kept the smaller of his tools. As she'd expected, they were gone, replaced by the wheelwright's equipment. Why hadn't she noticed the smell of fresh-cut wood and shavings before? Still, there had to be something here she could use. Chisels, awls, a mallet.

She had just put her hand out to sort through the tools when someone seized her elbow and spun her around, flinging her hard against the wall.

"I thought I'd—" Gower's eyes narrowed in recognition. "You," he said with such feeling that Alys knew he saw beyond the boy's clothing and filthy face of the "injured boy" who'd been his houseguest. "Ahh," he continued, "now I understand what's been going on."

This was no time to be meek. "Do you think people will believe you?" Alys demanded. "Wheels that fall apart, wife ready to run off with the first handsome young stranger, daughter dabbling in magic—have they started to talk yet?"

By the way he shook her, she knew they had. "You'll come with me, girl, and everyone'll know you're behind it all soon's they see you. All they got to do is catch one look at you in them boy's clothes. Soon's they start wondering how you got away from that dragon, they won't care about any wheels." He started to pull her toward the door.

Alys dug her heels into the floor. "Selendrile rescued me from the dragon." That much was certainly true. "And as for coming back here, that proves my innocence. If I was really a witch, I'd have cast a spell and been done with all of you. There'd have been no reason to come back. Etta's the witch."

Gower paused while he tried to reason it out. Then, "No," he said, tugging again, "they'll know it was you."

"I'll deny it. And there'll always be that

doubt. Any time anything goes wrong, they'll wonder." She caught hold of the doorway before he could drag her outside. "But it doesn't have to be that way."

He tugged and it felt as though her fingers were going to fall off.

"Gower, it doesn't have to be that way."

He finally hesitated. "What are you saying?"

"I'll admit to everything. I'll clear your name, restore your family's reputation."

"In exchange for what?"

"For you letting me go."

"What?" Once again he started yanking at her, even while she said, "I'll come back, on my honor I will."

"The honor of a witch?" he scoffed. "A witch who's given herself to the devil—"

Alys held on to the door and looked him in the eyes. "You know I'm not a witch," she said.

It was Gower who looked away.

"Come with me, if you're afraid I'll run off," she said, which was casting away any last chance at freedom. "We'll be back here in time for the noonday meal. And I'll remove all trace of doubt from your name. I'll even confess to being a witch, so that no one will ever be able to claim you had an innocent girl put to death. No one will ever come after Etta."

Gower repeated: "In exchange for what?"

"Selendrile's in trouble."

"Is he now?" Gower interrupted with a snort.

"Inquisitor Atherton took us to the same place where you left me for the dragon. He shackled him to the same stake." The rest, she thought, it was better if he didn't know.

"I see," Gower said. "I go with you out to the wilds between here and Griswold, rescue your friend who promptly thanks me by slitting my throat—"

"He won't. I'll tell him not to, that you and I have come to an agreement."

He was considering it, she could tell.

"If we don't get there by dawn, the deal is off," she warned. "You saw how easily the villagers turned on me—do you think it'll be any different for Etta?"

"Let me think."

"If we don't get there by dawn, the deal is off," she screamed at him. Thinking was the last thing she wanted him to do. How much time had he wasted already?

"You swear I'll come to no harm?"

"Yes!"

"You swear you'll tell them you're a witch and that you arranged—"

"Yes!"

He was determined to get it all out. "—that you arranged for the wheel to break, that you bewitched my wife and daughter?"

"Yes, yes!" Then, as he paused to make sure he hadn't left anything out, she said, "Now, Gower."

Slowly he nodded.

"They're iron shackles," she said, lest she give him time to change his mind. "What do you have that'll cut through them?"

"Is it high-grade iron?"

"I don't know," she cried. "Gower!"

"All right, all right." He fetched a metal file. "This should work."

"Fine. Let's go."

Gower tucked the file into his belt. "Soon's I tell Una, so she doesn't worry."

From what she'd seen, Alys didn't think Una would worry if she found her husband sprouting tree branches from his head, but this didn't seem the time to say so. She trailed after

Gower, praying he wouldn't give enough details that either he or Una would start to question his decision.

Apparently Una wasn't so worried that she had stayed awake. Watching from the doorway, Alys saw Gower nudge his wife. "I'll be back," he told her.

Una grunted, which might have meant, "All right," or "Leave me alone." In any case, Gower lit a torch from the night-fire and came right back out.

"Hurry up," Alys told him.

"Listen, if he's shackled, he's not going anywhere. We'll be there soon enough."

"We'll be there before dawn," Alys repeated.

Gower scowled, but began walking faster.

Chapter 15

THE SKY WAS getting lighter, Alys was certain. If they'd been back at Saint Toby's with its open view, she'd have seen pink and orange streaks creeping up from the horizon. Instead, she and Gower were surrounded by trees that were steadily becoming more distinct, and by glimpses of sky shading from black to gray. Before, while she'd been hurrying in the opposite direction, she'd played a mental game with herself, saying, "If I get to here before the sky starts to lighten, then I'll be able to reach Selendrile in time." She'd said it just beyond the edge of the clearing where she'd left him, giving herself ample time to struggle with getting the shackle off. She'd said it further and further out, having to assume the shackle would be easier and easier to remove. She'd said it the last time at a point where she'd have had to run faster than she'd ever run before and where the shackle would have to drop off at a touch.

But now she and Gower had not even reached that point yet, and as the sky paled she was faced with the certain knowledge that there was no way she could reach Selendrile in time.

"It's not fair!" she cried out, and Gower gave her a wary look. It wasn't fair if Selendrile died from helping her. "Hurry up!" she told Gower, though they were both panting already.

He stopped to shift the torch to his left hand.

"Hurry up!" she came back to tell him.

He caught hold of her arm. "Why the rush?" he demanded.

"Not now." She tried to shake him loose, but he'd been put off and ordered around long enough.

"Why the rush?"

"Let go of me!" She was being foolish, she knew it but couldn't help herself. Gower wasn't preventing her from getting to Selendrile in time—there *was* no time. And yet to stand here bickering with the wheelwright while Selendrile

died alone . . . as he had been afraid he would. . . .
As—

The realization struck her that he would have no way of knowing that she had even tried. For all he knew, she may have never intended to return. *Could* he think that of her? Yes, he could, for, really, that would have been the most sensible thing for her to do, it would have been a *dragon* thing to do, and she remembered the expression on his face. "Selendrile!" she shouted with all her might, still trying to pull free of Gower. "I'm coming!" The important thing was not to convince him that she'd reach him in time; the important thing was to let him know she was coming back for him.

But it was hopeless in either case. Her voice could no more travel those extra miles to the clearing than she could.

"Girl . . ." Gower shook her.

With her free hand, she slapped him.

Looking more startled than hurt, he loosened his grip just as she once more tugged, and she tumbled into the weeds by the side of the path. This was the fourth time this night that she'd found herself sprawled on the ground.

There wasn't time to scramble to her feet and elude Gower, who was even now coming toward her; the best she could do was to once again yell Selendrile's name from where she lay, flat on her back.

Just as she opened her mouth, she heard, faintly: "Alys."

It was impossible. There was no way Selendrile could yell loud enough from the clearing that she could hear him here. Only her imagination told her otherwise.

But Gower had paused midstride, his head cocked, listening.

"Alys," Selendrile's voice called again, fainter, but this time she was waiting for it.

And suddenly Alys knew: Of course he hadn't followed her instructions—he *never* followed her instructions. Instead of staying in the clearing searching for the key, he had started to come after her.

She jumped to her feet and began running down the path, Gower right behind.

She found Selendrile sprawled in the middle of the road, moments away from where she had given up. Without pausing to think, she threw her arms around him and gave him a hug, simultaneously trying to get him to sit up so that Gower could more easily get to the shackle.

He seemed barely conscious and sagged heavily against her. "There's not enough time," he murmured weakly.

"Everything's all right," she said. "Gower's here to help."

That got his eyes open. She felt the muscles in his back and shoulders tighten.

Gower remained out of arm's reach, watching everything suspiciously. His torch cast flickering shadows onto their upturned faces.

There wasn't time to explain it all. Above, the sky was getting pink, and in the forest around them songbirds roused themselves to greet the dawn. "Selendrile," she said, mindful of her promise, "it's all right. Gower and I have come to an agreement. He's a partner now."

"Gower?" He spat out the name.

She gave his shoulder a rough shove. "Enough! I told him I wouldn't let you hurt him."

His expression shifted to something she couldn't recognize, his dragon look. But then he said again, "There isn't enough time."

Gower must have taken that as agreement, for he handed Alys the torch and pulled the file from his belt. "This is *not* as you led me to believe," he grumbled. "He was supposed to be fastened to the stake."

"Just hurry up," Alys said. She lifted Selendrile's right arm and saw that the wrist and hand were bleeding and swollen. Despite her queasiness at the open wounds, she tightened her hug around his shoulders to reassure him. Selendrile shook his head, but she had no idea what he was trying to tell her.

Gower raised his eyebrows when he saw the arm, but wordlessly set file against shackle.

Selendrile flinched at the touch of the metal, sucking in his breath with a hiss.

Of course it had to be iron to cut through iron, but she hadn't thought of it.

Gower looked up, but only said, "Hold the torch steady." He pressed down hard and began moving the file back and forth in a sawing motion.

Alys listened for the snap of metal separating, but there wasn't one. The file put a small dent into the edge of the iron band, nothing more.

Selendrile pulled away from her. "This isn't going to work," he told her, his breathing strained and unsteady. "There isn't time. Don't touch me. You're too close."

"What's going on?" Gower demanded, sitting back on his heels.

"Just cut the shackle." Alys tightened her hold on Selendrile.

After a moment's hesitation, in which Alys watched the sky take on a whole new hue of pink, Gower once again placed the file against the iron band. Alys saw the cords on his neck stand out with the strain, and it seemed his teeth must crack he had them set so tight; but after a massive effort, the file hadn't cut quite halfway through.

Selendrile had his eyes closed as he fought a wave of pain.

Gower flexed his fingers and wiped his hands on his tunic, then once again gripped the file's handle. Grunting with concentration, he cut farther into the iron.

This time Alys thought he was going to make it. But not quite. He stopped just short of severing the band. "Damnation," he muttered, blowing on the palms of his hands.

Before Gower could take up the file again, Selendrile moaned and doubled over.

Alys cast a quick glance at the sky, which showed a hint of blue amidst the pink. She tried to get him to straighten, but he pushed her away. "No time," he gasped.

Gower was suddenly standing up, backing away. He held his hands out, indicating he'd had enough. "That's it," he said. "I'm not getting any closer."

Alys dropped the torch, which wasn't helping anymore anyway, and snatched up the file. There was just a sliver holding the band together. Surely she could manage that. Selendrile was fighting her, and it was only the fact that he was so weak that allowed her to take his hand and saw the file back and forth on the damaged shackle. She closed her eyes against the strain of pressing, pressing, pressing.

Selendrile jerked his arm back at the same instant the band snapped, at the same instant the first ray of the sun fell on her face, at the same instant something slammed into her and threw her, yet again, to the ground.

She opened her eyes to see bits of cloth falling through the air, settling to the ground. *Oh no,* she thought, *oh no.* She closed her eyes quick.

But then she heard something.

An awful cry. Like a huge bird of prey.

Alys jerked her head up in time to see the dragon clear the top of the trees, sunlight glinting on its golden scales. Then with another fierce cry, it disappeared in the direction of the sun.

So much, she thought, for what he thought of her getting a new partner.

Gower made a quick sign of the cross. Then he stood, shading his eyes, staring into the sky. "Yes, well, and thanks to you, too," he shouted into the morning light.

But of course there was no answer.

Chapter 16

ALYS DIDN'T GET Gower back to Saint Toby's by the noonday meal after all, but the fault was his own: He insisted on traveling the rest of the way to the clearing where Alys had originally told him Selendrile would be.

While her common sense warned her he would find the Inquisitor's body where they'd left him, she'd been unable to bring herself to say anything. *Just in case...*, she'd told herself. Just in case, hope against hope, he wasn't really dead and had returned home to Griswold. That was downright stupid. Just in case animals had gotten to the body and carried it off. She couldn't bring herself to think they'd eat it then and there. Just in case Selendrile had had the foresight to remove the evidence. Almost as stupid as hoping Atherton wasn't really dead.

Of course the body was still there.

She hung back, unwilling to approach within clear sight, while Gower crouched beside it. He didn't have to look long to determine what had happened. "Your dragon friend do this?"

Alys nodded. There were explanations, but none seemed adequate.

Gower didn't say any of the things he could have said, either. Instead he told her, "It's indecent to leave his body out like this." So, since they had no tools to dig a proper grave, they gathered stones and piled them atop him, like the old pagan burial cairns that dotted the countryside. It wasn't the Christian rite, but she hoped it was sufficient to set his soul—if he still had one—to rest.

By the time they returned to Saint Toby's—hungry, tired, hands and backs sore, fingernails torn and filthy—the villagers had obviously begun to worry about Gower's disappearance during the night and were setting out to search for him. She saw the look on the face of the first person who recognized her despite the dirt and the boy's clothing, and after that kept her face down. She had thought that it would be easier this time, that—having lived through the past four days—nothing could reach her and nothing could frighten her.

It wasn't easier.

Their hate still tore at her heart.

She was terrified all over again.

Members of the search party, fresh and eager to spread the news, hurried back to Saint Toby's so that when she and Gower reached the center of the village, everyone was there, waiting. Gower, pleased to be the center of attention, had refused to answer any questions along the way. Now, standing with thumbs hooked self-importantly around his belt, he waited for total silence before announcing, "She has something to say."

He had kept his part of the bargain, had proved to be more loyal than Selendrile. But she didn't have to give them any more than the least. "It was true," she said, never looking up, "everything everybody said about me. Then I came back with magic and lies against Gower and his family."

There was a moment of silence, Gower expecting more, the villagers taking in what she'd already said.

"The broken wheels...," Gower prompted.

"My doing."

"My wife and daughter..."

"Bewitched. I made an image of myself and put it with Etta's things so you'd blame her for what I did myself."

The crowd was beginning to murmur and stir.

Gower was getting annoyed with this lack of cooperation masking as cooperation. "Tell them about that Inquisitor from Griswold."

"Dead. My doing also. I bewitched the dragon, too, got him to take on human shape to help me hurt you. That's why I came back."

A voice from the crowd said, "That doesn't sound like you, Alys." Risa's mother.

Alys jerked her head up.

Too late.

Four days too late.

Alys pretended the movement had simply been the first part of a shrug. If she didn't let herself believe, they couldn't hurt her. She refused to look up again, answered their questions as briefly as possible, freely took the blame for every ill imagined or real which had befallen the village for the past fifteen years. *There,* she thought at Gower. *There.* She even let him take credit for ridding the village of the dragon. "I killed it," Gower claimed. "It won't be bothering us again," and she let even that pass.

For all that she agreed to everything they said, it took all the afternoon and into the evening for the villagers to decide, as Alys had known they would, that it was up to them to carry out the sentence the murdered Atherton had decreed. The only difference was that this time the method must be more certain.

Another stake was fashioned and set up in full view of the village. Wood was gathered, torches made. *This is what I deserve,* Alys told herself as she let them lead her to the stake, as she put her back to it before they could force her to. Maybe her death would be sufficient repayment for causing Atherton's death in her quest for revenge. But she couldn't bear to watch their faces as they set the kindling about her and called for rope. She set her gaze above their heads, beyond the people to the homes and buildings of the village itself.

And that was when she saw the old witch of the glen, lurking at the edge of the crowd.

It can't be her, Alys told herself. It had to be some other old woman, perhaps Hildy's grandmother, who rarely left the house and got stranger and stranger as the years went by. The old witch had no reason to leave Griswold, having finally acquired a soul to replace her own lost one.

But then the witch saw her looking, and gave a smile of such malicious glee that Alys couldn't fight the truth of it: This *was* the old witch, and the reason she had traveled to Saint Toby's was to watch Alys burn.

It didn't make sense, if it was the witch's soullessness that made her wicked. The only way Alys could work it out was that people couldn't really give up their souls. They only *acted* as though they didn't have one until, eventually, they forgot what it was like *not* to be soulless. Atherton had no more sold his soul to the old witch than the old witch had sold hers to Satan.

Alys watched the old witch come closer and closer, elbowing people aside to stand gloating next to Una in the circle of those closest to the stake. But then Gower came through the crowd also, with the rope to tie Alys, and she had to close her eyes so they couldn't see her panic. She held herself tight to control the shaking.

In her self-imposed darkness, she could smell the pitch as the torches were lit. Gower pulled her hands to the back of the stake. Someone screamed.

Alys tensed even more, assuming that the scream meant an overeager villager had set torch to kindling before Gower had had a chance to bind her.

But then there was another cry of fear.

Before Alys had a chance to open her eyes, she was knocked to the ground, falling into the still-unlit bundles of kindling. The stake, which had broken with a sharp crack, landed on top of her, knocking the breath out of her.

By the time she could see straight, the villagers were fleeing, screaming in terror, Una and the old witch both lost in the panic. Just as Alys got up onto her hands and knees, a blast of wind flattened her again. Her forearms were seized and she was lifted up, up into the air.

But then Selendrile swooped low, so that she could see Gower staggering groggily, too confused to look up. Selendrile dipped so low that

Alys's dangling legs almost dragged on the ground. The rush of air from his wings caused Gower to lose his footing again. He fell, sitting, and Selendrile circled again, close enough that Alys could see in Gower's eyes the moment he realized what was happening, could see him brace himself for the death he was sure was coming.

Which didn't come.

Once again Selendrile took to the air, circling the village, demonstrating to the villagers that there was no hope of outrunning him, no matter which direction they chose. Then again he swooped in close, his wings pulled in tight so that he hurtled between their houses, Alys's feet just barely clearing the street.

He roared, sending flames shooting down the street, licking at the heels of the fleeing villagers. Closer. Closer. Then at the last moment, up and above their heads.

Again he returned to the stake, fallen and abandoned. This time he roared directly at it, and the brittle wood burst into flame whose heat Alys could feel on her legs as they passed over.

Gower had almost reached the edge of the village when Selendrile caught up. He breathed a crescent of flame to block the wheelwright's way, close enough that Gower's eyebrows were probably singed. Gower turned.

Then, with Gower watching, Selendrile breathed fire. Not at Gower, but at the tin shop Gower had fought so hard to possess. For a moment, Alys felt an overwhelming sense of loss for her childhood home.

But only for a moment.

She had seen last night that it was no longer hers. She felt nothing as Selendrile shot over Gower's head and carried her into the darkness of the surrounding night.

AFTER FLYING LONG enough that Alys's arms were beginning to ache, Selendrile let her drop.

She landed flat on her back on ground that was prickly but bouncy. A haystack, she realized, probably the same one he'd dropped her into that first night. She'd given up trying to keep track of how often she'd been knocked down or fallen over in the past day—she probably couldn't count that high anyway.

Selendrile skidded to a stop beside her, transforming to human shape even before the shower of hay settled. He grabbed her by the shoulders, forcing her to sit up, looking intently at her as though searching for something in her face. She saw that his right wrist was almost entirely healed; the left had no mark of the shackle at all. She remembered how he had referred to human bodies as being fragile, and considered, once again, that dragons lived for hundreds of years. It wasn't fair of her to wish he was human just because she was.

"Thank you for rescuing me," she said.

Eventually he let go of her shoulders. Eventually he said, "You're welcome."

The moonlight glinted on his golden hair, long and loose. "So," he said in a voice that gave no clue to his thoughts, "does this mean no more revenge?"

"No more revenge."

He continued to look at her without saying anything.

"I didn't like it," she said. "I felt worse after than before. And I'm very, very sorry Atherton died."

No reaction at all.

"I assume it works out better for you," she

asked, "when you get revenge on those who hurt you?"

His eyes narrowed and his nostrils flared. But he was the one who looked away first. He sighed, shaking his head, probably more at her than in answer to her statement. "Do you want to go back?" he asked.

She thought about it. But then she said, "No. They'll never be able to forgive me."

He looked amused at the thought that she could be concerned with forgiveness. "Then," he said, "is there some other place you'd like me to take you?"

Now Alys sighed. "There were several kind people in Griswold who were willing to take me on. I may go back there." She sighed again. "Or, I could find a new place entirely. I don't think that's as impossible as I used to think it was."

"Ah," he said in that knowing way of his.

Alys rested her head against her knees.

"Or," Selendrile said, not quite looking at her, "you could stay with me."

Startled, she tried to gauge his sincerity from his bland expression. Aware of a hundred reasons why it wouldn't work, she asked, "Do you mean it?"

Selendrile paused to consider. "Perhaps," he said.

"I see," Alys answered.

The dragon-youth took a deep breath. "Yes." He said it quickly and decisively. "Yes, I mean it."

"Well, then," she said, "in that case, I will."